ISBN 978-1-330-64454-6
PIBN 10086694

English
Français
Deutsche
Italiano
Español
Português

www.forgottenbooks.com

Mythology Photography **Fiction**
Fishing Christianity **Art** Cooking
Essays Buddhism Freemasonry
Medicine **Biology** Music **Ancient
Egypt** Evolution Carpentry Physics
Dance Geology **Mathematics** Fitness
Shakespeare **Folklore** Yoga Marketing
Confidence Immortality Biographies
Poetry **Psychology** Witchcraft
Electronics Chemistry History **Law**
Accounting **Philosophy** Anthropology
Alchemy Drama Quantum Mechanics
Atheism Sexual Health **Ancient History**
Entrepreneurship Languages Sport
Paleontology Needlework Islam
Metaphysics Investment Archaeology
Parenting Statistics Criminology
Motivational

Kau

2 S. C
-) vols

h.n.
o.

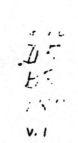

THE BORDERS

OF THE

TAMAR AND THE TAVY.

1770 - 1853

" I own the power
Of local sympathy that o'er the fair
Throws more divine allurement, and o'er all
The great more grandeur, and my kindling muse,
Fired by the universal passion, pours
Haply a partial lay."

CARRINGTON'S *Dartmoor*.

THE BORDERS

OF THE

AMAR AND THE TAVY;

THEIR NATURAL HISTORY,

𝕸𝖆𝖓𝖓𝖊𝖗𝖘, 𝕮𝖚𝖘𝖙𝖔𝖒𝖘, 𝕾𝖚𝖕𝖊𝖗𝖘𝖙𝖎𝖙𝖎𝖔𝖓𝖘, 𝕾𝖈𝖊𝖓𝖊𝖗𝖞, 𝕬𝖓𝖙𝖎𝖖𝖚𝖎𝖙𝖎𝖊𝖘,
𝕰𝖒𝖎𝖓𝖊𝖓𝖙 𝕻𝖊𝖗𝖘𝖔𝖓𝖘, 𝖊𝖙𝖈.

IN A SERIES OF LETTERS TO THE LATE

ROBERT SOUTHEY, ESQ.

BY *Anna Eliza (Kempe) Stotha*

MRS. ^BRAY,

AUTHOR OF "JOAN OF ARC;" "FITZ OF FITZFORD;" "THE TALBA;" "DE FOIX;"
"THE LIFE OF STOTHARD, R.A." "TRIALS OF THE HEART;" ETC.

Tavistock Abbey Gateway.

A NEW EDITION.   IN TWO VOLUMES.

VOL. I.

LONDON:

W. KENT AND CO., 23, PATERNOSTER ROW.

PLYMOUTH: W. BRENDON AND SON, GEORGE STREET.
MDCCCLXXIX.

NOTICE BY THE PUBLISHERS.

THE late Mr. Richard King, of Crediton, a gentleman well known and of high estimation in the literary world, had undertaken to write a Preface to these volumes, and was on the point of fulfilling his purpose when it was put an end to by his lamented death. Mr. King was specially qualified for the task, not only by his knowledge of the county of Devon, and by the general bent of his tastes and pursuits, but also by the warm interest he felt in Mrs. Bray's treatment of the subject. The loss of his introductory remarks will therefore, it is feared, be but inadequately supplied by those which the publishers are desirous of offering in their place.

The compression of the three volumes of the original work into the two of the present edition has been made by Mrs. Bray herself, who has curtailed only such matter as, from lapse of time and change of circumstances, would be without value to the reader of the present day. The biographical, historical, antiquarian, and descriptive portions have merely undergone careful revision ; and it is hoped that their interest has been enhanced by the addition of a considerable number of wood-cut illustrations.

All but one of the sketches for these (made on the spot) have been kindly supplied by a relative of Mrs. Bray's, Mr. C. N. Kempe; that of Sheeps Tor and the valley beneath by her old and much esteemed friend Sir Robert P. Collier.

It being Mrs. Bray's particular desire that attention should be drawn to her late husband's, the Rev. E. A. Bray's, Dartmoor researches, and her feelings being deeply interested in this, the publishers think it best to quote what she herself has written to them on the subject.

"It is but justice to state that my lamented husband, then a very young man, was the first who personally commenced those researches, which have thrown so much light on the antiquities of the Western limits of Dartmoor. Many have since followed, but he led the way. Mr. Bray's notes and observations, with the sketches he made on the spot of several of these antiquities, will be found in the following pages, and are now more than ever of interest and value; as it is much to be feared that many of the originals no longer exist, from the destruction which for the last few years has unfortunately been allowed on Dartmoor."

It is understood to have been Mr. King's intention to introduce into his Preface the letter of Southey, in which he suggested to Mrs. Bray the idea which she has realised in these volumes, and to follow this up with extracts from other letters addressed by that eminent man to the author during the progress of her task. In accordance with this intention the following are given from the selection of letters published in 1856, by the late Rev. J. W. Warter, Southey's son-in-law. Over and above their relation to the present publication they have an interest in connection with the mind and character of their distinguished writer, which it is believed will render any apology for their introduction unnecessary.

"Keswick, February 26th, 1831.

"I should like to see from you what English literature yet wants—a good specimen of local history, not the antiquities only, nor the natural history, nor both together (as in White's delightful book about Selbourne), nor the statistics, but everything about a parish that can be made interesting—all of its history, traditions, and manners that can be saved from oblivion (for every generation swoops away much); the changes that have been and that are in progress; everything in short that belongs to the pursuits either of historian, biographer, naturalist, philosopher, or poet, and not omitting some of those 'short and simple annals' of domestic life which ought not to be forgotten. Such works in general have been undertaken by dull men; but there are few tasks upon which a lively, and feeling, and spiritual mind might be more agreeably or usefully employed."

This was the first suggestion, but from various causes the commencement was not made until the following year, 1832.

On Mrs. Bray expressing a wish to adopt the form of letters addressed to Mr. Southey, and to introduce Mr. Bray's papers relating to Dartmoor, Mr. Southey replied :

"Keswick, March 14th, 1831.

. . . . "I am very glad that my suggestion has pleased you. What you do willingly you are sure to do well, and with the singular advantage of such a helpmate as Mr. Bray, and his previous collections and knowledge of the recondite parts of the subject, you will find it equally agreeable and easy. The epistolary form is at the same time pleasing and convenient; it allows of as much miscellaneous matter as you like to introduce, and transitions are made in it from one subject to another with less difficulty and more grace than in any other mode of composition. Of course I cannot but feel gratified at your proposal of addressing them to me; and I may as well take this opportunity of saying that letters of any weight will reach me, if they are sent under cover to . . . . So you see I may receive the letters as letters, and return them through the same channel, with any comments, should any occur, which may seem useful." . . .

In a letter dated Keswick, March 14th, 1832, the receipt of Mrs. Bray's first letter is thus referred to.

"It" (the MS.) "did not remain a single hour unread. We have all been greatly pleased with it, and without doubt you will make it a very attractive book, and set in it a very good and meritorious example. You have given me a great desire to see Dartmoor, which I only know by having skirted it from Moreton to Ashburton on foot, with a knapsack across my shoulders and Coleridge for my companion, on Thursday, September 12th, 1799. We had slept the preceding night at that inn where Mr. Bray's father was detained by the snow. I had not then industry or patience enough to make minute journals when travelling, and trusted too much to a vivid memory; and this I have often had occasion to regret. But in turning to the short notes which were made that day I find mention of Bovey and Manaton, Becky Fall, &c.

"Your salting story exceeds any that I ever met with for its combination of the shocking and the comical. I had inserted more specimens of Mary's poetry[1] than are found in the 'review;' but in these things you know an

---

[1] Alluding to a review he wrote for the *Quarterly* of Mary Maria Colling's poetry; which Mrs. Bray had recently edited and published for Mary's benefit. A portrait of Mary was given as frontispiece.

editor uses his own discretion. Every one from whom I hear of it is delighted with the book, and with you and with Mary Colling, and with Mary Colling's sweet face, which I can assure you has been greatly admired at Copenhagen."[2]

Under date Keswick, June 12th, 1832, he writes:

"Your pixies are pleasant creatures; I knew them of old by Coleridge's poem about them, which was written before he and I met in 1794, but your stories were new to me, and have amused my fireside greatly. We have no playful superstitions here, or if there are any they have not come to my knowledge; but I much suspect that the popular superstitions of the mountainous countries are generally of a sterner character than such as belong to milder regions. . . . . Your country abounds in Druidical remains more than any other part of the island; but I was ignorant of this till you informed me of it, and, indeed, the honour of having established this curious fact belongs to Mr. Bray. Poor Smith's is a very affecting story;[3] and there are too many such tragedies in real life which it is more easy to compassionate than to prevent or even relieve." . . .

"Keswick, July 14th, 1832.

"There is no reason why I should detain your letters after my womankind have enjoyed them. . . . . These extracts from Mr. Bray's Journal will certainly have the effect of bringing many curious travellers to Dartmoor. . . . The drawings excellently illustrate the Journal; Mr. Bray's reasoning about the artificial formation of the basins is conclusive."[4]

"Keswick, May 26th, 1833.

"I am much pleased with your account of Mr. Doney, and so will every one who reads it.[5] Poor man, were he in

[2] The Rev. Mr. Warter was at that time English chaplain at Copenhagen. [3] Vol. i. p. 183. [4] Vol. i. p. 214. [5] Vol. ii. p. 21.

comfortable health dearly should I like to hear him talk, and to take a pinch of snuff out of his snuff-box and offer him one out of mine; for although not an habitual snuff-taker, I carry a box when travelling. . . . . Your garden and all its accompaniments is most inviting in description. If I had wings, or the wishing-cap, I should be there as quickly as they could transport me. My wishes are not much more reasonable than those of the lover who was for annihilating time and space. I want to be in several places at the same time, and do many things at once."

"Keswick, October 13th, 1833.

"Your last packet has been detained thus long, because I have been working as hard in maritime war[6] as if I were a galley-slave myself. . . . . These letters which are now returned are very interesting; the biography, the stories, the superstitions—in short, the whole. I return them, as you direct, through Sir Francis Freeling. Franks are scarce at . . . . at this time."

"Keswick, January 30th, 1834.

"If I had been less interested with your concluding packet, I should have been in more haste to return it. Its whole contents are remarkably attractive; and there are few things of the kind which I have read with so much pleasure as your account of Mr. Bray.[7] A great deal of pleasure is produced by *vers de société*—a phrase which may with sufficient propriety be rendered by social verses, or social poetry. I suppose that in most countries the number of such poems will be in proportion to the degree of civilization, or rather of refinement; that there may be civilization without refinement the Americans are taking great pains to teach us. Such verses, independent of the immediate gratification which they impart, derive their value

[6] Mr. Southey was engaged with his *Naval History*.
[7] Vol. ii. p. 302.

from time. We gather from them some indications of the personal character and personal history of the writer, and they show the manners and opinions which prevailed when they were written. You see that I am far from thinking meanly of such verses; and in their class Mr. Bray's are what they should be. 'Life' is, indeed, a very striking hymn.

"Moreton was the birthplace of my old friend Lightfoot, and for his sake I have always felt some regard for the place. Such a punch-bowl tree as you describe I have seen by the road side near Breda, perhaps they are still common in the Low Countries; this one I particularly remember, having passed it several times. Some of the persons with whom Mr. Bray associated during his London life I also met with many years ago. Dr. Shaw was one, the learned Shavius he was called, some foreign naturalist having Latinized his name thus unluckily for English ears. Shield I met at Mrs. Barbauld's seven or eight and thirty years ago, and many years afterwards had occasion to communicate yearly with him as Poet Laureate, my verses and his music being for many years duly composed, lest they should be called for, till happily the custom fell into such disuse that we spared ourselves any further trouble. Barry I also knew; Combe (Dr. Syntax) I have met with—but perhaps this was not Mr. Bray's Combe—Flaxman, and Kemble. Browne, the traveller, was a native of this country. I am acquainted with his relations. Their account corresponds with yours. He was a man who let out nothing in conversation, and seems to have inspired as little attachment as he felt. Walking Stuart I have heard so much of that it was very agreeable to me to hear more of him.

"And now I hope your book will not be long before it finds its way to the press; and if you have as much pleasure in reading a proof-sheet as I have, I may wish you joy of your employment." . . . .

The last extract refers to the arrival of the printed volumes from the publisher, Mr. Murray.

"Keswick, February 28th, 1836.

"You will have rightly supposed that, being in daily expectation of your book, I delayed writing till it should have arrived. It has now been eight and forty hours in Keswick, and, as I cut the leaves myself, I refreshed my memory with what had been read before, and perused what was new to me. The book is more than interesting, it contains a great deal of curious matter, and a great variety of information. You have brought together in it many things well worthy of preservation, which must otherwise have been forgotten, because there would have been none to collect them, and you have collected them just in time. And no one could have done this except yourself; for no one else could have had such assistance from Mr. Bray. Such gleanings of tradition are very delightful to me. How often have I had cause to wish that I had, while it was possible, preserved all that the elders of my own family could have told me of their elders, and of the little circle in which they lived, of their own times and the times before them. But it is long since I have had any of these oracles to consult; for many years (with the exception of a good old aunt living at Taunton) I have been the eldest of my race."

In the following year Southey reviewed the work in the *Quarterly*.

The considerations which have led to the present republication may be stated very briefly.

The book has been a long while out of print and difficult to procure, even in the libraries of the chief towns in the county, while the inquiries for it have been increasing in number and frequency. Many circumstances have of late years drawn more and more attention to Dartmoor, and awakened a keen interest in it and its neighbourhood. The tide of summer touring, swollen by the extraordinary facilities of the day for locomotion, has found channels that have carried it to districts within our own shores, attractive for their wildness, their picturesque beauty, their healthfulness, or whatever other allurements are strong enough to draw our dwellers in towns away from the bustle, the bricks, and the mortar, of their ordinary life. The tract of country which is embraced in these volumes is certainly amongst the foremost of those 'pleasant places;' and in the annually increasing number of its visitors there must be many too little acquainted with its localities not to stand in need of information about them, and at the same time of minds too inquiring to be satisfied with what they can learn from the necessarily limited contents of the best of guide books. It has consequently appeared to the publishers that they would supply an obvious want by placing in the hands of such persons a work which they may read at home, as preparatory to or recollective of their Western excursions, or carry with them in those excursions, as *compagnon de voyage*, for days of detention and evenings of rest.

ILLUSTRATIONS TO VOLUME I.

TAVISTOCK ABBEY WALLS.

LETTER I.

TO ROBERT SOUTHEY, ESQ.

Allusion to the original Plan of the Work being suggested by the Laureate—Sources to be employed in its progress—Climate, situation, and natural advantages of the Town—Anecdote of Charles II.—Dartmoor Heights, Rivers, and Streams: their character—Weather: humourous lines on the same—Mildness of the Climate; Vegetation; Laurels, &c.—Myrtles: account of some extraordinary ones at Warleigh—House Swallows, or Martins—Story of a deep Snow: a Gentleman imprisoned by it—Origin of the name of Moreton Hampstead—Frozen Swans—A Christening Anecdote of the last Generation—Snow in the lap of May—Pulmonary Consumption unknown on Dartmoor—Snowdrops; Strawberry-plants; Butterflies at unusual Seasons—Blackbirds and Thrushes—Winter Weather—Monumental Stones of Romanized British Chiefs—Reasons given by the Writer for going at once to Dartmoor—Vestiges of the Aboriginal Inhabitants of that Region.

Vicarage, Tavistock, Devon, Feb. 11, 1832.

EVER since you so kindly suggested that, according to a plan which you yourself pointed out, I should attempt giving an account of this place and neighbourhood, I have felt exceedingly desirous to begin the task, that, previous to your honouring Tavistock with the promised visit, you may know what objects, possessing any interest in themselves, or in relation to past times, may be found here worthy your attention; and though to do justice to such a work as you have suggested to me would require your own powers fully to execute it, and conscious as I am how inadequate I must be to the undertaking, yet I will attempt as far as I am able to meet your wishes, well knowing, by my own experience, that you are one of those who receive with kindness and indulgence any information that may be gleaned, even from the humblest source.

Nor shall I forget that it is your wish I should give not only all the history and biography of this place, and gather up whatever of "tradition and manners can be saved from oblivion," but also (again to quote your own words) state "everything about a parish that can be made interesting, . . . not omitting some of those 'short and simple annals' of domestic life which ought not to be forgotten." Whilst I attempt therefore to give to subjects of historical import the serious attention they demand, I shall likewise endeavour to vary and lighten those more grave parts of my letters, by stating sometimes even trifling things, in the hope they may not be altogether void of interest or amusement ; for a traveller, though he sets out on a serious pursuit, may be pardoned if he now and then stoops to pick up a wild flower to amuse his mind for a moment as he journeys on his way. In the accounts which I purpose transmitting to Keswick, I shall not only give you such information as I have myself been able to collect, but I shall also, when I come to speak of Tavistock Abbey, derive some assistance by occa-

sional references to a series of papers written by
my brother,[1] respecting that monastic foundation.

I have, I believe, before mentioned to you, that at a
very early period of life Mr. Bray entertained some
thoughts of writing a history of his native town,
including descriptive excursions in its vicinity, the
latter more particularly embracing the western limits
of Dartmoor. Though, from living retired, and not
meeting with that encouragement which is so useful
and so cheering to young authors, he never threw into
a regular form his purposed work; yet he made for it
a considerable body of notes, principally derived from
his personal observations on the scenes and antiquities which excited his interest and attention. Some of
these papers have now become exceedingly valuable,
because, unfortunately, many of the memorials of
past times, which they most minutely describe, have
of late years been seriously injured, or entirely destroyed. In my letters therefore I propose, from time
to time, to transmit to you very copious extracts from
these papers, as it would be both needless and pre-
sumptuous in me to attempt giving my own account
of these vestiges of antiquity and picturesque scenes,
which have already been so carefully investigated and
faithfully delineated by my husband.

Before I enter therefore upon any historical notices
of Tavistock, I shall say something respecting the
climate, situation, and natural advantages of our
neighbourhood, since I am much disposed to think
that the monks, who knew so well how to choose
their ground whenever an abbey was in question,
were induced to fix on this spot on account of its
many and most desirable localities for the erection of

[1] Alfred John Kempe, F.S.A.

that noble pile, whose existence gave celebrity to the place, and was as a refuge of honour and security to the learning, science, and piety of those times, which now, with more flippancy than truth, it is so much the fashion to rank under the name of the 'dark ages,' though our own boasted light was caught from that flame which they had saved from extinction.

I have invariably found, with persons who rather choose to see the faults and deficiencies than to trace the advantages, either of the natural or the moral world, that whenever I speak in praise of Devonshire they oppose to such commendation the climate; and ask me how I can be partial to a place so constantly exposed to rain. The objection has received even the sanction of royalty, since it is traditionally averred that whilst Charles II. was in Tavistock (in his father's lifetime, during the civil wars) he was so annoyed by wet weather, that ever after, if anybody remarked it was a fine day, he was wont to declare "that, however fine it might be elsewhere, he felt quite sure it must be raining at Tavistock."

That we have a more than due proportion of wet I will not deny; but it is, I believe, a fault common to mountainous countries; and if we have some discomforts arising from this circumstance, I am convinced that we owe to it many of our advantages also. I have never seen your majestic mountains and lakes; but, judging from a beautiful collection of drawings,[2] in my own possession, of Cumberland and Westmoreland, I am induced to believe that a very great resemblance may be traced between the valleys of those fine counties and our own; and I rather think that you also have no want of showers.

[2] By the late lamented C. A. Stothard, F.S.A.

Our Dartmoor heights are frequently distinguished
by bold and abrupt declivities of a mountainous character; our verdure is perpetual—and we owe to
those watery clouds, which so much annoyed the
lively young prince, not only our rich pastures, but
the beauty of our numerous rivers and matchless
mountain streams. Of these I shall have occasion to
speak hereafter, since, go where we will, they meet us
in our walks and rides at every turn—and always like
pleasant friends, whose animation and cheerfulness
give an additional delight to every surrounding object.
So much, indeed, do I feel prejudiced in their favour,
that, after having become for so long a time familiar
with the tumult and the beauty of our mountain
rivers, I thought even the Thames itself dull, and
very far inferior to the Tavy or the Tamar.

Tavistock owes much of its humidity to the neighbourhood of Dartmoor; for there the clouds, which,
owing to the prevalence of the westerly winds in this
quarter, pass onward from the Atlantic ocean, are
attracted by the summits of its granite tors, and,
spreading themselves in every direction, discharge
their contents not only on the Moor itself, but for
many miles around its base. Some ingenious person
(whose name I do not know, or it should find a record) has described our weather with much humour in
the following lines :

"The west wind always brings wet weather,
    The east wind wet and cold together,
    The south wind surely brings us rain,
    The north wind blows it back again.

"If the sun in red should set,
    The next day surely will be wet ;
    If the sun should set in grey,
    The next will be a rainy day."

Thus you see, my dear sir, poets will sometimes be libellers, and help to keep alive a popular prejudice; for let the weather-grumblers say what they will, I can aver that our climate, (whose evil reputation is taken for granted, without sufficient inquiry into its truth,) bad as it may be, has, nevertheless, its redeeming qualities; and, amongst others, assuredly it teaches us to know the value of a good thing when we have it, a virtue getting somewhat scarce in these times. A real fine, dry, sunshiny day in Tavistock can never pass unnoticed. All living things rejoice in it; and the rivers run and leap and sparkle with such brilliancy, and offer so much to delight the eye and cheer the spirits, that the clouds and the damp and the rain that helped to render them so full and flowing are all forgotten in the gladness of the genial hour; and the animals, and the birds, with the insect tribe, (which is here so numerous and varied) play, or sing, or flutter about, with a vivacity that would almost make one believe they hailed a fine day as truly as would King Charles, could he have met with such a recreation on the banks of old Tavy.

The mildness of our climate is so well known, that it needs no eulogy of mine; our laurels and bays are the most beautiful evergreens in the world, and never fade. Our myrtles, too, flourish in the open air; and we used to boast of some very fine ones that grew in our garden. In a hard frost, however, they should be carefully matted; for the severe weather of January, 1831, killed ours, in consequence of their having been neglected in this particular. I cannot give a stronger proof of the mildness of our climate, than by mentioning the following circumstance, which I received from my esteemed friend, Mrs. Radcliffe, of Warleigh.

That lady says, in her letter to me, "Four myrtle trees grew in the open air, in the recesses of Warleigh House, from twenty-seven to thirty feet in height, the branches spreading nearly from the roots. One was a foot and a half in circumference at the base, and proportionably large to the top. The other three were nearly as high, and one of them was two feet in circumference near the root. Two of the four were of the broad-leaved kind, one small-leaved, and the other double-blossomed, the flowers of which might be gathered from the windows. They were cut down in 1782, from the apprehension of their causing the walls of the house to be damp. The late Mr. Radcliffe, who cut them down, remarks, in a memorandum, 'I have been the more particular in describing these myrtles, as I doubt not they were the largest in England. Four-and-twenty faggots of the usual size were made of the brushwood. The stem, main branches, and principal parts of the roots were in weight 452 lbs.' Tea-caddies made from the wood, and a block of it, remain in our possession at Warleigh."

I here also may add (as another proof of the mildness of our air) the following particulars, which I have seen stated in Dr. Moore's catalogue, lately published, of the birds of Devon. The Doctor says, "Of the house swallow, or martin, I have seen the old birds feeding their young on the 20th of September, 1828, at Warleigh; and have been assured, by a good observer, that martins have frequently been seen flying during mild weather even in the *Christmas week*, at Plympton. These birds build in the hollows of the rocks under Wembury Cliffs, as well as about the houses in this neighbourhood."

Our winters are seldom severe; and when we have snow it does not lie long upon the ground. But Dartmoor, from its great elevation, is far more liable to snow-storms and hard weather than we are, who live in a less elevated country. Mr. Bray recollects that, when he was a boy, returning from school at Christmas, three men with shovels went before the carriage as it crossed the Moor, in order to remove the snow-heaps which, in particular places, would otherwise have rendered it impassable.

The severest winter that I have heard of within the memory of persons now living, occurred about twenty years since, when my husband's father met with an adventure that was a good deal talked of at the time, and found its way into the public prints. Had you crossed the Moor to visit us when you were last with your friend Mr. Lightfoot, it is not impossible you might have had a somewhat similar one, since I perfectly well recollect then hearing that, for several days, the road from Moreton to Tavistock was exceedingly difficult of access on account of the drifted snow. I here give you Mr. Bray's adventure.

That gentleman had been at Exeter to take the oaths as portreeve of the borough of Tavistock, and was returning by the nearest road through Moreton Hampstead, situated about twelve miles from Exeter and twenty from home. There was a hard frost on the ground, and the evening being exceedingly cold, Mr. Bray determined to pass the night at a little comfortless inn, (the only one, I believe, which could then boast such a title in the place,) and to continue his journey across Dartmoor on the following morning.

He retired to a bed that was anything but one of down, and lay shivering all night, wishing for the hour that was to convey him to his own home, where warmth and comfort might be found at such a season. Morning came; but what was his amazement, when, on getting up, the first thing he beheld was the whole face of the surrounding country covered by such a fall of snow as he had never before witnessed in Devon, his native county. How to get home was the question; and, like many other puzzling queries, it was more easily started than answered.

With much eagerness Mr. Bray now consulted landlord and drivers on the practicability of so desirable an object. After much deliberation, every possible expedient being suggested and discussed, the thing was found to be impossible, for the roads were literally choked up with snow; not one could be found passable, either on horseback or in a carriage; nothing less than a whole regiment of labourers, could they have been found, to dig out a passage for many miles, could have effected the object; and even then, so thickly did the skies continue to pour down their fleecy showers, such efforts might have been unavailing. To reach Tavistock was out of the question; and he next inquired if it might be practicable to get back to Exeter. But the road in that direction was equally choked up; and the drivers assured him, in their Devonshire phrase, that "not only so thick was the fall of snow, but so hard was the frost, that the *conchables*" (meaning icicles, probably derived from the conch shell, to which indeed they bear some fanciful resemblance) "hung from the horses' noses as they stood in the stables."

There was nothing to be done; and as people must submit to mischances when they cannot run away from them, he was condemned to exercise Job's virtue, as many others do, because he could not help it. Finding this to be the case, he now began to think how he should contrive to pass the time during his imprisonment, and the landlady was called up and consulted as to what recreations or comforts her house could afford to a distressed gentleman under such circumstances: the prospect was a dreary one, for neither books nor company were to be found. Mr. Bray's situation, however, being communicated to the clergyman and squire of the place, he became indebted to both for the kind attentions with which they endeavoured to cheer the time of his detention at Moreton Hampstead, that lasted during the space of *three weeks;* and at length, when he did escape, he was obliged to reach his own home by travelling through a most circuitous road.

Thus in regard to him are verified all the constituents that are said to have given rise (but with what etymological accuracy I will not vouch) to the name of Moreton Hampstead: *i.e.*, "a town on the Moor instead of home;" for tradition says that it was so denominated from the circumstance of persons returning after Exeter market being oftentimes compelled to pass the night in a few wretched hovels, on the spot where the town now stands, in lieu of home; these hovels having originally been colonized by certain vagabonds and thieves who broke out of Exeter gaol in days of old.[3]

I have heard, likewise, of one or two other instances of the effects of hard weather in this neighbourhood, which I deem worthy of record in the annals of our

---

[3] I speak here, of course, only of the country tradition; for the real etymology must be from the Saxon *ham stede; i.e.* 'the place of the house,' &c.

town, because they are rare. The first relates to some favourite swans of the above-named gentleman. These fine birds were in possession of a piece of water, which had formerly been part of the stewponds of the Abbey. One morning, during a hard frost, the swans were seen, like the enchanted inhabitants described in one of the Arabian tales, who had become, all on a sudden, statues of marble. There the birds were—white, beautiful, but motionless. On approaching near them, they were found to be dead and frozen—killed during the night by a sudden and severe frost.

I add the following anecdote, not only as a very remarkable circumstance in this my letter on frost and snows, but also as forming the very first I can meet with in the life of my husband, whose claim to being ranked among the worthies of Tavistock I intend by-and-by to establish, when I come to my biographical department. But as I like my characters, whenever they can do so, to speak for themselves, I shall tell this story in Mr. Bray's own words. It may also afford a useful hint to those who are fond of observing the gradual changes in the manners and customs of polished society; since our modern fine ladies will be somewhat surprised at the politeness of the last generation, on occasions of emergency. Here is the extract from Mr. Bray's letter, addressed to myself when I was in London last year.

"You must allow this is a very cold May, though a dry one. Mrs. Sleeman, with whom I dined at Whitchurch the other day, told me that it was a common saying among her friends, when any one remarked that the weather was cold in *May*, 'But not so cold as it was at Mr. Bray's christening, when, on the *first of May*, so much snow fell in the evening, that the gentlemen who were of the party were obliged to carry home the ladies in their arms."

These instances of hard weather are not, however, common ; for so celebrated is the mildness of the climate in this part of the West, that when the doctors can do no more with their consumptive patients, they often send them into Devon, and many have recovered, whose cases were considered hopeless. I have heard it repeatedly asserted, and from a careful inquiry believe the assertion to be true, that no person born and bred on Dartmoor was ever yet known to die of pulmonary consumption ; a certain proof that, however bleak and rainy that place may be, it cannot be unhealthy. This, indeed, is easily accounted for, since the land is high, the air pure, and the waters are carried off by mountain-torrents and streams.

As additional proofs of the mildness of our climate, I may add, also, a few facts that have come under my own observation. I have seen in our garden (which is very sheltered) snowdrops as early as the first week in January. We have some strawberry plants, (I think called the Roseberry, but am not certain) that grow under the windows of the parlour where I am now writing to you ; and so late as the 14th of last November, did I pluck a few well-flavoured strawberries from these plants. The slugs devoured some others that were remaining before they were half ripe. The Rev. Dr. Jago, of Milton Abbot, who is a most intelligent observer of Nature, informs me that on the 18th of last December he saw in his garden the yellow butterfly, an insect seldom seen in midland counties before the month of March.

I confess that, though a great admirer of birds, I am not sufficiently acquainted with the feathered tribes to understand critically their 'life and conversation,' a circumstance which renders White in his *Selborne*, and the author of the *Journal of a Naturalist*, so truly delighted; but I believe it is no wonder, though it may be as well to mention it, that our blackbirds and thrushes sang to us at Christmas their carols, so lightly and so sweetly that I, who had the concert for nothing, was as well pleased with it as an amateur might be to pay the highest price to hear Signor Paganini play his violin.

And now what shall I add more in favour of our poor abused climate and its weather? Shall I tell you that I have often, in the 'hanging and drowning' month of November, found lively spirits, sunshine, and beauty on the banks of the Tavy? and that in December, when the good people of London are lost in fog, in 'the dark days before Christmas,' as they call them, and substitute gas lights for the sun's beams, I have often enjoyed a lovely walk to Crowndale, the birthplace of Sir Francis Drake, and have experienced that pleasure which I can describe in no language so well as you have done it, in your own winter excursion to Walla Crag; which will be read with delight so long as there are hearts alive to nature, truth, and feeling. "The soft calm weather has a charm of its own; a stillness and serenity unlike any other season, and scarcely less delightful than the most genial days of spring. The pleasure which it imparts is rather different in kind than inferior in degree: it accords as finely with the feelings of declining life, as the bursting foliage and opening flowers of May with the elastic spirits of youth and hope." [4]

I am aware that some of my worthy friends in this part of the world, who find consolation in charging all their infirmities to the score of the weather, would be apt to exclaim against me, and say that I have given too favourable an account of that at Tavistock; but I confess that I like, literally speaking, to be *weather-wise*, and to look on the cheerful side even of the most unpromising things; and if we have so much rain, and cannot help it, surely it is as well to consider the bounties which flow upon us from the skies, as to find nothing in them but sore throats and colds, and to fancy that our Devonshire showers fall, like the deluge, on no other errand than that of destruction.

And now, my dear Sir, having commenced my letters, like a true native of England, with talking about nothing but the weather, I shall give you my reasons for proposing to take you, in the next, to Dartmoor, before I set you down amongst the ruins of our Abbey. First, then, Tavistock owes not only many of its advantages but its very name to its *river*, which rises on Dartmoor. And though the glory of our town in after ages was its stately Abbey, yet as the river Tavy has associated its appellation with the place from times beyond human record, that fact is a sufficient presumption that it possessed in the aboriginal age a certain degree of importance.

This, indeed, we may consider as confirmed by the inscribed monumental stones of Romanized British chiefs that have been found in this neighbourhood,

----

[4] See *Colloquies*, vol. i. p. 116.

two of which are still preserved as obelisks in our garden. On Dartmoor, where this river rises, we find such abundant vestiges of the aboriginal inhabitants of this part of the West, that very imperfect would be any history of Tavistock which commenced in the Saxon era. I know there are those who have been sceptical about the Druidical remains on the Moor; but no one should venture to deny the existence of what they have never seen, only because they have never heard of it. We will begin, therefore, upon Dartmoor in the next letter; and I trust you will find it not altogether unworthy your attention.

LETTER II.

TO ROBERT SOUTHEY, ESQ.

Dartmoor—Origin of its Name—Made into a Forest by King John—
Henry III. gave it Bounds—Edward III. bestowed it on the Black
Prince—Its Extent—Granite Tors—Sunshine unfavourable to Moor-
land Scenery—Various Effects produced by Clouds, Times, and
Seasons—Rivers, their Character, &c.—Variety and Beauty of
Mosses and Lichens—Channels worn by the Rivers—Crags and
Cliffs—Tavy Cleave, its Grandeur—Scenery of the Moor where
combined with Objects of Veneration, their Founders the Druid
Priests and Bards—The Moor Barren of Trees—Soil—Various
Rocks—Pasture for Cattle—Peat—A Hut—The Crook of Devon—
Peasantry of the Moor, Children, &c., described—Language of the
People—Snow-storm on the Moor, and the Adventures of a Tra-
veller, with a Traveller's Tale.

Vicarage, Tavistock, Feb. 20, 1832.

DARTMOOR, or the Forest of Dartmoor, (as it is still
called in all grants and deeds of the Duchy of
Cornwall) is situated in the western limits of the
county of Devon. It is thirty miles in extent from
north to' south, and fourteen from east to west.
Few places, perhaps, are really less known, and
few are more deserving of attention. It derives
its name from the river Dart, which rises on the
Moor, in the midst of a bog at Cranmere Pool.
This river, which is sometimes written Darant, is
supposed to be called the Dart from the remarkable

rapidity of its course. "Dartmoor was," says Risdon, "made into a forest by King John, and not only confirmed by King Henry III., but had bounds set out by him in a charter of perambulation." And Edward III. gave it to his son, the Black Prince, when he invested him with the title of Duke of Cornwall.

This vast tract of land, which has been computed to contain 100,000 acres,[1] is distinguished by heights so lofty and rugged, that they may in some parts be termed mountainous; and though a large portion of the high road, over which the traveller passes in crossing it, presents an unvaried scene of solitariness and desolation, yet to those who pursue their investigation of the Moor beyond the ordinary and beaten track, much will be found to delight the artist, the poet, and the antiquary.

By a mind alive to those strong impressions which the vast and the majestic never fail to create, Dartmoor will be viewed with a very different feeling to that experienced by the common observer, who declares it is 'all barren.' To him, no doubt, it is so: since, in its bleak heights, he is sensible to nothing but the chilling air; in its lofty tors, still rude as they were created, he sees nothing but bare rocks; and in its circles of stones, its cairns, and its fallen cromlechs, he finds no associations to give them an interest by connecting them with the history and manners of ages long passed away.

The feelings inspired by visiting Dartmoor are of a very different order from those experienced on viewing our beautiful and cultivated scenery. The rich

---

[1] There are said to be 20,000 acres in addition to this, distinguished by the name of the Commons.

pastures, the green hills, the woodland declivities of Devon; its valleys, alive with sparkling streams, and skirted by banks whose verdure never fails, studded as they are with cottages and farms, convey to the mind that sense of pleasure which renders the spirits cheerful and buoyant. There is nothing in such scenes to raise a thought allied to wonder or to fear; we know that we could dwell among them in security and peace; they delight and soften the mind, but they seldom raise in it those deep and impressive reflections, which scenes such as Dartmoor affords rarely fail to create.

The peculiar character of the Moor is derived from its granite tors; these are mostly found on the summits of its numerous heights, and lie piled, mass on mass, in horizontal layers. Some portion of dark iron-stone is found amongst them. There are also slate rocks, and several that are considered by geologists to be of volcanic fusion.

No one who would wish to view the Moor in all its grandeur should go there on a very fine or rather sunny day; for it then possesses none of those effects produced by that strong opposition of light and shadow, which mountain scenery and rugged rocks absolutely require to display the bold character of their outline, and the picturesque combinations of their craggy tops. Indeed, most scenery derives its pictorial effect principally from the clouds, and even the most beautiful loses half its beauty when viewed in unbroken light. I have seen Dartmoor under most of the changes produced by sunshine, cloud, or storm. The first shows it to disadvantage; for the monotony of its barren heights then becomes predominant. A gathering storm gives it a character of sublimity;

but a day such as artists call a 'painter's day' is that which gives most interest to moorland scenery.

The pencil is more adapted than the pen to delineate such scenes as will then be found on the Moor. I have often seen it when, as the clouds passed slowly on, their shadowy forms would fall upon the mountain's breast, and leave the summit glittering in the sun with a brilliancy that might bear comparison with the transparent hues of the richest stained glass. The purple tints of evening here convey to the mind visions of more than natural beauty; so ethereally do the distant heights mingle themselves with the clouds, and reflect all those delicate and subdued tints of sunset, that render the dying day so glorious.

And often have I seen the Moor so chequered and broken with light and shade, that it required no stretch of the imagination to convert many a weather-beaten tor into the towers and ruined walls of a feudal castle. Nay, even human forms, gigantic in their dimensions, sometimes seemed to start wildly up as the lords and natural denizens of this rugged wilderness. But who shall picture the effects produced by a gathering tempest, when, as the poet of such scenes so truly describes, "The cloud of the desert comes on, varying in its form with every blast; the valleys are sad around, and fear by turns the storm, as darkness is rolled above"? In these moments the distant heights are seen in colours of the deepest purple; whilst a solitary ray of the sun will sometimes break through the dense masses of cloud and vapour, and send forth a stream of light that resembles in brilliancy, nor less in duration, the flash of 'liquid fire.'

The rivers, those veins of the earth that, in their circulation, give life, health, and vigour to its whole frame, here flow in their greatest purity. So constant is the humidity produced by the mists and vapours which gather on these lofty regions, that they are never dry. Sometimes they are found rising, like the Dart, in solitude and silence, or springing from so small a source that we can scarcely fancy such a little rill to be the fountain that sustains the expansive waters of the Tavy and the Teign. But all these rivers, as they pass on, receive the contributions of a thousand springs, till, gathering as they flow, they become strong, rapid, and powerful in their course. Sometimes, bounding over vast masses of rock, they exhibit sheets of foam of a dazzling whiteness, and frequently form numberless little cascades as they fall over the picturesque combinations of those broken slabs of granite which present, growing on their surface, the greatest variety of mosses and lichens to be found throughout the whole of Devon.

Often do the waters play upon rocks literally covered with moss, that has in it the blackness and richness of the finest velvet. In others, the lichen is white as the purest marble, or varied with the gradations of greys, browns, and ochres, of the deepest or the palest tints. There is also to be found on the Moor a small and beautiful moss of the brightest scarlet; and nothing can be more delicate than the fibrous and filigree formation of various other species, that can alone be compared to the most minute works in chased silver, which they so much resemble in colour and in form.

There are scenes on the Moor, where the rivers

rush through the narrow channels which they have
torn asunder at the base of the finest eminences of
overhanging crag and cliff. Such is Tavy Cleave.
There, after heavy showers or sudden storms, is heard
the roar of the Tavy, with a power that renders the

TAVY CLEAVE.

observer mute whilst he listens to it. The waters flow
wildly forward as their rush is reverberated amidst
the clefts and caverns of the rocks ; and, as they roll
their dark and troubled course, they give to the surrounding scene that character of awe and sublimity
which so strongly excites the feelings of an imaginative mind ; for there the deepest solitude to be
found in Nature is broken by the incessant agitation
of one of the most powerful of her elements. Such
a contest of waters—of agitation amidst repose—
. might be compared, by a poet, to a sudden alarm
. of battle amidst a land of peace.

Indeed, the whole of the river-scenery of Dartmoor is full of interest, more especially where it becomes combined with those objects of veneration which claim as their founders that 'deathless brotherhood,' the Druid priests and bards of the most ancient inhabitants of the West. Except in a few instances, the Moor is totally barren of trees; but they are not wanted; since its vastness,—its granite masses,—its sweeping outlines of height or precipice, are best suited to that rugged and solemn character which is more allied to grandeur and sublimity than to the cheerfulness and placidity of a cultivated or woodland landscape.

The soil of the Moor is of a deep black colour, and in most parts it is merely a formation of decayed vegetable matter, covering a foundation principally of granite; for it is not altogether confined to this rock, as occasionally there are others of differing formation. Though there are some bogs as well as marshes on the Moor, yet the soil affords the finest pasture for cattle in summer, and produces a vast quantity of peat, that supplies fuel throughout the whole of the year; whilst the sod also is useful in another way, since a good deal of it is employed in the building of huts, generally composed of loose stones, peat, and mud, in which the few and scattered peasantry of the Moor are content to make their dwelling. A hardy and inoffensive race, at no very remote period they were looked upon as being little better than a set of savages; and to this day they are assuredly a very primitive people. A Dartmoor family and hut may be worth noticing; and a sketch of one will, generally speaking, afford a tolerable idea of all, though there are exceptions, a few comfortable cottages being scattered here and there upon the Forest. Imagine a hut, low and irregular, composed of the materials above-named, and covered with a straw roof, or one not unfrequently formed with green rushes, so that at a little distance it cannot be distinguished from the ground on which it stands. Near the hut there is often seen an out-house, or shed, for domestic purposes, or as a shelter for a cart, if the master of the tenement is rich enough to boast such a convenient relief to his labour in carrying home peat from the Moor.

But this cart is a very rare possession; since the moormen most commonly convey their peat, and all things else, on what is called a *crook*, on the back of a poor, patient, and shaggy-looking donkey. You will say, 'What is this crook?' and I must answer, that I can really hardly tell you; unless (as did Mr. Bray for the late King, when he was Prince of Wales, at the request of Sir Thomas Tyrwhitt) I make a drawing of it, and send it in my letter. Try if you can understand such an account as the following, which I confess is an attempt to describe what is indescribable. Imagine the poor donkey, or a half-starved horse, laden first with a huge pack-saddle, never intended to bear anything else but a crook; and across this saddle is placed that very machine, which is made of wood, and so constructed as to keep from falling to the ground any load of peat, firewood, &c., that is frequently piled up twice as high as the poor beast that bears it. At either side of this machine arise two *crooked* pieces of wood, turning outward like the inverted tusks of the walrus. These in themselves have a somewhat formidable appearance, but more so when, after they are unloaded, the thoughtless

driver, as too frequently happens, places his pitchfork
in an oblique direction from the saddle to one of the
shafts of the crook : for thus, whilst the animals
are advancing at a brisk pace and in no very regular
order, the prong of it may lacerate the leg of any
unhappy horseman that meets them, and has not
time or dexterity to avoid their onset. The crook
is here known by the name of the Devil's Tooth-
pick.

I may here perhaps be permitted to mention an
anecdote of the late Mr. Bray, connected with the
present subject. On ascending a hill in an open
carriage near Moreton, he overtook a man on foot
who had the care of several horses, laden with faggots on crooks. From the steepness of the acclivity,
he was obliged to guide his horse in a somewhat
sinuous direction, and he soon found that some or
other of the crook horses invariably crossed him on
the road, and considerably impeded his progress.
This he was satisfied was owing to two words of the
driver, namely, *gee* and *ree*, which he took a malicious
pleasure in calling out contrary to what he ought—
making them go to the right when they should have
gone to the left, and *vice versâ*. Mr. Bray remon-
strated, but in vain. At length, when he reached the
brow of the hill, he said to the churl, " You have had
your frolic, and now I will have mine;" and, not only
whipping his own horse but the others also, he put
them into a full gallop. The consequence was that
they all threw off their loads one after the other, the
driver begging him in vain to stop, and receiving no
other answer than " You have had your frolic, and
now I have mine." '

The manners of the peasantry may in some measure be estimated by their dwellings. These are not over clean; and though they are surrounded on all sides by mountain-streams and rills of the purest water, I have generally found, close to their doors, as if they delighted in the odour it produced, a pool into which are thrown old cabbage-leaves and every sort of decaying vegetable matter.

Out of these huts, as you pass along, you will see running to gaze upon you, some half-dozen or more of children, not overburdened with clothes, and such as they have, like Joseph's coat, being often of many colours, from the industrious patching of their good mothers. The urchins, no doubt, are not bred up as Turks, since frequent ablution makes no part of their devotion. Now and then, however, you find a clean face, which is as rare as a dry day on Dartmoor; and when this is the case it is generally found worth keeping so, as it discloses a fine, fat, round pair of cheeks, as red,—I must not say as roses, for the simile would be much too delicate for my Dartmoor Cupids,—but as red as a piece of beef, which is a great deal more like the cheeks in question. Legs and arms they have that would suit the infant Hercules; and if they had any mind to play off the earliest frolic of that renowned hero, the Moor would supply the means; since snakes and adders it has in abundance, and a good thing it would be if they were all strangled.

The hair of these children, which, to borrow the language of Ossian, 'plays in the mountain winds,' is generally the sole covering of their heads. This sometimes is bleached nearly white with the sun; and as you pass along, there they stand and stare at you with all their eyes. One token of civilized life they invariably give, as they salute you with that sort of familiar bob of the head now become a refined mode of salutation in fashionable life, so widely differing from the bowing and bending of the days of Sir Charles Grandison, when no gentleman could salute another as he ought to do without removing from his head a little three-cornered cocked-hat, and when the management of a lady's fan was an essential part of her good manners in the dropping of a courtesy.

But I am digressing: to return then to the subject. A peasant, born and bred on the Moor, is generally found to be a simple character, void of guile, and, as Othello says of himself,—

> " Rude in speech,
> And little versed in the set phrase of peace;"

and to this may be added, very unintelligible to all who are not accustomed to the peculiar dialect of the Moor. It is not English; it is not absolutely Devonshire, but a language compounded, I should fancy, from all the tongues—Celtic, Saxon, Cornish—and in short from any language, that may have been spoken in these parts during the last two thousand years. I would attempt to give you a few specimens, but I cannot possibly guess how I am to *spell* their words so as to convey to you any idea of them. I have been assured that they retain some British words which resemble the Welsh, and that now and then they use the form of the old Saxon plural, for they sometimes talk about their hous*en* and their shoo*en*.

Though it certainly is a great libel on the poor people of Dartmoor to consider them, as was the case

about a hundred years ago, to be no better than
savages, yet no doubt they are still of 'manners
rude,' and somewhat peculiar to themselves; but as
an instance, like a fact in law, carries more weight
with it than a discussion, take therefore the following
as an illustration. It was related to me but last night
by my husband, who had it from a gentleman who, I
conclude, received it from the gentleman to whom
the circumstance occurred; and as all these parties
who related it were, as Glanville says of his relators
when telling his tales about old witches, "of undoubted
credit and reputation and not at all credulous," I do
not know that you will receive it anything the worse
for coming to you at the fourth hand. Well, then,
once upon a time, as the old story-books say, there
was a gentleman who, mounted on a horse, (at the
breaking up of a very hard and long frost, when the
roads were only just beginning to be passable) set
out in order to cross over Dartmoor. Now, though
the thaw had commenced, yet it had not melted the
snow-heaps so much as he expected: he got on but
slowly, and towards the close of day it began to
freeze again. The shades of night were drawing all
around him, and the mighty tors, which seemed
to grow larger and taller as he paced forward,
gradually became enveloped in vapour and in mist,
and the traveller with his horse did not know what
to do.

To reach Tavistock that night would be impossible,
as a fresh snow-storm was fast falling in every direction, and would add but another impediment to the
difficulties or dangers of his way. To stay out all
night on the cold Moor, without shelter or food, must
be certain death, and where shelter was to be found

somewhat puzzled the brains of our bewildered
traveller. In this dilemma he still paced on, and at
length he saw at a distance a certain dark object but
partially covered with snow. As he drew nearer his
heart revived ; and his horse, which seemed to understand all the hopes and fears of his master, pricked
up his ears and trotted, or rather slid, on a little faster.
The discovery which had thus rejoiced the heart of
man and beast was not only that of the dark object
in question, but also a thick smoke, which rose like a
stately column in the frosty air from its roof, and
convinced him that what he now beheld must be a
cottage.

He presently drew nigh and dismounted ; and the
rap that he gave with the butt-end of his whip upon
the door, was answered by an old woman opening
that portal of hope to him and his distresses. He
entered and beheld a sturdy peasant, that proved to
be the old woman's son, and who sat smoking his
pipe over a cheerful and blazing peat fire. The
traveller's wants were soon made known. An old
outhouse with a litter of straw accommodated the
horse, which, it is not unlikely, ate up his bed for
the want of a better supper; but this is a point not
sufficiently known to be asserted.

Of the affairs of the traveller I can speak with
more certainty; and I can state, on the very best
authority, that he felt very hungry and wanted a
bed. Though there was but one besides the old
woman's in the house, the son, who seemed to be a
surly fellow, promised to give up his own bed for the
convenience of the gentleman ; adding that he would
himself sleep that night in the old settle by the
chimney-corner. The good dame busied herself in

preparing such food as the house could afford for
the stranger's supper; and at length he retired to
rest.   Neither the room nor the bedding were such
as promised much comfort to a person accustomed
to the luxuries of polished life; but as most things
derive their value from comparison, even so did
these mean lodgings, for they appeared to him to
be possessed of all that heart could desire, when he
reflected how narrowly he had escaped being perhaps
frozen to death that night on the bleak Moor.   Before
going to rest he had observed in the chamber a large
oak-chest: it was somewhat curious in form and ornament, and had the appearance of being of very great
antiquity.   He noticed or made some remarks upon
it to the old woman, who had lighted him up stairs in
order to see that all things in his chamber might be
as comfortable as circumstances would admit for his
repose.   There was something, he thought, shy and
odd about the manner of the woman when he observed the chest; and after she was gone he had
half a mind to take a peep into it.   Had he been a
daughter instead of a son of Eve he would most
likely have done so; but as it was he forbore, and
went to bed as fast as he could.

He felt cold and miserable; and who that does so
can ever hope for a sound or refreshing sleep?   His
was neither the one nor the other, for the woman
and the chest haunted him in his dreams; and a
hollow sound, as if behind his bed's head, suddenly
startled him out of his first sleep, when a circumstance
occurred which, like the ominous voice to Macbeth,
forbade him to sleep more.   As he started up in bed,
the first thing he saw was the old chest that had
troubled him in his dreams.   There it lay in the

silvery silence of the moonlight, looking cold and
white, and, connected with his dream, a provoking
and even alarming object of his curiosity. And then
he thought of the hollow sound which seemed to call
him from his repose, and the old woman's odd manner when he had talked to her about the chest, and
the reserve of her sturdy son, and, in short, the
traveller's own imagination supplied a thousand subjects of terror; indeed so active did it now become
in these moments of alarm that it gave a tongue to
the very silence of the night, and action even to the
most inanimate things; for he looked and looked
again, till he actually fancied the lid of the chest
began to move slowly up before his eyes!

He could endure no more; but, starting from his
bed, he rushed forward, grasped the lid with trembling hands, and raised it up at once. Who shall
speak his feelings when he beheld what that fatal
chest now disclosed?—a human corpse, stiff and cold,
lay before his sight! So much was he overcome with
the horror of his feelings, that it was with extreme
difficulty he could once more reach the bed.

How he passed the rest of the night he scarcely
remembered; but one thought, but one fear, possessed and agonized his whole soul. He was in the
house of murderers! he was a devoted victim! there
was no escape: for where, even if he left the chamber,
at such an hour, in such a night, where should he find
shelter, on the vast, frozen, and desolate Moor? He
had no arms, he had no means of flight; for if plunder
and murder might be designed, he would not be
suffered to pass out, when the young man (now, in
his apprehension a common trafficker in the blood
of the helpless) slept in the only room below, through

which he must pass if he stirred from where he was.

To dwell on the thoughts and feelings of the traveller during that night of terror would be an endless task; rather let me hasten to say that it was with the utmost thankfulness, and not without some surprise, that he found himself alive and undisturbed by any midnight assassin, when the sun once more arose and threw the cheerful light of day over the monotonous desolation of the Moor. Under any circumstances, and even in the midst of a desert, there is pleasure and animation in the morning; like hope in the young heart, it renders all things beautiful. If such are its effects under ordinary circumstances, what must it have been to our traveller, who hailed the renewed day as an assurance of renewed safety to his own life? He determined, however, to hasten away; to pay liberally, but to avoid doing or saying anything to awaken suspicion.

On descending to the kitchen he found the old woman and her son busily employed in preparing no other fate for him than that of a good breakfast; and the son, who the night before was probably tired out with labour, had now lost what the gentleman fancied to have been a very surly humour. He gave his guest a country salutation, and hoping 'his honour' had found good rest, proceeded to recommend the breakfast in the true spirit, though in a rough phrase, of honest hospitality; particularly praising the broiled bacon, as "mother was reckoned to have a curious hand at salting un in."

Daylight, civility, and broiled bacon, the traveller now found to be most excellent remedies against

the terrors, both real and otherwise, of his own imagination. The fright had disturbed his nerves, but
the keen air of those high regions, and the savoury
smell of a fine smoking rasher, were great restoratives.
And as none but heroes of the old school of romance
ever live without eating, I must say our gentleman
gave convincing proofs that he understood very well
the exercise of the knife and fork. Indeed so much
did he feel re-assured and elevated by the total extinction of all his personal fears, that, just as the
good woman was broiling him another rasher, he out
with the secret of the chest, and let them know that
he had been somewhat surprised by its contents;
venturing to ask, in a friendly tone, for an explanation
of so remarkable a circumstance.

"Bless your heart, your honour, 'tis nothing at all,"
said the young man, "'tis only fayther!"

"Father! your father!" cried the traveller, "what
do you mean?"

"Why you see, your honour," replied the peasant,
"the snaw being so thick, and making the roads so
cledgey-like, when old fayther died, two weeks agon,
we couldn't carry un to Tavistock to bury un; and
so mother put un in the old box, and salted un in:
mother's a fine hand at salting un in."

Need a word more be said of the traveller and his
breakfast; for so powerful was the association of
ideas in a mind as imaginative as that of our gentleman, that he now looked with horror upon the
smoking rasher, and fancied it nothing less than a
slice of 'old fayther.' He got up, paid his lodging,
saddled his horse; and quitting the house, where
surprise, terror, joy, and disgust had, by turns, so
powerfully possessed him, he made his way through

every impediment of snow and storm. And never could he afterwards be prevailed upon to touch bacon, since it always brought to ·mind the painful feelings and recollections connected with the adventure of 'salting un in.'

LETTER III.

TO ROBERT SOUTHEY, ESQ.

Wild Animals in ancient times on the Moor—Old custom of Fenwell rights—Banditti once common—Road across the Moor; mode of travelling before it was made—Thunder and Lightning not common —Tradition of Conjuring Time noticed—Witchcraft still a matter of belief—Extremes of Heat and Cold—Shepherd lost; his Dog— Two Boys lost in the Snow—Hot Vapour on the Moor, its appearance—Scepticism respecting the Druidical Remains noticed; its being wholly unsupported by reason, knowledge, or enquiry—The Damnonii, their origin with the rest of the ancient Britons; their history, &c. &c.—Camden quoted—Aboriginal Inhabitants of the Moor; the Druids, &c.—Orders of the Bards—Poetry—Regal power assumed by the Priesthood—Priests and Bards distinct Orders—Sacred Groves, &c.—Allegory of Lucian—Tacitus quoted, and other authorities respecting the Druids—Their Customs, Laws, &c., briefly noticed—Vestiges of British antiquity at Dartmoor— Spoliation there carried on—An assault on the Antiquities of the Moor.

Vicarage, Tavistock, February 23rd, 1832.

I HAVE somewhere seen it asserted that, in former times, Dartmoor was infested by many wild animals; amongst them the wolf and the bear; for the latter I have found no authority that would justify me in saying such was the case; but Prince, I see, mentions in his *Worthies of Devon,* that, in the reign of King John, the Lord Brewer of Tor Brewer received a licence from his sovereign to hunt the fox, the wild cat, and the wolf throughout the whole of the county of Devon: Dartmoor, no doubt, afforded a fine field for such a chase. And I may here notice that there is a tradition (mentioned also by Polwhele) amongst the people on the borders of the Moor, which they state to have derived from their forefathers, "that the hill country was inhabited whilst the valleys were full of serpents and ravenous beasts."

There is likewise an old custom, commonly referred to as the 'Fenwell rights,' which supports the truth of the assertion respecting the *wolves:* since the '*Venwell* rights,' as the peasantry call them, are nothing less than a right claimed by the inhabitants of a certain district, of pasturage and turf from the fens free of all cost: a privilege handed down to them through many generations, as a reward for services done by their ancestors in destroying the wolves, which, in early times, so much infested the forest of Dartmoor.   Many stories and traditions are, indeed, connected with these wild regions: some of which in due season I purpose giving you ; and many remarkable customs, now falling fast into decay, were there practised ; whose origin, as I shall endeavour to show, may be traced back even so far as the earliest times of which we have any authentic records, subsequent to the invasion of Britain under Cæsar.

It is nothing wonderful that such an extensive waste as the Moor, so full of rocks, caverns, tors, and intricate recesses, should have been in all ages the chosen haunt of banditti ; and in former days they did not fail to avail themselves of its facilities for conveying away plunder, or for personal security against detection ; whilst the gentry of those times, unless in a numerous and armed company, feared to cross the Moor, so dangerous was it known to be from lawless men, and so reputed to be haunted by the spirits and pixies of credulity and superstition.

There is now an excellent road across the Moor ;
as I trust you will find when you next travel westward.
This road was made between sixty and seventy years
ago ; and till that work was executed it was most
perilous to the traveller : for if he missed his line of
direction, or became entangled amidst rocks and
marshy grounds, or was enveloped in one of those
frequent mists, here so much to be dreaded, that prevented him even from seeing the course of the sun
above his head, he had no alternative but to follow, as
well as the difficulty of the way would admit, the
course of a river or stream ; and if this last resource
failed, he was likely to be lost on the Moor, and in the
depth of winter to be frozen to death, as many have
there been.

The atmosphere of Dartmoor deserves particular
notice ; it is nearly always humid.   The rain, which
frequently falls almost without intermission for many
weeks together, is generally small; and resembles
more a Scotch mist than a shower.   Sometimes, however, it will pour down in torrents ; but storms attended with thunder and lightning are not very
common : and whenever they do occur, one would
think that the peasantry still retained the superstitious
awe of the aboriginal inhabitants of the Moor, who
worshipped thunder as a god under the name of
Tiranis ; for they call a storm of that description
conjuring time, from the thorough persuasion that such
effects are solely produced by the malice of some
potent spirit or devils : though, mingling their Pagan
superstitions with some ideas founded on Christianity,
(just as their forefathers did when, on their first conversion, they worshipped the sun and moon as well as
the cross) they make a clergyman to have some con-

cern in the business: for while 'conjuring time' is
going on, he, in their opinion, is as hard at work as
the devils themselves, though in an opposite fashion ;
since on all such occasions they say, " that somewhere
or other in the county there's a parson a laying of a
spirit all in the Red Sea, by a talking of Latin to it ;
his clerk after each word saying Amen."

Indeed, our superstitions here are so numerous, and
so rooted amongst the poor and the lower classes,
that I think, before I bring these letters to a close, I
shall have it in my power not a little to divert you.
Witchcraft is still devoutly believed in by most of the
peasantry of Devon ; and the distinctions (for they
are nice ones) between a witch and a white witch,
and being bewitched, or only *overlooked* by a witch,
crave a very careful discrimination on the part of
their historian.

The extremes of cold and heat are felt upon the
Moor with the utmost intensity. Many a poor creature
has been there found frozen to death amidst its desolate ravines. I remember having heard of one instance, that happened many years ago, of a poor
shepherd who so perished, and was not found till some
weeks after his death: when his dog, nearly starved,
(and no one could even conjecture how the faithful
animal had sustained *his* life during the interval) was
discovered wistfully watching near the body of
his unfortunate master.

I have also learnt that a few. years since two lads,
belonging to a farm in the neighbourhood, were sent
out to look after some strayed sheep on the Moor.
A heavy fall of snow came on, and the boys not
returning the farmer grew uneasy, and a search after
them was commenced without delay. They were

both discovered nearly covered with snow, benumbed and in a profound sleep. With one of the poor lads, it was already the sleep of death; but the other was removed in this state of insensibility, and was at length, with much difficulty, restored to life.

On a sultry day, the heat of the Moor is most oppressive; as shade or shelter are rarely to be found. At such a time there is not, perhaps, a cloud in the sky: the air is perfectly clear and still; yet, even then, you have but to look steadily upon the heights and tors, and, to your surprise, they will appear in waving agitation. So thick, indeed, is the hot vapour which on such sultry days is constantly exhaled from the Moor, that I can only compare it to the reeking of a lime-kiln. The atmosphere is never perhaps other than humid, except in such cases, or in a very severe frost. I have heard my husband say that the wine kept in the cellars of his father's cottage on Dartmoor (for the late Mr. Bray built one there, and made large plantations near the magnificent river-scenery of the Cowsick) acquired a flavour that was truly surprising; and which, in a great degree, was considered to arise from the bottles being constantly in a damp state. This perpetual moisture upon them was wont to be called 'Dartmoor dew;' and all who tasted the wine declared it to be the finest flavoured of any they had ever drunk.

Before I enter upon a minute account of the British antiquities of Dartmoor, it will, perhaps, be advisable to offer a few remarks which, I trust, may assist in throwing some light upon a subject hitherto treated with slight notice, and not unfrequently with absolute scepticism; since some, who have never even investigated these remains upon the Moor,—who have never even seen them,—have, notwithstanding, taken upon themselves to assert that there are none to be found. But assertion is no proof; and those who shun the labour, patience, and inquiry, which are sometimes necessary in order to arrive at truth, must not wonder if they often miss the path that leads to it; but they should at least leave it fairly open to others, who are willing to continue the search.

It is not my purpose in this letter to enter upon any discussion as to who were the first settlers in this part of Britain. Wishing to inform myself upon the subject, many and opposite opinions have I examined; and the only impression that I received from these discussions was, that the writers themselves were too much puzzled in the mazes of controversy to convince their readers, however much they might have been convinced that each, exclusively, entertained the right opinion.

It seems to me, therefore, the wisest way to rest satisfied that the Damnonii had one common origin with the rest of the ancient Britons; and without attempting to penetrate that obscurity which has defied for so many ages the ingenuity of the most patient investigators, to admit without scepticism the commonly-received opinion—namely, that the first settlers in this part of the West were, like the people of Gaul, descended from the Celtæ, a branch of the nations from the East. Devonshire, according to Camden, was called Duffneynt, 'deep valleys,' by the Welsh; and certainly a more appropriate name could never have been chosen for a country so peculiarly characterized by the beauty and richness of its valleys, watered as they are by pure and rapid rivers or mountain streams.[1]

The Damnonii, perhaps, were less warlike than the inhabitants of other kingdoms of the Britons; since they readily submitted to the Roman power, and joined in no revolts that were attempted against it: a circumstance which, according to some historians, was the cause that so little was said about them by the Roman writers. The Damnonii were distinguished for the numbers and excellence of their flocks and herds. It is possible that this very circumstance might have rendered them less warlike than their neighbours, since the occupations of a pastoral life naturally tend to nourish a spirit of peace; whereas the toils, the tumult, and the dangers, to which the hunters of those days were constantly exposed in the chase, which so justly has been called 'an image of war,' must, on the contrary, have excited and kept alive a bold and restless spirit, that delighted in nothing so much as hostile struggles and achievements in the field.

But still more probable, perhaps, is the conjecture that the Damnonii, from their long and frequent intercourse with the Phœnicians, who traded to their coast as well as to that of Cornwall for tin, had become more civilized than the inhabitants of the other kingdoms of Britain. Possibly, indeed, they had learnt to know the value of those arts of peace to which a

[1] Camden says, "The hither country of the Damnonii is now called Denshire; by the Cornish Britons Dennan; by the Welsh Britons Duffneynt,—that is, 'deep valleys;' because they live everywhere here in lowly bottoms; by the English Saxons, Deumerchine, from whence comes the Latin Devonia, and that contracted name, used by the vulgar, Denshire. It was certainly styled Dyfneint by the Welsh." See RICHARDS, *in voce.*

warlike life is so great an enemy. Hence might have
arisen their more willing submission to their Roman
conquerors, who were likely to spread yet further
amongst them the arts and advantages of civilized
society. This is mere conjecture, but surely it is
allowable—since there must have been some cause
which operated powerfully on a whole kingdom to
make it rest satisfied with being conquered; and we
have no evidence, no hint even given by the earliest
writers, to suspect the courage or manly spirit of the
aboriginal inhabitants of Devon.

So celebrated were the British priesthood at the
time of the invasion of the Romans under Cæsar,
and so far had their fame extended into foreign lands,
that we know, on the authority of his writings, "such
of the Gauls as were desirous of being perfectly
instructed in the mysteries of their religion (which
was the same as that of the Britons) always made a
journey into Britain for the express purpose of ac-
quiring them." And in these kingdoms, as in other
nations of Celtic origin, it is most likely that those
who preferred peace to tumult,—who had a thirst
after the knowledge of their age,—or who liked better
the ease secured to them by having their wants
supplied by others than the labour of toiling for
themselves, became the disciples of the Druids.
Their groves and cells, appropriated to study and
instruction, afforded security and shelter; and there,
undisturbed by outward circumstances, they could
drink of that fountain of sacred knowledge which
had originally poured forth a pure and undefiled
stream from its spring in the Eastern world, but had
become turbid and polluted as it rolled through the
dark groves of Druidical superstition.

In these groves, it is believed, they learnt the secret
of the one true and only God, the immortality of the
soul, and a future state of rewards and punishments.
But this was held too excellent for the people, who
it was deemed required a grosser doctrine, one more
obvious to the senses. To them, therefore, it was
not fully disclosed; it was not to be shown in
all its simple and natural lustre; the doctrines
which 'came of men' were added to it; and these
being of the earth, like the vapours which arise
thence, ascended towards Heaven only to obscure
its light.[2]

The poetry of the ancient British priesthood has
ever been a subject of the highest interest; and its
origin, perhaps, may be referred to the most simple
cause. Nothing of import was allowed to be written
down; nor is there any possible means of knowing
when symbols, or written characters, were first introduced among them. To supply this defect, it became
absolutely necessary that the laws, both civil and
religious, should be placed in such a form as most
readily to be committed to memory, and so trans-
mitted to their posterity. For this purpose no means

[2] There can be little doubt that the Druids, Celts, and Cyclops were
all of the same origin. The Druids, in fact, were nothing more than
the priesthood of that colony of the Celtic race established in Britain.
There cannot be a stronger proof of the truth of this assertion, than
that all Celtic works, in whatever kingdom they are found, are exactly
similar. Dr. Clarke, in his delightful *Travels*, mentions several
antiquities of Celtic date in Sweden and elsewhere, the same in their
construction as those found on Dartmoor. He tells us, that old Upsal
was the place renowned for the worship of the primeval idolatry of
Sweden; that a *circular range of stones* was the spot where its ancient
kings went through the ceremony of inauguration. "This curious
circle exists in the plains of Mora, hence it is called Morasteen, the
word *mora* strictly answering to our word *moor*."—CLARKE'S *Travels*,
vol. ix. p. 216.

could be so effective as those of throwing them into the form of apophthegms in verse: the triads are an example.

In process of time, however, what at first was had recourse to as a matter of necessity, became a subject of delight and emulation; and poetry in all probability was cultivated for its own sake: for its capability of expressing the passions of the soul, for the beauty of its imagery, and the harmony of its numbers. Those who had most genius would become the best poets; and giving up their time and attention to the art in which they excelled, it is not improbable that they were left to the full exercise of their talent, and became a distinct, and at last a secondary, order of the Druids. Those graver personages who did not thus excel in verse, retained and appropriated to themselves the higher order of the priesthood,— that of performing the rites and ceremonies of religion, sitting in judgment on the criminal, and acting the part both of priests and kings: for certain it is that though the regal title was still retained by the princes of the Celtæ, all real power was soon usurped by the priests; and it is not a little remarkable that, both in ancient and modern times, this tendency to encroachment on the part of the priesthood has always been observable in those who were followers of a false or corrupted religion. Where God, on the contrary, prevails in all the purity of his worship, respect, submission, and a willing obedience to civil government, for conscience' sake, invariably accompany the holy function and its order.

To return from this digression to the bards: and as I am writing from the very land they once inhabited, I feel a more than ordinary interest in my subject, which I trust will plead my apology if I somewhat dwell upon it.

Supposing, then, that at first there was but *one* order of the Druidical priesthood, (and I have found nothing to contradict this supposition, which seems most natural) and that in such order some of the members excelled others in the readiness of throwing into verse the laws and customs of their religion and government, and that this talent at length was their sole occupation, till they became in some measure secularized priests, it would naturally follow that in process of time the Druids absolutely divided and separated themselves into *two* orders—priests, and bards. And amongst the latter another division soon, perhaps, arose; for some of these excelled in composing the verses connected with the religion and rites of the sacred festivals, whilst others probably took more delight in celebrating the actions of chiefs and kings, and in singing the fame of their heroes who had fallen in battle. Hence came the *third* order. Those who celebrated the praises of the gods, of course, stood higher in a land of superstition, than those who merely sung the praises of men. The former, therefore, were called hymn-makers, or vates; and the latter, bards. So great was the power of this priesthood, whether wholly or separately considered, that its members not only exercised all rites of a sacred nature, but determined upon and excited war,—interfered to command peace,—framed the laws and judged the criminal; and also held within their hands the most useful as well as the most delusive arts of life. They cured the sick,—foretold the events of futurity,—held commerce with invisible spirits,—exercised augury

and divination,—knew all the stars of Heaven and
the productions of the earth; and were supreme in
all controversies of a public or of a private nature:
whilst their wrath against those who displeased them
vented itself in their terrific sentence of excommunication,—a religious sentence which has scarcely a
parallel in history, if we except that of excommunication as it was once enforced by the church of
Rome.

In the sacred groves, the disciples learnt the fearful
rites of human immolation to the deified objects of
human craft; and, mingling in their study of poetry
the beauty and innocence of fiction with some of its
worst features, they also made hymns in praise of the
seasons, of the birds and the plants, and celebrated
the seed-time, and the 'golden harvest,' in the
numbers of their verse. Here, likewise, they learnt
to frame those war-songs of impassioned eloquence,
which depicted the hero in such glowing colours that
they who listened caught the inspiration and rose to
emulate his deeds; and their kings and chiefs were
sent forth to the battle "with a soul returned from
song more terrible to the war."

The refinements of polished life and education
were not theirs; but their imagination, unfettered
by rules, and impressed from infancy by the wild
grandeur of the scenes in which they lived, was
strong and bold as the martial spirit of their race.
Those arts which teach men to subdue or to hide
their feelings were unknown; and, following the
impulse of Nature, they became masters in the true
eloquence of the heart. Hence arose the power of
the bards, in whose very name there is so much of
poetry, that in our own language we could find

no other term so suited to express the feathered
songsters of the air, and therefore were they called
'the *bards* of the woods.' [3]

The power of oratory was eminently displayed in
all their compositions; and so highly was that art
esteemed by the Druids of the Celtæ, that it gave
birth to the beautiful allegory told by Lucian, who
says that, whilst he was in Gaul, he saw Hercules
represented as a little old man, who was called by
the people 'Ogmius;' and that this feeble and
aged deity appeared in a temple dedicated to his
worship, drawing towards him a multitude who were
held by the slightest chain fastened to their ears and
to his tongue. Lucian, wondering what so strange
a symbol was intended to denote, begged that it
might be explained to him; when he was presently
told, "that Hercules did not in Gaul, as in Greece,
betoken strength of body, but, what was of far
greater power, the force of eloquence; and thus,
therefore, was he figured by the priests of Gaul."
Lord Bacon possibly might have had this image in
his mind when he so emphatically declared that
'knowledge is power.'

All the Celtic tribes appear to have studied these
arts with extraordinary success. The Germans, as
well as the Gauls and Britons, did so; for "they
abound," says Tacitus, "with rude strains of verse, the
reciters of which are called bards; and with this barbarous poetry they inflame their minds with ardour in
the day of action, and prognosticate the event from
the impression which it happens to make on the
minds of the soldiers, who grow terrible to the enemy,

[3] Most of the peasantry in Devonshire still pronounce this word
(birds) *bards.*

or despair of success, as the war-song produces an animated or a feeble sound."

The genius for poetry evinced by their bards was one of the most remarkable qualities observable among the ancient priesthood of Britain : so simple, yet so forcible, was the imagery they employed,—so feeling the language of their productions,—that, even at this day, such of their poems as have come down to us can never be read with other than the deepest interest, by those in whose bosom there is a responsive chord, true to Nature and to feeling. The passions which they expressed in these poems were rude but manly; their indignation was aimed against their foes—against cowardice and treachery; whilst the virtues of courage—of generosity—of tenderness—of the 'liberal heart' and 'open hand,' were honoured and praised by the Sons of Song; and the brave man went forth to battle, strong in the assurance that, if he conquered or if he fell, his fame would be held sacred, and receive its honours from the harp of truth.

The learning of the British priesthood has been frequently spoken of by ancient authors in terms of commendation ; and in this particular they have been ranked with the nations of the East. Pliny compares them to the magi of Persia, and says they were the physicians as well as the poets of the country. Cæsar observes that they had formed systems of astronomy and natural philosophy. Twenty years of study was the allotted time for rendering a novice competent to take upon him the sacred order ; and when initiated, the education of the sons of the British nobles and kings, the mysteries of religion, legislation, and the practice of the various arts that were exclusively theirs, must have afforded ample scope for the constant exercise of that learning which had been acquired with so much diligence and labour.

That they exercised their genius also, on matters of speculative philosophy, cannot be doubted; since Strabo has recorded one of their remarkable opinions respecting the universe;—"that it was never to be destroyed, but to undergo various changes, sometimes by the power of fire, at others by that of water." And Cæsar mentions their disquisitions on the nature of the planets, "and of God, in the power he exercised in the works of his creation." Many opinions, purely speculative, have been broached to account for the choice of a circular figure in their temples. Some have supposed it was designed to represent that eternity which has neither a beginning nor an end. But it is not improbable that, as they taught the multitude to worship visible objects, the form of their temples might have had a reference to those objects; and the heavenly bodies they so much studied (the sun and moon, in particular, as the chief amongst their visible deities) might have suggested an imitation of their form in the circular shape of the temples dedicated to their worship.

The use of letters was not unknown to the Druids of Britain; for Cæsar states "that in all affairs and transactions, excepting those of religion and learning," (both of which belonged to the mysteries of Druidism) "they made use of letters, and that the letters which they used were those of the Greek alphabet."[4] There was no want, therefore, of that

[4] The Rev. Edward Davies, in his most interesting account of the Lots and the Sprig Alphabet of the Druids, has very satisfactorily

learning which is requisite for the purposes of history, had they chosen to leave a written record of the public transactions of their country. But in these early times the poet was the only historian; and his verses were committed to memory, and were thus handed down from age to age. The laws were framed and preserved by the same means; so that in those days what are now the two most opposite things in the literature of modern nations,—law and poetry,—went hand in hand; and the lawyers of the ancient Britons were unquestionably the wearers of the long blue robes instead of the black ones.[5]

It was, indeed, a favourite practice with the nations of antiquity to transmit their laws from generation to generation merely by tradition. The ancient Greeks did so; and the Spartans, in particular, allowed none to be written down. The Celtæ observed the same custom; and Toland mentions that in his time there was a vestige of it still to be found in the Isle of Man, where many of the laws were tradition-ary, and were there known by the name of *Breast*

shown that many antiquaries, by an inattentive reading of a particular passage in Cæsar, adopted the erroneous notion that the British priests allowed nothing to be written down; whereas Cæsar only states that they allowed their *scholars* to commit nothing to writing. The symbols, or sprigs, chosen from different trees, gave rise to the sprig alphabet of Ireland; and Toland, in his very learned work on the Druids of that country, established the fact of their having some per-manent records, by a reference to the stone memorials of Ireland, which in his day, about a century ago, still bore the vestiges of Druidical inscriptions.

[5] In the *Triads* the bards are described as wearers of this par-ticular dress, which no doubt was adopted to distinguish them from the white robed Druids. "Whilst Menu lived, the memorial of bards was in request; whilst he lived the sovereign of the land of heroes, it was his custom to bestow benefits and honour and fleet coursers on the wearers of the *long blue robes*."

Laws. When speaking of the jurisprudence of these primitive nations, Tacitus gives a very striking reason for the administration of the laws being confined to the priesthood. " The power of punishing," says that delightful historian, "is in no other hands : when exercised by the priests, it has neither the air of vindictive justice nor of military execution ;—it is rather a *religious sentence.*" "And all the people," says Strabo, " entertain the highest opinion of the justice of the Druids : to them all judgment, in public and private, in civil and criminal cases, is committed."

We learn also from the classical writers, that the Druids had schools or societies in which they taught their mysteries, both civil and religious, to their disciples ;—that such seats of learning were situated in forests and groves remote from, or difficult of, general access; since secrecy and mystery were the first rules of their instructions. Had they taught only truth, neither the one nor the other would have been required ; since it is only falsehood that seeks a veil, and when that is once lifted, she is sure to be detected. False religions, or those corrupted by the inventions of men, have always observed the same kind of mysticism, not only in rude but in polished ages also. No one was suffered to lift the sacred mantle of the goddess Hertha, except the priest : the people were charged to believe in her most terrific superstitions, but none could see her and live.[6]

To enlarge on the frauds, the arts of magic, soothsaying, and divination, practised by the Druids to blind and lead the multitude, would extend much beyond the proposed limits of this letter. Should it never go farther than Keswick, all that I have said

[6] See *Manners of the Germans.* MURPHY'S *Tacitus*, page 351.

respecting the ancient priesthood I know would be unnecessary. But should these papers so far meet your approval as to sanction their hereafter appearing in print, I must consider what might be useful to the mere general reader; and it is possible that some one of that class may not have troubled himself much about the early history of that extraordinary priesthood, who once held a power so truly regal in the islands of Great Britain. To such this sketch, slight as it is, may not be unacceptable, should it only excite in them a wish to consult better authorities; and I trust, also, it may serve the chief purpose which I now have in view—namely, that of raising some degree of interest by speaking of the Druids, to lead my readers, should they have the opportunity, to an examination of those ancient vestiges and structures that still remain on the wilds of Dartmoor. Of these I shall speak in the subsequent letters; and in doing so I shall endeavour to execute my task with fidelity, since not the least motive in prompting me to it is the wish I entertain to throw some light on a subject which has hitherto been involved in much obscurity; and even my labours, like those of the 'little busy bee,' may bring something to the hive, though they are gathered from the simplest sources around me.

I may also add, that in pointing out to this neighbourhood in particular the connection that really exists between the remains of British antiquity (so widely scattered on the Moor) and the early history and manners of the first inhabitants of their country, it is to be hoped that a sufficient interest may be excited in favour of those vestiges, to check the unfeeling spoliation which has of late been so rapidly carried on. When we find on Dartmoor masses of

granite buried under the earth and resting upon its
surface,—here lying close to the road, and there
impeding the culture of its soil—surely it would
be better to serve the purposes of commerce from
sources like these, than to despoil (as they are now
doing) the summits of its eminences,—of those very
tors that give beauty and majesty to the desolation
of the Moor.   The cairns,—the obelisks—the circles,
and the poor remains of British huts, might be permitted to last out their day, and to suffer from no
other assaults than those which are inevitable—time
and tempest; and these are enemies that will not
pass over them in vain.

Dartmoor has, indeed, been a field to the spoiler;
and many of its most interesting memorials have
been destroyed within the last twenty or thirty
years; for during those periods vast walls of stones,
piled loosely together without cement, and extending
in every direction for many miles, have been placed
up as boundaries or enclosures for cattle.   This great
demand for stones caused the workmen to remove
those which lay, as it were, ready to their hand; you
may judge, therefore, what havoc it made with the
circles, cairns, and cromlechs.   Others—such as were
straight and tall—have been carried off (so the people
of the Moor tell me) to make rubbing-posts for cattle,
a rubbing-post being sometimes called 'cow's comfort' in Devon.

One assault on the antiquities of Dartmoor was so
atrocious that it must not here be passed in silence.
Many years ago, a young man of this place celebrated
his freedom from his apprenticeship by leading out a
parcel of young fellows, as wanton and as silly as
himself, to Dartmoor, for no other purpose than that

of giving themselves the trouble to do what they
could in destroying its antiquities. As if, like the
ancient inhabitants of the Moor, they had been wor-
shippers of the god Hu,—the Bacchus of the Druids,—
they commenced the day with a libation, for they
made punch in the rock-basins, and roared and sang
as madly as any of the old devotees might have done,
during the riots of a saturnalia in honour of Hu
himself in the days of his pride. This rite accomplished, and what small remains of wit they might
have had being fairly driven out by these potent
libations, they were ungrateful enough to commence
their havoc by destroying the very punch-bowl which
had served them, and soon set about the rest of their
work. They were a strong and a willing band; so
that logans were overturned, obelisks knocked down,
and stones rooted from their circles, till, work as hard
as they would, they found the Britons had been too
good architects to have their labours shaken and upset
in a day. They left off at last for very weariness,
having accomplished just sufficient mischief to furnish
the moralizing antiquary who wanders over Dartmoor
with the reflection their wanton havoc suggests to his
mind,—that wisdom builds not without time and
labour ; but that folly overturns in a day that which
it could not have produced in an age—so much easier
is it at all times to effect evil than to do good.[7]

[7] I am the more induced to dwell on this circumstance, since, even
in our own day, a naval officer overturned the celebrated Logan in
Cornwall ; and, much to the credit of government, was compelled to
set it up again, which he effected with extreme difficulty.

LETTER IV.

TO ROBERT SOUTHEY, ESQ.

Vicarage, Tavistock, Feb. 25, 1832.

THE earliest records respecting the history of Dartmoor must be sought on the Moor itself, and that
with no small diligence and labour. And as I
presume no reasonable person would deny that the
Damnonii, as indeed all the other inhabitants of
Britain, upheld the priesthood of Druidism, I shall
proceed to show that, throughout the whole county,
no place was so fitted to the august rites of their
superstition, to the solemn courts of their judicature,
or to the mystery and retirement which they sought

in the initiation of their disciples, as amid the rugged
and rock-crowned hills of Dartmoor.

We know that the Druids not only held it unlaw-
ful to perform the rites of their religion within
covered temples, but that they preferred, whenever
these could be found, eminences and lofty heights for
that purpose; as such situations gave them a more
open and commanding view of those planets which
they studied as philosophers and worshipped as
idolaters.

Dartmoor abounds in heights that, in some instances, assume even a mountainous character; and
when we find that many of these retain to the present
hour the very names of those false gods (though corrupted in their pronunciation, as are the names of
towns and villages, by the lapse of years and the
changes in language) to whom altars were raised by
the priesthood of Britain, surely this circumstance
alone becomes a strong presumptive evidence that
the Moor itself was a chosen spot for ·the ancient
and idolatrous worship of the Damnonii. I shall here
give a few of the most prominent examples; and it
is not unlikely that any one learned in the old British
tongues—the Cornish or Welsh—would be able to
find a significant meaning in the names of various
other heights and tors on the Moor, that now sound
so strange and whimsical to unlearned ears like my
own.

The Britons worshipped the Almighty, or, as he
was not unfrequently called, the God of Battles,
under the name of Hesus. On Dartmoor we find a
height called *Hessory Tor*. The sun, that universal
object of adoration even from the earliest times with
heathen nations, was also held sacred by the Druids,

and the noblest altars and temples were dedicated
to his honour. The sun was adored under various
names, but none more commonly than that of Belus,
or Bel;[1] and on Dartmoor we have *Bel Tor* to this
day. The sun, and also the moon, were sometimes
worshipped under the names of Mithra or *Misor:* on
the Moor we have *Mis Tor*, a height on whose consecrated rocks there is found so large and perfect a
rock-basin as to be called by the peasantry *Mis Tor
Pan.* Ham, or Ammon, was ranked amongst the
British deities: on Dartmoor the heathen god still
possesses his eminence, unchanged in name, as we
there find *Ham Tor* to this day; and my venerable
and learned friend, the Rev. Mr. Polwhele,[2] in his
History of Devon, refers to the worship of that
deity all the numerous *Hams* of this county.[3] We
have also a spot which you must visit—*Baird-down*,
(pronounced Bair-down) which Mr. Bray conjectures
to mean 'the hill of bards;' and, opposite to it, Wistman's, or (as he also conjectures) *Wiseman's* Wood,
of which I shall presently speak in a very particular
manner, as embracing some of the most remarkable
points of Druid antiquity to be found throughout the
whole range of the Moor.

We learn from Cæsar, and other classical writers,
that the Druids lived in societies and formed schools,
in which they taught the mysteries of their learning,
their religion, and their arts. We find, also, that such
seats of instruction were situated in forests and groves,

---

[1] Borlase notices these tors on Dartmoor as still bearing the names of
Druid gods.   [2] Since deceased.

[3] According to Kennet's *Glossary*, however, *hamma* is from the
Saxon *ham*, a house; hence *hamlet*, a collection of houses. It sometimes meant an enclosure; hence to *hem* or surround. This is the sense
in which it seems chiefly used in Devonshire, as the South-hams, &c.

remote from or difficult of general access; since secrecy and mystery accompanied all they taught. Where, therefore, could the priesthood of the Damnonii have found, throughout the whole of the West, a place more suited to these purposes than Dartmoor?

It was a region possessed of every natural advantage that could be desired in such an age and by such a people. It was surrounded and girded by barrier rocks, hills, and eminences mountainous in their character. No enemy could approach it with any hostile intent, without having to encounter difficulties of an almost insurmountable nature; and such an approach would have been announced by the flaming beacons of the hundred tors, that would have alarmed and called up the country to prepare for defence in every direction.

Though Dartmoor is now desolate, and where the oak once grew there is seen but the lonely thistle, and the 'feebly-whistling grass,' and its hills are the hills of storms, as the torrents rush down their sides, yet that it was once, in part at least, richly clothed with wood cannot be doubted. The very name, so ancient, which it still bears, speaks its original claim to a sylvan character—the *Forest* of Dartmoor;[4] and though of this antique forest nothing now remains but the wasting remnant of its days, in the 'lonely wood of Wistman,' (as Carrington has designated it) to show where the groves of the wise men or Druids once stood, yet evidence is not wanting to prove what it has been: since in bogs and marshes on the Moor, near the banks of rivers and streams, sometimes

[4] " Foresta *q. d. Feresta*, hoc est ferarum statio." Vide DU CANGE *in voce*, who defines it also " *Saltus*, Silva, *Nemus*," evidently inclining to the opinion that it should be a woody tract.

imbedded twenty feet below the surface of the earth, are found immense trunks of the oak and other trees.[5]

These rivers and streams, which everywhere abound on the Moor, afforded the purest waters; and many a beautiful and bubbling fountain, which sprang from the bosom of that earth, once worshipped as a deity by the Celtic priesthood, (and to which they ascribed the origin of man) became, no doubt, consecrated to the mysteries of her circle and her rites. It is not improbable that one or two springs of this nature, still held in high esteem on the Moor, may owe their sacred character to the superstitions of the most remote ages: such, perhaps, may be the origin of that estimation in which Fice's well is still held; but of this more hereafter.

The groves of oak, whose "gloom," to use the language of Tacitus, "filled the mind with awe, and, revered at a distance, might never be approached but with the eye of contemplation," were filled with the most varied tribes of feathered inhabitants. Some of these were of an order sacred in the estimation of Druid superstition. The raven was their tenant, whose ill-omened appearance is still considered as the harbinger of death, and still is as much dreaded by the peasantry as it was in the days of ancient augury and divination. The black eagle, that native of the Moor, long spread her sable wing and made her dwelling amidst the heights and the crags of the rocky tors, when she had been driven from the valleys and the more cultivated lands. She is still said to revisit the Moor, like a spirit of other times, who may be supposed to linger around the scenes in which she

[5] A very large trunk of an oak tree so found on Dartmoor is now preserved in the vicarage gardens of Tavistock.

once proudly held her sway; but her nest is nowhere
to be found.⁶   There also the "white-breasted bird of
Oxenham,"⁷ so fatal to that house, still appears with
her bosom pure and unsullied as the Druid's robes,
and like him raises a cry of augury and evil.   Her
mission done, she is seen no more till she comes
again as a virgin mourner, complaining before death.
There, too, may be found the heath poult, or moor
blackbird, once held sacred : so large is it, and sable
in colour, that it might at a little distance be mistaken for the black eagle.   Her eye, with its lid of
the brightest scarlet, still glances on the stranger who
ventures on the recesses of the Moor; and, like a
watchful genius at the fountain, she is chiefly seen to
make her haunt near the source of the river Dart.

   No place could have been better adapted for
observing the flight of birds in Druid augury, than
the woods and heights of Dartmoor.   I have often
there seen them in flocks winging their way at a
vast elevation across its hills.   Sometimes they would
congregate together, and with a sudden clamour that
was startling, rush out from the crags and clefts of
one of the granite tors, with the utmost velocity.
At others, they would pause and rest for a moment

   ⁶ "I have been told," says Mr. Polwhele in his *Devon*, "by a gentleman of Tavistock, that, shooting on Dartmoor, he hath several times
seen the black eagle there, though he could never discover its nest."
   ⁷ "There is a family," says Prince, speaking of Oxenham, in his
Worthies of Devon, "of considerable standing of this name at South
Tawton, near Oakhampton in this county; of which is this strange and
wonderful thing recorded.   That at the deaths of any of them, a bird,
with a white breast, is seen for a while fluttering about their beds, and
then suddenly to vanish away.   Mr. James Howell tells us that, in a
lapidary's shop in London, he saw a large marble-stone, to be sent into
Devonshire, with an inscription, 'That John Oxenham, Mary, his sister,
James, his son, and Elizabeth, his mother, had each the appearance of
such a bird fluttering about their beds as they were dying.'"

among the rocks, or skim along the rivers and foaming streams, and dip their wings and rise again with restless rapidity.

The vast quantity of rock, the masses of granite which are everywhere strewn throughout the Moor, the tors that crowned the summits of every hill, must have afforded such facilities for the purpose of their altars, circles, obelisks, cromlechs, and logans, that no part of this kingdom had, perhaps, a more celebrated station of Druidism than Dartmoor: not even Mona, Classerness, nor the plains of Abury and Salisbury. But they who, like the Druids themselves, have been accustomed to pay an almost idolatrous worship to that primitive and most noble structure Stonehenge, may here exclaim—"If this be true, how is it that you have no such memorial of equal magnitude on Dartmoor?"

To this I answer, Stonehenge (like Carnac in Brittany, which I have cursorily visited and described[8]) stands on a plain: it required, therefore, such a structure to give to the ceremonies of Druidical worship that awful and imposing effect which Tacitus so repeatedly implies to have formed the chief character of their religious mysteries. On the plains of Salisbury Nature had done nothing for the grandeur of Druidism, and art did all. On Dartmoor the priests of the Britons appropriated the *tors themselves as temples*, erected by the hand of Nature, and with such majesty that their circles were only memorials of their consecration: so that what in level countries became the most imposing object, was here considered as a matter of comparative

---

[8] In *Letters written during a Tour through Normandy and Brittany in* 1818.

indifference.   In such scenes a Stonehenge would
have dwindled in comparison with the granite tors
into perfect insignificance ; it would have been as a
pyramid at the foot of Snowdon.   The architects of
Egypt, like the Druids of Salisbury Plain, had a
level country to contend with, and they gave to it
the glory of mountains, as far as art may be said to
imitate Nature in the effect of her most stupendous
works.

Whoever attentively examines the tors and vestiges
of antiquity on Dartmoor will soon be convinced that
art was but very slightly employed on the masses of
granite which crown the heights that were consecrated
to the divinities of British idolatry.   In Vixen Tor,
that Sphinx of the Moor, the mass was so completely
formed by Nature to suit their desires, that three
basins, chiselled on the very summit of this lofty and
insulated rock, are the only mark left of its having
been selected for any one of the numerous rites of
Druidical superstition.

On Dartmoor, then, we may fairly conclude that
whatever was most advantageous to the hierarchy of
the ancient Britons was most amply to be found ;
and in my next letter I shall proceed to a more
minute examination of what use was made of such
advantages, by describing what still remains to
interest us as records of the being, the history, and
the religious rites of the priests of the Damnonii.
Nor can I conclude these remarks without observing
that on the Moor the Druid moved in the region of
the vast and the sublime : the rocks, the winter
torrent, the distant and expanded ocean, the works
of the great God of Nature, in their simplest and in
their most imposing character, were all before his

view; and often must he have witnessed, in the
strife of elements, that scene so beautifully described
by our poet, who has celebrated the Moor with a
feeling true to Nature, and with a boldness and
vigour suited to the grandeur of the subject he
portrayed.

> " Fierce, frequent, sudden is the moorland storm ;
> And oft, deep sheltered in the stream-fed vales,
> The swain beholds upon the lessening tor
> The heavens descend in gloom, till, mass on mass
> Accumulated, all the mighty womb
> Of vapour bursts tremendous.   Loud resounds
> The torrent rain, and down the guttered slopes
> Rush the resistless waters.   Then the leap
> Of headlong cataract is heard, and roar
> Of rivers struggling o'er their granite beds—
> Nor these alone—the giant tempest passed,
> A thousand brooks their liquid voices raise
> Melodiously, and through the smiling land
> Rejoicing roll."

And here, ere I say farewell, let me pause a moment
to express my regret for that indifference with which
many persons, in this part of England, look on Dartmoor.   Carrington found in it a subject for a poem
that has ranked his lamented name amongst the first
of our British bards.   And though all are not poets,
nor have the feelings that are allied to poetry, yet all
might find some pleasure, would they but learn to
value it,—a pleasure pure as it is powerful,—in the
heights and valleys of the lonely Moor.

A morning's walk there in the spring or the summer is attended with a freshness, from the bracing
temperature of the air, which gives cheerfulness to
the mind and content to the heart. A thousand
circumstances in Nature everywhere lie around to

interest him who views her with a kindly and a
feeling eye. The mists which hang about the tors are
seen gradually dispersing ; and the tors themselves,
as we watch them, seem to put on a thousand forms,
such as fancy suggests to delight the mind in which
she dwells. The cattle are seen around, grazing on
the verdant pastures, studded with myriad drops of
dew. As we look on them, they call to mind some
of the bronze works of antiquity that so nobly
represented those creatures: for in symmetry of form
and limb, as well as in richness of colour, the cattle of
Devon are models of beauty in their kind. The wild
horses and colts, with their unshorn and flowing tails
and manes, recall also to our recollection the forms of
antique sculpture. To observe them in action as they
bound, race, or play together, in the very joy of their
freedom, affords a spectacle of animal delight that is
replete with interest. The horse thus seen in his
natural state, before he is ridden by man, becomes a
perfect study for a painter.[9] And the poor ass, that
useful and patient drudge,—an animal, like the goat,
of the most picturesque nature,—is seen quietly
browsing on the grass, waiting the hour of labour in
the service of his master.

The instinct of the lambs and the care of their

[9] The following circumstance, respecting a pony that was one of a
very fine breed the late Mr. Bray had on the Moor, is worth noticing
here. It is also mentioned by Mr. Burt in Carrington's poem. The
late Ca   Cotgrave, who was engaged in some duty at the French
prison,   d seen a pony he wished to detach from the herd at Bair-
down. In the endeavour to effect his object, the animal was driven on
some blocks of granite by the side of a tor. A horseman instantly
rode up in order to catch it, when, to the astonishment of all who
witnessed the feat from below, the pony fairly and completely leapt
over horse and rider, and escaped with a fleetness that set at defiance
all further pursuit.

mothers have often interested me, as I have observed the perseverance with which one of the latter would range around the flock till she found her own off spring, to give it the earliest meal of her milk. And the bleating of some other poor little straggler, as it would stand still and call upon its dam, was so like the cry of infancy, that it could not fail to raise a feeling of pity for so helpless and harmless an animal.[1]

The rivers and streams, as they run in the morning light, have something so exhilarating that it glads the heart and the eye to look on their lively and sparkling waters as they flow,

" Making sweet music with the enamelled stones."

And then the fresh air of the Moor, which renders the very step light as we inhale it, and the clear blue skies, and the varying and changing clouds, now white, now roseate, or opening and closing before the view, are all objects of the highest enjoyment. And the insect world, that starts at once, as it were, into its ephemeral being,—a world of which none in Nature presents a greater variety,—all useful, all governed by a beautiful economy in their order and their kind,— can never be seen with indifference by those who have once given such subjects even but a slight attention. We are pleased to see around us, reviving into life, even our most familiar acquaintance, the common house-fly; and the very insects that love rivers and haunt pools add some degree of animation to the hour. No place will afford a more interesting

[1] Early lambs are never reared on Dartmoor, on account of the coldness of the air. Those that come late, however, are considered to do well there. These are called *cuckoo lambs*, as being contemporary with the appearance of that bird.

field for the entomologist than the hills and vales of
Dartmoor.   There too we meet in spring, upon a
sunny day, the pale yellow butterfly, usually the
tenant of the garden and the flower-bed ; and it is
often seen, like infancy by the side of age, sporting on
the front of some old grey rock, or settling on the
wild thyme, or on the golden furze,—as its wings
vibrate with a quickness that will sometimes dazzle
the sight.

And how beautiful is 'the song of earliest birds,'
the thrush that never tires, or the lark that sings
first and soars highest, like youth who thinks the
world a region of pleasure to be compassed on the
wing of hope.   Dartmoor is rich in birds, and those
often of an uncommon kind.[2]   The pretty little
wheatear, or English ortolan, builds its nest amongst
the old rocks, whose colour it so resembles in the
black and grey of its wings, that you sometimes do
not observe it perched upon the clefts till you hear its
small cry.   There too has been seen the goshawk, so
rare in Devon ; and the kite, that is now seldom found
in its peaceful and inhabited valleys, still prowls like
a bandit about the Moor, as if he came to make his
prey with impunity amidst its unfrequented wilds.
And the honey-buzzard, rare as it is in this county,
has there, nevertheless, been marked chasing the
dragon-fly, as that beautiful insect endeavoured to
evade its enemy, and would

> " Dart like a fairy javelin by."

And the ring-ousel finds its dwelling in the hollows
and cavities of the rocks, and the poor little reed-wren
makes them her home ; and the robin, that favourite of

[2] Dr. Moore, of Plymouth, has lately published a catalogue of all
the birds that frequent the different parts of the county of Devon.

old and young, there need fear no pilfering youngster
—since so much is this pretty bird the familiar friend
of children in our neighbourhood, that the boys will
pelt any one of their companions who may steal but
an egg from 'poor Cock Robin's' nest. The snow-
bunting and the stormy petrel are sometimes found
on these hills; and even the bittern will make her
cry amidst their desolation. But these are birds of a
melancholy season; since the first we know by its
name comes in the dreary time, and the petrel,
suffering from the storm that gives her a claim upon
our commiseration, has been driven to land, and
found dead upon the Moor.

But on a spring or a summer morning no birds are
seen but those which give delight. They are not
vain monitors; for all their occupations are divided
between rejoicing and industry. They sing in the
gladness and thankfulness of their existence, or they
labour to find food and shelter for their young. To
them nothing is indifferent within the range of their
capacity. The straw or the fallen leaf,—the tuft of
wool that hangs on the briar as it was torn from the
sheep,—a very hair, is treasured and placed to the
account of what is useful in the internal structure
exhibited by the little architect in its nest.

To watch the economy of birds,—to mark the
enjoyment of the animal world,—to view with an
eye of interest and contemplation the fields with
'verdure clad,' and every opening blossom bursting
into beauty and life, are enjoyments that instruct
and delight youth, middle, and old age. They supply
us with a source of innocent employment, to which
none need be dead but those who wilfully become so,
by keeping their eyes closed before that book of

Nature which is everywhere spread around, that we should read in it those characters of an Almighty hand that lead the mind to wonder at and adore his goodness, and the heart to acknowledge and to feel his power, as a Father, who in his 'wisdom has created' and preserves them all.

LETTER V.

TO ROBERT SOUTHEY, ESQ.

Bair-down supposed to have been the Hill of Bards—Inscriptions on the Rocks: how cut—House on the Eminence—Beautiful Ravine: Bridge over the River Cowsick—Trees planted in the Ravine by the late Mr. Bray—Remarks on the Etymology of Bair-down, and Wistman's Wood—Observations on the English Distich— Merlin's Cave in the Rocks—Wand or Rod—Rural Inscriptions on the Granite.

Vicarage, Tavistock, March 2, 1832.

HAVING given you in my former letters a general account of Dartmoor, I shall now proceed to a more particular description of its localities, and in doing so I shall principally avail myself of the Journals of my husband, written at different intervals so far back as the year 1802 down to the present period. I purpose beginning with Bair-down: first, because it was enclosed by the late worthy and respected Mr. Bray, who there built a house, and was fond of retiring to it during the summer and autumn; and secondly, because, as you will presently find, my husband considers Bair-down to have been 'the hill of bards.' In addition to my former allusions on this subject, I may here state, that should it be thought he is incorrect in his view of the *original* claims of the hill to a bardic character, he has now at least fully established them, by the *inscriptions* on the granite with which he has partly covered several of those enormous masses that arise, with so much magnificence, in the midst of the river Cowsick, that flows at the foot of the eminence on which the house was built by his father.

Some of these inscriptions are now so moss-grown, so hidden with lichen, or so worn with the weather and the winter torrents, that a stranger, unless he examined the rocks at a particular hour of the day when the sun is favourable, would not be very likely to discover them. Others, though composed by him for the same purpose, were never inscribed, on account of the time and labour it required to cut them in the granite. The mode he adopted with those which have been done was as follows: he used to paint the inscriptions himself, in large characters, upon the rocks, and then employ a labourer with what is here called a pick (pickaxe) to work them out. Some of these inscriptions were in triads, and engraved on the rocks in the bardic character of the sprig alphabet, as it is given by the Rev. Edward Davies in his *Celtic Remains.*

As a further motive to the task, he wished to indulge his fancy by peopling, as it were, a wilderness with his favourite authors to enliven its solitude: and when I shall presently tell you the number of poems he wrote at that early period of his life, (which, a few only being ever printed, still remain in manuscript[1]) as he delighted to cultivate the poetical visions of a youthful fancy on the Moor, you will not wonder that he should have attempted, with somewhat the same sentiments as those so beauti-

[1] A selection of these was published after the decease of the Author by Messrs. Longman, in 1859.

fully described by Shakspere, to give a tongue to
the very rocks, so that there might be found, even in
the midst of a desert,

> " Books in the running brooks,
> Sermons in stones, and good in every thing."

The eminence of Bair-down, on which stands the
cottage erected by his late father, is situated about
eight miles from Tavistock, near the Moreton road.
It is extensive, and to one approaching it from this
quarter is seen surrounded on the north and east
by lofty tors. In the latter direction it declines
gently but deeply, where flows the Dart; whilst the
descent is more sudden at the south, and on entering
the grounds from the turnpike road, presents itself
most unexpectedly as a ravine, its sides picturesquely
clothed with wood, through which, amid innumerable
rocks, rushes the foaming Cowsick. As you continue
to advance, the path winds by the side of this ravine,
which gradually opens and presents a scene of the
most peculiar and romantic kind,—a scene so beautiful that, though I have often viewed it, it always
affords me that delight which is generally supposed
to be the result of novel impressions. The Cowsick
rushes down this ravine over the noblest masses of
granite, broken into a thousand fantastic forms, and
scattered in every direction. A picturesque bridge
of a single, lofty arch, crosses the river at that spot
where the fall is most striking and precipitous: after
heavy rains it there presents a combination of water-
falls that are of the greatest beauty. In the midst
of the stream, at some short distance from the bridge,
the river branches off in two rocky channels, as it is
there interrupted by a little island, on which stands a
thick grove of trees. On either side the banks of

this steep ravine are seen a number of trees of various kinds, all in the most flourishing state, on account of their being so sheltered from the bleak winds of the Moor.

Such is Bair-down. All the trees were planted by my husband's father, who built the house and the bridge, and who raised the loose stone walls as enclosures for cattle for many miles in extent; and, in short, who literally expended a fortune on the improvements and enclosures on this estate. In the barn behind the cottage, for two years, divine service was performed every Sunday, by one of the Prince of Wales's chaplains, under a dispensation from the Bishop of Exeter. This estate is now let by Mr. Bray to a respectable farmer named Hannaford, (of whom you will hear more in these letters) for a very trifling rent. I now take my leave of you; for all that here follows is from the pen of my husband. The only share I have in it is that of transcribing it, verbatim, from his old Journals.

REMARKS ON THE ETYMOLOGY OF BAIR-DOWN, RURAL INSCRIPTIONS, &c.

By Edward A. Bray, 1802.

"The most obvious idea as to the origin of this name is, that it either has a reference to Bear, the substantive, or Bare, the adjective. But though a vague rumour, which can hardly be styled tradition, states that it was so called because it was the spot where the *last bear* was destroyed on the Moor; I should rather think that some recent poetical spirit has thus given 'to an airy nothing, a local habitation and a name.' And the second supposition can hardly be supported, when we come to consider that this part

of the Moor, so far from being *bare*, or void of
vegetation, is perhaps nearly the best land in the
whole of this extensive desert. Rejecting, therefore,
those ideas as equally unfounded, we must derive our
information from other sources ; and fortunately these
sources are immediately at hand. On the opposite
side of the river Dart, which bounds my father's
property, stands Wistman's Wood—the only remaining vestige of the ancient forest. *Wist* is the preterit
and participle of *wis*, from pissan, Saxon, *wissen*,
German, to know; and is not at present altogether
obsolete, as it is still used in Scripture in this sense.
From the same etymon comes also *wise :* 'sapient ;
judging rightly; having much knowledge'—(Johnson's *Dict.*)   Thus Wissman's or Wistman's Wood
signifies *Silva Sapientium*,[2] 'the wood of wisemen.'
The Druids and bards were unquestionably the
philosophers or wisemen of the Britons. We may
naturally conjecture, therefore, that this was their
principal or their last place of assembly; and the
many stone circles on Bair-down immediately opposite the wood confirm the opinion. I am not ignorant
that Wistman's Wood is sometimes called also *Welshman's* Wood : the one name may easily be the
corruption of the other; but if not, and they are
distinct appellations, the conclusion will be pretty
much the same.

"When the ancient inhabitants of this country were
subjugated by the Romans, some retired into Wales,
and others into Cornwall. Cornwall was considered

[2] See STUART'S *View of Society*, p. 337, to prove that the Wites
were the same as the Sapientes; and LL. Anglo-Saxon ap Wilkins
there referred to. See also a curious supplication del County de
Devonshire to Edward III. COKE'S 4. *Institute*, p. 232. *Barons
and Autres Sages*, &c.

as part of Wales, and, from its form, was called
Cornu, Walliæ, 'the horn of Wales.' Indeed it is
frequently styled West Wales by the British writers.
(See Rees's *Cyclop.*) The inhabitants, therefore, of
Cornwall, as well as Wales, might be called Welsh.
And in this supposition I am confirmed by Borlase,
who states that the Saxons 'imposed the name of
Weales on the Britons driven by them west of the
rivers Severn and Dee, calling their country, in the
Latin tongue, Wallia.' It is not improbable that
in the centre of Dartmoor, a colony might still be
permitted to exist, either from their insignificance or
their insulated situation ; and that this colony might
be called by the other inhabitants Welshmen, from
their resemblance to the inhabitants of Cornwall and
Wales.

" No colony can be supposed to have existed among
the ancient Britons without having their Druids or
wisemen, who, indeed, had the whole of the spiritual,
and the greater part of the temporal, power in their
hands. Bair-down then, from its commanding situation, and its gently-ascending acclivities, on which
were spread their sacred circles, must without doubt
have been frequently resorted to by them.

" *Dun*, now altered to down, signifies a hill. We
may naturally imagine, therefore, that it was originally called Baird, or Bard-dun, *Bardorum-mons*, 'the
hill of bards.' And the etymology of the word bard
will confirm this opinion : it is derived by changing
u into *b*, which is by no means uncommon, particularly as the German *w* is pronounced like our *v*,
from *waird*, whence comes the modern English *word*.
This, like the Greek ϵπος, signified not only *verbum*,
a word, but *carmen*, a song. The bards then were so

called from being singers, or persons who celebrated in songs the achievements of warriors and great men. What, therefore, was originally pronounced Baird-down may easily be supposed, for the sake of euphony, to be reduced to Bair-down.

"P.S. On further inquiry I find that some derive bard from *bar*, a fury. The analogy between this and the *furor poeticus* of the Romans must strike every one. The plural in Welsh is *beirdd*. Taliesin is called Pen Beirdd, *i.e.* 'the prince of *the bards*.' Thus Beirdd-dun is literally the 'hill of the bards.'

"The Druids were divided into vacerri, beirdd, and eubages. The second order, or bards, subsisted for ages after the destruction of the others, and indeed were not totally extirpated by the bloody proscription of Edward.

"RURAL INSCRIPTIONS ON THE ROCKS OF BAIR-DOWN.

"In stating the reasons by which I was actuated in the composition of these inscriptions, and in confining myself to their present form, it will be necessary to mention the ideas that suggested themselves to me upon the subject. At first the idea occurred to *me*, that nothing more would be required than to select passages from my favourite authors, and I actually laid some Latin and Italian poets under contribution for that very purpose; but I found that the long hexameter lines of Virgil could not easily be brought within the compass of a rude granite stone, where capitals only could be used, and those too of no small dimensions; that many of the most appropriate passages were of some length; and that, were I to have followed the example of Procrustes, however they might still be discovered to be *disjecti membra poëtæ*, the sight would have given more disgust than satisfaction to the eye of the spectator. A consideration of no small importance likewise occurred ; namely, that though I traced them myself beforehand upon the surface, it was not probable that the person I employed to cut them into the solid granite would be so attentive as not to commit blunders, especially as his labours were only proceeded with during my absence. It was obvious that fewer mistakes would probably occur in English, of which, at any rate, he may be presumed not to be so entirely ignorant as he certainly is of the former, being only a common mason. In addition to which inscriptions of this kind have been so frequently repeated that I could not hope to attract attention by any novelty of application. On further reflection, however, I made a great alteration in my original design, and, considering poetical inscriptions as of subordinate consequence, resolved to consecrate particular rocks to particular persons. As the name alone of Theocritus or of Virgil could not fail to communicate to a poetical mind a train of pleasing associations, I did nothing more, at first, than inscribe upon a few rocks 'To Theocritus,' 'To Virgil,' &c. This of itself, in so wild and solitary a scene as Dartmoor, was not without its effect : it seemed to people the desert ; at any rate one might exclaim, 'The hand of man has been here!' I then conceived that it would give more animation to the scene by adding something either addressed to, or supposed to be uttered by, these fancied genii or divinities of the rock ; and accordingly, for the sake of conciseness as well as a trial of skill, composed them in couplets.

I certainly should have found it much easier to have expanded them into quatrains, or any indefinite number of lines ; but I chose to impose this task upon myself for other reasons as well as those above stated, which, however, I cannot help thinking are sufficient.

"I entertain a higher opinion of the English language than to think it so deficient in conciseness as to be unable to adapt itself to the form of a distich. I am rather inclined to think that the moral distichs of Cato might be very adequately translated in the same form.   D'Avanzati's translation of Tacitus has acquired great reputation for its conciseness ; but, for the sake of curiosity, I have proved that it may be more concisely translated into English than Italian. I may possibly have failed, however, in showing its superior excellence in this particular by my inscriptions, but these I have not the vanity to imagine as just criteria of its powers.

"In the island, to which I would appropriate the name of the Isle of Mona, I propose to put none but Druidical inscriptions, principally in the form of triads.   These shall be in bardic characters, as they are represented in Davies's *Celtic Researches.*   By way of amusement to those who may wish to decipher them, I shall mark this simple alphabet on a white rod, and call it the *virgula divinatoria,* or the diviner's wand, which is still so celebrated among the miners, so that literally few, if any, will be able to understand it without the assistance of this magic rod.   It will add to the effect to call a recess, or kind of grotto, that is contiguous to this island, Merlin's Cave, and on a rock, which may be considered as his tomb, to inscribe—

" These mystic letters would you know,
     Take Merlin's wand that lies below.

It will be right, perhaps, to have two wands, of equal
length; one to be a kind of key to the other; one to
be marked with the bardic letters, and the other at
corresponding distances with the English alphabet,
thus—

ΛѴ‹›ЈΛᐸhIJΚΛⴸⵏ◁ᒋℾⴼ↑ℾⵢⵈⴸⴸ.

A B C D E F G H I K L M N O P R S T U V W Y "

INSCRIPTION THE FIRST.
To my Father.

Still lived the Druids, who the oak revered,
(For many an oak thy peaceful hands have reared)
The hill of bards had echoed with thy name,
Than warrior deeds more worthy songs of fame.

No. II.
To the Same.

Who gilds the earth with grain can bolder claim
The highest guerdon from the hands of Fame,
Than he who stains the martial field with blood,
And calls from widowed eyes the bitter flood.

No. III.
To the Same.

This tender sapling, planted now by thee,
Oh! may it spread a fair umbrageous tree;
Whilst seated at thy side I tune my lays,
And sing beneath its shade a father's praise.

DRUIDICAL AND OTHER INSCRIPTIONS.
No. I.

Ye Druid train these sacred rocks revere,
These sacred rocks to minstrel spirits dear!
If pure your lips, if void your breast of sin,
They'll hear your prayers, and answer from within.

No. II.

Read only thou these artless rhymes
Whom Fancy leads to other times;
Nor think an hour misspent to trace
The customs of a former race:
For know, in every age, that man
Fulfils great Nature's general plan.

No. III.

Oh! thou imbued with Celtic lore,
Send back thy soul to days of yore,
When kings descended from their thrones
To bow before the sacred stones,
And Druids from the aged oak
The will of Heaven prophetic spoke.

INSCRIPTIONS ON THE ROCKS OF BAIR-DOWN, IN THE RIVER COWSICK, &C.

To Merlin.

Born of no earthly sire, thy magic wand
Brought Sarum's hanging stones from Erin's land:
To me, weak mortal! no such power is known,
And yet to speak I teach the sacred stone.[3]

INSCRIPTIONS IN TRIADS, &C.

No. I.

Though worshipped oft by many a different name,
God is but one, and ever is the same,
To him at last we go, from whom at first we came.

---

[3] It is pretended that Merlin was the son of an incubus and a vestal. He is said, by the power of magic, to have brought from Ireland those immense masses of granite that form Stonehenge, which means, according to some antiquaries, *hanging-stones;* or stones hanged, hung, or connected together; or as the poet says, 'poised by magic.' The *hinge* of a door may probably be referred to the same origin. Merlin's original name was Ambrosius. It is thought that Amesbury, or Ambresbury, near Stonehenge, took its name from Ambrosius Aurelius. a British Prince. May not the credulous vulgar have confounded him with Merlinus Ambrosius, and thus ascribed this probably Druidical monument to the supernatural powers of this celebrated enchanter?

No. II.

Know, though the body moulder in the tomb,
That body shall the living soul resume,
And share of bliss or woe the just eternal doom.

No. III.

Proud man ! consider thou art nought but dust;
To Heaven resign thy will, be good, be just,
And for thy due reward to Heaven with patience trust.

No. IV.

Their earthly baseness to remove,
Souls must repeated changes prove,
Prepared for endless bliss above.

No. V.

Adore great Hu,[4] the god of peace;
Bid war and all its woes to cease;
So may our flocks and fruits increase.

No. VI.

To Odin[5] bow with trembling fear,
The terrible, the God severe:
Whose bolt, of desolating fire,
Warns not, but wreaks his vengeful ire;
Who roars amid the bloody fight;
Recalls the foot that turns for flight;
Who bids the victor's banners fly;
And names the name of those to die.

INSCRIPTIONS TO THE BARDS ALLUDED TO BY GRAY.

To Cadwallo.

Mute is thy magic strain,
'That hushed the stormy main.'

To Hoel.

Thy harp in strains sublime expressed
The dictates of thy 'high-born' breast.

---

[4] Hu Gadran, 'the peaceful ploughman.' One of the names of the
Deity among the Celtæ.

[5] Odin, the deity of the Goths and other Northern nations.

To Urien.

No more, awakened from thy 'craggy bed,'
Thy rage-inspiring songs the foe shall dread.

To Llewellyn.

Mid war's sad frowns were smiles oft wont to play
Whilst poured thy harp the 'soft' enamoured 'lay.'

To Modred.

Thy 'magic song,' thine incantations dread,
'Made huge Plinlimmon bow his cloud-topt head.'

ADDITIONAL TRIADS.

No. I.

From Mela.

Ut forent ad bella meliores;
Æternas esse animas,
Vitamque alteram ad manes.

The soul's immortal—then be brave,
Nor seek thy coward life to save;
But hail the life beyond the grave.

ANOTHER FROM DIOGENES LAERTIUS.

Σέβειν Θεούς,
καὶ μηδὲν κακὸν δρᾶν,
καὶ ἀνδρείαν ἄσκειν.

Adore the Gods with daily prayer,
Each deed of evil shun with care,
And learn with fortitude to bear.

ALLUDING TO THE DRUIDS' BELIEF IN THE METEMPSYCHOSIS.[6]

Here all things change to all—what dies,
Again with varied life shall rise:
He sole unchanged who rules the skies.

[6] Cæsar speaking of the Druids (Lib. 6, Sec. 13) says,—In primis hoc volunt persuadere, non interire animas, sed ab alias post mortem transire ad alias: atque hôc maximè ad virtutem excitari putant, metu mortis neglecto.

ALLUDING TO THE DRUIDICAL SPRIG ALPHABET.

Hast thou the knowledge of the trees?
Press then this spot with votive knees,
And join the sacred mysteries.

A TRIAD.

Founded on the Maxims of the Druids in RAPIN'S *History of England*,
vol. i. p. 6, Introduction.

None must be taught but in the sacred grove:
All things originate from Heaven above;
And man's immortal soul a future state shall prove.

TO MY FATHER.

Inscribed on a rock in the River Cowsick, the banks of which he had planted.

Ye Naiads! venerate the swain
Who joined the Dryads to your train.

INSCRIPTION FOR AN ISLAND IN THE RIVER COWSICK, TO WHICH I HAVE GIVEN THE NAME OF MONA.

Ye tuneful birds! ye Druids of the grove!
Who sing not strains of blood, but lays of love,
To whom this Isle, a little Mona's given—
Ne'er from the sacred spot shall *ye* be driven.

INSCRIPTION FOR A ROCK ON THE LOWER ISLAND.

Who love, though e'en through desert wilds they stray,
Find in their hearts companions of the way.

FOR THE SAME ISLAND.

To thee, O Solitude, we owe
Man's greatest bliss—ourselves to know.

INSCRIPTION ON A ROCK IN THE WOODS NEAR THE COWSICK.

The wretch, to heal his wounded mind,
A friend in solitude will find;
And when the Blest her influence tries,
He'll learn his blessings more to prize.

For a Rock on Bair-down.

Sweet Poesy! fair Fancy's child!
Thy smiles imparadise the wild.

Inscription for an Island in the Cowsick, to which I have given the name of Vectis.

When erst Phœnicians crossed the trackless main
For Britain's secret shore, in quest of gain,
This desert wild supplied the valued ore,
And Vectis' Isle received the treasured store.

For a Rock in Wistman's Wood.

The wreck of ages, these rude oaks revere;
The Druid, Wisdom, sought a refuge here
When Rome's fell eagles drenched with blood the ground,
And taught her sons her mystic rites profound.

For the Same.

These rugged rocks, last barrier to the skies,
Smoked with the Druids' secret sacrifice;
Alas! blind man, to hope with human blood
To please a God, all merciful, all good.

Inscription for a Rock on Bair-down.

Mute is the hill of bards, where erst the choir,
In solemn cadence, struck the sacred wire:
Yet oft, methinks, in spells of fancy bound,
As swells the breeze, I hear their harps resound.

Inscription near the Island.

Learning's proud sons! think not the Celtic race,
Once deemed so rude, your origin disgrace:
Know that to them, who counted ages o'er,
The Greeks and Romans owe their learned lore.
                          (*Celtic Res: passim.*)

Inscription for a Rock near the Cowsick.

Here, though now reft of trees, from many an oak
To Druid ears prophetic spirits spoke;
And, may I trust the muse's sacred strain?
Reviving groves shall speak of fate again.

Near the Same.

Ye minstrel spirits! when I strike the lyre,
Oh, hover round, and fill me with your fire!

To Boadicea.

Roused by the Druids' songs, mid fields of blood,
Thine arm the conquerors of the world withstood.

To Caractacus.

Imperial Rome, that ruled from pole to pole,
Could never tame, proud chief, thy mighty soul.

To Taliesin.

How boiled his blood! how thrilled the warrior's veins!
When roused to vengeance by thy patriot strains.

To the Cowsick.

To thee, fair Naiad of the crystal flood,
I offer not the costly victim's blood;
But as I quaff thy tide at sultry noon,
I bless thee for the cool reviving boon.

To Æsop.

E'en solitude has social charms for thee,
Who talk'st with beast, or fish, or bird, or tree.

To Thomson.

To Nature's votaries shall thy name be dear,
Long as the seasons lead the changeful year.

To Shakspere.

To thee, blest bard, man's veriest heart was known,
Whate'er his lot—a cottage or a throne.

To Southey, for a rock in Wistman's Wood.

Free as thy Madoc mid the western waves,
Here refuged Britons swore they'd ne'er be slaves.

To Savage.

What! though thy mother could her son disown,
The pitying Muses nursed thee as their own.[7]

---

[7] See Johnson's *Life of Savage*, and his poem of the 'Bastard.'

To Spenser.

The shepherd, taught by thine instructive rhyme,
Learns from thy calendar to husband time.

To Shenstone.

Nurtured by taste, thy lyre by Nature strung,
Thy hands created what thy fancy sung.

To Browne.

I bless thee that our native Tavy's praise
Thou 'st woven mid Britannia's pastoral lays.

To Burns.

Long as the moon shall shed her sacred light,
Thy strain, sweet bard, shall cheer the cotter's night.

I have now given you a very numerous collection
of Mr. Bray's inscriptions for the rocks of Bair-down
and the river Cowsick; yet, numerous as they are,
there remain not less than one hundred and fifteen in
distichs, which would have been too many for inser-
tion in these letters. In the next I purpose taking
you to Wistman's Wood, where I trust you will find
some objects worthy your attention.

LETTER VI.

TO ROBERT SOUTHEY, ESQ.

Vicarage, Tavistock, March 6, 1832.

I NOW take up my pen to give you some account of Wistman's Wood, which, if you will allow the expression, we have always considered as the *posterity* of a Druid grove; and I cannot help thinking that when I shall have stated the various circumstances which induce us to come to this conclusion, you will admit it is not wholly without probability or reason.

Every one at all conversant with history is aware that no community of the British priesthood was without its sacred grove, a custom derived from the most remote countries and ages, for the Bible informs us that such groves were the resort of Eastern idolatry in its most fearful rites, and that such were generally found on eminences or 'high places.' We read in the Second Book of Kings, that when "the children of Israel did secretly those things that were not right against the Lord their God, they built them high places in all their cities," they "set them up images and groves on every high hill and under every green tree, and there they burnt incense in all the high places." And again we find these corrupt Israelites "left all the commandments of the Lord their God, and made a grove, and worshipped all the host of Heaven, and served Baal."

The Druid priesthood did the same in after ages; and their groves, their altars and 'high places,' are still remaining, though in the last vestige of their decay, as witnesses of their idolatry, in the extensive wilderness of Dartmoor. How striking a resemblance does the following passage of Scripture bear to the superstitions and practices of Celtic nations! Speaking of Ahab, it is recorded that "he reared·altars for Baal, and made a grove; and worshipped all the host of Heaven and served them;" and that "he made his son pass through fire, and observed times and used enchantments with familiar spirits and wizards." And when Josiah conquered these infidels, it is written that he destroyed the "groves and vessels made for Baal,—for the sun, the moon, and the planets, and put down the idolatrous priests who had burnt the incense to them on high places;" and that "he defiled

Tophet, which is in the valley of the children of
Hinnom, that no man might make his son or his
daughter to pass through the fire to Moloch. And
he took away the horses that the kings of Judah
had given to the sun."[1] How much does this superstition (of the horses given to Baal, or Bel, the god of
the Sun) agree with a passage in Tacitus, where,
speaking of the manners of the ancient Germans, he
says, "a number of milk-white steeds, unprofaned by
mortal labour, are constantly maintained at the public
expense, and placed to pasture in the religious groves!
When occasion requires, they are harnessed to a
sacred chariot; and the priest, accompanied by the
king, or chief of the state, attends to watch the
motions and the neighings of the horses. No other
mode of augury is received with such implicit faith by
the people, the nobility, and the priesthood. The
horses upon these solemn occasions are supposed to
be the organs of the gods, and the priests their
favoured interpreters."

Cæsar and Diodorus both speak of the Druid
groves of superstition; and Tacitus does the same
in regard to the Germans, who, as well as the Gauls
and Britons, were followers of the Celtic idolatry.
"Their deities," says that admirable historian, "are
not immured in temples, nor represented under any
kind of resemblance to the human form. To do
either were, in their opinion, to derogate from the
majesty of supreme beings. Woods and groves are
the sacred depositaries, and the spots consecrated to
their pious uses: they give to that sacred recess the

[1] In the same chapter we read, that Josiah "slew all the priests of
the high places that were there upon the altars, and burnt men's bones
upon them."

name of the divinity that fills the place." So numerous are the allusions of the classical writers to the
groves of Druidism, that it is not necessary to recite
examples; since no fact is more clearly established
than that no society of the Celtic priesthood was
without its grove, for the purposes of instruction,
retirement, augury, and numerous other religious
rites. The custom of cutting the misletoe from the
oaks of these sanctuaries is too generally known to
need any particular notice; since the commonly-
received idea of a Druid, with those who scarcely
read at all, presents itself to the mind under the
figure of an old man with a long beard, who cuts
misletoe from the oaks with a golden hook.

In order to ascertain how far the conjecture is
founded on probability that Wistman's Wood, on
Dartmoor, is the posterity of a Druid grove, we must
consider its known antiquity[2]—its localities—the
extraordinary appearance and actual state of the
dwarf and venerable trees, that still flourish in decay
amidst the rudest storms, and in one of the rudest
spots throughout the whole of the Moor;—the probable age of these oaks, and how far one tree would
be likely to succeed another;—and though last, not
least, their relative situation with the other British
antiquities, by which they are in fact surrounded, and
that close at hand. Mr. Bray's derivation of the
name of Wistman's Wood, given in the last letter,

---

[2] In the office of the Duchy of Cornwall there is preserved a
Perambulation of the Moor, of very high antiquity, by which it appears
that Wistman's Wood was nearly in the same state as at present at
the time of the Norman Conquest. This is a very curious fact, and
it should be borne in mind by the reader, as it goes far to establish the
opinion the writer has ventured to give on this most interesting vestige
of the Forest.

must also be borne in mind ; since this most curious
antiquity in the vegetable world is very near Bair-
down : so that if he is right in his derivation in both
instances, the hill of bards and the wood of the
wisemen, or Druids, were contiguous.

Wistman's Wood, then, lies on the side of a steep
hill, opposite Bair-down ; at its base runs the western
branch of the river Dart. Let me fancy for a moment
that you are with us—(a dream I one day hope to see
realized)—join our excursion, and, whilst attempting
to visit this eminence, are helping me along from
Bair-down; a friendly arm being a very necessary
support to a female who ventures on the expedition ;
which to one like myself is a task of no small labour,
though replete with interest.

The farmer, Hannaford, is our guide; and after
having passed up and down hill, and over one of the
boundary-walls, or enclosures, some of the stones of
which he removes (and builds up again) to afford us
an easier way of clambering over it, we have managed, by jumping from rock to rock, in part to ford
the river Dart, the waters not being so high as to
prevent our doing so, till at length we come to one
place so puzzling—so difficult—that our Herculean
guide can see no other way of getting me over but
that of taking me up, and putting me across with as
much ease and good will as Gulliver would have
displayed in assisting the Queen of Lilliput in crossing a puddle. At last we are landed on the opposite
bank, and there lies Wistman's Wood, rocks and all,
before us ;—an inviting object to curiosity and specu-
lation with those who love to indulge in visions of
the ' olden time.'

The summit of the eminence cannot be seen, on

account of its steep ascent; and huge piles, mass on
mass of granite blocks, seem to rise and grow before
us as we pace upward towards the wood. Every
step requires wary walking, since to stumble amidst
such rocks, holes, and hollows might be attended
with an accident that would prevent all further investigation; and the farmer says, "'Tis a wisht old
place, sure enough, and full of adders as can be."
This last communication somewhat cools my enthusiasm about Druid groves; but the farmer offers
and supplies a speedy remedy,—one also of most
mystical origin, and not a little heathenish, being
derived from the very Druids upon whose haunts
we are about to intrude; for he transfers to my
hand the ashen bough or sprig that he was carrying
in his own, and initiates me on the spot into the
pagan rites of charming adders, to render them
harmless as the poorest worm that crawls upon the
earth. He tells me that the moment I see an adder
I have nothing to do but to draw a circle with an
ash rod round it, and that the creature will never go
out of it; nay, if a fire were kindled in the ring, it
would rather go into the fire itself than pass the
circle. He believes, also, that an animal bitten by
this venomous reptile may be cured by having a
kind of collar woven of ash-twigs suspended round
his neck. He likewise mentions having, a year or
two ago, killed a very large adder that had been
tamed by the above charm, when he took fifteen
young ones from its belly.

To return to our expedition: these superstitions
(as we pause a moment to take breath before we
continue the rough ascent) become the subject of our
conversation; and we cannot help remarking how

appropriate they are to the place of Druid antiquity, since the one may be traced to the serpent's egg, and the other, very probably, to the *virgula divinatoria*, or diviner's rod. Indeed all magicians and sorcerers are described, from the earliest ages, as being armed with a wand or rod : we read of this, too, in the Bible, where the rods of the magicians were turned into serpents, and the rod of Moses, so transformed, swallowed them up. That the Druids professed magical arts cannot be doubted, since Pliny calls that priesthood "the magi of the Gauls and Britons;" and of this island he says, "Magic is now so much practised in Britain, and with so many similar rites, that we cannot but come to the conclusion that they immediately derived it from the magi of the Persians." The bard Taliesin thus speaks of the magic wand of the Druids: "Were I to compose the strain, were I to sing, magic spells would spring, like those produced by the circle and wand of Twrch Trwyth." I think I have somewhere read, that the sophists of India also pretended to possess the power of charming venomous reptiles ; and there can be little doubt the art was long practised in Britain, since it has been supposed that the caduceus seen in the hand of Mercury had its origin in the British Isles, where the Druids exercised the arts of charming serpents. And Toland, who, in his very learned work, has brought to light so much curious information respecting Druidism, informs us that in the Lowlands of Scotland many glass amulets were found, which the people of that country called 'adder stanes.' The Druids, we know, carried magic amulets about their persons ; and it may also be remarked, that the adder itself was held as a symbol of the Helio-arkite god, and therefore of his priest, who took his station on the sacred mount, or in the no less sacred diluvian lake.[5]

Now all these things considered induce me to believe, that as Dartmoor must from the earliest times have been most prolific in vipers, the mode of charming them with an ashen wand, still retained by the peasantry, is nothing less than a vestige of the customs of Druid antiquity.

Having paused a moment to consider the origin of the ashen wand and the adders, we once more turn our attention to Wistman's Wood ; and near its commencement, on the south side, we find a spring of the clearest and the purest water, which Hannaford, the farmer, tells us never fails. It bursts from beneath a rock, and, like most of the blessings of Providence (whether we avail ourselves of them or not) it still pours its limpid fountain in fruitful abundance, amidst the wildness and desolation of the spot, and nourishes a thousand beautiful mosses and flowers, that render the Moor, though a desert in one sense of the word, a rich wilderness for Flora and her train.

We now view with surprise the oaks before us : and such is their singular appearance, that, without stopping to reason upon the subject, we are all disposed to think that they are really no other than the

[5] The serpent's egg, which the Druids pretended to catch in the air, in order to impose upon the multitude, was held as a mystery. They wore this egg round their necks ; no one in Britain except themselves knew the secret of manufacturing this kind of glass. "The priests," says Davies, "carried about them certain trinkets of vitrified matter, and this custom had a view to Arkite mysteries." The great Druid temple at Carnac (which I visited in early life) is, I am informed, now ascertained to be in the form of a *serpent*. Might it not, therefore, have had reference to the mysteries of the diluvian Helio-arkite god? Carnac stands very near the sea-shore.

last remnant of a Druid grove; or rather the last
vestige of its posterity. You, being a poet, (for I
must still be allowed to fancy you by my side) think
of Lucan; and repeat the passage in his *Pharsalia*,
where he describes the impression made on the
Roman soldiery under Cæsar, on their entering
beneath the gloom and solemnity of a Druid grove;
their horror, their silent dread to touch with the axe
that old and honoured wood : till Cæsar, snatching it
from their trembling hands, aimed the first blow and
violated the oaks so long held sacred to a dark and
sanguinary superstition.

When you have finished your quotation from
Lucan, I tell you that Rowe, who was his translator
into English verse, is said to have been born in
Lamerton, only three miles from Tavistock; of which
pretty little village his father was the incumbent.
And Mr. Bray, who has long been an enthusiast
about Dartmoor and the Druids, is ready to follow
your quotation by repeating the noble lines from
Mason's *Caractacus* descriptive of a Druid grove;
whilst I, determined to have my share of poetical
feeling, recite the sonnet, written by my husband
when very young :

To Wistman's Wood.

Sole relics of the wreath that crowned the Moor !
  A thousand tempests (bravely though withstood,
    Whilst, sheltered in your caves, the wolf's dire brood
Scared the wild echoes with their hideous roar)
Have bent your aged heads, now scathed and hoar,
  And in Dart's wizard stream your leaves have strewed,
    Since Druid priests your sacred rocks imbrued
With victims offered to their gods of gore.

In lonely grandeur, your firm looks recall
    What history teaches from her classic page ;
How Rome's proud senate on the hordes of Gaul
    Indignant frowned, and stayed their brutal rage.
Yet Time's rude hand shall speed, like theirs, your fall,
    That selfsame hand so long that spared your age.

Whilst these poetical feelings prompt each to some suitable expression of them, the farmer, a matter-of-fact man, looks as if he thought us all "a little mazed," as they say in Devonshire, "about the wisht old trees;" and it being now his turn to say something, he gives us his own legend about them; which is that according to tradition, or as he expresses it, "as the people do tell, that the giants once were masters of all the hill country, and had great forests, and set up their cairns (he calls them by their right name) and their great stones and circles, and all they old ancient things, about the Moor."

As we advance we again contemplate with wonder and interest the extraordinary object before us. It is altogether unlike anything else. There is a steep height, to toil up which I compare to going up the side of a pyramid.

The ascent to Wistman's Wood is strewn all over with immense masses of granite, that lie scattered in every direction. The soil about these rocks is very scanty, and appears, the same as in many other parts of the Moor, to be composed of decayed vegetable matter. In the midst of these gigantic blocks, growing among them, or starting, as it were, from their interstices, arises wildly, and here and there widely scattered, *a grove of dwarf oak trees*. Their situation, exposed to the bleak winds, which rush past the side of the declivity on which they grow, and through the valley of the Dart at their base, (a valley that acts like a tunnel to assist the fury of the gust) the diminutive height of the trees, their singular and antiquated appearance, all combine to raise feelings of mingled curiosity and wonder. The oaks are not above ten or twelve feet high, thus stunted is their growth by the sweeping winds to which they stand exposed; but they spread far and wide at their tops, and their branches twist and wind in the most tortuous and fantastic manner; sometimes reminding one of those strange things called mandrakes; of which there is a superstition noticed by Shakspere—

" Like shrieking mandrakes, torn from out the earth."

In some places these branches are literally festooned with ivy and creeping plants; and their trunks are so thickly embedded in a covering of fine velvet moss, that at first sight you would imagine them to be of enormous thickness in proportion to their height. But it is only their velvet coats that make them look so bulky; for on examination they are not found to be of any remarkable size. Their whole appearance conveys to you the idea of hoary age in the vegetable world; and on visiting Wistman's Wood it is impossible to do other than think of those 'groves in stony places,' so often mentioned in Scripture as being dedicated to Baal and Ashtaroth. This ancient seat of idolatry seems to have undergone, also, a great part of the curse that was pronounced on the idolatrous cities and groves of old; for here, indeed, do 'serpents hiss,' and it shall never be inhabited; 'neither doth the shepherd make

his fold there;' 'but the wild beasts of the desert
and the owl dwell there,' and 'the bittern' still screams
amidst its 'desolation.'

Many of the immense masses of granite around
and under the trees are covered with a cushion of
the thickest and the softest moss; but to sit down
upon them would be rather too hazardous; since
such a seat might chance to disturb from their comfortable bed a nest of adders that are very apt to
shelter in such a covert, and few persons, now-a-days,
would feel quite so confident as honest Hannaford in
the power and efficacy of the ashen wand to render
them innocuous. The oaks, though stunted and
turning from the west winds, to which they are most
exposed, are by no means destitute of foliage; and
the good-natured farmer cuts me down a branch to
carry home in triumph, after having achieved the
adventure of a visit to Wistman's Wood. This
branch has upon it several acorns, the smallest I
ever saw; but the leaves are of the usual size, and as
vigorous as most other trees of the same kind.

I shall now give you a short extract from a very
brief entry in Mr. Bray's Journal of August 9th,
1827, concerning this wood. He says as follows:—
"Tradition relates that Wistman's Wood was planted
by the celebrated Isabella de Fortibus, Countess of
Devon.⁴ But I do not hesitate to say that, to any
one who has visited the spot, it is evident no other
hand has planted it than that of God. No one
would or could have planted trees in the midst of

⁴ Among the peers of Henry the Second was William de Fortibus,
Earl of Albemarle, created Earl of Devon in right of his wife Isabel,
sister and heiress to Baldwin de Redvers, or Rivers, eighth Earl of
Devonshire. The title thus created in 1262 became extinct in 1270.

such rocks.[5]   They unquestionably can be no other than the remains of the original forest ; which, though in its original acceptation (according to Du Cange, *in voce Foresta*, it comes from *feris*, that is, *ferarum statio*, a station for wild beasts) it means but 'a wild uncultivated ground *interspersed* with wood,'[6] must yet have had some trees, at intervals, in every part of it.   At present (except here, and in some modern plantations, of which those of my father are the finest) there are none, though the trunks of trees are occasionally found in the bogs. It is not improbable that these trees were first very generally destroyed by fire, in order to extirpate the wolves.   The few that remained were destroyed by cattle afterwards pastured there ; and it is only, perhaps, owing to their being so surrounded and interspersed with rocks that those of the wood in question have been preserved from a similar depredation.

"At the late Visitation at Tavistock, on the 31st of May, Archdeacon Froude, a gentleman possessed of considerable antiquarian information, told me that he had lately obtained part of a tree from this wood, with a view, if possible, to discover its age by the number of circles from its centre to the circumference ; that, by the aid of a microscope, he had counted some hundreds, but that at times the divi-

[5] That Wistman's Wood was *not* planted by Isabella de Fortibus is proved by the fact before noticed, that the record of a Perambulation of the Moor (made immediately after the Norman Conquest) is still preserved in the office of the Duchy of Cornwall, by which we find that Wistman's Wood was even at that remote period much the same as it now appears.

[6] TODD's *Johnson's Dictionary*.   See also there the *legal* sense of the word.

sions were so minute as hardly to be distinguishable ;
that, different from any other trees he had ever seen,
the circles were more contracted, and in a manner
condensed, on one side than on any other; and that
he supposed this was the side the most exposed to
the beat of the weather.   On consulting Evelyn's
Silva, I found the following passages in his second
volume, which may throw some light upon the
subject :—

"'The trunk or bough of a tree being cut transversely plain and smooth, sheweth several circles or
rings more or less orbicular, according to the external
figure, in some parallel proportion, one without the
other, from the centre of the wood to the inside of
the bark, dividing the whole into so many circular
spaces . . . . by the largeness or smallness of the
rings, the quickness or slowness of the growth of
any tree may, perhaps, at certainty be estimated."
—page 201.

"'The spaces are manifestly broader on the one
side than on the other, especially the more outer, to
a double proportion, or more; the inner being near
an equality.

"'It is asserted that the larger parts of these rings
are on the south and sunny side of the tree (which is
very rational and probable) insomuch, that by cutting
a tree transverse, and drawing a diameter through the
broadest and narrowest parts of the ring, a meridian
line may be described.

"'It is commonly and very probably asserted, that
a tree gains a new ring every year.   In the body of
a great oak in the New-Forest cut *transversely even*
(where many of the trees are accounted to be some
hundreds of years old) three and four hundred have

been distinguished.' These and other remarks, he attributes (p. 204) to 'that learned person, the late Dr. Goddard.'[7]

"My tenant, Hannaford, said that his uncle had found a few silver coins, about the size of a sixpence, in some of the cairns on the Moor, and promised, if possible, to obtain for me a sight of them. He further informed me that he had lately destroyed what he called *a cave*,[8] which he described as composed of a large oblong stone supported, as a cover, by others set on edge at the head and foot, and on either side; and that among the stones and earth within he found some human hair clotted together, but no bones or other vestige of the body. Hair, it is said, will grow as long as there is any moisture in the body; but whether it will last longer than bones is a question that seems hardly yet decided. Might it not have been the scalp of an enemy, or hair offered up to the manes of the departed, or to some deity of which this might be the altar? The remains of one of these British monuments still exist on Bair-down; but the ancient circular enclosures (of which there are so many near Wistman's Wood) that I myself remember there, were unfortunately destroyed when my father erected his ring-fence."

I have already given you Mr. Bray's conjectures as to the etymology of Wistman's Wood; and the opinion of its having been a grove sacred to the

---

[7] For the age of trees, see CLARKE'S *Travels*, vol. vii. p. 312. 4th edition.

[8] Or kieve: which signifies, I believe, any large vessel, from a puncheon to a caldron. There is a waterfall in Cornwall called St. Nathan's Kieve, probably from the basin into which it falls.

rites of Druidism obtains no inconsiderable support from its immediate localities; since, notwithstanding the spoliation of successive ages, there still remain close to it many British antiquities. Such for instance as three cairns, (and several others have been destroyed within the last twenty years to supply stones for the boundary walls, &c.) some hut rings, and the circles noticed by Mr. Bray in his Journal: these are all near the wood; whilst to the south of it lies Crockern Tor, the undoubted seat of British jurisprudence on the Moor, and of which I shall speak at large in my next letter. To the west, separated only by the narrow valley which is watered by the river Dart, is found Bair-down, or 'the hill of bards.' And Littleford Tor is also not far distant from Wistman's Wood, contiguous to which is seen a group of above sixty hut circles. Thus then do we find that this venerable grove, situated in the very heart of the Moor, is on all sides surrounded by vestiges of Druid antiquity.

Before I conclude this account of the wood, (in which there is not one circumstance fictitious, excepting my having indulged in the fancy of your being of the party when I visited it in 1827) I ought to mention that Mr. Bray conjectures that it was very probably one of the last retreats of the Druids of Damnonia, after they were exposed to the persecution of the Roman power. There appears to me nothing improbable in this conjecture; for we all know how long after that epoch the bards sought shelter and existed, in Caledonia, Armorica, Wales, and Cornwall. Dartmoor, so near the last-named retreat, from its mountainous character, its want of roads, its deep recesses, its loneliness and general difficulty of access, must long have stood as an impenetrable barrier against persecution. [9]

On the Moor, shelter and even safety might be found for those who, to the last, struggled to maintain their power; and who, rather than yield up the sacred privileges of that priesthood in which they had been trained from their earliest years, fled to rocks and deserts as their retreat; and there still preserved their sway, though reduced in numbers and confined within a comparatively small space for their dominion.

That such men were long welcome to and upheld by the British people, is proved by the circumstance of the bards having existed for so many generations in Scotland, Ireland, Cornwall, and Wales, when they were extinct in all other parts of Great Britain. The natives of the soil, it cannot be doubted, long maintained a veneration for their ancient customs and superstitions; and their bards possessed that feeling, that tenderness, which is ever the companion of poetry; and without which real genius, in any branch of literature, surely cannot exist : for if Plato's definition of genius be really true, that even in its highest order it is nothing more than 'extent of sympathy,' the bards might claim it as their own. Hence arose their power, and hence it was that they kept alive, by their pathetic appeals to the hearts of the Britons, all the pity that their own persecuted state was likely to call forth. They were, it is true, 'fallen from their high estate,' and from their ac-

[9] Mr. Polwhele considers that the Romans never penetrated into Dartmoor; and that this circumstance is the cause of no Roman barrows or antiquities being there found; all that have hitherto been discovered being undoubtedly British.

knowledged power ; they were seared and blighted—
yet from that very cause were they become but the
more cherished and honoured ; even as the ancients
hallowed those spots of earth that had been blasted
by the lightning and the thunder-bolt of Jove—
misfortune had touched them, and they were sacred.
Long, therefore, were the bards cherished ; long did
they survive, honoured in their ruin and in their fall ;
and now, perhaps, in the lonely and melancholy wood
of Wistman, we behold one of the last decaying
vestiges of their retreat.

LETTER VII.

TO ROBERT SOUTHEY, ESQ.

Vicarage, Tavistock, March 9th, 1832.

I PURPOSE in this letter giving you some account of a place on Dartmoor which, it is most probable, was used in the days of the Britons as a tribunal of justice. Unhewn stones and circles of the same, it is generally admitted, were raised for courts of this description; and we have the most ancient and undoubted authority—the Bible, for considering that fabrics of unhewn stone derive their origin, like the more rational parts of the religion of the Druids, from those eastern nations of which the Celtæ were a branch.

We find that the custom of erecting or of consecrating monuments of this nature, as memorials of a covenant, in honour of the dead, as places of worship, &c., prevailed even from the earliest times. Jacob and Laban made a covenant in Gilead; and no sooner was this done, than "Jacob took a stone and set it up for a pillar." Joshua in passing over Jordan with the ark caused a heap of stones to be raised, that they should be "for a memorial unto the children of Israel for ever." And certain tribes also "built there an altar by Jordan, a great altar to see." And after Joshua had destroyed Achan, "they raised over him a great heap of stones unto this day." The Jewish conquerors did the same by the King of Ai; and on Absalom "did they heap stones:" and Rachel's monument, the first we read of in the Bible, was of stone, for Jacob "set up a pillar upon her grave."[1]

There cannot, I think, be a doubt that the courts as well as the temples of unhewn stone, had their origin in the East. And as the laws of the British people were delivered to them by the Druids, not as secular ordinances, but as the commands of the gods whom they adored, this circumstance no doubt added to the solemnity of their administration: so that it is not improbable the spot appointed for the Gorseddau or Court of Judicature was chosen with a view to the most advantageous display of its august rites.

[1] *Vide* HERODOTUS for the stones set up by Sesostris.

Hence an elevated station, like the temples of their worship, became desirable ; and there must have been a more than ordinary feeling of awe inspired in the mind of the criminal, by ascending heights covered, perhaps, with a multitude, to whose gaze he was exposed, as he drew nigh and looked upon those massive rocks, the seat of divine authority and judgment. How imposing must have been the sight of the priesthood and their numerous train, surrounded by all the outward pomps and insignia of their office ; as he listened, may be, to the solemn hymns of the vates, preparatory to the ceremonial of justice, or as he stepped within the sacred enclosure, there to receive condemnation or acquittal, to be referred to the ordeal of the logan, or the tolmen, according to the will of the presiding priest ! As he slowly advanced and thought upon these things, often must he have shuddered and trembled to meet the Druid's eye, when he stood by 'the stone of his power.'

The Druids not only adjudged, but with their own hands executed the terrific sentence which they had decreed. The human victims which they immolated to appease or to render propitious their deities, (particularly those offered to Hesus the god of battles, and to Bel, or the Sun) were generally chosen from criminals; unless when the numbers demanded by the sacrifice induced them to mingle the blood of the innocent with that of the guilty, to supply their cruel rites. And as these sacrifices were not merely confined to the eve of a battle, or to make intercession for the calamities of a kingdom, but were frequently offered up at the prayer of any chief or noble afflicted by disease, it is not unlikely that the condemned criminal was hurried from the Gorseddau to suffer as a victim to the gods, against whose supreme will all crimes were held to be committed that were done upon the earth.

That these ancient courts of justice were kept in the open air seems to be the most probable opinion, since such was the custom with many of the nations of antiquity; the Areopagus of the Greeks is an instance. And in earlier ages we find it to have been much the same; as we read in the Bible of the elders pronouncing judgment 'sitting in the gates.' These gates were at the entrance of a town or city; a court that must have been in some measure held in the open air. With the Celtic nations it was unquestionably a practice that long prevailed amongst their posterity; since, in the ancient laws of Wales, the judge was directed " to sit with his back to the sun or storm, that he might not be incommoded by either." [2]

One of these primitive courts, handed down as such by successive ages from the earliest times, through the various changes of government and religion, is to this day found on Dartmoor: it is known by the name of Crockern Tor,[3] the most curious and

[2] Dr. Clarke when describing the Celtic remains at Morasteen, near old Upsal, says, " We shall not quit the subject of the Morasteen (the circle of stones) without noticing that in the *central stone* of such monuments we may, perhaps, discern the origin of the Grecian (Βῆμα) Bêma, or *stone tribunal*, and of the 'set thrones of judgment' mentioned in Scripture and elsewhere, as the places on which kings and judges were elevated; for these were always of *stone*."

[3] Mr. Polwhele says, in his *Devon*, " For the Cantred of Tamare we may fix, I think, the seat of judicature at *Crockern Tor* on Dartmoor; here, indeed, it seems already fixed at our hands, and I have scarce a doubt but the Stannary Parliaments at this place were a continuation even to our own times of the old British Courts, before the age of Julius Cæsar."

remarkable seat, perhaps, of Druidical judicature throughout the whole kingdom. It remained as the Court of the Stannaries till within the last century, and hence was it commonly called Parliament-rock. On this spot the chief miners of Devon were, by their charters, obliged to assemble. Sometimes a company of two or three hundred persons would there meet, but on account of the situation, after the necessary and preliminary forms had been gone through, they usually adjourned to Tavistock, or some other Stannary town, to settle their affairs. The Lord Warden, who was the supreme judge of the Stannary Courts, invariably issued his summons that the jurors should meet at Crockern Tor on such a day; and by an accidental reference to an old magazine, I find a record of a meeting of this nature having been there held so late as the year 1749. If this was the last meeting or not I cannot say, but I should think not, and that the custom died gradually away, till it was altogether abolished.

Some powerful motive, some deep veneration for ancient usages, or some old custom too well established to be easily set aside, must have operated to have caused these Stannary Courts, in comparatively modern times, to be held on such a spot as Crockern Tor; whose rocks stand on the summit of a lofty height open on all sides to the bleak winds and to the weather, affording no shelter from a storm, remote from the habitations of men, and, in short, presenting such a combination of difficulties, and so many discomforts to any persons assembling on matters of business, that nothing can be more improbable, I had almost said impossible, that such a place should have been chosen for the Stannary Courts, had it not been handed down as a spot consecrated to justice from the earliest ages.

Having offered these few introductory remarks on the subject of Crockern Tor, I now give you the following extracts from Mr. Bray's Journal of his survey of the western limits of Dartmoor, so long ago as the year 1802; when, though a very young man, he was the first person who really examined and brought into notice many of those curious Druidical antiquities in which it abounds. He spoke of them in various quarters; and some persons were induced by what he said cursorily to explore them. Of these a few now and then published some account, and though not unfrequently availing themselves of Mr. Bray's information, I do not know, excepting in one instance, that any person ever did him the justice to acknowledge the obligation, or even to mention his name as having been the first to lead the way to an investigation of what was still to be found on the Moor.

"September 20th, 1802. Crockern Tor, or Parliament-rock, is situated on Dartmoor, near the turnpike-road leading from Moreton to Tavistock, at the distance of about eleven miles from the former, and nine from the latter. Prince, in his *Worthies of Devon*, p. 168, in his account of the family of Crocker, after informing us that Crockernwell received its name from them, says—'There is another famous place in this province, which seems to derive its name also from this family, and that is Crockern Tor, standing in the Forest of Dartmoor, where the parliament is wont to be held for Stannary causes; unto which the four principal stannary towns, Tavistock, Plimton, Ashburton, and Chagford, send each twenty-four burgesses, who are summoned thither when the lord warden of the Stannaries sees occasion; where they enact statutes, laws, and ordinances, which, ratified by the lord warden aforesaid, are in full force in all matters between tinner and tinner, life and limb excepted. This memorable place is only a great rock of moorstone, out of which a table and seats are hewn, open to all the weather, storms and tempests, having neither house nor refuge near it, by divers miles. The borough of Tavestock is said to be the nearest, and yet that is distant ten miles off.'

"I am not inclined to agree with Prince about the origin of the name of this rock, nor, from the present appearance of it, do I think his a correct description. The first thing that struck me was a rock, with a fissure in the middle, with one half of it split, either by art or nature, *into four pretty regular steps*, each about a foot and a half high and two feet broad.[4] Whether these were used as seats of eminence at the assembly of the tinners, I cannot pretend to say.

[4] The following very curious passage from Clarke's *Travels*, vol. iv., will be found most interesting here:—"Along this route, particularly between Cana and Turan, we observed basaltic phenomena; the extremities of columns, prismatically formed, penetrated the surface of the soil, so as to render our journey rough and unpleasant. These marks of regular or of irregular crystallization generally denote the vicinity of a bed of water lying beneath their level. The traveller, passing over a series of successive plains, resembling in their gradation the order of a staircase, observes, as he descends to the inferior *stratum* upon which the water rests, that where rocks are disclosed, the appearance of *crystallization* has taken place; and then the *prismatic* configuration is vulgarly denominated *basaltic*. When this series of depressed surfaces occurs very frequently, and the *prismatic* form is very evident, the *Swedes*, from the resemblance such rocks have to an *artificial flight of steps*, call them *trap:* a word signifying, in their language, a *staircase*. In this state science remains at present concerning an appearance in nature which exhibits nothing more than the common process of *crystallisation*, upon a larger scale than has hitherto excited attention."—p. 191.

"Before this mass, towards the north, is a short ledge of stones evidently piled up by art, which might have been a continued bench. On ascending higher I arrived at a flat area, in which, though almost covered with rushes, I could plainly trace out four lines of stones forming an oblong square, twenty feet in length and six in breadth, pointing nearly east and west. The entrance seems to have been at the north-west corner. At the north side, four feet distant, is another imperfect line, and ten feet on either side is a straight natural buttress of rock.

PARLIAMENT-ROCK

Possibly the table might have stood in the centre of this area, and these lines may be vestiges of the seats around it. I can hardly suppose the stone was so large as to rest on these as its foundation, though there are no stones in the middle that might have answered that purpose. Whilst the Lord Warden and Stannators presided at this table, probably the rest of the assembly filled up the remainder of the area, or climbed the rocks on each side.

"As an instance of the powers of the Stannary Court, I have been informed that a member of the House of Commons having spoken in it of the Stannaries in a manner that displeased the Lord Warden, as soon as the offending member came within the jurisdiction of his court he immediately issued his precept, arrested him, and kept him in prison on bread and water till he had acknowledged his error and begged pardon for his transgression.

"Tin, on being melted, is put into moulds, holding generally somewhat above three hundred weight, (then denominated *block-tin*) where it is marked as the smelters choose, with their house-mark [that brought to Tavistock bears, I have generally observed, an Agnus Dei, or lamb holding a pennon] by laying brass or iron stamps in the face of the blocks while the tin is in a fluid state, and cool enough to sustain the stamping iron. When the tin is brought to be coined, the assay-master's deputy assays it by cutting off with a chisel and hammer a piece of one of the lower corners of the block, about a pound weight, partly by cutting and partly by breaking, in order to prove the roughness [query toughness?] and firmness of the metal. If it is a pure good tin, the face of the block is stamped with the duchy seal, which stamp is a permit for the owner to sell, and at the same time an assurance that the tin so marked has been examined and found merchantable. The stamping of this impression by a hammer is *coining* the tin, and the man who does it is called the *hammer-man*. The duchy seal is argent, a lion rampant gules, crowned or, with a border garnished with bezants."

The punishment for him who, in the days of old, brought bad tin to the market, was to have a certain quantity of it poured down his throat in a melted state.

Tin was the staple article of commerce with the
Phœnicians, who used it in their celebrated dye of
Tyrian purple, it being the only absorbent then
known. This they procured from the island of
Britain. Its high value made the preservation of its
purity a thing of the utmost consequence; any
adulteration of the metal, therefore, was punished
with barbarous severity. The Greeks were desirous
of discovering the secret whence the Phœnicians
derived their tin, and tracked one of their vessels
accordingly. But her master steered his galley on
shore, in the utmost peril of shipwreck, to avoid
detection; and he was rewarded, it is said, by the
State for having preserved the secret of so valued
an article of national commerce.

The next extract I here send you is from Mr.
Bray's Journal of June 7th, 1831.

"My wife, her nephew, and myself, set out from
Bair-down, between twelve and one o'clock, for
Crockern Tor. In addition to the wish she had long
felt of seeing it, her curiosity was not a little raised
by my tenant's telling her that he could show her
the *Judge's Chair*. And I confess that my own was
somewhat excited to find out whether his traditionary
information corresponded with my own conjectures,
made many years ago, as to this seat of the President
of the Stannators. He took us to the rock (situated
somewhat below the summit on the south side of the
Tor) which bears the appearance of rude steps, the
highest of which he supposed to be the seat. It
seems to be but little, if at all, assisted by art, unless
it were by clearing away a few rocks or stones.
Below it is an oblong area, in which was the table,
whilst around it (so says tradition) sat the Court of

Stannators: whence it is also known by the name of Parliament-rock. This stone, I had been informed, was removed by the late Judge Buller to Prince Hall; but my tenant told me that it was drawn by twelve yoke of oxen to Dennabridge, now occupied by Farmer Tucket, on the Ashburton road, about ten miles from Tavistock. It is now used, he said, as a shute-trough, in which they wash potatoes, &c.

"From this, as far as I can comprehend his meaning, I should conceive that it serves the purpose of a lip, or embouchure, to some little aqueduct that conveys the water into the farmer's yard. The Tor itself is of no great height, and is now much lower than it was, by large quantities of stone having been removed from its summit for erecting enclosures and other purposes. It could not be chosen, therefore, for its super-eminent or imposing altitude; though possibly it might be so for its centrical situation; but I am disposed to think that it was thus honoured from being used as a judicial court from time immemorial. My reasons I shall mention hereafter. I shall remark here, however, that it is the first tor of any consequence that presents itself on the east side of the Dart, upon the ridge that immediately overhangs its source.

"We then proceeded along this ridge to Little Longaford, or Longford Tor. This, in Greenwood's map, which is defective enough in regard to names, is thus distinguished from a larger one; whilst the tors that follow Crockern Tor in succession are there called Littlebee Tor, Long Tor, Higher-white Tor, and Lower-white Tor. White Tor, or Whiten Tor, as my tenant pronounced it, we did not visit; and as I have some doubts about the real names of the tors,

I shall only say that the first (a small one) that we approached had something in its appearance which so much reminded me of Pew Tor, that I asked the guide if there were any basins in it; at first he replied in the negative, but afterwards said he thought he had once observed a basin on one of these tors. This was enough to ensure a search, and we were not long in finding one. It was in the shape of a rude oval, terminating in a point or lip, about twenty inches long, eighteen wide, and six deep. A square aperture among the rocks here, somewhat like a window, suggested the idea of its possibly having been used as a tolmen, through which children, and sometimes, I believe, grown people, were drawn to cure them of certain diseases. The second tor was much less, but large enough to afford Mrs. Bray, who felt fatigued, sufficient shelter from the sun and wind whilst we proceeded; and there we left her busied with her sketch-book.

"Between this and the great tor we found several pools of water, though it was the highest part of the ridge, and though the season had been so free from rain (a circumstance not very common in Devonshire) as not only to render the swamps of Dartmoor passable, but almost to dry up the rivers. Longford Tor is more conical than most of the eminences of the Forest, having very much the appearance of the keep of a castle. Unlike also the generality of tors, which mostly consist of bare blocks of granite, it has a great deal of soil covered with turf, and only interspersed with masses of rock, whilst the summit itself is crowned with verdure. Towards the north is White or Whiten Tor: for the Devonians soften, or as some may think harden, words by the introduction of a consonant, but more frequently of a vowel ; and they are laughed at for saying Black-a-brook instead of Blackbrook, though we perceive nothing objection-able in black-a-moor, which is precisely upon the same principle of euphony.   On this tor, some years ago, were found some silver coins, and, I believe, human hair.   And on Stennen Hill, which lies below it, if I may trust my informant, are many barrows, in one of which was supposed to have been found 'a pot of money,' whilst two men of the name of Nor-rich and Clay were employed in taking stones from it.   The former, it is said, discovered it without com-municating it to his companion, but sent him to fetch a 'bar-ire,' or crow-bar, whilst he availed himself of the opportunity to appropriate the contents to himself. The inference seems principally to be drawn from the circumstance that he afterwards was known to lend considerable sums of money at interest.

"The greatest extent of view from Longford Tor is towards the east and south-east.   In that direction, as far as I could collect, you see Staple Tor, (so that there seem to be two of this name on the Moor) High or Hay Tor, Bag Tor, Hazel Tor, &c.   On Hay Tor, which is commonly called Hay Tor Rocks, though at so great a distance, is visible a kind of white land or belt about its base, made by the removal of granite: so that we can more easily account for it than the belts of Jupiter.   Of the tors that lie towards the south and south-west, Hessory is certainly higher than Longford (which my guide at first doubted), as also Mis Tor.   Nearer are Bair-down and Sidford Tors.   Bair-down Man (which, however, we could not see) is a single stone erect, about ten feet high. To these succeeded, towards the north, Crow or

Crough Tor, and Little Crow Tor. I learnt from my guide that at a place called Gidley there are circles much larger and far more numerous than near Merrivale. There are also two parallel lines about three feet apart, which stretch to a considerable distance. In order to see them, you must go to Newhouse, about twelve or thirteen miles on the Moreton road from Tavistock, and there turn off into the Moor for about four or five miles. I also learnt that near the rabbit warren there is something that goes by the name of the King's Oven.

"We again on this day visited Wissman, Wistman, or Welshman's Wood (concerning the etymology of which I made some remarks in my former papers): it is about half a mile in extent, and consists principally of oaks, but is here and there interspersed with what is called in Devonshire the quick beam or mountain-ash. I conceive it to have been 'the wood of the wise-men,' and Bair-down, on the opposite side, 'the hill of bards.' On the latter were formerly many circles, which, I am sorry to say, were destroyed by the persons employed by my father in making his enclosures. Would they have given themselves but a little more trouble they might have found a sufficient supply among those stones or rocks which are thickly scattered on a spot opposite the wood, and to which they give the name of the Grey Wethers. I think that the same name has been given to some stones at Abury, with which is supposed to be erected Stonehenge. If so, the coincidence is not a little remarkable. They possibly may be so called from resembling at a distance a flock of sheep. The resemblance indeed had struck me before I heard the name.

"I shall now state the reasons why I think Crockern

Tor was chosen by the miners as the chief station for holding their Stannary Courts. It is but little more than a mile from what I venture to consider as 'the hill of bards' and 'the wood of wisemen,' or Druids. On, or near each of these are numerous circles, which, whether they were appropriated to domestic or religious purposes (most probably to both) clearly indicate that it must have been a considerable station. This was not only supplied with water from the river, but two or three springs arise from the rocks at the bottom of the wood itself. Well sheltered and well watered, (for not only had they trees to screen them from the storm, but they had also a comparatively snug valley, open only to the south) it is no wonder that the aborigines here fixed their habitation. The circles, the wood, the existing names, all seem to lead to the supposition that some of the high places in their immediate neighbourhood were originally those of superstition and judicature, where priest, judge, and governor were generally combined. The tor that we may thus imagine was appropriated by the ancient Britons, might afterwards (from traditionary veneration for the spot) be used by the Saxons for assembling together their Wittenagemot, or 'meeting of wisemen,' and lastly, for a similar reason, by the miners for their Stannary Courts."

Before I give you Mr. Bray's account of Dennabridge Pound, which will be the next extract from his Journal, it may not be amiss to observe that there is on Dartmoor another remarkable vestige and one better known, of like antiquity, called Grimspound. Like that of Dennabridge, this truly cyclopean work is an enclosure, consisting of moor-

stone blocks, piled into a vast circular wall, extending round an area of nearly four acres of ground.
Grimspound has two entrances, and a spring of
water is found within, where the ruins of the stone-
ring huts are so numerous as to suggest the idea of
its having been a British town. It is well known that
the foundations of all these primitive dwellings were
of stone, though their superstructure, according to
Diodorus and Strabo, was of wood. For they "live,"
says the former, "in miserable habitations, which are
constructed of wood and covered with straw." And,
when speaking of the Gauls, the latter says, "They
make their dwellings of wood in the form of a *circle*,
with lofty tapering roofs."

In some instances it is not improbable that the
larger stone circles are vestiges of enclosures made
for the protection of cattle. The Damnonii were
celebrated for their flocks and herds; and the wolves,
the wild cats, and the foxes, with which this country
once abounded, must have rendered such protection
highly necessary for their preservation. I have often
remarked on Dartmoor two or three small hut-rings,
and near them a larger circle of stones; the latter I
have always fancied to have been the shelter of the
flocks, and the former the dwellings of their owners.
There is nothing perhaps very improbable in this
conjecture, since many tribes of the ancient Britons
were, like the Arabs, a wandering and a pastoral
people; and it is also worthy of observation, that to
this day the Devonians never fold their sheep, but, on
Dartmoor in particular, still keep them within an enclosure of stone walls set up rudely together without
cement. Where extensive stone circles are found
near what may be called a *cursus*, or *via sacra*, (of

which I shall have somewhat to say hereafter) or near cromlechs and decaying altars, we may fairly conclude such to have been erected not as the habitations of individuals, but as temples sacred to those gods whose worship would have been considered as profaned within any covered place, and whose only appropriate canopy was held to be the heavens in which they made their dwelling.

The circles within Grimspound are different from these; and that this vast enclosure (as well as Dennabridge Pound) was really a British town, seems to be supported by the accounts given of such structures by Strabo and Cæsar. The latter describes them as being surrounded by a mound or ditch for the security of the inhabitants and their cattle. And Strabo says, "When they have enclosed a very large circuit with felled trees, they build within it houses for themselves and hovels for their cattle."[5]

That the people of Dartmoor should prefer granite to felled trees for such an enclosure is nothing wonderful, inasmuch as the Moor abounds with it; in fact it must have been then, the same as in the present day, a much easier task to have piled together the blocks and pieces of stone, strewed all around them, than to have felled trees for the purpose of forming their walls; and how much greater was the security afforded by a granite fence, to one of mere timber! In other parts of Britain, such as Cæsar saw and

[5] "The universality of Celtic manners, at a very remote period, is proved by the existence of conical thatched houses, as among the Britons, and rude stone obelisks, adjacent tumuli, and Druidical circles, in Morocco."—*Gentleman's Magazine*, July, 1831. Dr. Clarke, the celebrated traveller, gives a very interesting account of vestiges similar to those found on Dartmoor, in Sweden, and other northern countries. See the ninth volume of his *Travels*.

described, rock or stone was not so easily or so plentifully to be found. The Britons, therefore, very naturally availed themselves of what the country would most readily afford; and the wild and vast forests supplied materials for their public walls as well as their private dwellings.

Stones, however, it is probable, were in all places considered as indispensable in the erection of those structures sacred to the rites of religion; and hence is it that we often see such enormous masses piled on places where it seems little less than miraculous to find them: for no stones of a similar nature being seen in their immediate neighbourhood, gives rise to the belief that they must have found their present stations by being moved from a distance, and not unfrequently to the summits of the loftiest hills and mountains: such, for instance, is that most extraordinary cromlech called Arthur's Stone on the eminence of Cevyn Bryn in South Wales.[6] That most of these structures were of a sacred nature cannot well be doubted. No impulse either on the public or the private mind is so strong as that dictated by a feeling of religion, even when it is misdirected: no labours, therefore, have ever equalled those of man when he toils, in peace or in war, for the honour or the preservation of his altars.

That Grimspound and Dennabridge sheltered both the Britons and their cattle seems the more probable when we recollect the general customs of that people, and of the Damnonii in particular; since, in every way, their flocks must have been to them of the

[6] An account of this ancient British monument was laid before the Society of Antiquaries by my brother, Alfred J. Kempe. It may be found in the twenty-third volume of the *Archæologia*.

highest value. They were allowed to be the most excellent in Britain; the constant verdure of this county no doubt rendered them such. They were not merely useful at home, but an article of commerce abroad; and Cæsar says, that "the Britons in the interior parts of the country were clothed in skins." It is not improbable, therefore, that the Damnonii found their account in the wool and skins of those flocks for which they were so famed, as a convenient clothing for their neighbours.

Their tin traffic with the Phœnicians had early initiated them into a knowledge of the advantages and benefits of commerce. And as I have long taken a pleasure in busying myself to trace out, in connexion with ancient times, whatever may be found in Nature or in art on Dartmoor, I amuse myself with fancying that I have discovered an allusion in Pliny to the beautiful and scarlet moss still found on the Moor, which, not many years ago, was used as a dye for cloth. Indeed, it is not improbable that, as such, it became an article of commerce even in the days of the ancient Britons; for Pliny says, when speaking of British dyes, that they were enriched by "wonderful discoveries, and that their purples and *scarlets* were produced only by certain wild herbs."

How sadly have I rambled in these pages! It is a good thing that in letters there is no sin in being desultory, or how often should I have offended! But letters are something like the variations of an air of music; you may run from major to minor, and through a thousand changes, so long as you fall into the subject at last, and bring back the ear to the right key at the close. Once more, therefore, I fall back on

DARTMOOR HORSES. [LET.

... found, and here follows the extract

... Journal : --

... ...th of July, 1831, I set out in search of

... on the Moor; namely. the table said to

... removed from Crockern Tor, and Denna-

... and, which (like all or most others on the

... understood was on the site of a Celtic

... ...ing up the hill beyond Merrivale Bridge,

... and colts, almost wild, that were in an

... ...ar the road, came galloping towards us,

... from curiosity or the instinctive feeling of

... kept parallel with the carriage as far as

... One of them was of a light

... whilst its mane, which was almost

... formed a fine contrast, but added

... to the picturesque effect of the whole

... clusters waving and floating, now in

... its neck, and now over its forehead,

... ...s and ears I could not help thinking

... our horses by cropping their manes

... cruelly depriving them of their

... against flies. And enthusiastically

... taste of the Greeks, particularly in

... cannot but confess that, if I may be

... consult my own eyes, they seem to have

... taste and rejected a rich embellishment,

... as on the Elgin marbles in the

... Museum all their horses with hogged manes.

... ...s run from painting to sculpture, and

... ...ard to Greece, though it may still, perhaps,

... association of ideas, I must return to

... ...ts of our present pursuit, without further

... for these digressions.

... bridge over which we had passed, I observed, on the right of the road, a circle seven paces in diameter, with a raised bank around, and hollow in the centre. Having come about ten miles from Tavistock, which I had understood was the distance of Dennabridge Pound, I entered a cottage near to make inquiries, but could gain little or no information, finding only a girl at home who had not long resided there. I had observed on the map that there was not only Dennabridge Pound, but also a place called Dennabridge, which I learnt from this girl was about a quarter of a mile distant. Seeing nothing at the former place that at all corresponded with the object of my search, I resolved on proceeding to the latter; not without hopes that I should meet with some kind of primitive bridge, consisting perhaps of immense flat stones, supported on rough piers, which was the ordinary construction of our ancient British bridges.

"Seeing a person whom I considered one of the natives near a cottage, I pointed to a lane that seemed to lead towards the river, and asked if it was the way to Dennabridge. The answer I received was, 'This, Sir, is Dennabridge.' My informant seemed as much surprised at my question, as I was at his reply. No signs of one being visible, I inquired where was the bridge that gave name to the place? He said that he knew not why it was so called, but that there was no bridge near it. Observing, however, at some distance down the river, what seemed not unlike the piers of one, of which the incumbent stones or arches might have fallen, I asked if a bridge had ever stood there? He believed not, but said that they were rocks; situated, however, so near each other, that it was the way by which persons usually crossed the river. Under-

standing that the spot was difficult of access, particularly for a lady, we did not go to it; but I am
rather disposed to think that the place is not so
called as in *lucus a non lucendo*, but that these
rocks were considered as a bridge, or at least *quasi*
a bridge.   And perhaps it deserved this name as
much as that which is thus mentioned by Milton in
his description of Satan's journey to the earth—

> "'Sin and Death amain,
> Following his track, such was the will of Heaven,
> Paved after him a broad and beaten way
> Over the dark abyss, whose boiling gulf
> Tamely endured a bridge of wondrous length,
> From Hell continued, reaching the utmost orb
> Of this frail world.'

"On further conversation with this man, I learnt
that he lived at Dennabridge Pound, where there
was no stone of the kind I inquired for, but that at
Dennabridge itself, hard by, was a large stone that
possibly might be the one in question.   I asked if
he had ever heard that it had been brought thither
by the late Judge Buller.   He said that it must
have been placed there long before the Judge's time;
that he knew the Judge well, and had lived in that
neighbourhood forty years or more.   Perhaps I might
have obtained the information I wanted long before,
had I asked for what I was told to ask; namely, for
a stone that was placed over a *shoot*.   But, absurdly
I confess, I have always had an objection to the word;
because in one sense at least it must be admitted to
be a vulgarism even by provincialists themselves.
The lower classes in Devonshire almost invariably
say *shoot* the door, instead of *shut* the door.   And
when it is used by them to express a water-pipe, or

the mouth of any channel from which is precipitated a stream of water, I have hitherto connected it with that vulgarity which arises from the above *abuse* of the word. But if we write it, as perhaps we ought, *shute*, from the French *chute*, which signifies *fall*, we have an origin for it that may by some perhaps be considered the very reverse of vulgar, and have at the same time a definite and appropriate expression for what otherwise, without a periphrasis, could hardly be made intelligible.

"At the entrance of the farm-yard adjoining is, I doubt not, the stone I had gone so far in search of, though I could not gain such satisfactory information as I anticipated. The farmer who lives on the spot exonerates the Judge, as did my first informant, from having committed the spoliation with which he has been charged. He says that it has been there, to his own knowledge, for fifty years; and that he has heard it was brought from Crockern Tor about eighty years ago. He further says that it was removed by the reeve of the manor. His wife, who is the daughter of this reeve, (or of his successor, I do not remember which) says that she also always heard that it had been brought from Crockern Tor, but she does not think that it could have been the table, as she remembers that her father used to take persons to the spot as a guide, and show them the table, chair, and other objects of curiosity on the Tor. I thought I could perceive that the reeve of the manor was at any rate considered a great personage, and not the less so, perhaps, from being the cicerone, or guide to the curiosities of the Forest; for this is the word by which the inhabitants are fond of designating the treeless Moor. I do not know whether the reeve, with the spirit of an antiquary, had any veneration for a cromlech, and therefore wished to imitate one; but if such were his intention he succeeded not badly: for the stone (which is eight feet long by nearly six wide, and from four to six inches thick) is placed, as was the quoit in such British structures, as a cover, raised upon three rude walls about six feet high, over a trough, into which by a *shute* runs a stream of water. And probably the idea that the removal of this stone

STANNARY TABLE.

was by some one in authority, may have given rise to the report that such person could be no less than Judge Buller, who possibly might be supposed to give sentence for such transportation (far enough certainly, but not beyond sea) in his judicial capacity: to which, perhaps, some happy confusion between him and the judge or president who sat in the Stannary Court may have contributed. Nay, possibly the reeve or steward may have considered himself to be the legal representative of the latter, and so have removed it to his own residence. We thence returned to Denna-bridge Pound. On clambering over the gate, I was

surprised to find close to it a rude stone seat. Had
I any doubt before that the pound was erected on
the base of an ancient British, or rather Celtic circle,
I could not entertain it now; for I have not the
slightest doubt of the high antiquity of this massive
chair. It is not improbable that it suggested the
idea of the structure over the trough. And it is
fortunate that the reeve had not recourse to this
chair, instead of the stannary table, for the stone he
wanted. It certainly was handier; but possibly it

DRUIDICAL STONE CHAIR.

would have deprived him of showing his authority
and station by occasionally sitting there himself.
But I am fully convinced that it was originally designed for a much greater personage; no less perhaps
than an Arch-Druid, or the President of some court
of judicature. Two upright stones, about six feet
high, serve as sides or elbows. These support
another, eight feet long, that forms the covering
overhead. The latter, being in a sloping direction
to give greater shelter both from wind and rain, ex·
tends to the back, which consists also of a single
stone. In front of it are two others, that supply the

immediate seat, whilst a kind of step may be considered as the foot-stool.

"The enclosure, pound, or circle, is about 460 paces
in circumference on the inside.   The wall of it has a
double facing, the external part being a little higher
than the inner.   Though far beyond the memory of
man, *this superstructure* is unquestionably modern,
when compared with the *base or foundation*, which is
ruder, and of larger stones.   There are a few rocks
scattered about in the area.   I thought, however,
that I could distinguish the vestige of a small circle
near the centre, through which passed a diametrical
line to the circumference, but somewhat bent in its
southern direction towards the chair.

"On reaching Bair-down I was told by my tenant
Hannaford, that there could be no doubt but I had
seen the right stone, and that he believed the report
of its being removed by Judge Buller was wholly
without foundation.   On referring afterwards to Mr.
Burt's notes to Carrington's poem on Dartmoor, I
find he treats it as 'a calumny.'   I believe that by
our different conversations with Hannaford we have
made him a bit of an antiquary, and I was no less
surprised than delighted when he informed me that,
only a few days before, he had brought home an oak
that he had discovered in a bog, at a place called
Broad-hole, on Bair-down.   I have heard Sir Thomas
Tyrwhitt say that he had found alders and willows in
a bog near Tor Royal; but I do not remember to
have heard of any oak being so found, at least of
such dimensions.   The tree thus discovered, which
consists of the trunk, part of the root, and also of a
branch, is ten feet long, and, at its lower extremity,
is nearly five feet in girth.   The whole of the trunk

is perfectly sound, but not altogether so dark or solid as I should have expected ; for generally, I believe, and particularly when it has been deposited in a bog, it is as hard and as dark as ebony.   A branch of it had for some time been visible in the bank of the river Cowsick, and this induced Hannaford to examine it, and finally to exhumate it from the depth of eight feet.   It is not improbable that this is a vestige of the antediluvian forest of the Moor.   Distant from Wistman's Wood about two miles, and by the side of another river, it could never have formed part of it ; indeed it is probably larger than any there : and we have no account for ages of any other oaks existing on the whole of this extensive desert.   A day or two after he brought it to Tavistock, and it is now in my possession.

"I learnt from him that some years since some oak bowls[7] were found in a bog, between the Ashburton and Moreton roads, by a person called John Ash.

"On crossing the bridge which was erected by my father over the Cowsick, Mrs. Bray expressed a wish that I would point out to her some of my inscriptions on the rocks below, which, from some strange circumstance or other, she had never seen ; and even now I thought that without much search we should not have found them ; not recollecting, after so long a period, where I had placed them.   But on looking over the parapet she observed, on one of the rocks

[7] Bowls formed of oak were used by the ancient Britons.   Mention is made of them in Ossian ; and in the *Cad Godden ; or, The Battle of the Trees*, by Taliesin, the following passage occurs :—"I have been a spotted adder on the mount" (alluding to the serpent's egg) ; "I have been a viper in the lake.   I have been stars among the supreme chiefs ; I have been the weigher of the falling drops," (the water in the rock basins) "dressed in my priest's robe, and furnished with my bowl."

beneath, the name of her favourite Shakspere.
Perhaps under other circumstances it might have
altogether escaped notice; but the sun was at that
instant in such a direction as to assist her in deciphering it, as it did some of our English officers in
Egypt, who thus were able to interpret the inscription
on Pompey's Pillar which the French savants had so
long attempted in vain.   Many an officer (for a large
body of troops had guarded for years the French
prison on the Moor) no doubt had visited Bair-down
and probably fished on the river, and yet these inscriptions seem never to have attracted their notice,
nor, indeed, that of other persons; or, if they have,
it has never reached my ears.   But I have long been
taught to sympathise with Virgil, when he exclaims—

'Rura mihi, et rigui placeant in vallibus amnes,
   Flumina amem sylvasque inglorius.'—*Geo.* l. ii. 485.

"Had my name been so renowned as '*virûm volitare
per oras,*' I doubt whether I should have experienced
greater pleasure than I felt when my wife first discovered my inscription on the rock, and expressed the
feelings it excited in her.   I question whether, for the
moment, she felt not as much enthusiasm as if she
had been on the Rialto itself, and there had been
reminded of the spirit-stirring scenes of our great
dramatist in the *Merchant of Venice.*   I have somewhere read that a philosopher having been ship-
wrecked on an island which he fancied might be
uninhabited, or, what perhaps was worse, inhabited by
savages, felt himself not only perfectly at ease but
delighted at seeing a mathematical figure drawn upon
the sand; because he instantly perceived that the
island was not only the abode of man, but of man in

an advanced stage of civilization and refinement.   It certainly was a better omen than a footstep; for the impression of a human foot might have excited as much fear, if not surprise, as that which startled Crusoe in his desert island.   Perhaps I had fondly anticipated that, long ere this, on seeing these inscriptions, some kindred being might have exclaimed, 'A poet has been here, or one at least who had the feelings of a poet.'   I would have been content, however, to remain unknown still longer, thus to be noticed as I was by one so fully competent to appreciate those feelings, which no doubt to most would have appeared ridiculous, if not altogether contemptible."

As, since the days of Sir Charles Grandison, it is quite inadmissible for ladies to write to their friends the fine things that are said of them, I certainly should have stopped short before I came to this compliment about myself.   But my husband, who was pleased to pay it, insisting that if I took anything from his Journal I should take all or none, I had no choice.

LETTER VIII.

TO ROBERT SOUTHEY, ESQ.

Vicarage, Tavistock, April 10*th,* 1832.

WE have on Dartmoor, at a short distance from
Merrivale Bridge, and nearly four miles from Wistman's Wood, some very remarkable vestiges of the
cursus, or *via sacra*, used for processions, chariot
races, &c., in the Druidical ceremonies. This *cursus*
is about 36 paces in breadth, and 217 in length. It
is formed of pieces of granite that stand one, two,
or sometimes three feet above the ground in which
they are imbedded: a double line of them appears
placed with great regularity on either side, as you
will see in the drawing of the ground-plan. A circle

in the middle of the *cursus* breaks the uniformity of
line in part of it. There are, near this extensive
range of stones, many remains of Druidical antiquity ;
such as a fallen cromlech, a barrow, an obelisk, a
large circle, and several foundations of the round

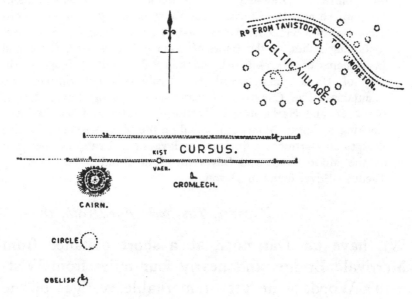

MAP OF THE GREAT CURSUS, CIRCLES, ETC., NEAR MERRIVALE BRIDGE.

huts or houses of the Britons. A *cursus* of this
nature is found near Stonehenge ; Borlase, I believe,
mentions one at Classerniss in the Isle of Lewis,
another is seen in Anglesea, and we have this remarkable vestige on Dartmoor.

Processions formed a distinguished part of the
ceremonies observed in Druidical festivals. According to Davies, the sacred ship of glass was borne
along the *cursus* with the utmost pomp on the day
of observing the mysteries of the Helio-arkite god.
The procession of Godo, the British Ceres, was no
less splendid : it took place in the evening, as that
of the solar deity did in the morning. And the
cursus at such moments must have presented scenes

like those exhibited by the abominable priests of Baal, of whom we read in the Bible : for in the midst of their wild dances they cut and lacerated their bodies in honour of her mystic rites. "Let the thigh be pierced with blood," says Taliesin. And Aneurin thus describes the ceremonies of the procession sacred to Hu, the British Bacchus : " In honour of the mighty king of the plains, the king of the open countenance, I saw dark gore arising on the stalks of plants, on the clasp of the chain, on the bunches, (alluding to the flowers on the necks of the oxen) on the king himself, (the god Hu[1]) on the bush, on the spear. Ruddy was the sea-beach, whilst the circular revolution was performed by the attendants of the white bands (the Druids) in graceful extravagance." The bard thus continues : " The assembled train were dancing after their manner, and singing in cadence with garlands on their brows."[2]

Chariot races, as well as the above-noticed processions, were also common with our British ancestors : they were likewise performed in the *cursus ;* and it is not improbable that they became a part of the religious ceremonies of the festivals. In Germany we know they were so ; as the sacred chariot of the goddess who ruled over the affairs of men, its procession, and race, is most strikingly described by Tacitus in his delightful book on the manners of the Germans. I forbear to transcribe the passage, as I wish to mention one less known, that occurs in the very curious and ancient Welsh poem of *Gododin :* a poem which, like the chronicles of Froissart,

[1] Hu was the great demon god of the British Druids. Has he not ever been the same? For what passions are more demoniacal than those excited by a devotion to the god of wine?

[2] From the Rev. E. Davies's translation of Aneurin's song.

affords the most lively picture of the manners of the times to which it relates. *Gododin* is a poetical narrative, or history, of the conduct of Hengist and Vortigern in the cruel slaughter of the ancient Britons.

This act of treachery, the poet tells us, took place in the *cursus* near the great temple of Stonehenge; which he calls 'the area of the sons of harmony,' no doubt in allusion to the bards. In addition to the light which *Gododin* throws on ancient manners, its incidents would afford the finest subject for a poem in the style of *Madoc*. The time, the place, the variety of character, the cold-hearted cunning of the wily Saxon, or of the 'Sea-drifted Wolf,' as Hengïst is styled by the Welsh poet; the distracted state of the Druid, who, casting the lots just before the feast begins, and finding their presage fatal to the Britons, fears to warn them, as he meets the eye of Hengist fixed sternly upon him; the frankness and honest confidence of the betrayed British chiefs; the sudden and fearful catastrophe, as the bowl with the flowing mead is raised to the lip; the resolute conduct of the bards who perish in defending the temple; the magnanimity of Eidiol (the young hero of the tale) who escapes at last from a host of enemies; all these and many other circumstances are highly dramatic, and would afford materials for a poem of great power and interest. So minutely does the Welsh bard describe everything connected with his subject, that he mentions even the amber beads worn as a wreath on the brows of Hengist; a circumstance whose correctness is ascertained by the heads of many Saxon princes being seen thus adorned in sundry coins that have been found in England.

I mentioned, at the commencement of this letter,

that there is, near the remains of the ancient *cursus*
on Dartmoor, a fallen cromlech. I shall here, therefore, before I proceed to the account of it, venture to
offer a few observations respecting the purposes to
which cromlechs were devoted ; since, though I have
always delighted in pursuits connected with antiquity,
I never yet could find any amusement in looking
upon an old stone, or any other rude vestige, unless I
could in some measure trace out its history, or understand what relation it might bear to the manners
and customs of former ages : for without this connexion to give it an interest, to admire anything
merely because it is old seems to me an absurdity.

I am well aware that antiquaries differ in their
opinions respecting the purposes to which cromlechs
were applied. Far be it from me to suppose that I
could throw any additional light on the subject ; but
as I have attentively read many of those opinions,
and some were wholly opposite, I have been led to
conclude that each may be in the right, though not
exclusively, and that cromlechs were applied to *more*
than *one* purpose ; that they were sometimes used as
altars of sacrifice, at others as sepulchral monuments,
and not unfrequently as a mark of covenant. Mr.
Owen considers them in the latter view, as the Grair
Gorsedd or 'altar of the bards,' placed within the ring
of federation. To them, therefore, may be applied
those lines of the poet—

> "Within the stones of federation there,
>   On the green turf, and under the blue sky,
>   A noble band, the bards of Britain stood,
>   Their heads in reverence bare, and bare of foot,
>   A deathless brotherhood."[3]

[3] *Madoc.*

Those cromlechs under which are found urns and human bones were most likely sepulchral.

All cromlechs with wells or springs beneath them were most probably stones of federation; since the forms of initiation with the bards invariably took place at a cromlech, where water might be found, as necessary to the mysteries. This initiation represented *death*, and a renovation from the dead; for the aspirant of Druidism was obliged to pass the river of death in the boat of Garan Hu, the Charon of Britain. Sometimes he was immersed in the water, or at others buried, as it were, beneath the cromlech; since, says Davies, "it was held requisite that he should have been mystically buried as well as mystically dead." And cromlech, according to Logan, is a Punic word, and signifies 'the bed of death.' The cells sometimes found under these antiquities no doubt were used as the temporary burial-places of the bards, previous to the ceremonies of initiation; ceremonies that might differ according to the particular attributes or character of the god to whose honour and worship the bard more immediately devoted his life. This act of burial in the cells was considered as a necessary trial of his patience and his fortitude; it was seldom, if ever, dispensed with, and as it took place the day or night previous to initiation, it reminds us in some measure of that ceremony of later times, the vigil of arms practised by the novitiate of chivalry, on the night before he paid the vows, and received the honours of knighthood.

By far the finest cromlech on Dartmoor is near Drewsteignton[4]—the very name speaks its high claim

---

[4] *Drew*, in the Celtic, and *drus*, in the Greek, signified an oak. The oak was sacred to the great god of the Druids. From Drewester,

to veneration ; and on the noble pile of rocks in that neighbourhood may be seen some rock basins that remain entire even to this day.

The fallen cromlech on the Moor, which I mentioned, derives its chief value from its immediate vicinity to the *cursus*, or *via sacra* of the Druidical processions. From its situation it is more likely to have been a place of sacrifice than a stone of federation, or a memorial for the dead. And this conjecture I think will not be found far-fetched, when we recollect that Godo, the British Ceres, on the day of her festival, not only had her procession in the *cursus*, but also her sacred fire kindled in her temple or on her stone, which was never to be extinguished for a year and a day. It was, in fact, like that of Vesta, (originally derived from the Magi) a perpetual fire. I have found one reference that bears upon this point in the translation of the ancient poems of the bards by Davies. It occurs in *Gododin*, before noticed, where the sacred fire near the *cursus* of Stonehenge is called the perpetual fire.[5] This very circumstance, therefore, renders it still more probable that the fallen cromlech in question, near the Dartmoor *cursus*, was a stone of sacrifice, where offerings were made to the sacred fire of the British gods.

'priest of the oak,' we have the word Druids. The oak god was sometimes styled Buanaur, 'the quickener,' before whom heaven and earth trembled. " A dreadful foe, whose name in the *Table Book* is Dryssawr, 'the deity of the door.'" This, says Davies, " must apply to the deified patriarch, who received his family into the ark, and his connected votaries into the Druidical sanctuary." Acorns were held as offerings from the bards. Taliesin speaks of the " proud, the magnificent *circles* round which the majestic oaks, the symbols of Taronuy the god of thunder, spread their arms."

[5] Stonehenge was a temple of the Sun ; and fire was invariably used in the worship of that deity.

I mentioned also that the line of the great *cursus* on Dartmoor was in one part broken by a stone circle. On circles, in their general character, I have before ventured some remarks in my former letters. But respecting *this*, found on the *line* of stones which *forms the via sacra*, I am inclined to think it was more immediately connected with the ceremonies of the Helio-arkite procession. The idea struck me when I found that Davies, in his very learned work on the mythology of the British Druids, so clearly proves that the Caer Sidi was no other than a figure of the sacred vessel in which the mythological Arthur and his seven sons escaped the general deluge. The Caer Sidi was, in fact, the ark of Noah. But as in process of time the British priests, like most other idolaters, blended their worship of the planets with whatever vestiges they might retain of true religion, (derived to them through Gomer the son of Japhet, and the father of the Celtic nations) even so did they transfer the name of the ark to that 'great circle' in which those luminaries, "emblems of their gods, presided and expatiated. In British astronomy it was become the name of the Zodiac." [6] In the most ancient songs of the bards, this Caer Sidi, or sacred circle, is constantly alluded to, sometimes as a ship preserving what was left of the inhabitants of the old world; at others as a celestial circle; and often as the temple of Druidical worship; and the circle of the Helio-arkite god is spoken of when the procession of the sacred ship becomes the theme of song. [7]

[6] DAVIES's *Celtic Remains.*

[7] "With the circle of ruddy gems on my shield do I not preside over the 'area of blood, which is guarded by a hundred chiefs?" So writes Taliesin in his poem of *Cad Godden.* "This shield," says Davies, "was of the Helio-arkite god, and of his priest, having the

Not far from the *cursus* there is seen a barrow, no doubt the grave of some chief or noble of the Damnonii; as it is well known that heaps of earth (sometimes containing a kistvaen, or stone chest for the body, and at others only an urn) or barrows were the burial-places of the ancient Britons. Of these tumuli Mr. Polwhele (whose learning entitles his opinions to be received with the utmost respect) says *none are Roman.* That gentleman also tells us that in the year 1790, a friend with whom he held a literary correspondence opened some of the barrows on Dartmoor; and found in them "urns filled with ashes or the bones of a human body, together with ancient coins, and instruments, sometimes of war." This account reminds us of the manner in which the ancient inhabitants of Caledonia made their graves: for if a warrior became the tenant they placed his sword by his side, and the heads of twelve arrows; and not unfrequently the horn of a deer, as a symbol of the deceased having been a hunter.

The Britons, also, sometimes erected a single stone in memory of the dead. Possibly the obelisk seen near the *cursus* (which has no inscription) may be a memorial of this nature, and if so of very high antiquity; since, judging by two noble funereal obelisks of Romanized British chiefs (now preserved in our garden) I should imagine that after the Romans had overrun Britain, and not before, the Britons inscribed their monumental stones and pillars. On this point, however, I shall have more to say when

image of Caer Sidi, the Zodiac, or of the Druidical temple, formed of gems and set in gold." The device still may be seen upon old British coins. The hierarch presided in the *area of the altar*, which was guarded by the priests and drenched with human blood.

I come to the subject of inscribed stones found in this neighbourhood, both of the British and the Saxon period.

OBELISK AND CIRCLE.

I have before noticed what a fine field Dartmoor must have afforded the Druids for the augury of birds; and as I do not wish to break in upon the extracts from Mr. Bray's Journals, which will supply matter for many of my letters, before I take my leave of the Druids I wish to offer a few desultory remarks that will not, I trust, be found altogether misplaced. Certain it is that in this neighbourhood, and on the Moor in particular, birds are still considered as ominous of good or evil, more especially of the latter; and no reasoning will operate with the people who have imbibed these prejudices from their infancy, to make them consider such opinions as an unhallowed credulity.

Augury indeed seems to have been a universal superstition even in the earliest ages; and I have always thought that, like most other heathenish customs, it took its rise in truth; for surely it is not improbable that the dove of Noah bearing back to the ark the olive-branch, in token of the flood having ceased, might have given birth to the confidence reposed in all auguries of the feathered tribes, a confidence which extended itself throughout the known world. The Egyptians, the Greeks, the Romans, the Gauls and Britons, and many other nations of antiquity, consulted the flight and appearance of birds. In Wales the custom long held sway, and the bards sometimes celebrated these omens in their songs. Taliesin thus alludes to them, when he makes a priest say, "A cormorant approaches me with long wings. She assaults the *top stone* with her hoarse clamour : there is *wrath in the fates !* Let it burst through the stones ! Contention is meet only amongst the grey wolves."

I have noticed, likewise, that there are certain springs on the Moor which appear to have been considered with more than ordinary interest, such as Fitz's or Fice's Well. And where we find so many vestiges of Druidical antiquity, it is most natural to conclude that even these springs were held in veneration at a very remote period. Water, we know, was used for many sacred purposes by the Druids ; it was in fact essential in many of their religious rites. The celebrated cauldron of Ceridwen (which, according to Davies, implied not a *single vessel* used for one simple purpose) was nothing more than water taken from a sacred fountain and impregnated with a decoction of certain potent herbs. The 'cheerful and placid vervain' was chief amongst these ; and this decoction was used, like the holy water of the Church of Rome, for purification or sprinkling. The cauldron of Ceridwen was placed in two vessels within the circle or temple, east and west, and the priests moved round them reciting hymns or prayers. Pliny bears testimony to the use of vervain : as he says it was used by the Druids in their sortilege or lots of divination. And Tacitus, also, gives a particular account of the manner in which the German priests practised this custom of casting lots. I cannot immediately find the passage; but if I recollect right he mentions branches or twigs, as well as *herbs*, as being used in sortilege. Some of the latter it was likewise usual to gather near a sacred fountain.

The purposes to which the water secured in *rock basins*, as it fell from the clouds, might have been applied, has I am aware long been a subject of dispute with antiquaries. But it is not improbable that the water in the rock basins, like the disputed cromlechs, was applied to more purposes than merely that of lustration or sprinkling. My reason for thinking so is grounded on certain passages in the poems of the bards; and if we reject the writings of the bards as authorities, where shall we supply their place? We might surely with as much reason reject the authority of Froissart for the manners and customs of the Middle Ages. Taliesin speaks of the mystical water as being the fountain of his own inspiration; and Davies (whose profound learning in Celtic antiquity cannot be too highly appreciated) tells us that in a mythological tale, describing the initiation of that celebrated bard, the goddess Ceridwen prepared the water from the sacred rock, and placed in it her potent herbs that had been collected with due observance of the planetary hours.

Rocking or logan stones are still found on Dartmoor, notwithstanding the havoc that has been made amongst them during so many ages. There can, I think, be no doubt that these stones were engines of cunning in the hands of the Druids; who most probably made the multitude believe that they possessed a power more than natural, and could alone be moved by miracle at the word of the priest. One of their tricks respecting the secret means of setting a logan in motion on Dartmoor was accidentally discovered by Mr. Bray, in a way so remarkable, that I shall forbear any other mention of it in this place, purposing hereafter to send you his own account of the circumstance. The logan was in all probability not only resorted to for the condemnation or acquittal of the accused, but the very threatening, the mere apprehension, of its supernatural powers in the detection of guilt, might have led the criminal to a full confession of those offences with which he stood charged.

Amongst the British antiquities of the Moor, I must not forget to mention the rude vestiges of its primitive bridges.

The construction of these bridges is exceedingly simple, being nothing more than masses of granite piled horizontally, and thus forming the piers, on a foundation of solid rock that Nature has planted in the midst of the stream. The piers being thus formed, the bridge is completed by huge slabs of moorstone laid across and supported from pier to pier. Some few of these picturesque and primitive bridges still remain entire; others are seen in ruins. It is not unlikely they are unique in their construction; at least I can say that, though I have visited in England, South Wales, and Brittany, many places celebrated

for Celtic remains, I have never yet seen anything
like our ancient Dartmoor bridges. They appear to
have been placed in those spots where, on ordinary
occasions, stepping-stones would have answered the
purpose: but the sudden and violent rains with which
the Moor is visited render stepping-stones very in-
sufficient for the convenience or security of the passen-
ger. No person but one who is accustomed to witness

BRITISH BRIDGE.

the sudden swell, the turmoil, rapidity, and force, of
a river or torrent in a mountainous region during
heavy rains, can have the least idea of the violence
with which a traveller, attempting to cross from rock
to rock, would be carried off and overwhelmed by
one false step or slip in his hazardous passage. So
sudden, sometimes, is the rush and swell of our Dartmoor rivers in storms of rain, that immense masses
of granite, generally standing aloft above the waters,
will be in a moment covered with a sheet of foam

that resembles those fearful breakers at sea which always indicate hidden and fatal reefs of rock.

On the Moor, also, are several ancient trackways, together with stream-works of very high antiquity. Mr. Bray is disposed to consider them of the same date with the Druidical remains. The art of working metals was known to the Britons; and the mines of Dartmoor, though now fallen into neglect, were for many successive ages worked with considerable profit. Leland mentions them; and Mr. Polwhele says, "We are informed from *records* that all the old mines on Dartmoor are on its western side towards the Tamar; there are strong marks both of shode and stream works." Leland speaks of these, and adds "that they were wrought by violens of water." Mr. Polwhele is of opinion that the Damnonii carried on their tin traffic with the Greeks of Marseilles, and that the port Ictis in all probability was the Isle of St. Nicholas in Plymouth harbour.[8] I have heard (though I have never been fortunate enough to see any) that in breaking into old mines in this neighbourhood, heads of axes and other antiquities made of flint have been found: flint indeed has been the primitive material for most implements, not only with the ancient Britons, but with uncivilized nations even to the present day.

Of any minute particulars respecting the commerce of the Damnonii, nothing I believe is known. Like that of the other kingdoms of Britain, it principally consisted in hides and tin. But as Tacitus expressly declares that Britain produced both gold and silver, as well as other metals, it is not improbable that, even so early as the Roman Conquest, the silver mines of

[8] Pinkerton is of opinion that the Cassiterides did not mean exclusively the Scilly Isles, but also Great Britain.

this neighbourhood were not unknown to the Britons. The silver of Devon in later times was held in high estimation. Edward III. derived from it such considerable benefit, that it assisted him to carry on his brilliant and chivalrous career in France. These mines at one period were conducted by the Jews, who rendered them so flourishing that the reigning monarch (if I remember right it was Edward II.) banished them the kingdom from motives of suspicion, as a reward for their skill, labour, and success. In the days of Elizabeth several veins were discovered; and that great princess, with her accustomed wisdom, pursued a very different policy to that of Edward II., for finding her crown mines had fallen into neglect, and that foreigners understood the mining art better than the English, she invited and allured them from Germany and elsewhere, by liberal offers of reward, to pass over sea and teach their craft to the miners of Devon. A cup weighing 137 ounces was presented to the city of London by Sir Francis Bulmer; it was formed from the silver of the Coombe-Martin mines in the north of our county.

My letter has extended to such a length that I must forbear to add more, reserving for some future opportunity what I may have to say, not only about our Dartmoor minerals, but also concerning certain vestiges of ancient customs still found to linger, though in decay, amongst the peasantry of the Moor; and, though last not least, a word or two respecting the life and adventures of those merry little pixies and fays, which though never seen are here still averred to have a local habitation as well as a name, and to do all those various petty acts of mischief, which in a family or amongst domestics in other

counties have, whenever inquiry is made respecting
them, 'Nobody' for their author: not so is it in
Devon; our 'Somebody' is never wanting; and as
it is a being who can slip through a keyhole, sail on
a moonbeam, and, quite independent of all locks and
bolts, enter closets and cupboards at will, we are never
at a loss to hear who it is that pilfers sweatmeats, or
cracks cups and saucers, to the annoyance of staid old
housekeepers, who may think that both should be held
sacred, and that tea-cups, like hearts, were never made
to be broken.

LETTER IX.

TO ROBERT SOUTHEY, ESQ.

Account of the Circles of Stone near Merrivale Bridge—Walls, or
Stone Hedges, how formed on the Moor—Account of Forty contiguous Circles of Stone—Traditionary account and vulgar Error
respecting the Circles near Merrivale Bridge—Plague at Tavistock
in the year 1625—Temporary appropriation of the Circles at that
period to a Market gave rise to the Error—Borlase quoted ; his
opinion of the Circular Temples of the Britons—Further account
of the Great Cursus near Merrivale Bridge—Barrow—Cromlech—
Kistvaen, or Sepulchral Stone Cavity—Origin of the word Cromlech—Obelisk near the Cursus—Hessory Tor—View from it—
Curious Rock on the summit of the Tor answering in every
respect to a Druidical Seat of Judgment—Rundle Stone.

Vicarage, Tavistock, April 18th, 1832.

THIS evening, on looking over some notes made by
my husband at the time he first explored the western
limits of Dartmoor, I find he notices, more particularly
than I have done, the circles and *cursus* near Merrivale Bridge. I think, therefore, before I enter on any
other subject, to give you the following extract from
his papers :

" October 7th, 1802.—This morning we paid a
visit to the stone circles, which are about five miles
from Tavistock, on the hill beyond Merrivale, or
Merrivill, Bridge, over the river Walkham. They
are on each side of the Moreton road, by which
indeed two of them are intersected. The first (which,

as well as many others, has been partly destroyed, in order to build a neighbouring stone hedge) is twenty feet in diameter. I here, perhaps, may be allowed to remark, that the hedges on Dartmoor are formed of stones piled on each other without any mortar, or even earth, to the height of about five feet. These walls are found better in many respects than any others; for, by admitting the winds through their interstices, they are not liable to be blown down by the storms which are here so tremendous; and, by being of so loose a texture, the cattle are afraid to come near, much more to break over them, for fear of their falling upon them.

"Finding the circles were so numerous, I measured the remainder by the shorter method of pacing them. They consist in all of about forty: six being on the left side of the road, and the remainder on the other. The greater number of them are about eight paces in diameter, though one is sixty, in which are enclosed two or three small ones. This is about the centre of the whole. There are two or three of an oval form; many of them have two upright stones at the entrance, which is generally towards the south. The other stones are mostly placed on their edge, lengthways, and are frequently ranged in double rows. Within the largest circle is one of about eight paces, enclosing a much smaller, of which it forms a part. Close to it are some flat rocks, about a foot or two high. This was perhaps the central altar. Towards the north-east and south-west sides are two ill-defined circular lines of stone, which might probably be the circum-vallation or boundary of the holy precincts.

"The account given by tradition respecting these circles requires some notice here. I shall preface it with saying, that one of the four great plague years in London was 1625, in which about 35,000 of its inhabitants perished. And this is the year in which this fatal malady most raged at Tavistock. The burials in our register at that period amount to 522. In the following year they had decreased to 98 ; and in the preceding year (in the latter part of which it probably in some degree prevailed) they amounted but to 132 ; the very number, save one, that were buried in one month (namely September) in the year of this awful visitation. Of this, or a similar one, another memorial remains in these circles on Dartmoor near Merrivale Bridge, (though they certainly are of far greater antiquity, and are either Druidical, or the vestiges of a Celtic town) for they are stated by tradition to be the enclosures in which, during the plague at Tavistock, (that they might have no intercourse with its inhabitants) the country-people deposited the necessary supply of provisions, for which within the same the townspeople left their money.

"That these circles may have been applied to this purpose is not improbable ; particularly as the spot is still known (and indeed is so distinguished in some maps) by the name of the 'Potato Market.' Nor is it altogether improbable that it was during the plague in question. For the potato was first brought from Virginia by Sir Walter Raleigh (the contemporary, nay fellow-soldier, of our great townsman, Sir Francis Drake, and himself also a native of Devonshire) 'who, on his return homeward in the year 1623, stopping at Ireland, distributed a number of potatoes in that kingdom. These having been planted multiplied accordingly ; and in a few years the cultivation of them became general. It may be noticed that the discovery of this inestimable root has been of the greatest con'sequence to mankind, as it is now almost universally cultivated, though at first its introduction was very much opposed.   It has been remarked that, with the greatest propriety, it may be denominated the *bread-root* of Great Britain and Ireland.'[2]   Indeed by our neighbours, the French, it is called by a name to which *earth-apple* would be synonymous in our own language.

"Nor is it, perhaps, to be wondered at, that the era of this cautious traffic should be no longer known, or almost as little remembered as the purposes to which these granite circles were originally applied. From our long immunity we have been induced to think that the plague was no more likely to return to us than the barbarous superstitions of our Celtic ancestors.   But of the sons of men who shall say to the pestilence, 'Hitherto shalt thou come, but no farther'?

"It is absurd to imagine that any circles would be formed of such vast stones solely for the purpose of a market during the time of the plague, though being on the spot they might have been so applied. If they were designed only to be boundaries to distinguish the property of different persons, a circular line or trench on some spot free from stones, might have been formed with greater ease.   It has been suggested by some, that these enclosures were made to defend the flocks from the wolves.   This idea, though more specious at first, is equally objectionable; for if this were the case, they must have been built to some height, and at least parts of the walls must have remained in an erect position, or the

[2] REES'S *Cyclopædia.*

ruins have been still found below. But this is not the case ; not one stone, in most instances, being on the top of another.

"It is natural to conclude then, that like the other vestiges on the Moor, they must have been the works of the Britons or the Druids ; and this last conclusion will presently be supported by some other remains found near them, and which (after mentioning the purposes to which Druidical circles were applied) I shall endeavour to describe. They may be considered as temples or places set apart by the Druids for the purposes of religion. Borlase considers that 'some might be employed for the sacrifice, and to prepare, kill, examine, and burn the victims.' 'Others,' he conjectures, 'might be allotted to prayer;' for the station of those selected as the victims, and some for the feastings of the priests. Thus, whilst one Druid was preparing the victim in one circle, another might be engaged in his devotions, or in 'describing the limits of his temple, and a third be going his round at the extremity of another circle of stones.' Nor is it unlikely that many other Druids were occupied in these mysterious evolutions. Some perhaps were busy in the rites of augury, and at the same time all employed, each in his proper place, in the ceremonials of idolatry, 'under the inspection of the high priests, who, by comparing and observing the indication of the whole, might judge of the will of the gods with the greater certainty.'

"The circles above described are on the slope of a hill. On the top of it, which spreads into a plain of some length, are two parallel double lines of stones, stretching south-west by north-east. The remains of a circle are at the commencement of one,

where is also an erect stone.   This line is 198 paces
in length, at the end of which is a stone, now fallen,
nine feet long.   The stones that form the line are
about two feet apart, and the same space exists between the two rows.   From this to the opposite
double line are thirty-six paces.   The last is imper-
fectly extended to the length of seventy-four paces
more; there are two stones, one erect, the other
fallen.   Returning from the point opposite the other,
where is also a stone erect, after walking seventy-one
paces I came to a low circular mound which I conjecture is a barrow, with a kistvaen on the top of it.
This I shall describe hereafter.   From this circle, at
the distance of forty-seven paces, I met with a large
stone, which served as an index to a cromlech fourteen paces distant.   Sixty-nine paces farther brought
me to two large stones; and thirty paces from these
I reached the end, where is a stone erect.   Thus,
including the additional line, this is 217 paces in
length.   To the other, which it here also somewhat
surpasses, are twenty-six paces; so that these lines
of stone are ten paces nearer at the north-east end
than they are at the other.   But, considering the
length, they may be looked upon as parallel.   The
area between, as well as the space without them, for
some distance is free from stones.

"For what purpose this avenue, or *cursus*, was used
it is now impossible to determine; though the several
adjacent remains, known to have been frequently
erected by the Druids, are a strong confirmation of
the opinion that it must have been the work of one
and the same people and period.   This avenue,
which was probably subservient to religion, might
possibly have been appropriated for the sacred pro-

cessions of the priests. It might be used, also, to bear the funeral pomp of their departed brethren, as by the side of the south-west end of it is seen a circular heap of stones sixty-five paces round. This was probably a barrow, or place of burial. From the end of this line at the south-west, at the distance of seventy-one paces, we found another barrow, mentioned above. It is in the centre of the two lines, and is twelve feet in diameter. In the middle of it is a hollow in the form of a diamond, or lozenge, which is undoubtedly a kistvaen, or sepulchral stone cavity. It was almost concealed with moss, but with some difficulty we dug to the depth of three feet; and discovering nothing thought it useless to dig farther, as in appearance we had reached the natural stratum, which was of a clayey substance, below the black peat. It is probable that nothing was deposited there but ashes.

"The cromlech which we afterwards visited is fallen, but bears evident signs of having been in an erect position. This, also, is supposed to be a sepulchral monument. The word cromlech is derived from *krum* 'crooked' and *lêch* 'a flat stone;' as it consists of a flat stone, generally of a gibbous or convex form, supported on other stones in an erect position.

"Many are the opinions respecting cromlechs. Borlase says, 'that the use and intent of them was primarily to distinguish and do honour to the dead, and also to enclose the dead body, by placing the supporters and covering-stone so as they should surround it on all sides.' The quoit or covering-stone of this on the Moor, one end of it being buried in the ground, is ten feet and a half long, six feet and a half

wide, and one foot and a half thick. Under it are
three or four stones now lying prostrate, but undoubtedly they formerly were in an erect position, as
its supporters.

"At some distance, towards the south of the parallel
lines, is a circle of nine low stones, twelve paces in
diameter, rising from the smooth surface of the ground.
Near it is an erect stone ten feet and a half high.
From its connexion with the circle it was probably
placed there by the Druids, and might have been one
of their idols. At some distance from the other end
of the parallel lines we perceived some stone posts
about five or six feet high, stretching in a line to the
south-east, but having no connexion with what has
been described. On going up to them we found on
one side the letter T, and on the other A. On inquiring afterwards we learnt that they served as
guide-posts from Tavistock to Ashburton, before the
turnpike-road was made over the Moor.

"We next visited two tors to the south, but saw
nothing worthy remark, and then turning to the east
ascended Hessory Tor, which is six miles from Tavistock, and is reckoned the highest part of the Forest.
There we had a most extensive view in every direction. The sea was visible over the summits of the
lofty tors towards the south and south-west. Towards
the north-west, also, we thought we could distinguish
it, as we perceived a horizon evidently too straight
to be land. On the top of this Tor is a curious rock,
which, from its shape, I should be inclined to think
was not unknown to the Druids. Its front, towards
the south-east, was thirty-two feet. At the height of
eight feet from the ground are two canopies, projecting nine feet. At the distance of eight feet is a kind

of buttress, twenty in length, and four in height.   It
answers in every respect to the idea we entertain of a
Druidical seat of judgment.   Descending to the road
we reached it near a high stone post, which is commonly called Rundle Stone.   This is considered as
the boundary of the Forest, and the letter B on the
south side of it may refer to the limits of the Moor."

LETTER X.

TO ROBERT SOUTHEY, ESQ.

Bogs on the Moor called Dartmoor Stables—Mists on the Moor, their density—Popular belief among the Peasantry of being *Pixy-led*—Fairies and Pixies of the Moor—Lines from Drayton—Duergar or Dwarfs—Their origin by some attributed to the Lamiæ—Derivation of the word *Pixy*—Pixies a distinct genus from Faries—The reputed Nature, Character, and Sports of Pixies—Traditionary Tales respecting them—Said to change Children in the Cradle—Story of a Changeling — Pixy Houses, where found — Lines from Drayton's *Nymphidia—Conrade and Phœbe*, a Fairy Tale in Verse—The wild waste of Dartmoor haunted by Spirits and Pixies—Causes assigned by the Peasantry for these Spirits not being so common as in former Days—Pixy-led Folk--Turning Jackets and Petticoats, a practice to prevent the Disaster—Legend of the Old Woman, the Tulip-bed, and the gratitude of Pixies.

Vicarage, Tavistock, April 24th, 1832.

I BELIEVE I have not yet said much about our bogs on the Moor, which, from some luckless horse or other being now and then lost in them, have obtained, as their popular name, that of the 'Dartmoor stables.' These bogs in old times must have been exceedingly formidable and perilous; since, to borrow an expression from the poetaster who celebrated the roads of General Wade in the Highlands, I may truly say of the Moor, " Had you travelled its roads before they were made," you would have blessed the good fortune that enabled you to cross such a wilderness without being lost. For even now that we have a passage

through it, which displays all the happy results of
Mr. MacAdam's genius, yet nevertheless, if a mist
suddenly comes on, the stranger feels no small apprehension for his own safety.

Mr. Bray assures me that when he used, in early
life, to follow up with enthusiasm his researches on
the Moor, not heeding the weather, he has frequently
been suddenly surprised and enveloped in such a
dense mist, or rather cloud, that he literally could
scarcely see the ears of the animal on which he rode.
Once or twice he was in some peril by getting on
boggy ground, when his horse, more terrified than
himself, would shake and tremble in every joint, and
become covered with foam, from the extreme agony
of fear.   If such adventures have now and then
happened even in these latter days, how far more
frequently must they have occurred, when there was
no regular road whatever across the Moor! How
often a traveller, if he escaped with life, must have
wandered about for hours in such a wilderness, before he could fall into any known or beaten track, to
lead him from his perils towards the adjacent town
of Tavistock, or the villages with which it is surrounded!

I mention this because I think there cannot be a
doubt that similar distresses gave rise to the popular
belief still existing, not only on the Moor, but throughout all this neighbourhood, that whenever a person
loses his way he is neither more nor less than '*Pixy-
led.*' And as I wish to give you in this letter some
little variety of subject, suppose we leave for a while
the old Druids and their mystic circles, and say something about the fairies or pixies of the Moor; though,
as I shall presently state and give my reasons for so

doing, I consider the latter to be a distinct race of genii from the former. You are a poet, and have therefore no doubt a very friendly feeling towards those little pleasant elves that have supplied you with many a wild and fanciful dream of fairy land. You will listen then with good will to one who proposes in this letter to become the faithful historian of sundry freaks and adventures they are said to have played off in our neighbourhood, the remembrance of which without such record might become lost to posterity ; and as fairies or pixies often do as much mischief in their supreme career as greater personages, I do not see why they should not claim some celebrity, as well as other spirits of evil who may have exhibited their achievements on a larger and more important scale. To borrow an expression from Drayton, that exquisite poet of fairy land (who, perhaps, is not inferior even to Shakspere for the frolics of his Pigwiggin, in the *Nymphidia*) I would say that as no historian has here been found to record the acts of our pixies, I, unworthy as I may be to accomplish the task, will nevertheless adventure it—

> " For since no muse hath been so bold,
>   Or of the latter, or the old,
>   Their elvish secrets to unfold,
>   Which lie from other's reading,
>   My active muse to light shall bring
>   The court of a proud fairy king,
>   And tell there of the revelling ;
>   Jove prosper my proceeding."

However, as I wish to model my historical records of the pixies on the very best examples, I shall bear in mind that it is usual in all grave histories, before reciting the heroic or other actions of individuals, to

say something of the origin, rise, and progress of the
people to whom they belong.   Thus then, before I
relate the frolics of

> " Hop and Mop, and Drop so clear,
>   Pip, and Trip, and Skip, that were
>   To Mab, their sovereign dear,
>   Her special maids of honour,"

it may not be amiss to tell what I have been able to
glean about the accredited opinions and traditions
concerning the fairy race in general, ere we come to
particulars.   And who knows but such a task may be
more liberally rewarded than is usual with luckless
authors, even by—

> " A bright silver tester fine
>   All dropped into my shoe."

Dr. Percy gives it as his opinion that these 'elves
and demi-puppets' are of much older date in this
country than the time of the Crusaders, to whom
some writers have referred their introduction on British
ground.   This opinion receives no small confirmation
from the known credulity and numberless superstitions
of the Anglo-Saxons.   Amongst other wonders of
the unseen world of spirits, they believed in the
existence of a certain race of little devils, that were
neither absolutely spirits nor men, called *duergar* or
dwarfs ; and to whose cunning and supernatural skill
they attributed sundry petty acts of good or evil that
far exceeded the power of man.   They were considered so far to partake of human nature that their
bodies were material, though so light and airy that
they could at will pass through any other created
substance, and become indistinct and even invisible
to the sight.

Some writers have affirmed that the fairies derive their origin from the *lamiæ*, whose province it was to steal and misuse new-born infants; and others class them with the fauns or sylvan deities of antiquity. And a very learned and meritorious author[1] considers that the superstition respecting fays is founded on the *abrunæ* of the Northern nations, *i.e.* their penates. Amongst the ancient Germans, he states, they were merely images made of the roots of the hardest plants, especially the mandragora. These little images were about six or seven inches or a foot high. They mostly represented females or Druidesses; and remind us of a child's doll of modern days. They were usually kept in a little box, and offered meat and drink by their possessors: occasionally they were taken out and consulted in the telling of fortunes; when, not improbably being managed by some wire or machinery like the puppets that now delight childhood, they would bow their heads and raise their arms in answer to a question. These penates were considered as lucky for the household in which they had their abode; and they were held to have a marvellous power in the cure of diseases or pains.

The Druids are supposed to have worshipped fairies, amongst their many deities; and certain it is they are often mentioned by the most ancient Welsh bards, by whom they were called 'the spirits of the hills.' There can be no doubt that these little beings were considered as a race of genii by the Northern nations, as the *duergi* or *pigmies*. May not this have given origin to the word *pixies*, the name by which

---

[1] The Rev. Thomas Dudley Fosbroke, in his excellent and laborious work, the *Encyclopædia of Antiquities*, gives a very interesting account of the fairies of different nations.

they are to this day known in the West of England?
Brand's derivation seems improbable.[2] The pixies
are certainly a distinct race from the fairies; since to
this hour the elders amongst the more knowing
peasantry of Devon will invariably tell you, if you
ask them what pixies really may be, that these native
spirits are the souls of infants, who were so unhappy
as to die before they had received the Christian rite
of baptism.

These tiny elves are said to delight in solitary
places, to love pleasant hills and pathless woods; or
to disport themselves on the margins of rivers and
mountain streams. Of all their amusements, dancing
forms their chief delight; and this exercise they are
said always to practise, like the Druids of old, in a
circle or ring. Browne, our Tavistock poet, alludes
to this custom, when he writes—

> " A pleasant mead,
> Where fairies often did their measures tread,
> Which in the meadows make such circles green."

These dainty beings, though represented as of exceeding beauty in their higher or aristocratic order,
are nevertheless in some instances of strange, uncouth
and fantastic figure and visage: though such natural
deformity need give them very little uneasiness, since
they are traditionally averred to possess the power of
assuming various shapes at will; a power of which
Ariel exhibits a specimen, who, as well as being able
to 'ride on the curled clouds,' to 'flame amazement,'
and to mock and mislead the drunken Trínculo and

---

[2] He says, "I suspect pixy to be a corruption of *puckes*, which
anciently signified little better than the devil, whence in Shakspere the
epithet of 'sweet' is given to Puck by way of qualification." Surely
pixy is more like pigmy than 'puckes.'

his companions, could transform himself into a harpy, and clean off a banquet with his wings. But whatever changes the outward figure of pixies may undergo, they are amongst themselves as constant in their fashions as a Turk; their dress never varies, it is always green.

Their love of dancing is not unaccompanied with that of music, though it is often of a nature somewhat different to those sounds which human ears are apt to consider harmonious. In Devonshire that unlucky omen, the cricket's cry, is to them as animating and as well timed as the piercing notes of the fife, or the dulcet melody of rebec or flute, to mortals. · The frogs sing their double bass, and the screech owl is to them like an aged and favoured minstrel piping in hall. The grasshopper, too, chirps with his merry note in the concert, and the humming bee plays 'his hautbois' to their tripping on the green. The small stream, also, on whose banks they hold their sports, seems to share their hilarity, and talks and dances as well as they in emulation of the revelry; whilst it shows through its crystal waters a gravelly bed as bright as burnished gold, the jewelhouse of fairy land; or else the pretty stream lies sparkling in the moonbeams, for no hour is so dear to pixy revels as that in which man sleeps, and the queen of night who loves not his mortal gaze becomes a watcher.

It is under the cold and chaste light of her beams, or amidst the silent shadows of the dark rocks where that light never penetrates, that on the Moor the elfin king of the pixy race holds his high court of sovereignty and council. There each pixy receives his especial charge: some are sent, like the spirit

Gathon of Cornwall, to work the will of the master
in the mines; to show by sure signs where lies the
richest lode; or sometimes to delude the unfortunate
miner who may not be in favour, with false fires, and
to mock his toils by startling him with sounds within
the bed of the rocks, that seem to repeat, stroke for
stroke, the fall of the hammer which he wields, whilst
his labours are repaid by the worst ore in the vein;
and then the elfin will mock his disappointment with
a wild laugh, and so leave him to the silence and
solitude of his own sad thoughts, and to those fears
of a power more than natural, not the less apprehended because it takes no certain or distinct form,
and is liable to be regulated by so much wanton
caprice. Other pixies are commissioned on better
errands than these; since, nice in their own persons,
for they are the avowed enemies of all sluts or idlers,
they sally forth to see if the maidens do their duty
with mop and broom; and if these cares are neglected—

> "To pinch the maids as blue as bilberry,
>   For Mab, fair queen, hates sluts and sluttery."

The good dames in this part of the world are very
particular in sweeping their houses before they go to
bed, and they will frequently place a basin of water
by the chimney nook to accommodate the pixies, who
are great lovers of water and sometimes requite the
good deed by dropping a piece of money into the
basin. A young woman of our town, who declared
she had received the reward of sixpence for a like
service, told the circumstance to her gossips; but no
sixpence ever came again; and it was generally believed the pixies had taken offence by her chattering,

as they like not to have their deeds, good or evil, talked over by mortal tongues.

Many a pixy is sent out on works of mischief, to deceive the old nurses and steal away young children, or to do them harm. This is noticed by Ben Jonson in his *Masque of Queens.*

> " Under a cradle I did creep
>   By day ; and, when the childe was a-sleepe
>   At night, I sucked the breath ; and rose
>   And plucked the nodding nurse by the nose."

Many also, bent solely on mischief, are sent forth to lead poor travellers astray, to deceive them with those false lights called will-o'-the-wisp, or to guide them a fine dance in trudging home through woods and waters, through bogs and quagmires, and every peril ; or as Robin Goodfellow says, to

> " Mislead night wanderers, laughing at their harms."

Others, who may be said to content themselves with a practical joke, and who love frolic more than mischief, will merely make sport by blowing out the candles on a sudden, or kissing the maids 'with a smack,' while they 'shriek out, Who's this?' as the old poet writes, till their grandams come in, and lecture them for allowing unseemly freedoms with their bachelors. Some are dispatched to frolic or make noises in wells ; and the more gentle and kindly of the race will spin flax and help their favourite damsels to do their work. I have heard a story about an old woman in this town, who suspected she received assistance of the above nature, and one evening, coming suddenly into the room, spied a ragged little creature, who jumped out at the door. She thought she would try still further to win the services of her elfin friend ; and so bought

some smart new clothes, as big as those made for a
doll. These pretty things she placed by the side of
her wheel : the pixy returned and put them on ; when
clapping her tiny hands in joy, she was heard to
exclaim these lines (for pixies are so poetical, they
always talk in rhyme)—

> " Pixy fine, pixy gay,
> Pixy now will run away."

And off she went ; but the ungrateful little creature
never spun for the poor old woman after.

The wicked and thievish elves, who are all said to
be squint-eyed, are dispatched on the dreadful errand
of changing children in the cradle. In such cases (so
say our gossips in Devon) the pixies use the stolen
child just as the mortal mother may happen to use
the changeling dropped in its stead. I have been
assured that mothers who credited these idle tales,
(and it must be allowed they are very poetical and
amusing) have been known sometimes to pin their
children to their sides in order to secure them ;
though even this precaution has proved vain, so
cunning are the elves. I heard a story not long ago
about a woman who lived and died in this town, and
who most solemnly declared that her mother had a
child that was changed by the pixies, whilst she, good
dame, was busied in hanging out some linen to dry in
her garden. She almost broke her heart on discovering the cheat, but took the greatest care of the
changeling; which so pleased the pixy mother that
some time after she returned the stolen child, who
was ever after very lucky.

A pixy house (and presently I shall give an account
of a grand one which Mr. Bray visited at Sheeps
Tor) is often said to be in a rock : sometimes, how-

ever, a mole-hill is a palace for the elves; or a hollow nut, cracked by the 'joiner squirrel,' will contain the majesty of pixy-land. And Drayton, who writes of these little poetical beings as if he were the chosen laureate of their race, thus describes their royal dwelling:

> "The walls of spiders' legs are made.
> Well morticed and finely laid,
> He was the master of his trade
>   It curiously that builded:
> The windows of the eyes of cats,
> And for a roof, instead of slats,
> Is covered with the skins of bats,
>   With moonshine that are gilded."

And then for the royal equipage of fairy-land we have the following beautiful description, which is so similar to that of Shakspere's Queen Mab, that we are almost tempted to conclude, either that Drayton borrowed from Shakspere, or our great dramatist from him: both, it will be recollected, wrote and died in the reign of James I.

> "Her chariot ready straight is made,
> Each thing therein is fitting laid,
> That she by nothing might be staid,
>   For nought must be her letting:
> Four nimble gnats the horses were,
> Their harnesses of gossamere,
> Fly Cranion, her charioteer,
>   Upon the coach-box getting.

> "Her chariot of a snail's fine shell,
> Which for the colours did excel,
> The fair Queen Mab becoming well,
>   So lively was the limning;
> The seat the soft wool of the bee,
> The cover (gallantly to see)
> The wing of a pied butterflee,
>   I trow 'twas simple trimming!

"The wheels composed of crickets' bones,
　And daintily made for the nonce,
For fear of rattling on the stones
　　With thistle-down they shod it:
For all her maidens much did fear
If Oberon had chanced to hear
That Mab his queen should have been there,
　He would not have abode it."

Her attendants are thus mounted :—

" Upon a grasshopper they got,
　And what with amble and with trot,
For hedge nor ditch they spared not,
　　But after her they hied them;
A cobweb over them they throw,
To shield the wind if it should blow,
Themselves they wisely could bestow,
　Lest any should espy them."

I know not how it is, but Drayton seems to have
fallen into sad neglect; yet let any one but open his
fairy tale of 'Pigwiggin,' and if he can close the book
before reading it to an end, that man must have but
little poetry in his soul.　In the legend of the 'Owl'
also, though somewhat tedious perhaps at the commencement, the terse and animated manner in which,
in a few lines, he paints the character of the various
birds, is such as White, the immortal author of *Selborne*, would have fully appreciated, had he had the
good luck to be acquainted with that poem.

Before I quit the subject of fairy verse, I cannot
resist observing that Mr. Bray, when a youth, was so
much delighted with the pixy lore of his native
county, that he wrote some elfin tales which would
not have disgraced an older or more practised poet.
He then had never seen the works of Drayton: but
in one of the tales called *Conrade and Phœbe* (which

I would give here, but he says it is too long for my letter), I find the following description of a fairy car, that I think bears some resemblance to the *spirit* of Drayton. The elfin queen is about to transport Conrade, an unfortunate, but favoured mortal, to recover his lost mistress :—

> " Her ivory wand aloft she rears,
> And sudden from the sky appears
>   A silver car in view;
> By dragons drawn, whose scales were gold,
> It lightened as their eyes they rolled,
>   And through the ether flew.
>
> " With Conrade in the car she springs,
> The dragons spread their radiant wings,
>   And, when she slacks the reins,
> Swifter than lightning upward rise;
> Then dart along the yielding skies,
>   And spurn the earthly plains.
>
> " Her train, as dew-drops of the morn,
> Suspended on the flowery thorn,
>   Hang round the flying car;
> Young Conrade, though he soared on high,
> Still downward bent his wondering eye,
>   And viewed the earth afar.
>
> " As oft the eagle, 'mid the skies,
> Below a timid dove espies,
>   And darts to seize his prey,
> The dragons thus, at length, no more
> With heads to heaven directed soar,
>   But earthward bend their way."

However I am digressing, and talking about Drayton and my husband, when I ought to be "telling about nothing but a real pisgie tale," as the children say here when they sit round the fire and listen to the legends of their grandmothers. In collecting these anecdotes respecting the pixy race, I must acknowledge my obligations to Mary Colling, the amiable young woman whose little verses you so kindly noticed, and whose artless attempts have also been so favourably received by her friends and the public.[3] Mary, to oblige me, chatted with the village gossips, or listened to their long stories; and the information thus gained was no small addition to my own stock of traditions and tales 'of the olden time.' Some of these will be given in the course of my letters to Keswick, though a few I must hold back, because having already commenced a series of Tales of the West, *founded on tradition*, of which *Fitz of Fitzford* was the first, I must not spoil what little interest I may raise in any such works, by telling the leading point of the story beforehand; a custom which, though rendered popular by a great and successful example, injures, perhaps, the interest of what follows in the narrative.

It is reported that in days of yore, as well as in the present time, the wild waste of Dartmoor was much haunted by spirits and pixies in every direction; and these frequently left their own especial domain to exercise their mischievous propensities and gambols even in the town of Tavistock itself, though it was then guarded by its stately Abbey, well stocked with monks, who made war on the pixy race with 'bell, book, and candle' on every opportunity. And it is also averred that the devil (who, if not absolutely the father, is assuredly the ally of all mischief) gave the pixies his powerful aid in all matters of delusion; and would sometimes carry his audacity so far as to encroach even upon the venerable precincts of the

[3] See *Fables and other Pieces in Verse.* By Mary Maria Colling. Published by Longman and Co., London.

Abbey grounds, always, however, carefully avoiding the holy water : a thing which, like the touch of Ithuriel's spear to the toad in Paradise, would infallibly transform him from any outward seeming into his own proper shape and person. But of late years the good people here affirm, that by means of the clergy being more learned than formerly, and the burial service being so much enlarged to what it was in other days, the spirits are more closely bound over to keep the peace, and the pixies are held tolerably fast, and conjured away to their own domains.

The pixies, however much they may have been deified by the Druids, or northern nations, were never, I believe, considered as saints in any Catholic calendar; though it is affirmed that they have so great a respect for a church that they never come near one. Some very good sort of people, calling themselves Christians, do the same even in these days : but whether it be from so respectful a motive is perhaps somewhat questionable. Pixies then are said to congregate together, even by thousands, in some of those wild and desolate places where there is no church. Various are the stories told about these noted personages : amongst others that in a field near Down-house there is a pit which the pixies, not very long ago, appropriated for their ball-room. There in the depth of night the owl, who probably stood as watchman to the company, would hoot between whiles ; and sounds such as never came from mortal voice or touch would float in the air, making 'marvellous sweet music ;' whilst the "elves of hills, brooks, standing lakes, and groves," would whirl in giddy round, making those "rings, whereof the ewe not bites," that have for ages puzzled the conjectures of the wisest and most grave philosophers, to account for them according to the natural order of things.

Whitchurch Down (a favourite ride with me and my pony ; for it sometimes is a hard matter to get him into any other road) is said to be very famous for the peril there incurred of being *pixy-led :* for there many an honest yeoman and stout farmer, especially if he should happen to take a cup too much, is very apt to lose his way ; and whenever he does so he will declare, and offer to take his Bible oath upon it, " That as sure as ever he lives to tell it, whilst his head was running round like a mill-wheel, he heard with his own ears they bits of pisgies, a laughing and a *tacking* their hands, all to see he led astray, and never able to find the right road, though he had travelled it scores of times." And many good old folks relate the same thing, and how the pisgies delight to lead the aged a-wandering about after dark.

But as most evils set men's wits to work to find out a remedy for them, even so have we found out ours in this part of the world against such provoking injuries. For whosoever finds himself or herself pixy-led has nothing more to do than to turn jacket, petticoat, pocket, or apron inside out. A pixy, who hates the sight of any impropriety in dress, cannot stand this ; and off the imp goes, as if, according to the vulgar saying, he had been " sent packing with a flea in his ear." Now this turning of jackets, petti-coats, &c., being found so good as a remedy, was like a quack doctor's potion, held to be excellent as a preventive : even so do our good old townsfolk practise this turning inside out, ere they venture on a walk after sun-down near any suspected place, as a certain preventive against being led astray by a pixy. But pray listen to a tale that is as true, (so at least I am assured) aye, as true as most tales that are told by gossips over the 'yule clog,' to make the neighbours merry or sad on a Christmas-eve.

Once upon a time there was, in this celebrated town, a Dame Somebody, I do not know her name. All I with truth can say is that she was old, and nothing the worse for that; for age is, or ought to be, held in honour as the source of wisdom and experience. Now this good old woman lived not in vain, for she had passed her days in the useful capacity of a nurse; and as she approached the term of going out of the world herself, she was still useful in her generation by helping others into it—she was in fact the *Sage-femme* of the village.

One night about twelve o'clock in the morning, as the good folks say who tell this tale, Dame Somebody had just got comfortably into bed, when rap, rap, rap, came on her cottage door, with such bold, loud, and continued noise, that there was a sound of authority in every individual knock. Startled and alarmed by the call, she arose, and soon learnt that the summons was a hasty one to bid her attend on a patient who needed her help. She opened her door; when the summoner appeared to be a strange, squint-eyed, little, ugly old fellow, who had a look as she said very like a certain dark personage, who ought not at all times to be called by his proper name. Not at all prepossessed in favour of the errand by the visage of the messenger, she nevertheless could not or dared not resist the command to follow him straight and attend upon 'his wife.'

"Thy wife!" thought the good dame: "Heaven forgive me; but as sure as I live I be going to the birth of a little divel." A large coal-black horse, with eyes like balls of fire, stood at the door. The ill-looking old fellow, without more ado, whisked her up on a high pillion in a minute, seated himself before her, and away went horse and riders, as if sailing through the air, rather than trotting on the ground. How Dame Somebody got to the place of her destination she could not tell; but it was a great relief to her fears when she found herself set down at the door of a neat cottage, saw a couple of tidy children, and remarked her patient to be a decent-looking woman, having all things about her fitting the time and the occasion.

A fine bouncing babe soon made its appearance, and seemed very bold on its entry into life, for it gave the good dame a box on the ear, as, with the coaxing and cajolery of all good old nurses, she declared the "sweet little thing to be very like its father." The mother said nothing to this, but gave nurse a certain ointment with directions that she should "strike the child's eyes with it." Now you must know that this word *strike*, in our Devonshire vocabulary does not exactly mean to give a blow, but rather what is opposite, to "rub, smooth down, or touch gently." The nurse performed her task, though she thought it an odd one: and as it is nothing new that old nurses are generally very curious, she wondered what it could be for; and thought that, as no doubt it was a good thing, she might just as well try it upon her own eyes as well as those of the baby; so she made free to strike one of them by way of trial; when, oh, ye powers of fairy land, what a change was there!

The neat, but homely cottage, and all who were

in it, seemed all on a sudden to undergo a mighty transformation; some for the better, some for the worse. The new-made mother appeared as a beautiful lady attired in white; the babe was seen wrapped in swaddling clothes of a silvery gauze. It looked much prettier than before, but still maintained the elfish cast of the eye, like its redoubted father: whilst two or three children more had undergone a metamorphosis as uncouth as that recorded by Ovid when the Cercopians were transformed into apes. For there sat on either side the bed's head, a couple of little flat-nosed imps, who with 'mops and mows,' and with many a grimace and grin, were 'busied to no end' in scratching their own polls, or in pulling the fairy lady's ears with their long and hairy paws.

The dame who beheld all this, fearing she knew not what in the house of enchantment, got away as fast as she could without saying one word about 'striking' her own eye with the magic ointment, and what she had beheld in consequence of doing so.[4] The sour-looking old fellow once more handed her up on the coal-black horse, and sent her home in a *whip-sissa*. Now what a whip-sissa means is more than I can tell, though I consider myself to be tolerably well acquainted with the tongues of this 'West Countrie.' It may mean perhaps, 'Whip, says he,' in allusion to some gentle intimation being feelingly given by the rider to the horse's sides with a switch, that he should use the utmost dispatch. Certain it is, the old woman returned home much faster than she went. But mark the event.

[4] It has been the popular belief of all ages that no mortal can *see* a fairy without his eyes being rubbed with a magic ointment. Cornelius Agrippa, if I remember right, though it is long since I have seen his book, gives a very amusing receipt for compounding such a salve.

On the next market-day, when she sallied forth to sell her eggs, who should she see but the same wicked-looking old fellow, busied, like a rogue as he was, in pilfering sundry articles from stall to stall.

"Oh! ho!" thought the dame, "have I caught you, you old thief? But I'll let you see I could set master mayor and the two town constables on your back, if I chose to be telling." So up she went, and with that bold free sort of air, which persons who have learnt secrets that ought not to be known are apt to assume, when they address any great rogue hitherto considered as a superior, she inquired carelessly after his wife and child, and hoped both were as well as could be expected.

"What!" exclaimed the old pixy thief, "do you *see* me to-day?"

"See you! to be sure I do, as plain as I see the sun in the skies; and I see you are busy into the bargain."

"Do you so!" cried he. "Pray with which eye do you see all this?"

"With the right eye to be sure."

"The ointment! the ointment!" exclaimed the old fellow: "take that for meddling with what did not belong to you—you shall see me no more."

He struck her eye as he spoke, and from that hour till the day of her death she was blind on the right side; thus dearly paying for having gratified an idle curiosity in the house of a pixy.

One or two stories more shall suffice for the present; and the following tale may somewhat remind you of a merry little rogue, who, if he was not immortal before, has certainly been rendered so by Shakspere— Robin Goodfellow. It is not unlike one of his pranks.

Two serving damsels of this place declared, as an excuse, perhaps, for spending more money than they ought upon finery, that the pixies were very kind to them, and would often drop silver for their pleasure into a bucket of fair water, which they placed for the accommodation of those little beings in the chimney corner every night before they went to bed. Once, however, it was forgotten; and the pixies, finding themselves disappointed by an empty bucket, whisked up stairs to the maids' bed-room, popped through the keyhole, and began in a very audible tone to exclaim against the laziness and neglect of the damsels.

One of them who lay awake, and heard all this, jogged her fellow-servant, and proposed getting up immediately to repair the fault of omission : but the lazy girl, who liked not being disturbed out of a comfortable nap, pettishly declared "that, for her part, she would not stir out of bed to please all the pixies in Devonshire." The good-humoured damsel, however, got up, filled the bucket, and was rewarded by a handful of silver pennies found in it the next morning. But ere that time had arrived, what was her alarm as she crept towards the bed, to hear all the elves in high and stern debate, consulting as to what punishment should be inflicted on the lazy lass who would not stir for their pleasure.

Some proposed 'pinches, nips, and bobs,' others to spoil her new cherry-coloured bonnet and ribands. One talked of sending her the toothache, another of giving her a red nose : but this last was voted a too vindictive punishment for a pretty young woman. So, tempering mercy with justice, the pixies were kind enough to let her off with a lame leg, which was so to continue only for seven years, and was alone to be cured by a certain herb, growing on Dartmoor, whose long and learned and very difficult name the elfin judge pronounced in a high and audible voice. It was a name of seven syllables, seven being also the number of years decreed for the chastisement.

The good-natured maid, wishing to save her fellow-damsel so long a suffering, tried with might and main to bear in mind the name of this potent herb. She said it over and over again, tied a knot in her garter at every syllable, as a help to memory then very popular, and thought she had the word as sure as her own name; and very possibly felt much more anxious about retaining the one than the other. At length she dropped asleep, and did not wake till the morning. Now whether her head might be like a sieve, that lets out as fast as it takes in, or if the over-exertion to remember might cause her to forget, cannot be determined; but certain it is that when she opened her eyes she knew nothing at all about the matter, excepting that Molly was to go lame on her right leg for seven long years, unless a herb with a strange name could be got to cure her. And lame she went for nearly the whole of that period.

At length (it was about the end of the time) a merry, squint-eyed, queer-looking boy, started up one fine summer day, just as she went to pluck a mushroom, and came tumbling, head over heels, towards her. He insisted on striking her leg with a plant which he held in his hand. From that moment she got well; and lame Molly, as a reward for her patience in suffering, became the best dancer in the whole town at the celebrated festivities of Mayday on the green.

The following tale will be the last I shall send in

this letter : it would afford, perhaps, a good subject for poetry.

Near a pixy field in this neighbourhood, there lived on a time an old woman who possessed a cottage and a very pretty garden, wherein she cultivated a most beautiful bed of tulips. The pixies, it is traditionally averred, so delighted in this spot, that they would carry their elfin babies thither, and sing them to rest. Often at the dead hour of the night, a sweet lullaby was heard, and strains of the most melodious music would float in the air, that seemed to owe their origin to no other musicians than the beautiful tulips themselves; and whilst these delicate flowers waved their heads to the evening breeze, it sometimes seemed as if they were marking time to their own singing. As soon as the elfin babies were lulled asleep by such melodies, the pixies would return to the neighbouring field, and there commence dancing, making those rings on the green which showed, even to mortal eyes, what sort of gambols had occupied them during the night season.

At the first dawn of light the watchful pixies once more sought the tulips, and though still invisible could be heard kissing and caressing their babies. The tulips, thus favoured by a race of genii, retained their beauty much longer than any other flowers in the garden; whilst, though contrary to their nature, as the pixies breathed over them they became as fragrant as roses; and so delighted at all this was the old woman who possessed the garden, that she never suffered a single tulip to be plucked from its stem.

At length, however, she died; and the heir who succeeded her destroyed the enchanted flowers, and converted the spot into a parsley bed, a circumstance which so disappointed and offended the pixies, that they caused it to wither away; and indeed for many years nothing would grow in the beds of the whole garden. But these sprites, though eager in resenting an injury, were, like most warm spirits, equally capable of returning a benefit; and if they destroyed the product of the good old woman's garden, when it had fallen into unworthy hands, they tended the bed that wrapped her clay with affectionate solicitude. For they were heard lamenting and singing sweet dirges around her grave; nor did they neglect to pay this mournful tribute to her memory every night before the moon was at the full; for then their high solemnity of dancing, singing, and rejoicing took place, to hail the queen of the night on completing her silver circle in the skies. No human hand ever tended the grave of the poor old woman who had nurtured the tulip bed for the delight of these elfin creatures; but no rank weed was ever seen to grow upon it; the sod was ever green, and the prettiest flowers would spring up without sowing or planting, and so they continued to do till it was supposed the mortal body was reduced to its original dust.

And of pixy legends I now, methinks, have given you enough to prove that the people of this neighbourhood, in the lower ranks of life (from whose chit-chat all these were gleaned) possess, in no small degree, a poetical spirit for old tales. The upper and more educated classes hold such stories as unworthy notice; and many would laugh at me for having taken the trouble to collect and repeat them; but however wild and simple they may be, there is so much of poetry and imagination in them, that I feel convinced you will consider them worthy of being saved, by some written record, from that oblivion to which in a few years they would otherwise be inevitably consigned.

LETTER XL

TO ROBERT SOUTHEY, ESQ.

Vicarage, Tavistock, April 30th, 1832.

I MENTIONED in my last letter the dense mists with
which travellers were often in danger of being enveloped during their journey over Dartmoor, and that
I had no doubt such mists occasioned those wanderings out of the right road, which gave rise to the
popular belief of being *pixy-led*. On looking over my
husband's papers about the Moor, I find a very interesting letter addressed to him by the late Mr. Edward
Smith, of this town, a young man who possessed
considerable natural talents, and who once intended
writing a history of his native place; for which
(although I have never seen them) he made, as I am
told, some collections.

We well knew poor Smith, who died I believe of a
broken heart; and whose sad sufferings and misfor-

tunes were in a great degree the result of imprudence. But he is gone—there are many who have dwelt upon his errors and his faults; let me, though I was not blind to these, rather here speak of his good qualities, for he had many. Ever since his death I have entertained a wish to pay some tribute of sympathy to his memory; and, now that he lies in an early grave, to ask for him what he can no longer ask for himself, mercy from the world for his errors, and that some charity be shown to one, who, in the midst of all his faults, had a heart capable of warm affections and sincere gratitude; feelings that never can exist where there is not at least a capability of virtue. Before I give you, therefore, a copy of Edward Smith's letter, (and it is the only one of his in our possession that would be likely to interest a third person) I shall say something about him. His family indeed, especially in two of its members, is deserving notice in the biography of this place; and though I mention him here, even if it be a little out of rule, it is not of much consequence, for you will read the letter with more interest when you know some few particulars respecting the deceased writer.

I have often heard him state that the Smiths of Tavistock were a very old family in the county of Devon. I do not know any minute particulars respecting this family at an early period; for little did I think when poor Smith told me, as we one day walked under the Abbey walls in our garden, the few anecdotes here mentioned, that I should ever live to become his biographer! He was then not five and twenty years old, and full of health, spirit, and ambition. I remember well that he used to say his maternal grandfather had been the parish clerk of

Tavistock. I believe it was one great object of his literary ambition (and who could blame him for it, had he lived to accomplish his views?) to show the world that he had still the spirit of his loyal ancestors within him, which had survived, in blood at least, their change of fortune.

I regret I did not learn the particulars of his early life. I know he held some station in the navy; but as, when we first knew him, he was falling under that cloud which finally overshadowed all his prospects, we felt reluctance to make inquiries that would have occasioned, perhaps, much pain to satisfy them. All I can with truth say is, that his gallant brother, the Major,[1] (who, dying suddenly at the inn here, chanced to pass the last evening of his mortal pilgrimage under our roof) told me that poor Edward was, he believed, truly kind and feeling at heart, but that he had been of a thoughtless, warm, and irritable temper; and by some neglect of his minor duties, and those forms of discipline which are as necessary to be observed by the gifted as by the common mind, had given offence to a superior, and had lost in consequence that golden opportunity which, when once forfeited by a young man in the outset of his career, seldom visits him again with the like prospect of success. The Major spoke this with every charitable allowance for his brother; and regretted he had died before he could retrieve himself in the eye of the world.

He also told me that Edward Smith was for some short time at Wadham College. I conclude his finances did not suffer him to remain there long

---

[1] Major Smith, of the Marines, who distinguished himself by quelling a mutiny.

enough to profit much by his studies. He could hear
of no situation ; and as he had good talents, and was
a respectable antiquary, he determined to turn author
for his support. This determination made him seek
the acquaintance and notice of Mr. Bray, who received
him with every kindness, and did what he could to
forward and assist his pursuits ; and Edward Smith
ever returned his kindness with the utmost gratitude
and respect. He thought of making his first work a
history of the antiquities of Tavistock : it was proposed to dedicate it to the Duke of Bedford, and to
publish it by subscription. Many names were obtained
in its support.

At that time he was frequently at the Vicarage ;
and we never saw him without having cause to
remark the lively and acute powers of his mind. He
was (what all authors ought to be) a great reader ;
and he read aloud with peculiar feeling and energy.
He had a strong memory, reflected on what he read,
and possessed so clear an arrangement of the knowledge he thus gained, that he could always apply it
with effect. He had been much abroad, and could
give a very interesting account of what he had
observed in his wanderings. The specimen I shall
here send you of his writing is one of the best I have
ever seen from his pen. Its merit, I am inclined to
think, arises from its *not having been written for publication ;* for Smith as a young author fell into a
common error, which time and a good critic would
have cured—he thought it necessary to write for the
public press in a different manner to that he would
have adopted if writing for a private or familiar
reader ; the consequence was (at least in the little I
ever heard him read of what he wrote) that his style

was somewhat inflated and affected, though he knew how to choose his matter well enough. To say whether the talents of Smith (which were most conspicuous in conversation) would, or would not, have produced any lasting fruits as an author, is now impossible to decide. He had certainly strong and original powers of thinking and expression; but he died before any work was completed. We see in the very highest order of writers, that excellence in composition shows itself at very different and unequal periods. Chatterton, that ‘marvellous boy,’ produced his extraordinary works and died before he was twenty. Young, on the contrary, did not produce his *Night Thoughts* till he was turned of sixty. Richardson (if my memory is faithful) was about that age when he wrote his first novel. Swift never wrote at all till he was four and thirty; and Pope produced his best work (for so Johnson considers his *Essay on Criticism*) when he was twenty. To say, therefore, what a person possessed of superior talents may or may not achieve, if he be cut off in his youth, is impossible.

Such were the misfortunes, perhaps I may add the imprudence, of Smith, that the necessities of to-day interfered with the prospects of to-morrow. He was obliged to solicit some of his subscriptions before the work could be committed to the press; and living on what he received, he could never find means to set the engravers and printers upon their task, for his work was not of that nature to secure publication on the bookseller's risk. The Duke of Bedford, I know, kindly sent him thirty pounds in the hope to forward it; his brothers, especially the Major, gave him frequent assistance; Mr. John Carpenter, of Mount

XI.] EDWARD SMITH.

Tavy, was to the last his benefactor; and he had other friends who did what they could to relieve him.

But to live entirely on the casual help of friends is neither wholesome for the moral nor the intellectual character: it blunts the best feelings of a man, by sinking in him the honest pride of independence, which is as the safeguard of honour; it sours and irritates the temper (especially in a mind conscious of superior talents) and makes the dependant acutely alive to every petty pain, so that he is on the watch to take offence. A word is often misconstrued, and received as a reproach to his necessities, when it is only intended as a warning to his imprudence.

Poor Smith suffered in every way by his early imprudence; since to add to his distresses he married a young woman of this place, who like himself had nothing. And two children brought with them an accession to their father's anxieties, and such an additional call on the assistance of his relatives and friends, that none could sufficiently help him, so as to set him free from his accumulated necessities.

Misery, also, had been to him like the hair shirt to the religionist of Rome; not a wound to kill, but a fretting and irritating suffering. It affected his temper, and made him take up imprudent arms in his own cause; for the slightest contempt he returned with bitterness. This bitter invective I believe was often deserved by his enemies: it was therefore the more keenly felt and resented; and those who triumphed over a superior mind because that mind was in misery, soon found they had nothing to fear; for the poor are generally the powerless. For my own part, I could never think of Smith, in his last

struggles with the world, without being strongly reminded of the poet Savage, whose life, from the pen
of Johnson, none but a heart of stone could read
unmoved. Savage lived to raise a great name as
an author; Smith died before his abilities produced
any lasting memorial of *his* name: but both have left
an example, the one in public, the other in private life,
that (to use the words of the admirable biographer
of the poet) "no superior capacity or attainments
can supply the place of want of prudence; and that
negligence and irregularity, long continued, render
even knowledge itself useless, and genius contemptible."

So far truth, for the sake of others, obliged even
the enlarged charity of Johnson—a charity that like
his piety and life did honour to human nature—to
declare of Savage, whom he pitied and regarded in
the midst of all his errors. But Johnson had that
discrimination as well as goodness, which could detect the germ of virtuous feelings amidst the wildest
growth that may be found in the sluggard's garden
of folly and of vice. The naturalist, in the darkest
night, will pause to look with pleasure on the solitary
ray of light emitted by the little glow-worm as it lies
on the lowly turf: the great moralist did the same—
one spark of good never escaped his searching eye.
So may it be with all (however inferior their powers
or their capacity) who attempt to record the character of the dead. For the example of the living, for
the honour due to God, for the just demands of truth,
no vice should be ever sophisticated into a virtue;
for such is but 'seeming.' But where human frailty
(the consequence more of imprudence than a wicked
heart) produces distress; where that frailty has been

exposed to suffer increase by the manifold temptations of poverty and want, *there*—in the name of Him
who was all mercy, who took on himself the lowest
estate to show an example of long-suffering to the
poor—*there* let charity be extended in the most enlarged degree.

After having given birth to two children, Smith's
wife, whose health was delicate, fell into a decline.
During the early part of her illness, as she and her
husband were one day playing with the eldest infant,
at the very moment it was in the father's arms it
suddenly and instantaneously expired. The shock
increased Mrs. Smith's illness; it was soon pronounced fatal; and I have heard that distress of mind
helped to bring on her first indisposition. And now
the amiable part of poor Edward Smith's character
showed itself in the most marked manner—he devoted himself to her comfort with the zeal of the
most ardent affection. So ill was she, yet so pain-
fully did she linger on, that I have been assured for
weeks before her death he never enjoyed one night's
repose.

At length his wife died; and left him with the
youngest helpless infant. It was affecting to hear
how the poor father, on the day of her death, would
take the child in his arms, endeavouring to recall the
living image of its mother by looking in its face;
unconscious as it was of the widowed grief and the
desolation of that father's heart. He was relieved of
this care; for, as the child was so very young, a
relation of the mother took it home. A deep melancholy settled on his mind from the hour of his wife's
death. For some little time, however, he endeavoured
to rally his spirits; and being universally pitied he

was not deserted in his misery; though he now shunned observation, and even kindness, as much as he could. But the earthly cup of sorrow, of whose bitterness he had tasted even to its brim, was not yet drained to the very dregs. His last child died; and that he followed to the grave. Well might he say of death, as did the melancholy poet of the night —

"Insatiate archer ! could not one suffice?
Thy shaft flew thrice ; and thrice my peace was slain !"

It is the custom in this town, for young women clothed in white, with a handkerchief drawn through the coffin rings, (underhand, as it is called) to act as bearers at a child's funeral. A young person, who assisted in performing this office at the burial of poor Smith's infant, gave me a very interesting account of his demeanour on that sad day. He attended the funeral, though all present were shocked to observe his altered appearance. His eye, that had in other and happier days possessed uncommon brightness and vivacity, was now sunk in his head—it was dim and downcast. He was very pale and thin; and all energy and spirit seemed dead within him. For some time he stood over the grave, after the ceremony was concluded, in silence, contemplating that earth which was about to close on the last nearest and dearest of his affections. The young person who gave me this account was his schoolfellow in their infant days; and had been well known to his deceased wife. From long habits of acquaintance, she ventured to speak to him, even in these moments, some words of sympathy. She held out her hand. He took it, grasped it, and looked at her with an expression of such heartrending distress, as she said she should never forget; but tears rose in his eyes, and looking once more on the grave, he said—'It will yet hold another!'

Soon, indeed, was that other numbered with the dead already gone before; for the blow had been struck that to him, I doubt not, in the end was one of mercy. Not long after he was seized with a fever, the consequence of the long-continued anxiety of his distresses. At first hopes were entertained of his recovery; but delirium came on, and all was soon over: for, on the 1st of January, 1827, he expired, in the 27th year of his age. He was buried in the churchyard of his native town of Tavistock. Since then his gallant brother has been laid to rest in the same ground.

I here give you the extract from Edward Smith's letter, addressed to my husband in 1823.

"On Tuesday, the 11th of August, about twelve o'clock, I set out on a fishing excursion to the river Walkham, above Merrivale Bridge. This part of that romantic river is situated entirely on Dartmoor. As soon as I reached the high lands under Cox Tor, my walk became highly interesting, from the peculiar state of the weather: being one instant enveloped in a blaze of light from an unclouded August sun, and almost in the next shrouded in an impervious fog.

"The weather, however, was favourable for fishing, and reaching Merrivale hamlet about half after one, I commenced; the sport excellent—but having promised to meet some friends at Prince Town to dinner at five, I shut up my rod as soon as I had reached the western foot of that immense hill, called, I believe, Mis Tor, whose eastern base conjoins with Rundle

Stone. At this spot I was probably about a mile or mile and a half (following the rough and sinuous course of the river) above Merrivale Bridge. An idea struck me that ere I could reach across the hill towards Prince Town, I might be caught in a fog, but with a carelessness which I subsequently lamented, I determined on risking it. Up the mountain, there-fore, I stretched, but scarcely had I reached a quarter of a mile ere a cloud, dense and dark and flaky, fell, as it were, instantly upon me. So sudden was the envelopment, that it startled me. On every side appeared whirling masses of mist, of so thick a con-sistency, that it affected my very respiration. I paused ; but impelled by some of those ill-defined feelings which lead men to action, they know not why, I determined to proceed—indeed, I fancied it would be impossible I could err in describing a straight line over the summit of the hill ; but in this I was sufficiently deceived.

"I stretched on, and the way seemed to lengthen before me. At last I descried a few of those immense fragments of granite with which the summit was strewed.   Their appearance, through the illusive medium of the fog, was wonderfully grand, wavy, fantastic, and as if possessing life. Although all plane with the surface, such was the optical deception that they appeared upright, each in succession perpendi-cular—until I should arrive so close, that it required almost the very touch to prove the deception. There were also some scattered sheep, one here and there. At the distance of twenty or thirty yards, for I am sure I could distinguish nothing farther, they had the appearance of a moving unshapen mass, infinitely larger than reality. Every now and then, too, one

of these animals would start from the side of a block
of granite close to my feet, affrighted—sometimes
with a screaming bleat, as if like myself filled with
surprise and awe.

"Arrived now as I considered on the summit, I
stood still and looked around—the scene was like one
of those darkly remembered dreams which illness,
produced by lassitude and grief, sometimes afflicts us
with—an obscure sense of a scene where we have
been darkly wandering on. There was above, beneath, and all around me, a mass, flaky, and at times
even rushing, of white fog—there is no colour by
which it could be named—a sombre whiteness—a
darkness palpable and yet impalpable—that Scrip-
tural expression best suits it, 'the very light was
darkness.'

"I bent my course onward: now amongst massy
fragments of granite, the playthings of the deluge,
and now amongst bogs and rushes. I became impatient to catch some object familiar to me. I quick-
ened my pace; but the farther I proceeded, the more
and more did the fog bewilder me. My eyesight
became affected, my very brain began to whirl, till
at length I sat down from sheer incapability to walk
on. My situation was now painful, the evening was
rapidly approaching—the fog increased in murkiness,
and all hopes that it would clear away had vanished.
I looked around for some large fragment of stone,
under shelter of which to take up my quarters for the
night. I had from exertion been hot even to excess,
I was now shivering and chilled. At length the idea
of maternal anxiety relative to where I might be
struck me, and I determined once more to advance.
Reflecting, from the boggy nature of the ground I

now trod, I had perhaps gone on towards the north,
I turned directly to the left and went swiftly forward.
The ground now began to incline, and I suddenly
found myself descending a steep acclivity—presently
I heard the distant rushing of water; I stopped to
calculate where it could be. At length I concluded
my former conjecture right, and that I had been all
this while toiling in a northerly instead of an easterly
direction from the mountain's summit, and that I
was approaching a stream called Blackabrook. The
sound, however, enlivened me; it was like the voice
of a conductor, a friend, and I pressed onward;
the descent however was still steep, very steep, and
this destroyed again the conjecture which I lately
thought sure: still I pressed on—when suddenly, so
instantaneously that I can compare it to nothing save
the lifting of a veil, the fog rushed from me, and the
scene which opened induced me almost to doubt my
senses. At my feet the river Walkham brawled
amongst the rocks scattered throughout its bed—at
my left was just sufficient of Merrivale open to show
the eastern arch of its picturesque bridge, whilst in the
distance the fantastic rocks of Vixen Tor were still
wreathed in mist. At my right, within two or three
hundred yards, was the very spot I had first quitted
to ascend the mountain; and in my front that grand
tor at the back of Merrivale hamlet rose frowningly
dark, its topmost ridges embosomed in clouds, whose
summits were gilded by the broad sun, now rapidly
descending behind them.

"The whole scene was like magic—even whilst
looking on, it appeared to me a dream. I doubted
its reality—I could not imagine, toiling up, then
across the summit, then down the sides of a rugged

mountain, how it was possible I could have returned to a spot *from whence* I even then felt almost sure I had been continually receding. I had, moreover, been full two hours and a half in progress, but still the stubborn certainty was before me.

"I had actually walked up the mountain, taken a complete circuit of its summit, and almost retraced my steps down to the spot I first quitted.

"In an instant the fog enveloped me again—by this time I had purchased experience. I therefore quickly regained the banks of the river, traced its stream, reached Merrivale Bridge, and on once more placing my foot on the beaten road, determined never again to try the experiment of finding my way across a trackless Dartmoor mountain when the clouds were low about it."

So concludes poor Smith's letter to Mr. Bray.

LETTER XII.

TO ROBERT SOUTHEY, ESQ.

Vicarage, Tavistock, May 2nd, 1832.

I SEND you in this Mr. Bray's account of a visit to Vixen Tor, extracted from his Journal of 1801.

"On the 17th of September, accompanied by a friend, I left Tavistock early in the morning, with the intention of spending the day in viewing some of the neighbouring tors of Dartmoor. As we approached the first, Cox Tor, we found its head covered with mist; but as the horizon was clear behind us, we concluded it was only a partial collection of vapours, so frequently attracted by the lofty eminences of the Forest,[1] and expected that the wind, which was very high, would soon dissipate them. However, on proceeding we found it was a wet mist, which soon spread over the country, and prevented us from seeing more than a few feet before us.

[1] Though the whole of this uncultivated tract of country, from Cox Tor, which is about three miles from Tavistock, is generally called Dartmoor, the Forest itself does not begin till we arrive at the distance of six miles; the intermediate parts being considered as commons belonging to the different neighbouring parishes.

" Before the turnpike road was made over the Moor, even those who acted as guides frequently lost their way on this almost trackless desert, through the sudden diffusion of the mist. When this was the case, they generally wandered about in quest of some river, as by following its course they were sure at last of finding an exit to their inhospitable labyrinth.

" Since we understood Cox Tor was principally entitled to attention for the extensive prospect it afforded, we knew it would be fruitless now to ascend it, and having determined to relinquish the design of visiting the tors in regular succession, proceeded to Vixen Tor, for the purpose of climbing to the top of that lofty rock. My friend had formerly effected it ; and the information he gave me of having found an excavation or circular hollow on its very summit, which coincided with the idea I had formed of a Druidical basin, powerfully excited my wish to accomplish it.

" Vixen Tor presents itself to the eye from the road leading from Tavistock to Moreton in a picturesque and striking manner. Three contiguous lofty rocks raise themselves from the middle of a spacious plain, and at different points of view assume a vast variety of fantastic appearances. Sometimes you may fancy the Tor bears a resemblance to a lion's head, at others to the bust of a man ; and when seen from the Moreton road it greatly resembles the Sphinx in the plains of Egypt,² whilst the mountains beyond may give no bad idea of the pyramids around it.

Ridiculous as it may appear, I can never view it from one particular point, without thinking on the con-

---

² Mr. Burt, in his Notes on Carrington's *Dartmoor*, published more than twenty years after this account was written, also compares Vixen Tor to the Sphinx.

venient but grotesque mode of riding on horseback,
which is, I believe, more generally practised in the
West of England than in any other part of the kingdom, called 'riding double.' A horse that carries
double is esteemed as valuable in this part of the

SPHINX VIEW OF VIXEN TOR.

world, as in any other may be one that serves in the
twofold capacity of a hackney and a draught horse. In
addition to its convenience, no person will deny that
it is a sociable method of riding, when he is informed
that the gallant may thus accommodate his fair one,
by taking her an airing *en croupe* on a pillion behind
him. Some ladies, who are not afraid of singularity,
will occasionally squire one another, when they are in
want of a beau; and this is called 'riding jollifant.'

"From the sketch I have made of Vixen Tor in
this whimsical view, an opinion may be formed whether
I have any excuse for entertaining such a fancied
resemblance. The gentleman, who has a cocked-hat
on his head, is rather short, but sufficiently prominent
in front. The lady, too, is rather of a corpulent size,
and proudly overlooks her husband; her cloak, however, may be supposed to be somewhat expanded by
the wind; whilst her head is sheltered with a calash.

Even the head of the horse and the handle of the
pillion behind may be distinguished with no greater
stretch of fancy.

"In addition to this, it cannot fail to attract the
traveller's eye as being the focus (if I may be allowed the expression) or principal object of a grand

WHIMSICAL VIEW OF VIXEN TOR.

and beautifully varied view. Before it is the rugged
foreground of the Moor, rough with stones and heath;
beside it is a deep valley, where flows the river Walkham; around it are a number of hills, all verging to
or meeting in this point, whilst on one of them the
tower of Walkhampton conspicuously elevates itself;
and behind the whole is a distant view of Plymouth
Sound, with the woody eminence of Mount Edgcumbe. On the south-west it is much increased in
its appearance of height by the abrupt declivity of
the ground. It here seems an immense ridge of
rocks, on which stand three lofty piles in an almost
perpendicular elevation. At the foot of this ridge are
some curiously-shaped masses of rock, one of which
projects for several feet in a horizontal direction.

"On the opposite side there is a perpendicular fissure, which we found large enough to admit us, and
attempted to climb through it to the top of the

loftiest pile; but the wind was so violent, and forced itself with such impetuosity up this narrow passage, that we at length gave up the attempt, but not till our eyes were filled with dust and moss. The roar occasioned by it was at times tremendous, but varied with our change of situation, from the dashing of a cataract to the soft whispers of the breeze.

" A rock to the north-west afterwards attracted our attention, which from its fancied resemblance to the form of that animal we called the Tortoise. At its northern end there is a projection of three feet, which forms the head of the Tortoise. Under it the green turf is enclosed with three stones; and this enclosure, from its wearing the appearance of art, first gave us the idea of its having been appropriated to the uses of Druidical superstition; probably as a hearth or receptacle for burnt-offering.

" Determining thoroughly to examine this rock, I climbed to the top, which is formed by a large flat stone, eleven feet from north to south, and nine from east to west, divided about the middle by a fissure. We discovered on the southern division the ill-defined vestiges of four basins, in which was some rain water, uniting with one another in a transverse direction. A little channel or dipping-place communicated with the southern extremity of the rock. On the other half a thorn bush was growing on a turf of mould, rising about three or four inches from the surface.

" By observing a little circular hollow at one end of it, I was induced to push in my stick, and though it met with resistance, I found it was not from stone. It occurred to us, therefore, that there might be a basin beneath, and we began with our sticks to dig into the

mould, which was of as firm a texture, being the de-
composition of decayed vegetable substances, as the
ground below.　Indeed, it was of the same black
colour as the peaty soil of the whole Moor, which
shows evident signs of its vegetable origin.　On
loosening the mould we gradually discovered that
our conjecture was well founded.

"We were more than an hour engaged in this
undertaking; and, for want of better instruments,
my friend sat down and made use of his heels in
kicking away the earth.　Whilst thus employed, I
was astonished to find that with every blow the
half of the stone on which he sat, though it was of
such large dimensions, shook, and was followed by a
sound occasioned by its collision with the rock below.
Having at length removed all the earth, we discovered
two regularly shaped basins, communicating with each
other, whilst a natural fissure served for the dripping
place.　The length of the largest was three feet,
width two, and depth eight inches.　The smallest
was only two feet long.

"I have no doubt that these basins have been
covered with earth for generations; as in no shorter
space of time could moss or other vegetable substances
be converted into so firm a mould.　Indeed from
other rocks near it we stripped off the moss, though
five or six inches thick, with perfect ease, and found
it of a texture almost as tough as a mat, but without
any particle of earth.　That the earth could not be
placed in this cavity by the hands of man, or deposited there by the wind, is I think pretty certain;
as at the bottom of the whole we found a thin coat
of intertwisted fibres, which, though stained by the
earth of a black colour above, was white beneath,

and kept the rock perfectly clean. The thorn bush likewise, which in so exposed a situation would not grow unless it had met with perfectly-formed earth, and then would not have attained any size till after a long period of years, indicates that the basin has not been exposed for a long period to the eye of day.

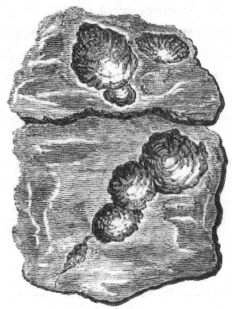

ROCK BASINS.

"It will not, I hope, be deemed a useless digression to mention what is supposed to have been the use of these rock basins. Borlase, in his *Antiquities of Cornwall*, informs us that they were designed to contain rain or snow water, which is allowed to be the purest. This the Druids probably used as holy-water for lustrations. They preferred the highest places for these receptacles, as the rain water is purer the farther it is removed from the ground. Its being nearer the heavens also may have contributed not a little to the sanctity in which it was held. The officiating Druid might have stood on these eminences and sanctified the congregation by this more than ordinary lustration, before he prayed or gave forth his oracles. 'The priest too,' says Borlase, 'might judge by the quantity, colour, motion, and other appearances in the water, of future events and dubious cases, without contradiction from the people below. By the motion of the logan stone the water might be so agitated, as to delude the inquirer by a pretended miracle, and might make the criminal confess, satisfy the credulous, bring forth the gold of the rich, and make the injured, rich as well as poor, acquiesce in what the Druids thought proper.'

"A logan signifies in Cornish a shaking rock. That the rock we visited is of this description, I hesitate not to affirm, as it was still capable of being moved, though the fissure was almost filled up with stones, some of which we with difficulty removed by means of a crooked stick. 'It is probable the Druids made the people believe, that they only, by their miraculous powers, could move these logan rocks, and by this pretended miracle condemned or acquitted the accused, and often brought criminals to confess what would in no other way be extorted from them.' It is possible they encouraged the idea 'that spirits inhabited them, and this motion they might insist on as a proof of it, and thus they became idols.' The Druids, by placing even a pebble in a particular direction, might render unavailing the attempts of others to move the rock, and, by taking it away and moving the immense mass with apparent ease themselves, convince others of their superior powers.

"On a rock at a little distance we discovered another basin, with a lip or dripping-place to the south-west, of a complete oval form, two feet and a half in length, and one foot nine inches in width.

The depth of it was about six inches; we found in it some rain water that seemed remarkably cold to the touch.

"On our return we visited several other rocks, but met with nothing worthy of remark, excepting some fine views of the vale through which flows the river Walkham, and some distant reaches of the river Tamar."

SECOND VISIT TO VIXEN TOR.

ALSO EXTRACTED FROM MR. BRAY'S JOURNAL.

"October 3.—We left Tavistock early in the morning with the intention of climbing to the top of Vixen Tor, and afterwards inspecting Mis Tor.

"We ascended the former on the north-east side, through a fissure of about two feet in width, made by a division between two of the piles. We reached with difficulty (for it was like climbing up a chimney) the top of the lowest rock, where we sat for some time to rest ourselves. From this, with a wide stride, we got a footing on the other, and at length attained the summit.

"The uppermost rock is divided into two or three masses, on parts of which we found moss and green turf, which, though damp with the dew, afforded us a seat. Facing the east are three basins—one four feet long, three feet two inches wide, and eight inches deep; this has a lip at the edge. Of the two remaining basins, which communicate together, one is four feet in diameter, and fourteen inches deep. The other is one foot and a half in diameter, and nine inches deep. They were the most regularly circular basins we had yet seen. And from these, also, a lip discharged the water over the edge of the rock.

"Though in the vale below we had not perceived it, yet here the wind was high. As the foundation of the rock is much lower on the south-west side, we wished to drop the line thence, in order to find its height. Having only a ball of thin packthread, to which was affixed a small lead bullet, we attempted to throw it over, as owing to a projection we could not drop it; but the wind blew the thread out of its proper direction, and we were unsuccessful in two or three attempts; at last we wound the thread round the bullet and secured it better; but could not tell, though the thread was all expended, whether it had reached the bottom. To satisfy ourselves as to this, though I stood in great need of the assistance of my companion, I resolved to get down by myself; in which, however, I succeeded better than I expected. My friend had intimated that he should be uneasy till he heard my voice at the bottom. Indeed it was no small satisfaction to myself when I was able to assure him of my safety by a loud shout, which was instantly returned by him.

"On finding that the line did not reach the bottom, and that he had no more, I requested he would throw down the stick to which it was tied; but the wind carried it away, and on striking against the moss the lead was not heavy enough to clear it. Though vexed that our labour was partly in vain, I took a sketch of the rock with my friend on the top of it, to show we had ascended it. Whilst thus employed, he startled me by throwing down one of his boots, and afterwards the other, in order to have a firmer footing in his descent. In his way down he was so fortunate as to recover the string, and as I had marked how far it reached I was in hopes, after all, to know the elevation of the rock. As, in folding it over, he had entangled it, we had the greatest difficulty in unravelling it; and though two or three times we cut this gordian knot, we were afraid our hopes would prove vain. My vexation, which I confess was great, though about a thread, conduced not to mend the matter. However, by cutting and tieing and making allowances for the entangled parts, we found the height of the central rock to be about one hundred and ten feet. We returned to the road on our way to Mis Tor, and arrived at Merrivale Bridge. It here began to rain : and as an inhabitant of the Moor, who was working on the road, informed us that if rain came on about half-past ten o'clock, which was then the hour, and did not clear up by eleven, it would prove a wet afternoon, we resolved to wait this eventful half hour, and sheltered our horses in a hovel near. But having waited till our patience was exhausted, we turned our horses towards Tavistock, where we arrived not in so dry a state as when we set out."

ADDITIONS BY MR. BRAY.

"In the autumn of 1831, within a few weeks, or possibly a few days, of thirty years since the above excursion, I took a young friend to Vixen Tor. He had heard of my getting to the top of it, but that no one else, it was believed, had done so since. I said that I wondered at it; particularly as I had often mentioned that I had left a twopenny piece in one of the basins; which at least, I thought, might have induced some shepherd boy to attempt it. On his asking how I ascended, I told him that I climbed through the fissure on the eastern side as up a chimney, by working my way with my arms and knees and back.

"He said he should like to try it himself, and would go to reconnoitre the spot. He instantly galloped up the hill amongst the rocks; and whilst I followed him on foot, not without some apprehension for his safety, he leapt his horse over a wall of loose stones, and, to my surprise, when I saw him again it was on the summit of the rock. We had previously seen there a raven pacing to and fro ; and I make no doubt it must equally have surprised the bird at any human being thus daring to 'molest her ancient solitary reign.' For that she might see him, either from her 'watch-tower in the skies,' or from the top of some neighbouring tor, is probable; as on a ledge of the rock we saw signs of its being the settled habitation of this feathered biped.

"He had thrown off his coat, and—being dressed in black—what with the contrastive whiteness of his sleeves, and his varied positions as he sought for the basin and the coin deposited in it, formed an object as picturesque as it was singular. He said that the greatest part of the surface was covered with grass or moss upon earth or mould of some depth, and that, therefore, he could distinguish but few vestiges of the basins, and nothing of the twopenny piece. To see him descend was still more picturesque, as the attitudes were still more varied and unusual, rendered also more graphically striking by being foreshortened. To this must be added the play of the muscles, as sometimes he hung by his arm, and at other times poised himself on his foot. Nor can I forget, on my part, the sense of his danger, which gave it a yet greater interest; for I felt no little fear as at length he found some difficulty in fixing his feet, and indeed stopped about half-way down to take off his boots, that he might secure a firmer footing. I may here, perhaps, be permitted to remark that we thus have some data as to the period of the formation of vegetable mould in basins, and on the tops of rocks."

So conclude Mr. Bray's observations on Vixen Tor. My next letter will contain various particulars about the Moor.

LETTER XIII.

TO ROBERT SOUTHEY, ESQ.

Vicarage, Tavistock, May 6th, 1832.

FROM Mr. Bray's Journal of September, 1802, I extract the following account of

PEW TOR ROCK.

"We once more resumed our excursions on the Moor, which, to my mortification, we were prevented from doing sooner by the unfavourable state of the weather. We proceeded over Whitchurch Down to Pew Tor, situated about two miles and a half from Tavistock.

" The ascent to this eminence is covered with rocks : among which are two that project in a pendent manner, several feet from the top of a buttress of the same material. On the summit of the Tor is a spacious area, level, and pretty free from stones, and of a form approaching to an oblong square. At each corner, which is nearly facing one of the cardinal points, is an elevation of massy rocks, with their fissures or layers in a horizontal direction, that gives them the appearance of rocks piled upon one another. From the opening at north-east to the corresponding one at south-west it measures twenty-seven, and from that at north-west to its opposite eighteen paces.

"The rock at the northern angle principally attracted our attention. From the form of it I could not hesitate to suppose that it was a Druidical seat of judgment. On the top is a large canopy stone, projecting about six feet, very like the sounding-board of a pulpit. Below it is a seat, projecting two feet and a half in the form of a wedge. A smooth stone supplies the back of this juridical chair; and a stone on each side may be considered as forming its elbow supporters. At its foot is a platform of rocks, somewhat resembling steps, elevated two or three feet from the ground, which is distant from the canopy about five feet.

"This curious rock is in every respect more perfect than the judgment-seat at Karnbrè, in Cornwall, described by Borlase.[1] The canopy is much larger, and the seat more easy to be distinguished. Before that at Karnbrè there is an area, whose outer edge is fenced with a row of pillars, probably so placed for the purpose of keeping the profane at an awful distance. *Here* the elevated platform answers the same end in a grander manner.

[1] *Antiquities*, p. 115.

"That this rock was appropriated by the Druids to their religious uses is without doubt; as it not only possesses the singularities above described, but also several basins on its top. A gentleman, whose residence is situated almost at the foot of the hill, informed me he had often visited this romantic spot, and admired the extensive prospects it affords; but had never seen or heard of these rock-basins. On my pointing them out, he immediately assented to their being a work of art.

"But before we proceed to their examination, I shall request permission to state my opinions respecting a Druidical seat of judgment. The Druids, we know, were possessed of almost sovereign sway; indeed in some respects of power superior even to their kings. For the monarch seldom dared to execute anything without consulting the Druids; whose supposed intercourse with their deities afforded them the pretence of arrogating to themselves a preternatural knowledge of futurity. Criminals, especially those guilty of sacrilege or any impiety, or where the accusation was doubtful, may be naturally supposed to have been brought before the venerable Arch-Druid. The awe which his presence must have inspired, increased by the stupendous tribunal on which he sat, doubtless frequently occasioned a conscientious confession from the guilty breast.

"To say that the Druids erected these amazing piles themselves, would be to grant them the powers which they made their superstitious votaries imagine they possessed. It is probable they selected those rocks that were naturally the best adapted to their purpose, and if they used art carefully concealed every trace of it, in order to make their followers imagine that they were piled and arranged for them by the gods themselves.

"The Druids may be supposed to have occasioned those singular forms of rock of which they were so fond, by breaking off parts of them, or detaching one mass from another, rather than by placing or piling them together in these immense heaps: though were I even to assert the latter, I might be greatly supported by the astonishing structure of Stonehenge, and also by what the Hindoos, almost equally unskilled in arts, have been known to effect in India. On the tops of some of their pagodas are amazing masses of rock. To place them in such elevated situations, they had recourse to aggeration; they took the laborious method, by accumulated earth, of forming an easy ascent or inclined plane to the top; by means of levers rolled them to the summit; and then removed the mound.[2]

"On the top then of this rock I had the pleasure of discovering the basins before alluded to, which confirmed the ideas I had already formed of the

---

[2] In a letter which I received from Mr. Southey, after this had been sent to Keswick, the following observations occurred; and I here venture to transcribe them, as I doubt not they will be found of interest to the reader—"If such of your tors as the drawings represent have not been formed simply by taking away parts of them, (as within living memory was done in this immediate neighbourhood, to make the Bolder stone appear wonderful) I think the stones are more likely to have been raised by mechanical means, than by the rude process of aggeration. The largest stone at Stonehenge might have been raised by a three-inch cable; and we know that the mischievous lieutenant, who threw down the rocking-stone at the Land's End, succeeded in raising it again. The Druids themselves may not have possessed either the skill or the means necessary for such operations; but the Phœnicians, with whom they traded, might have helped them; and both Dartmoor and Salisbury Plain are within easy reach of a sea-port."

purposes to which this Tor was applied. Of these, I counted four of a perfect, and five of an imperfect form. From north-west to south-east, the length of the rock is seventeen feet, and it is nine feet wide.

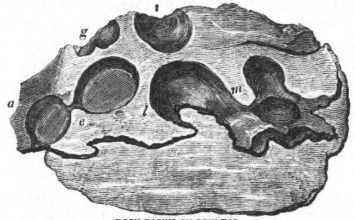

ROCK BASINS ON PEW TOR.

At *a* is an imperfect or shallow basin; into which communicates, at *e*, a larger one, in length three feet, width two, and depth ten inches. The bottom of this is flat and smooth. At *g* is a small imperfect one, the outward edge of which seems broken off. Near it, at *i*, is another, two feet in length, and eleven inches in depth. At *l m* is a basin, whose side is evidently broken off. This is three feet in length, and thirteen inches deep, and communicates with four others; two of which are perfect, and two imperfect.

"It is probable there were many more basins; as the rock on which these excavations are made, being thin, is broken, and the line of separation runs through the basins. No vestiges remain of the other part; which probably fell to the ground, and may now be covered with soil. The workmen must have taken great pains not to perforate or split the rock; as at the bottom of these basins it is but little more than an inch in thickness.

"It seems almost needless to prove these basins
are the work of art; but it may be proper to obviate
some objections started by persons who have never
seen, or never thoroughly examined them.   They say
these excavations are mere hollows in the rock, formed
by time and weather.   Setting aside their shape,
which is far too regular to be ascribed to these
causes, I would ask why they are confined to a few
particular rocks?   For as almost all the rocks on
Dartmoor are of the same description, namely, granite,
why should some yield to the effects of time sooner
than others?

"Granite, I believe, is seldom found to be carious,
and is more liable to be rendered smooth than
perforated by the above causes; as by being exposed
to the weather the sandy granulations of which it is
composed are worn off, and the edges as well as top
of the rock are moulded into a convex or gibbous
form.   How is it that moss and soil, formed of
decayed vegetable substances, are found in these
very hollows? surely if the rock cannot resist the
impetuosity of the weather, much less can the tender
vegetable.

"I allow that in rivers we frequently find rocks
with considerable perforations; but these are made
by the whirlpools or eddies of the torrent.   It surely
would be too absurd to think these basins were the
effect of the deluge; for nothing but the deluge
could cover the tops of such elevated mountains.
Besides, if the weather produced these wonders, they
would be continually increasing, and cease to be
novelties.   Can it be imagined, for an instant, that
Nature would select only those rocks that are singular
and remarkable enough in other respects, to add to

their peculiarities by forming basins on the tops of them? It is strange that men will have recourse to miracles to account for what may be explained by such simple means.

"By standing at the north-west opening, you have a perspective view of the four bastions, if I may be allowed the expression, and a distant prospect of Plymouth Sound. This curious Tor here wears so regular an appearance, that one might almost as easily assent to its being a work of art as of Nature: possibly it partakes of both. The area may be supposed to have been cleared, as there are only five or six stones within it; which probably served as altars. The four openings also seem to have been partly owing to art. But if the whole be the work of Nature, every one must allow that she has for once deviated from her accustomed plan.

"It is not improbable that this spot was used as a fastness, or stronghold, by the ancient Britons; and, with very little addition, it might now be rendered impregnable even to the improved system of warfare of the present day. A spot of this kind, whence is so extensive a view of the sea, and whence might be descried the approach of the enemy in every direction, could not surely have been entirely neglected; and it is well known that one and the same place was frequently converted to the purposes both of religion and war.

"We had been informed that at the bottom of the hill there was a curious cavern, which however by no means answered the expectations we had formed of it. The aperture, which is about four feet long and two wide, might be easily taken for the entrance of a rabbit burrow. With some difficulty we entered this

narrow passage, and found an excavation about fourteen feet in length, eight in width and five in height.
It terminated in a narrow hole; and was probably
the adit to a mine, or part of a stream-work; as
in the same direction there are several pits close
to it, which seem to have been opened in search
of metal.   I apprehend it has not unfrequently been
used by smugglers, as a secret deposit for their
liquors.

"In our way to Walkhampton, after descending a
most precipitous road, we passed over Huckworthy
Bridge, around which are a few cottages partially
concealed with trees. On ascending the opposite hill
we had a very picturesque view of this rural bridge,
with its arches partly covered with ivy, bestriding a
rocky river that owes its source to Dartmoor; one of
whose lofty tors closed this romantic scene. At Walkhampton, which is a small village, we gained directions
to Sheeps Tor, where we had heard there was an
excavation called the 'Pixies' Grot,' and to Stanlake,
near which we were informed the Dock-leat[3] formed
a fine cascade.

"After passing over some downs or commons of
no great extent we entered a road, at the bend of
which we had a view of Sheeps Tor, with its rocky
summit peering over a bridge almost covered with
ivy.   The banks of the rivulet beneath it were
fringed with willows; whilst beyond the ivied arch
appeared the tops of some lofty trees, which waved
their branches over the roofs of the cottages that
were visible between them. On reaching the little
hamlet of Sheeps Tor, we were informed by the
matron, whom from her age and appearance we

[3] Leat is used in Devonshire to signify a stream of water.

denominated the Septuagenarian Sibyl, that we might
easily find out the 'pixies' house,' where we should
be careful to leave a pin, or something of equal value,
as an offering to these invisible beings; otherwise
they would not fail to torment us in our sleep. After
thanking the good dame for her advice and information, we proceeded in search of it.

"By making a circuit we rode to the very summit
of this lofty Tor, on which is a spacious area of green
turf. We searched for some time amid this labyrinth
of rocks for the residence of the pixies, but in vain,
and lamented we had not taken a guide. We determined, however, to make a complete survey of the
Tor on foot, thinking that at least we should be
recompensed by the sight of the distant scenery, or
the nearer picturesque formation of the rocks.

"In the vale below, the little tower of the village to
which this eminence gives its name forms a pleasing
object. To the west is an extensive horizon; the
north is bounded by other equally lofty tors, one of
which is almost in the form of a regular cone or
pyramid. Below strays a little winding rivulet, content to wash the foot of the haughty mountain.[4]

"At the north side of the Tor we discovered a
narrow fissure, amid some large and lofty rocks; and
imagining we had at last found the object of our
search, squeezed ourselves into it with no little difficulty. The fissure was equally narrow all the way;
and as it took an angular direction, we got out with
as much labour on the other side. We did not,
however, follow the recommendation of our aged
informant, as we agreed that Oberon and his queen

---

[4] The leat that supplies Plymouth with its waters begins not far distant from the base of this tor.

Titania never could condescend to honour this spot
with their presence.

"On returning for our horses, we discovered near
the top of the Tor two stone ridges, almost covered
with turf, that intersected each other nearly at right
angles, and formed a cross. In the middle was a flat
horizontal stone. Measuring from this central point,
the ridge to the east was twelve paces, west six, north
seven, and south eleven. We afterwards discovered
a larger one below, at the south side of the Tor. At
first we conjectured they were sepulchral monuments;
and afterwards thought they might have been folds
for sheep; which at the same time was endeavouring
to account for the name of the mountain. But after
all, these conjectures are entitled to little attention;
as nothing can be accurately decided without more
minute examination than we were then capable of
giving.

"We returned to the village little satisfied with
our excursion; but on inquiry found, notwithstanding
all our search, that we had failed in discovering the
wonderful grotto. With a little boy for our guide,
we again ascended the mountain. Leaving our
horses below, we followed our conductor over some
rugged rocks, till he came to one in which was a
narrow fissure. On his telling us this was the entrance we laughed, and said none but the pixies and
himself could enter it; but on his assuring us it was
the spot, I resolved to make the attempt. With great
difficulty I succeeded, and found a hollow about six
feet long, four wide, and five feet high. It was
formed by two rocks resting in a slanting position
against another in a perpendicular direction. The
cavity was certainly singularly regular, and had

somewhat the form of a little hovel. A rock served for a seat, and the posture of sitting was the only one in which I could find myself at ease. A noise occasioned by the dripping of water is distinctly heard; and as the cause of it is out of sight, it produces at first a sensation somewhat approaching to surprise, till reflection tells us the occasion of it: which might possibly have prepared the mind to imagine it the resort of invisible beings.[5]

"We now returned about a mile and a half, and turning to the right, went in search of the cascade; which, as well as the cave just mentioned, is beyond measure indebted to the exaggerating tongue of fame. This is produced by the Dock-leat, flowing from the side of a hill across a little rivulet, over a bridge or aqueduct. The effect is not in the least picturesque, and by no means recompensed us for our trouble."

The following is extracted from Mr. Bray's Journal of the same year, written a few days after the above.

EXCURSION TO COX TOR,[6] ROOSE TOR,
AND STAPLE TOR.

"On ascending Cox Tor, which is on the left of the Moreton road, we observed several ridges, some of which are of a circular form. They do not seem

[5] The Rev. Mr. Polwhele, in his *Devon*, notices it, and in a note gives the following extract from a correspondent :—"Here, I am informed, Elford used to hide himself from the search of Cromwell's party, to whom he was obnoxious. Hence he could command the whole country; and having some talents for painting, he amused himself with that art on the walls of his cavern, which I have been told (says Mr. Yonge of Puslinch) by an elderly gentleman who had visited this place, was very fresh in his time. The country people have many superstitious notions respecting this hole." None of the paintings now remain on the sides of the rock.

[6] Cox Tor; possibly so called from the heath-cock, formerly very plentiful on Dartmoor.

however to be of Druidical origin, as they are too irregular, and are principally formed of mounds of earth; whereas the circles of the Druids were generally constructed of stones alone. They possibly may be the remains of enclosures to defend the sheep from the wolves, which at an early period are said to have been very numerous on the Forest.

"Towards the south of the Tor is an inclosure of this description of an oblong form; at the end of which is a singular rock, with two lines or fissures on its side, in the form of a cross. Hence is a grand and extensive view of the sea, the blue hills of Cornwall, the town of Tavistock situated in a deep valley, the lofty eminence of Brent Tor and the distant horizon beyond it. The top of Cox Tor spreads into a kind of plain; in the middle of which is a rocky prominence, that appears to have been a place of defence. Around it we traced the ruins of a circular wall. The foundations of a small building within it, eleven feet by eight, were plainly visible, as the walls were about four feet high. The entrance and fire-place could be clearly distinguished. By the side of it was a mound of stones, which is the loftiest point of the Tor, and probably was used as a beacon or signal-post.

"The declivitous sides of this Tor, to the north and east, are covered with either mole or ant-hills, as contiguous to one another as they can possibly be placed. We remarked, however, a few lines or belts without any, and on approaching these spots, found them wet and swampy. It is singular that this is the only Tor we have yet seen that possesses these excrescences. They seem to indicate a depth, and consequently comparative richness, of soil. Farther to the north is a mound of stones of a circular form, with a deep concavity in the middle. The circumference of this ridge measures twenty-nine paces. The stones of which it is composed are thickly covered with moss. At a little distance from it is a cairn, or heap of stones, flat at the top.

"Descending this mountain we crossed a narrow valley, and mounted the side of another Tor in a north-east direction. After passing near some pits or trenches, which we imagine are the vestiges of stream works, we met with an aged shepherd, who was collecting his flock, and informed us the hill we were ascending was

ROOSE TOR.

"This name may possibly be derived from *Rhôs* or *Rôo*, signifying in Welsh and Cornish, a 'heathy mountain.' At present, however, there is no heath near it; and indeed scarcely any is to be seen on the whole Forest, as it is constantly burnt almost as soon as it appears. By this means the heath-polts, which were here numerous, are nearly extirpated, whilst the sheep are benefited by the rich pasture that succeeds. The south side of the Tor has a grand and picturesque appearance. Two immense piles of rocks are of so pendent a form as to threaten every instant to fall upon the beholder. One of them is supported on its two extremities, about a couple of feet from the ground, by some low rocks, and seems as if it had been bent in the middle by its own weight. And this probably was the case, for a perpendicular fissure or hiatus, that extends from the convexity of the base into the body of the lower stratum, proves that rocks, on their formation, must have been of a soft, yielding nature.

"This first group of rocks showed no symptoms of
art; but on another pile, which was fifteen feet high,
we found two basins—one two feet by one and a
half; the other one foot in diameter. The rock consisted of seven layers, and the basins were on the
stone next to the top, which was small. Another pile,
though much lower, we ascended with the greatest
difficulty. On the top of it were a few imperfect basins.
But a mass of rocks near the latter afforded us a very
curious specimen of the works of the Druids.

ROCK BASIN ON ROOSE TOR.

"On the uppermost stone of the mass we discovered a basin, in depth a foot and a quarter, with
smaller ones surrounding it, and little channels communicating with others in a serpentine direction. On
this Tor we found a sheepfold between some rocks,
which were serviceable in the formation of it; and
were informed by another shepherd that it was still
used. A Tor, it seems, is generally appropriated to
a particular flock. Hence we proceeded to

STAPLE TOR,

probably corrupted from Steeple Tor, as it has two or
three piles of rock of a considerable height. On asking
the old shepherd whether he thought we could climb
them, he laughed at the idea. However, we determined to ascend the lowest first, which we did with

no great difficulty, and discovered on it a basin a foot
and a half in diameter and one foot deep. This,
contrary to all we had hitherto seen, was full of dirty
water, which was probably occasioned by decayed
moss. Over it hung a loftier pile, which we resolved
to ascend as high as we could, without much hope of
reaching the top. My friend, however, got to the
very summit, on which he informed me was a wide
but shallow basin. I followed him till I reached the

STAPLE TOR.

third stone from the top, which I could feel with my
hand, but was unable to summon resolution enough
to ascend higher.

"Whilst I was leaning with my breast against the
stone, he *moved* from his position, *and I felt the rock
shake under him.* On my mentioning this circumstance he did not seem to give it credit; but I soon
convinced him by shaking it myself, till with some
degree of apprehension he requested me to desist.

"I begged he would continue on the top, till I had
descended and taken a sketch of it, with himself on
the summit; but first gave him a plumb-line to let
down, and we found he was elevated thirty feet.
He not only stood upright, but stretched out his

hands and foot in the position of Mercury, and seemed rather like a statue on the top of a lofty column than a human being on the summit of a natural rock. Besides its elevation, it hangs considerably out of the perpendicular; which so blended

STAPLE TOR.

the feelings of fear for my friend and surprise at his firmness, that I felt the most indescribable sensations, and my fingers could scarcely hold the pencil.

"I again made an attempt to join him, but halted in my former situation; and the more he endeavoured to encourage me, added to my own attempts to overcome it, the more the perturbation of my mind increased; and, unable to bear it longer, I again descended. On letting himself down, I was obliged to direct my companion where to place his feet. Had he missed his hold, it would have been instant destruction. As he was now on the same spot where I had stood, I requested he would move the rock, thinking he could do it with greater ease, as he is much stronger than myself, and the rock must have been rendered somewhat lighter by his having removed from it. But my astonishment was great at his assuring me he could not move it in the least. This convinced us he must have acted as a poise; which was confirmed afterwards by our examining the inclination of the rock, and the point on which he stood. As one part of the rock projected considerably, it required something on the opposite side to balance it, and when this was removed it destroyed the libration; so that there was less danger of its falling when he was on it than otherwise. When he was half-way down, the shepherd again joined us, with the laugh of stupid wonder, and saying he had observed him on the top, asked how he could possibly get down.

TOLMEN, STAPLE TOR.

"On the same group of rocks is a singular Druidical monument, or tolmen, for such I am convinced it is. The word is composed of *tol*, a hole, and *mên*, a rock, in the Cornish language. After a description of this, which is different from any mentioned by Borlase, we will consider the purposes to which works of this description were applied. On the top of a rock, with a flat surface, a stone, nine feet long, and six wide, is supported by two other stones. One of the supports is placed on the very edge of the rock. Neither point of bearing is an inch in thickness, so that in all appearance a slight effort would remove it. Through this aperture I crept, not without apprehension, and took especial care not to touch its supporter even in the slightest manner.

TOLMEN, STAPLE TOR.

"The tolmen is denominated by Borlase a stone deity. By going under the rock, or through the passage formed by it, he thinks one acquired a degree of holiness; or that it was used to prepare for and initiate into the mysteries of Druidism, their future votaries. Some, too, he says, might be resorted to by people troubled with particular diseases, who by going through these passages left their complaints behind them.[7]

"After all, however, it is probable that *this* rock cannot come under such denomination, as tolmens in general are large orbicular rocks, supported from the ground by two small ones. And as nothing similar

[7] "Creeping under tolmens for the cure of diseases is still practised in Ireland, and also in the East, as is shown by Mrs. Colonel Elwood in her travels."—*Gentleman's Magazine*, July, 1831.

to it is to be found in Borlase's account of Druidical remains in Cornwall, I may be allowed, perhaps, to indulge my own conjectures.

"I am inclined, then, to think that *this* was designed as a kind of moral touchstone. The Druids might lead the accused to the spot, point out to him the apparently tottering rock, and by threatening to make him pass under it, when if guilty it would fall and crush him, extract from the delinquent the confessions of his fear. We know, though Borlase has unaccountably overlooked it, that ordeals of various kinds were used by the ancient inhabitants of this kingdom; and the rock ordeal may be supposed as effectual as any other. After examining some more rocks, where we found nothing remarkable, we returned, with the determination of soon visiting Mis Tor, which is the next to the north-east, and which our good shepherd informed us was the most curious on the Moor, and that we should there meet with what was called *Mis Tor Pan:* this we concluded must be a Druidical basin of a large size.

"I may here observe, that Vixon, or Vixen Tor, described in a former excursion, receives its name, as I am told, from vixen, the female of a fox; these animals resorting there from a neighbouring wood, near the Walkham, to breed among the hollows of the rocks."

In my next letter I propose giving you several other extracts from Mr. Bray's Journals.

TO ROBERT SOUTHEY, ESQ.

Mis Tor described—Tumuli and Circles near Mis Tor—Ashes found in
the Circles—Barrows—Stream-work, &c.—Brent Tor—Beacon
station with the Ancient Britons—Account of this most conspicuous
and remarkable Tor—Church on the very top of it—Its commanding
station—Legend respecting it—Another Tale respecting its Foundation—Most probable Tradition concerning its Erection—Brent Tor
a striking Object at a distance—Camden's notice of the Gubbins, a
rude race of Men inhabiting a neighbouring Village—Wherefore
called Cramp-eaters—Longevity, instance of it in Elizabeth Williams
—Geology of Brent Tor.

Vicarage, Tavistock, May 10*th,* 1832.

I SEND you in this Mr. Bray's account of an excursion,
made in the same year as the former, to

MIS TOR.

" This tor, which is situated about five miles from
Tavistock, we visited to view the *pan* already mentioned.[1] It lies to the left of the Moreton road,
near the river Walkham. A small rock, or tor,
probably Little Mis Tor, is near it : this we ascended.
It had nothing but its natural yet regular appearance, almost like that of masonry, to attract our
notice.

" On continuing our ride hence, we found the

---

[1] The popular legend respecting Mis Tor Pan is, that it was formed
by the devil, and used by him as a frying-pan on particular occasions.

ground swampy, and before we reached Great Mis
Tor crossed a stream-work of considerable extent.
Here there are four or five masses of regularly piled
rocks, on one of which, about the centre of the Tor,
is a basin, the largest we had yet seen, three feet in
diameter and six inches in depth. The bottom was
flat and smooth. It had a lip, with a channel to the
north-east. Near it on the same ridge is a singularly
formed rock; from its appearance we concluded it

MIS TOR PAN.

was a logan stone, but tried· in vain to move it. We
examined every part of the Tor but could find no
other work of art: if there ever had been any, it was
probably destroyed some years ago by the lawless
rout of idle young men, who sallied out and purposely
overthrew every rock they were able to move in this
neighbourhood. Whilst we were employed in these
investigations we sheltered ourselves from a shower
of rain, by entering a chasm amid the rocks, and made
them echo with the voice of song."

The next extract is from the same Journal, kept
by Mr. Bray during his excursions on the Moor.

TUMULI AND CIRCLES NEAR MIS TOR.

"Having occasion to pass over Dartmoor, without any intention of renewing my researches on it at that time, I thought I observed as I ascended Merrivale hill, a mound or two at the left hand, at some distance from the road. It was rather remarkable they had not before attracted my notice, particularly as, in our last excursion, I cast my eyes over it in doubt whether I should examine it more minutely or not.

"As I was not much straitened for time, I directed my course to the spot, which is an enclosure, and found the first barrow I came to was of an oblong square, thirty-five paces round the base, with shelving sides and flat at the top. It was covered with moss, rushes, and grass, and had a broad but shallow trench around it. It stretched east and west, or rather north-east and south-west. Another near it was of the same dimensions. A little beyond this was one thirty-seven paces round. They all pointed to the same quarter of the heavens. At a distance I perceived several others, and determined to return to my horse, which I had fixed to the hedge, and ride to them. I was convinced, from their shape and situation, that they were barrows or tumuli, which were in remote ages receptacles of the dead.

"Owing to enclosures I was obliged to return to the turnpike road, and near the circles above-mentioned found a man employed in building a hut, the foundations of which I had before remarked. He informed me that he had a grant from Mr. Lopes" (the late Sir M. Lopes) "of several acres around, and intended to reside there with his family. On my

asking him what he imagined the circles were designed for, he repeated the old story, that they were
used as a market during the plague at Tavistock, the
account of which he traced back to his great grandfather. He told me he would show me the spot
where the market-house stood, together with the
wraxelling ring, or place appropriated for wrestling.
The circles he conceived were *booths;* and said he,
'To prove they were, I've found many of their fire-
places with ashes in them.'

"This alone was wanting to corroborate my opinion
of their being used by the Druids in their sacrifices,
or as dwellings by the aboriginal inhabitants of the
Forest. He promised me he would let me know when
he had discovered any more. On accusing him of
having destroyed some of the circles, he said the
stones were very *handy* for him, and he did not know
what use they now were. But on my informing him that
I should endeavour to bring them into notice, which
might possibly induce the curious to visit them, and
that if he acted as their guide he might meet with
some remuneration, he promised he would restrain
his destroying hand. On finding he had resided for
most part of his life near Vixen Tor, I asked whether
he had ever been on the top of it, to which he replied
it was impossible ; and I could hardly persuade him
I had myself accomplished that feat.

"I thence directed my route in pursuit of the
remaining barrows towards Mis Tor, and leaving my
horse near the stream-work mentioned in one of my
former rambles, entered the enclosure, which reaches
from the river Walkham half way up the rocky side
of Mis Tor. The first barrow I arrived at was twenty-
seven paces round, the next twenty-seven, another

thirty-four. Near this was one thirty-eight, and another twenty-five. They were in general about four and a half feet high. Not far distant was the largest I had yet seen; the circumference of which was forty-eight paces, and its height six feet. Near this were two more, one twenty-eight paces, the other thirty-two in circumference. It may possibly be said that they are nothing more than old peat stacks, as where the turf has been removed the earth is very black, but this is the natural colour of the soil on the Moor. It would be absurd to imagine such pains would be taken to place them all in the same direction, or to make them all of nearly the same size. But the strongest proof till one of them be opened, (which at some future time I hope to do) is that the next I came to evidently had its sides faced with stone. This was twenty-four paces round. At the east end of it is a circle ten paces in diameter; it was different from any other I had before seen. Stones were piled upon each other to the height of two feet, which was about the width of the wall. The entrance was to the south, whence you have a fine view of the sea, Maker Heights, and Vixen Tor.

"Near this was another barrow, thirty-two paces round, more distinctly faced with stone. Thus in all there are thirteen tumuli within the space of less than half a mile; and since they are surrounded on all sides by such evident Druidical remains as basins and circles, we may surely attribute them to the same origin. Indeed, this spot seems to have been the sacred cemetery of the Druids.

"I forgot to mention above that an idea may be started, from their proximity to a stream-work, that these mounds were formed of the rubbish arising from them.   This, however, could by no means be the case, as they surely would not have carried it to such a distance from the work, nor was there any reason to form a trench around, or to make them in so artificial a shape.   Near these tumuli are several lines of stones stretching in various directions, some straight, and others in a circular direction.   To the north-east of them I found very unexpectedly a great number of circles, of all sizes from three or four paces to sixty or seventy in diameter.   The largest united three or four small ones, and had lines of connexion with some at a distance.   On the range of its circumferential line, a square is formed on the inside by three or four stones, which has an entrance from without.   This I conjecture to have been the sacred hearth or altar for burnt sacrifice.   And near one of the circles is a pit or cavity, which possibly might have been applied to the same purpose."

The next extract which I here send you from Mr. Bray's papers is an account of his excursion to

BRENT TOR.

"On my road I passed Hurdwick, about a mile from the town.   It was formerly the property of the Abbot of Tavistock; and the remains of a barn of considerable extent, with bold projecting buttresses, built probably about the same period with the abbey, prove it to have been a place of no mean consequence. Indeed, the Abbot was called to the *house of peers*, in the time of Henry VIII., by the title of Baron Hurdwick.

"At the northern extremity of Heathfield, Brent Tor is a conspicuous object.   In Gibson's edition of Camden's *Britannia*, we are informed that Brent Tor

is a name signifying 'a high rocky place.' As *Tor*
alone can lay claim to the greater part, if not the
whole of this definition, (for *tor*, tower, turris, are all
of the same import, meaning something elevated ;
and tor moreover is generally, at least in Devonshire, confined to a rocky hill) the *first* syllable, and
thus the very name of the place itself, is totally
omitted.

"*Brent* is the participle of *brennen*, to burn.   And
little doubt can be entertained that Brent Tor was an
ancient beacon, upon which wood, turf, or other rude
articles of fuel, were *burnt* by way of signal ; and we
know that the church upon its summit is even at
present 'a famous sea mark.'   Four or five tumuli
about a mile distant, on Heathfield, are still called
the Beacons.   It was probably in the time of the
early Britons a stronghold, or hill fort ; as on the
northern side may be traced two or three mounds,
that seem to have been raised for the purpose of
defence.

"The summit of this lofty eminence is generally so
damp and wet, that the very coffins are said to float
in the vaults.   This no doubt is greatly exaggerated :
but most of the hills on Dartmoor are so wet and
boggy, from being frequently covered with mist, that
they justly might be designated as 'cloudcapt tors.'
In addition to this the western winds, being here
the most prevalent, bring the clouds from the Atlantic
ocean ;   and these, surcharged with vapour from
crossing such an immense expanse of water, are
attracted and broken by the hills of Devonshire.
This in fact is the principal cause of the humidity,
but at the same time the perpetual verdure, for which
this country is so remarkable.

"The church on Brent Tor is dedicated to St. Michael. There is a tradition among the vulgar that its foundation was originally laid at the foot of the hill; and that the enemy of all angels, the prince of darkness, removed the stones by night from the base to the summit, probably to be nearer his own dominion, the air: but that, immediately on the church being dedicated to St. Michael, the patron of the edifice hurled upon the devil such an enormous mass of rock, that he never afterwards ventured to approach it. Others tell us that it was erected by a wealthy merchant, who vowed in the midst of a tremendous storm at sea, (possibly addressing himself to his patron, St. Michael) that if he escaped in safety, he would build a church on the first land he descried. If this was the case, he seems to have performed his vow with more worldly prudence than gratitude; as it is one of the smallest churches anywhere to be met with. Indeed, it frequently, and not inappropriately, has been compared to a cradle. The tower has but three small bells. It is a daughter church to Tavistock; and the Michaelmas fair, now held at the latter place, used formerly to be celebrated at Brent Tor, doubtless in honour of its tutelar saint. The stone still lies by the road side on which the pole with a glove, the usual concomitant of a fair, was erected. Probably, however, it was originally the base of a cross.

"The church stands on the very summit of the rock, within a few feet of the declivity, on its most precipitous side. These words, inscribed on a tablet, are seen on the south wall—'Upon this rock will I build my church.' There are no monuments; but the following rude inscription is worthy notice :—

"'Heare under this stone lyeth the bodie of John Cole, Jun. of Litton, who departed this life the 23d. of November, 1694, æta : 22. Also, Johan, his sister, who was burled the 1st of February, 1694, æta : 11.'

> "'If thou be serious (Friend) peruse this stone ;
> If thou be not soe : pray : let it alone.
> Against death's poison, vertue's the best art ;
> When good men seem to die, they but depart.
> Live well : then at the last with us thou'lt feele
> Bare dying makes not death, but dying ill.'

"Brent Tor is a pleasing object at a distance; here towering abruptly, there gently rising from the extensive plain of Heathfield; but when viewed near it is too void of foreground; though a projecting rock at the north-west end, under which is a little shed or stable, gives it a prominent feature, and in some degree supplies the deficiency: for as one passes along the road beneath, the form of the hill is perpetually varying; and the effect is totally changed, as the tower is seen on the one side or on the other of this impending cliff.

"In Camden the inhabitants of a neighbouring village, called the Gubbins, are stated to be 'by mistake represented by Fuller (in his *English Worthies*) as a lawless Scythian sort of people.' The writer contents himself with asserting that it is a mistake, though upon what authority does not appear; as even at the present day the term Gubbins is well known in the vicinity, though it is applied to the people and not the place. They still have the reputation of having been a wild and almost savage race; and not only this, but another name, that of *cramp-eaters*, is still applied to them by way of reproach.

"Instead of buns, which are usually eaten at

country revels in the West of England, the inhabitants of Brent Tor could produce nothing but cramps, an inferior species of cake; probably owing to the badness of their corn, from the poverty of the soil. Thus they were called 'cramp eaters,' as the whiskered warrior in the Batrachomyomachia, or battle of the frogs and mice, of Homer, was denominated Sitophagus, or 'cake-eater.' And if a *bad* pun may be allowed, they might be learnedly called cacophagi. We know that the gipsies are descended from the Egyptians; but notwithstanding Fuller's credit is thus fully re-established, we must not venture to suppose that the modern inhabitants of Brent Tor aspire to carry back their genealogy to the ancient Scythians; particularly as history informs us that their country was not held in high esteem, even by its natives. For a certain petulant Greek objecting to the celebrated Anacharsis that he was a Scythian, 'True,' says Anacharsis, 'my country disgraces me, but you disgrace your country.'

"If however longevity be a characteristic of savage nations, the inhabitants of Brent Tor will not, perhaps, be displeased at being compared to them in this particular. There is now living among them a woman called Elizabeth Williams, of the age of one hundred and six, who still retains the full possession of her faculties. She says she was married at the age of twenty-four, at Lamerton, and by the parish register of that place it appears that this occurred in April, 1736; so that, if this account be correct, she can be no more than ninety-eight years old. Her maiden name was Blatchford.

"It may not be uninteresting here to subjoin Mr. Polwhele's notice of Brent Tor rock, extracted from

his *Devon.* 'The summits of these (the Dartmoor)
Tors are found to be composed, in general, partly of
granite and partly of dark brown iron-stone, which in
some places appears to have been in a state of fusion.
Brent Tor, and several other tors on the west side of
the river, are undoubtedly volcanic. Brent Tor is
very curious; it being one mass of hill, rising to a
great height from a perfect plane, and entirely divested of everything of the kind besides itself, and
differing from all other tors which we visited. We
found it covered, between the rocks, with a fine
verdure, and every indication of a very rich soil, far
different from the heath which surrounds it. We
brought away some bits of the rock, which in
general is a deep rusty blue, inclining to black,
hard and heavy, with pores here and there as if
worm-eaten; some of the pores contain a little of a
brownish red earth, but whether of the ochre kind
we could not determine. Near the top of the Tor
some pieces were found more porous, even resembling a cinder, or piece of burnt bread, and very
light; we supposed it to be a variety of tophus.
Another observation was very striking, that this Tor
does not contain a single particle of granite, that we
could discover. In this it differs from most of the
other tors we visited, though we found some on the
west side of the river Lid, which contained stones of
a similar porosity. From the above observations, we
were led to believe that this remarkable Tor was the
effect or remains of some long-ago extinguished volcano; as, in its appearance, situation, soil, strata, &c., it
argues strongly for it. It bears, also, a great similarity
to the description in Brydone's *Tour through Sicily,*
of the hills which he calls the offspring of Etna.'"

LETTER XV.

TO ROBERT SOUTHEY, ESQ.

Source of the Tavy on Dartmoor—North of Crockern Tor—Account of
some very curious Circles found in this Excursion—Long Be Tor—
South Be Tor—Bel Tor, or Belle Tor—Excursion to Tavy Head—
Cranmere Pool—Source of the River Tavy—The tracks of Foxes
seen—A Hare chased by a Fox—Superstition respecting the Spirits
condemned to the Pool—The Guide's credulity—His account of
having been himself Bewitched by an old Woman—Extraordinary
Walking Race—Head of the river Walkham—Crossing the Fen—
Peter Tor, a fortified Stronghold.

Vicarage, Tavistock, May 13th, 1832.

I PURPOSE sending you in this letter an account of
the source of the river Tavy, which rises on Dartmoor,
and flowing through the adjacent country gives name
to Tavistock, which is situated on its banks. But
wishing to be as regular as I can, I shall continue
my extracts from Mr. Bray's Journal in the order in
which I find it written. The following brief notice
of some ancient vestiges comes before his account of
the source of the Tavy. It is dated—

"Sept. 20th, 1802. As the family had determined
on going to Bair-down this day, I was glad to be
of the party, to continue my observations towards
the north of Crockern Tor, which I had lately visited.
After passing Merrivale Bridge, we thought we saw
a circle or two on the right of the road, in a valley
where there are directing-posts from Tavistock to

Ashburton. As I had not been exactly on that spot before, we proceeded to it; and the first circle we found was fifty-six paces in diameter; including a smaller one to the westward, another to the south-east, and a third to the north-east. That to the westward had a diametrical line intersecting it. To the north and south were two or three large flat stones set on end; and in the circle were some rocks, which possibly might have served the purpose of altars.

"At a little distance from this is another circle, or rather three parts of one; for a portion is very rudely traced: it is one hundred and sixteen paces in circumference. Adjoining, but on the outside, is a smaller circle, with a diametrical line, and within it are two others, somewhat large, connected with the circumferential line. On the outside of this is a large flat rock, which serves as a back to what was once, I conjecture, an altar-hearth, as there are some stones, now partly thrown down, that form a square before it. Near this spot were three or four smaller ones, not deserving any particular notice.

"Continuing our route to the left, on the east we arrived at a small tor on the acclivity ascending to Hessory Tor, on which is a basin two feet and a half long and six inches deep. My father, who had never before seen a rock basin, was convinced, though this was by no means a regular one, that it must have been a work of art. We fell into the road again at Rundle Stone, on which, on the south side, is the letter R, in *alto relievo*. Hence I had often thought I perceived to the east-south-east a tower; and though every person who had heard me mention it considered it as suppositious, I by means of a glass now saw it very distinctly: from its direction as well as appearance, I think it must be Lord Courtenay's Belvidere.

"My father left me at Bair-down; and I resolved to visit by myself the tors, four in number, to the east of the Dart. The first tor is just above Wistman's Wood: it is called Long Betor. On one stone I found three imperfect basins; on another a shallow one; and on a third three more, also imperfect. This Tor bears evident marks of having suffered from some concussion of the earth; for the strata lie in all directions, and some piles of rocks have fallen from their perpendicular, and, though falling against others, have not separated. At South Betor, on the same ridge, there is a basin two feet and a half in diameter: it is shallow. Waydown Tor, though much the highest of the four, has nothing remarkable, excepting the view, which is very extensive. It is almost the only tor of such a height that is covered with grassy turf.

"Belle Tor (or Bel Tor)[1] has on its summit a circular mound of stones, hollow in the middle, with two little piles at the east and west. This is evidently artificial; as there are no loose stones near excepting those fallen from the top. A rock or two to the north had nothing worthy notice. In many places the ground was boggy; I was obliged when this was the case to tie my horse to some rushes, not without some degree of fear that he would eat himself loose."

[1] Supposed, as stated in a former letter, to derive its name from Bel, or Belus, the sun, worshipped by the Britons.

EXCURSION TO TAVY HEAD.

ALSO FROM MR. BRAY'S JOURNAL.

"Sept. 22.—Accompanied by my friend I set out to visit Tavy Head. We went first to the village of Peter Tavy, where my father had recommended me to make inquiry of a farmer of the name of Mudge. We met two men driving sheep to Tavistock market, and, on applying to them for information, found it was the farmer and his son. On learning who we were he insisted on accompanying us himself, and accordingly returned for a horse; and to be more expeditious mounted him without any saddle.

"We soon found he was well acquainted with all the western parts of the Moor. Indeed he was communicative in every respect; and informed us that he had a large family, which at times from misfortunes and losses he should not have been able to have brought up, had it not been for the many kindnesses of his landlord, who amongst others permitted him to pay his rent only just when it was convenient to himself. My companion asked him who his landlord was, and he replied that he was my father. I was greatly affected at the good farmer's expressions of affectionate gratitude to his benefactor.

"Near Peter Tavy is an upright stone, where was buried a man who some years ago poisoned himself in consequence of the infidelity of his mistress. We first rode to Limebarrow, which is an immense heap of stones with a little cavity on the top: in the centre is a large stone. It is eighty-five paces in circumference. The tor near it, a very low one, has nothing worth notice.

"About half a mile farther, we left our horses to the care of some persons who were employed in carrying away '*turves*' (peat) and proceeded on foot towards Cranmere Pool, the source of the river Tavy. If we had not taken a guide it would have been impossible to have attempted it; for even as it was we were half way up the leg every instant in crossing a bog, or morass, of two miles in extent, and another soon after of the same dimensions.   At a spot where the verdure was entirely carried away by water, and where there was nothing but soft black peat, we ascended a circular mound, seemingly artificial, whence we had an extensive view: to the south Bel Tor, and Waydown Tor, with the tors on Bair-down, and Hessory Tor; to the west Ger Tor, Fur Tor, West Han Tor, Sharpy Tor, and Sourton Tor; to the north Amarcombe, West Mil Tor and East Mil Tor, Row Tor, and others, with I believe Sheperton, Wild, and Watern Tors.

"To the north-east we perceived a flag on a hill about a mile distant, to which we went, and conjectured it was affixed there by those employed in the trigonometrical survey of the county; though one would think, from its not being worn, that it had been but lately erected.   The Dart rises at a little distance from it.

"We saw frequently the track of foxes; and our guide informed us that once he had seen a fox in chase of a hare.   This is a fact rather new, I believe, in natural history.   About a mile farther, in the midst of a bog of a considerable extent, we found Cranmere Pool.   It is not as represented in the map on the top of a hill, but in a low part of the bog; however the bog itself is on high ground.   The pool was dry, and through it we observed the foot-marks of a fox. I walked into it some little distance without sinking higher than my ankle. It does not appear to be more than a hundred feet in diameter; nor can the water itself be more than six or eight feet deep when it is full. I am inclined to think that its size must have been exaggerated by the fears of those who viewed it only at a distance; for in wet weather it cannot well be approached. Indeed at present we found many deep holes around it full of water, and partly covered with long grass, so thick that it required the utmost circumspection to wade along in safety.

"Our guide informed us that it is believed spirits are here condemned to suffer. Indeed, he was not very sceptical; for he said that an ill-minded old woman, who is still alive and lives near him, had *bewitched himself*, so that for seventeen weeks he never slept an hour, nor ate more than a biscuit or two; that he never felt hungry nor sleepy; that always at twelve o'clock at night, precisely, such pains as of pricking of pins would so torment him in his side, that he was obliged to be taken out of bed, and that then he would sit up till six o'clock in the morn-ing, when these tortures regularly left him!

"The Pool is about eight miles from Peter Tavy, and within three of Zeal, near Okehampton. On our remarking to our guide how lustily he walked, he informed us his age was sixty-five, but that he could never walk so well as his son, who, for the wager of a guinea, had run eleven miles in forty-five minutes, from Tavistock Bridge to Knackersknowle.

"Returning from Cranmere Pool, we again crossed the Tavy, which is here a little rivulet. We also saw

the head of the river Walkham. We mounted Fur
Tor, on which is a basin two feet and a' half in
diameter, and eight inches deep. There are also two
small contiguous basins, one of which has a perforation
communicating with the side of the rock.

"Hence we again waded to our horses, after walking about ten miles across the fen. We were not a
little heated and fatigued; but had it not been for a
pretty brisk wind we should have been much more
so. We rode about half a mile, and, coming to a clear
stream, went to dinner on a venison pasty, which I
had carried in my valise. Soon after we took leave
of our good old guide, and went to Peterstone Rock,
the highest stone of which, he said, had been split in
pieces by lightning about forty years ago.

"Peter Tor was evidently a fortified stronghold, as
it is surrounded by a mound of stones, and in the
midst three or four rocks are encompassed with the
same. Hence is a distant view of the Sound, &c.
The Tor is composed of black granite, covered with
moss. The layers are not, as usual, horizontal, but
jagged, and generally perpendicular. Below it is a
large oval ridge of stones, one hundred and thirty-
three paces long, with seven small internal circles.
From a tor near Peter Tavy is a very fine and extensive view—the winding river, Tavistock, Mount
Edgcumbe, Kit Hill, Brent Tor, &c."

In the first part of the above account, which I have
extracted from his old Journal, Mr. Bray mentions
the upright stone that marks the spot where a young
man was buried who had poisoned himself, in consequence of the infidelity of his mistress. That spot
is at the meeting of four cross-roads, now grass-grown;
it is known by the name of Stevens's grave.

I send you also some account, written by Mr. Bray, of our excursion to

TAVY CLEAVE.

"Sept. 8th, 1830.—In our progress towards Tavy Cleave, whilst stood before us two of the summits of those lofty tors that surround it, we saw between them, stretching to the remotest horizon, a number of intersecting hills, on which the light from the different distances was continually shifting, the tors

TAVY CLEAVE.

themselves being in the deepest shadow. It instantly reminded me of the effects produced by the gently alternating light and shadow of the diorama. It is seldom that such a scene is found in Nature, where the foreground remains fixed in gloom, and light and shade seem to chase each other over the varied landscape; because in general we see a continuation of extent, and the gradual and therefore almost imperceptible changes that take place; whilst here the different points of distance were so happily combined, that the eye, as it glanced from one to the other, beheld one illuminated and the other obscured, now in succession and now in opposition, as the flitting clouds passed over them.

"The rocks above Tavy Cleave are not so much composed of the usual layers of granite as they are a conglomeration of small disjointed parts. Immediately below one of the walls (for such therefore we may call them) of the summit, the stones appear to have been thrown by the hand of Nature into a circular direction. Indeed, one might almost fancy them to have been ejected from the crater of a volcano as in a whirlwind, and not to have lost their rotary motion on their descent. Most of them being on their edge, they look like petrified waves, and may be compared, perhaps, to the Mer de Glace, not however in ice, but granite.

"Two of these broad masses of rocks are divided by an aperture, through which with most advantage may be viewed the scene below. Between a bold declivity on the left, divided into two or three pointed eminences, and another less precipitous on the right, the Tavy winds in a deep ravine or cleft (which probably gives name to the spot) at first over some shelving rocks, that give rise to long filaments of foam, and then to a broad white belt in a transverse direction; till meeting with a ridge, or perhaps a fissure (for the cause is invisible) it assumes even amid its own dark waters the appearance of a cascade, equally white with foam; and at last transforms itself, as it were, into a deep black pool.

"When we approached the river, we were almost covered with what seemed showers of thistle-down;

but on coming closer we saw no spot on which thistles by any possibility could grow. We soon discovered, however, that it was the efflorescence or dry incrustation of foam, which had collected between and upon the rocks beneath what I have described as the cascade.

"The bed of the river here, being principally a horizontal stratum, seems part of the floor or original crust of the earth: and if it have undergone any alteration it is probably by a partial subsidence; whilst the tors around appear to have been elevated by a projectile force, and down their sides may still be seen what may be called, perhaps, cataracts of stones."

The next extract I shall here send will be an omitted passage from Mr. Bray's former Journal, with a notice of

SHARPY TOR.

"It well deserves the name, for some of the points, almost in a perpendicular direction, appear as sharp as the head of a spear. There are four eminences at a short distance from one another overhanging the Tavy. Air Tor, or Hare Tor, to the north of the former, commands a very extensive view, looking down upon Lydford Castle. On the very summit is seen a kind of natural mound of earth, where appears also something like a circle. It is however hollow in the centre, and there was in it the burrow of a rabbit or other small animal. On the south-west side the granite is coarse, mingled with a square-shaped white spar. Here is a small oval basin. In going to this Tor, I was obliged to leave my horse at a distance, owing to the boggy nature of the soil. On returning

I heard the bleating of a sheep very near, but looking around discovered no signs of one. I found, however, that it proceeded from nearly beneath me, and at length ascertained that it was a lamb which had got under the rocks. I at first, through the interstices of the rocks, saw its nose only; but at last succeeded in dragging it out by its legs. Thus, my journey, long and fatiguing as it was, would have been amply recompensed had it only afforded me the opportunity of saving the life of this harmless animal. I next visited the lower part of Air Tor to the north; and observed some few projecting nodules of shining mundic in the granite. Between this and the next tor there is a small artificial cairn with a concavity, and two sharp-pointed heaps on its edge. On riding down the hill my horse entangled his foot between the rocks, and by the violent effort he made in extricating himself, which was so great as to tear off his shoe, I was thrown over his head; but most providentially with no other hurt than slightly bruising my leg, and spraining my hand. This, of course, put an end to any further progress that day."

LETTER XVI.

TO ROBERT SOUTHEY, ESQ.

Excursion to the Warren in search of the King's Oven—Arrival at an
old House called an Inn—Invitation to the Traveller held out in
Verse—Romantic Story—Derivation of the word Merrivale—
A search after Antiquities under a broiling Sun—Ridges of Stones
—Circular Barrow seventy-six Paces in Circumference—The King's
Oven found—Probably a place used by the Aboriginal Inhabitants of
the Moor for their cookery—A Circle—A Stone Cross—Curious
Remains of a British Bridge examined and described, near a
Circular Enclosure like Dennabridge Pound—Visit to Fitz's Well
on the Moor—Account of the Well, with the tradition respect-
ing its History as connected with the Pixies and Sir John and
Lady Fitz.

Vicarage, Tavistock, May 26th, 1832.

MY next extract from Mr. Bray's Journal will yet
detain you on Dartmoor : it gives an account of our
excursion to the

WARREN AND KING'S OVEN.

" 27th July, 1831.—Accompanied by my wife, I set
out in search of the King's Oven, the name of which
certainly excited more than ordinary expectations.
On reaching New House, formerly an inn, I inquired
of a female who was standing at the door if there
were any room in the stable for my horses. Her
reply was that the stable was full of turf, by which
she meant peat. We had come fourteen miles, in

an extremely hot day ; but, anticipating no great accommodation for them, I had brought corn, and therefore directed my servant to lead them about, and to feed them in the best manner he could.

"Had the stable been empty it could afford, I believe, but little accommodation at the best, and the house itself, even in its better days, though it held out an invitation far more magnificent than the usual one, 'Entertainment for man and horse,' would perhaps have little exceeded that which is celebrated in poetry as the death-scene of the profligate Villiers, who is described as having died 'In the worst inn's worst room.' The inscription on the sign, which I think I must have seen myself when a boy, was as well as I recollect,—though, as I doubt not it was 'spelt by the unlettered muse,' I wish I could give it *verbatim et literatim*—

> " Here is cider and beer,
>   Your hearts for to cheer.
>   And if you want meat
>   To make up a treat,
>   There are rabbits to eat."

"New House (which Hannaford, when he mentioned to me that the King's Oven was at no great distance from it, seemed to consider a misnomer, for he said he believed it was one of the oldest houses on the Moor) is surrounded by a warren, which thus afforded an easy opportunity of fulfilling at least the latter part of the above promise, and they probably were able to give a Welsh-rabbit into the bargain. Having provided ourselves with sandwiches, in a kind of cartouch box, which originally however was made for botanizing, and a pocket pistol, *vulgo* a small bottle of brandy, (for I would not have my

readers expect any perilous adventures with banditti)
I made no lamentations on the absence or entire
annihilation of most of these eatables and drinkables,
but contented myself with inquiring of the representative of the *ci-devant* landlady, which was the
way to the King's Oven. She hardly seemed at first
to understand the question, and indeed was evidently
altogether so uninformed, that I was satisfied she
was not the person whom I thought I possibly might
find there, and of whom I had heard the following
story.

"A common pack-horse driver, or carrier, was in
the habit of putting up at a public-house on St.
David's Hill at Exeter, which, indeed, was a pretty
general rendezvous for persons of this description.
They there, over their beer, amused themselves with
singing. Whether the person above alluded to sang
the loudest or the sweetest I know not, but his voice
was so pre-eminently distinguishable from that of his
companions, as to attract the attention of the daughter of a clergyman who resided near. I presume not
to say who made the first advances : it is clear who
made the first impressions. The result, however, was
that she married him, and he took her as his bride to
this same house in the very heart of the Moor. I
made no inquiry about her of its present inhabitant,
as I thought she was as little likely to give any
information on matters connected with romance as
on those of antiquity.

"On asking, however, if she had never heard that
there was anything curious to be seen in the neighbourhood, she said that she had lived there no more
than two years, but that once a pedlar entered the
house, and remarking how much it was out of repair,

and that perhaps the wisest plan would be to pull it
down, advised her if such should be her resolution
to build it on a spot the other side of the road, where
a foundation for a similar purpose had been already
laid, or at least the ground dug out for it. He said
it was in a line with the corner of their field near
the *mire*, by which I afterwards found she meant
the bog.

"And here, at the risk of being charged perhaps
with digression, I must mention that on previously
passing Merrivale Bridge, and, farther on, Higher
Merripit and Lower Merripit, I had ventured to
account for the name of these places, by supposing
it derived from *miry*, corrupted into *merry*. They
all, especially the two latter, are near a bog. And
thus, if she were not the means of *giving* me information, she was, as not unfrequently happens, the means
of my *gaining* it, or at least of confirming my own
opinion, which I believe with most is considered
equivalent to information. Though her curiosity had
never led her there, she was good-natured enough,
however, to assist in gratifying mine, and offered to
accompany us to the spot which she thought was
meant by the pedlar. When I arrived there, however,
I was as wise as before, for I knew not whether I was
to see a mound or a cavity, and of each of these
there were many, as we were evidently surrounded
by the 'old workings' (as they are called in Devonshire) of a tin mine, which had subsequently been
converted into a warren. The day was extremely
hot, and as my companion was tired and almost faint-
ing with the heat, I resolved (though to think then of
looking for an oven seemed somewhat a work of
supererogation) to go in search of it alone.

"Sometimes thinking of the burning fiery furnace of Nebuchadnezzar, and sometimes of King Arthur's Oven, which I believe is a kind of cromlech in Scotland, I rambled about with an umbrella over my head in search of I knew not what. I thought also more than once of a wildgoose-chase, and was almost induced again and again to give it up; but tempted by the pleasure of exploring unknown regions I persevered.

"As I ascended the hill I perceived some ridges of stone, which whether they were the remains of inclosures or tracklines I could not tell. I found on an elevated point of view what seemed like the King's broad-arrow, which appeared to have been but recently made in the turf. And had it not been so long ago, I could have fancied it one of those marks made during the trigonometrical survey by direction of the Ordnance under Colonel Mudge. Soon after I came to something like a small rude circle, with what might have been an erect stone or pillar, but now fallen, and, whether by lightning or otherwise, split longitudinally and laterally into four parts, in nearly equal proportions. Advancing farther, I observed the outline of the summit of the hill somewhat rough with stones and rushes, and hastening towards it found as I conclude the object of my search.

"It is a circular barrow composed of small stones, seventy-six paces in circumference. Its form approaches but little to conical, being I should think but three feet high. I saw on it no lichen or moss, which is generally found on structures of this description that have remained in their original form, and I therefore should conclude that many of the stones have at a comparatively late date, been carried away.

It can boast of almost a panoramic view of consider-able extent, particularly towards the north-east and south. Near it is a kind of trench, about six feet long, with a shorter meeting it at right angles in the centre, the sides of which are lined with stone. And in the same direction are several pits, and one in particular of some extent in the shape of an inverted cone.[1]

"On our way homeward, a little before we came to Merripit, I observed a circle on my right hand inter-sected by the road; and a little farther on to the left, on the other side of the road, a stone cross, nine feet and three quarters long, now fallen, and lying near a circular pit. Its arms are very short, but the whole is of a more regular shape and better wrought than such crosses as are generally found on the Moor.

"At Post Bridge I got out of the carriage to measure one of the flat stones of that structure, which I found to be fifteen feet by five and a half. These immense slabs are supported on four piers, at either extremity one, two having originally been in the centre, of which one is fallen and now lies in the bed of the river. It was probably erected by the aboriginal Britons, and might almost be taken for the work of the Cyclops themselves. On passing over the new

---

[1] It is not improbable this was really the King's Oven, or used for the purpose of baking by some British chief—since it was a custom with the people of Britain as well as of Gaul to dig a *deep pit, line it with stones*, and make the stones hot by burning heath or wood upon them. In similar pits, says the editor of Ossian, "they laid venison at the bottom, with a stratum of stones above it, and thus did they alter-nately till the pit was full: the whole was covered with heath to confine the steam." Near these holes or pits there was generally also found a "heap of smooth flat stones of the flint kind," used perhaps for baking bread.

bridge, near which is another cross close to the road, I observed at some distance to the right a circular enclosure, somewhat similar to what I suppose was the foundation of Dennabridge Pound."

The next extract from Mr. Bray's Journal is an account of a visit to

FITZ'S WELL.

"August 10th, 1831.—Having many years since attempted to find Fitz's, or, as it is generally called, Fice's well, by crossing the Moor from Bair-down, when my horse, on getting into a bog, so trembled in every limb that I gave up the search, and from some circumstance or another never resumed it; I determined, this day, to renew my investigations.

"I directed my course to the house on the Moor near Rundle Stone, where a female offered to guide us to the well. We proceeded in a northerly direction, along the eastern bank of the leat that conveys the water to the prison. After we had gone about half a mile, we turned off at a right angle, following the direction of what appeared to be an old hedge or part of an enclosure, at no great distance to the left of which we reached the well, not, however, without some of the party getting wet in the feet, as it is nearly in the midst of a bog. It is situated on a gentle declivity, near Blackabrook, (over which, a little lower down, is an ancient foot bridge) the edifice about the well consisting of flat slabs of granite; the cover being three feet ten inches by three feet three inches. The height of this rude structure is about three feet. The well, according to Carrington's work, 'measures three feet square by two feet and a half deep.' On the front edge of the cover is the inscription, which I hesitate not to say is given very incorrectly in the vignette of his book.

"I am willing, however, to make every allowance for the artist, as he possibly might labour under similar disadvantages to myself, if not even greater; for the whole was in shadow, whilst the sun shone bright behind it. Had it been at noon, or an hour or two previous, for it faces nearly east, it would have been partially illumined, and the shadow of the letters, which are in relief, would have assisted in deciphering them. But I am sufficiently convinced that the letters 'I F' are *not* reversed, but in their natural order; and that instead of being 1168, it is 1568.

"I think it most likely that Fitz's Well was constructed by John Fitz, the old lawyer and astrologer of Fitzford; whose traffic with the stars in foretelling the fate of his only son is still the theme of tradition.

"John Fitz, the elder, was, if I may so express myself, a water-fancier as well as an astrologer; for he built the conduit-house at Fitzford; and I have in my possession his autograph. It is thus written: 'John Fytz;' and appears on the counterpart lease of a field, giving him liberty to convey water 'in pipes of timber, lead, or otherwise,' to his mansion-house at Fitzford. It is dated the 10th of Elizabeth. Now Elizabeth began to reign 1558, and the structure called Fitz's Well on Dartmoor was, as we have seen, erected in 1568."

Since Mr. Bray wrote the above notes in his Journal, I have learnt from Mary Colling, who is well acquainted with all the traditions of her native town, that the following is still told by the elders of Tavistock, respecting Fice's Well.

John Fitz the astrologer, and his lady, were once
pixy-led whilst riding on Dartmoor. After long
wandering in the vain effort to find the right path,
they felt so fatigued and thirsty, that it was with
extreme delight they discovered a spring of water,
whose powers seemed to be miraculous; for no sooner
had they satisfied their thirst than they were enabled
to find their way through the Moor towards home
without the least difficulty. In gratitude for this
deliverance, and the benefit they had received from
the water, old John Fitz caused the stone memorial
in question, bearing the date of the year, to be placed
over the spring for the advantage of all *pixy-led*
travellers. It is still considered to possess many
healing virtues.

LETTER XVII.

TO ROBERT SOUTHEY, ESQ.

Height of Southern Hills of Dartmoor—Luminous evaporations there seen—Tin Mines—Grey Granite; of what composed—Manganese found near Moreton Hampstead—Devonshire Marbles—Slate remarkably beautiful—The various uses to which applied in the County—Slaters called Helliers—Crystals, where found—Black Garnets—Spar, where found—Loadstone on Dartmoor—Brent Tor, its curiosity and Geology—Dartmoor a primeval Mountain Tract—Convulsions of Nature have been great on the Moor—Shock of an Earthquake felt—Full account of the Storm and its awful effects, at Widdecombe, in 1638—Low Towers of the Churches on the Moor—Botany, slightly noticed—Golden blossom of the Furze magnificent in Devon; admired by Linnæus—The Digitalis, or Foxglove, grows in the greatest luxuriance—Whortleberries—White Clover—Wild Flowers; poetical Names given to them by the Peasantry—Provincial Names for the Birds, &c.—The Finny Tribes—Reptiles—The Long-Cripple Snake and Toad seen together—Story of a remarkable Toad—Lizards—Adders common on the Moor—The Bat abundant in the Ruins of an old Tower in the Vicarage Garden.

Vicarage, Tavistock, June 1st, 1832.

On looking over the notes I have made for these Letters, I find several respecting Dartmoor that are of so miscellaneous a nature that I do not know very well how to throw them into any connected form; and yet I think they contain information on some points that ought not to be passed in silence. Will you, therefore, admit a letter which must, I fear, be little better than a string of unconnected paragraphs: for in what other way can I give you such notes as the following?

I find that the southern hills of that immense waste
called Dartmoor are about eleven hundred feet above
the level of the sea;[1] and that luminous mineral
evaporations and *ignes fatui* are commonly seen in
the valleys and hollows of the Moor in dark nights :
"some of these," says Polwhele, "are like balls of light
rising about five feet from the earth, then falling back
and rebounding." In former times the mines were
numerous ; at present very few are worked, though it
is conjectured that this vast tract is rich in its sub-
terranean product of metals and ores. Tin mines
are amongst these, particularly in the parish of
Sampford-Spiney ; and some years ago the sexton,
whilst digging a grave in the church of Whitchurch,
near Tavistock, struck into a lode of tin. I have in
these Letters repeatedly mentioned the grey granite
which so much abounds on the Moor. This consists
of white felspar, black mica, and quartz. It is remarkable that no sort of granite is more readily
rough-hewn, and none with greater difficulty brought
to receive a polish. Iron is found in it, and a large
vein of that metal was discovered in the Sampford-
Spiney mine. In the fissures of the granite there
are seen also two varieties of tin, *Stannum crystallis
columnaribus nigris*, and *Stannum amorphum rufori-
gricans*.[2] Manganese is found in abundance near
Moreton Hampstead.

Our Devonshire marbles, of which the most beautiful chimney-pieces are wrought, are too celebrated
to need much notice in this letter. The Drewsteignton

---

[1] The highest summit of one, Yes Tor, near Okehampton, is upwards
of 2000 feet.

[2] POLWHELE'S *Devon, passim.* These are both varieties of the oxide,
and now classed under the common name cassiterite.

marbles are chiefly black, or of the richest dark blues, and elegantly veined; they are capable of receiving the highest polish, and are sometimes found spotted with shells or other fossil remains, so hardened as to form a part of the marble. Our slate too is very celebrated: it is often of so deep a grey as almost to approach black. Chimney-pieces, highly polished, are made of it. The Rev. Mr. Evans, of Park Wood, has in his house one of this description, so exceedingly beautiful, that on first seeing it I took it for black marble. Some of the finest quarries are in our neighbourhood.

This slate is very valuable, and with us it is used not merely for a general covering against the weather, but for various other purposes. We have a hearth in our kitchen of one entire slab, that measures eight feet in length by four in breadth. In Devon it is often used for tombstones. When we visited the church of Launceston in Cornwall, about two years ago, we saw lying against the wall of the churchyard part of a memorial of this description, which ought to have been carefully preserved in the church itself, as one of the most curious and beautiful specimens of *carving in slate* perhaps in the whole kingdom. The arms and supporters of the deceased, the crest with many flourishing decorations, and the whole style of ornament, declared it to be a work of the time of Henry VIII., when simplicity was getting out of fashion. This broken slab of monumental slate, for the sharpness and perfection of its execution, and the delicacy of its finish, was equal to any sculpture I have ever seen in marble; and when we consider the brittle nature of the material in which it is wrought, there cannot be a doubt that as a work of art it is one of great value and curiosity. From the situation in which it stood when we saw it, I should fear that in a few years it will be totally destroyed. Slaters with us still retain that antique name by which, if I remember correctly, they are distinguished by Chaucer; for here they are called *helliers*, and the slate roof of a house is termed the *helling*.

But our granite, marbles, and slate are not the only productions of the earth for which we are famous: the earth itself is deserving notice for the vast variety of its tints, and the richness they add to the landscape. I need not tell you, who have been at Exeter, how brilliant is the red earth of that neighbourhood, and that it is always considered the best and most productive.[3] Rougemont Castle, in that city, derives its name from the colour of the soil on which it stands and the stone of which it is built. Mr. Polwhele mentions that crystals are found in it; and that the earth in which diamonds are discovered at Golconda is of the same nature.

Crystals also are sometimes seen on Dartmoor amongst the granite. In Sampford-Spiney above one thousand were discovered, "being all of a short thick column, with tapering pyramidal ends." These are very rare in England. "They are always met with in parcels in the same place, generally detached and single, though sometimes a few of them cohere together; they are beautifully transparent, and of

---

[3] Even in Otaheite it is so; for there we learn, by the accounts of recent travellers, that the poor savages have a tradition that the first man was made out of the *red earth* of a certain mountain. On my mentioning having read this to Mr. Bray, he remarked how much this tradition of a savage nation accorded with the Mosaic account of the creation; since the word *Adam*, the name of the first man, in the Hebrew signifies *red earth*.

extreme brightness." Semi-pellucid columnar quartz
crystals are frequently found in the fissures of the
Dartmoor granite ; and the black garnet is discovered
at Moreton Hampstead, like schorl crystals, and the
amorphous minutely granulated black schorl. We
have also on the Moor a compact species of spar,
that bears a fine polish and is capable of being
worked the same as marble. I observed a few days
since several rocks of this description, rising two or
three feet above the surface of the ground, near
Holwell, on Whitchurch Down. "In Devonshire,"
says Risdon, "is found the miraculous loadstone, not
discovered in this island till the sixteenth century :
the loadstone, though of an inferior kind, has been
found on Dartmoor." According to Prideaux, some
of the hills, or mountainous tracts of the Moor, attain
a height of nearly two thousand feet ; the valleys,
though they run in various directions, nevertheless
have a tendency to the north and south. The hills
are most elevated towards the borders, where the
granite seems of a harder and closer texture. The
colour here and there varies ; though its general appearance is grey, yet is it found "from almost black
with schorl, to pure shining white, and some occurs
of a rich red, superior in beauty to any Egyptian
granite, particularly where it contains tourmaline." It
is metalliferous, tin being common; copper is sometimes found. The granite, though rich in schorl, is
poor in mica, consequently containing less magnesia,
and the more subject to the operations of the weather
from that cause. The line of granite from the town
of Tavistock to Hay Tor may be pretty accurately
traced by the coppice, which, clothing the declivities of
the slate-rocks that abut against it, disappears sud-

denly on the gritty soil. Cox Tor is a mountain of trap, which runs in a northerly direction to Whiter Tor and Brazen Tor. "It is almost pure hornblende, in different degrees of compactness, and consequently of specific gravity." At Cox Tor and Whiter Tor it is seen in contact with clay-slate, at Brazen Tor with granite. This slate is likewise observed on the western sides of the first-named Tor, where it comes in contact with the trap. This preserves its laminar structure; it has assumed the aspect of flint, and gives fire on receiving a blow from the hammer. In some places it is become riband jasper, but finer as a mineral.[4]

Mr. Bray noticed in a former paper, that Brent Tor was considered by geologists to be a volcanic pro- duction; and as there is evidence of the action of fire on the Moor, so likewise is there of water. Alluvial tracts are here and there displayed; and though the nature of the granite rocks cannot be doubted, yet it is the opinion of Polwhele that the vast fragments of stone so wildly scattered everywhere around, or piled in the rudest heaps, clearly indicate some terrible wreck of a former world. The eminence, for instance, which arises above the logan stone at Drews- teignton, displays the boldest and the most marked vestiges of some great flood. It is the same in other parts, particularly near Hay Tor Rock. There "the hills are broken up or strangely rounded. The rocks along the sides of the hills are smoothed by the waters, or shattered by the force of the torrent: whilst an infinite number of pebbles are dashed around these abrupt masses. The valleys have on one spot an even surface, but gravelly and sandy.

[4] PRIDEAUX'S *Geological Survey, passim.*

On another they are ploughed up into the wildest irregularities; all around, indeed, the very entrails of the earth are laid open. These were not common floods; they were such as might divulse the whole strata of the hills, wash away the substances that had been accumulating for ages, and bring others instantaneously into their place."[5] An intelligent correspondent of the same author observes "that the convulsion which produced the mountain tracts of Blackdown and Haldon, raising themselves, perhaps, partly if not wholly from the sea, was not enough to throw off all their superficial strata from the clay-stones and shells that remain on them; they may therefore be called alluvial mountain tracts. But the convulsion being stronger that formed the heights of Dartmoor, all superficial strata were thrown off, and the granite, which is considered as a primeval stratum, appeared. This stratum has nothing upon it but a thin vegetable mould that it has since collected. This, therefore, in the language of a geologist, may be called a primeval mountain tract."

That Dartmoor has experienced at different periods many convulsions of Nature cannot be doubted by those who have examined with attention the features of that most interesting waste. The last convulsion of any extraordinary character occurred in the year 1752, when, on the 23rd day of February, a smart shock of an earthquake was felt at many places on the Moor, and its immediate neighbourhood—Manaton, Moreton Hampstead, and Widdecombe. In the last-named village some houses were injured, and one of the pinnacles of the tower of the church was thrown down. Widdecombe, indeed, seems destined to suffer

[5] POLWHELE'S *Devon.*

by the convulsion of the elements. The most fearful of these sufferings was alluded to in an extract from Mr. Bray's old Journal, given in a former letter. It deserves, however, a more particular notice; and the following account, founded on the authority of Prince, will I trust be not altogether devoid of interest, though it relates to a most melancholy subject.

On Sunday, the 21st of October, 1638, whilst the Rev. George Lyde was performing the evening service in his church of Widdecombe, he was suddenly surprised by such darkness that he could with difficulty proceed in his duty. This was followed by intermittent peals of thunder that sounded afar off like the discharge of artillery. The darkness so increased, as the tempest drew nearer, that the congregation could scarcely see each other; and whilst the hurricane raged without in fearful violence, the choristers sang one of the psalms in praise of Him "who maketh the clouds his chariot, who walketh upon the wings of the wind, who hath His way in the whirlwind, and in the storm." At length the whole face of the heavens became covered by dense and black clouds, and all was dark as midnight. In a moment this was fearfully dispersed, and the church appeared to be suddenly illumined by flames of forked fire. According to Prince, these terrific flames were accompanied with smoke, and "a loathsome smell like brimstone." A ball of fire also burst through one of the windows, and passed down the nave of the church, spreading consternation in its passage.

Many of the congregation thought it the final judgment of the world: some fell on their faces, and lay extended like dead men upon the ground; others beat their breasts, or cried aloud with terror: many

wept and prayed.   The reverend pastor continued in
his pulpit, amazed by this event, yet by Divine Providence unharmed himself, though a sad spectator of
the dreadful sufferings around him.   His wife was
scorched by the lightning, but her child, seated by
her in the same pew, received no injury.   A woman
who attempted to rush out was so miserably burnt
that she expired that night.   Many other persons
likewise, in a few days after, died from the same
cause.   One unhappy man had his skull so horribly
fractured, that the brains were found cast upon the
pavement in an entire state.   "But the hair of his
head," says the chronicler of this event, "stuck fast to
the pillar near him, where it remained a woful
spectacle a long while after."   Several seats were
turned upside down, yet those who were on them
received no injury.   One man, on rushing out at the
chancel, saw his dog, that ran before him, whirled
towards the door, where the animal fell down dead.
On seeing this the master stepped back, and his life
was preserved.   A beam from the roof fell between
the pastor and his clerk; neither was injured.   So
violently was the tower of the church shaken, that
vast stones were tossed from it, as if from the destroying hands of 'an hundred men.'   A pinnacle of the
tower in its fall broke through the roof, wounded
many, and killed a woman.   The pillar against which
the pulpit stood became black and sulphureous;
yet, though thus surrounded by danger on every
side, the undaunted minister of God never forsook
his station; and in reply to a proposal made by some
one present that all should venture from the church,
he exclaimed, "Let us make an end of prayer, since
it is better to die here than in another place!"

The affrighted congregation, however, seeing the building so fearfully shaken and tottering above their heads, dared not remain; and Mr. Lyde was left to finish the prayer with the dead and the maimed around him; four persons being killed, and sixty-two grievously burnt by the lightning, or wounded by the falling of the stones. Carrington thus alludes to this awful visitation in his poem of *Dartmoor*[6]:—

> " Far o'er hill and dale
> Their summons glad the Sabbath-bells had flung;—
> From hill and dale obedient they had sped
> Who heard the holy welcoming; and now
> They stood above the venerable dead
> Of centuries, and bowed where they had bowed
> Who slept below.   The simple touching tones

[6] The wildest tales respecting this storm, so severely felt in Widdecombe church, are still the theme of tradition with the peasantry of Dartmoor. One story is that the devil, dressed in black and mounted on a black horse, inquired his way to the church of a woman who kept a little public-house on the Moor. He offered her money to become his guide; but she distrusted him, on remarking that the liquor went hissing down his throat, and finally had her suspicions confirmed by discovering he had a cloven foot, which he could not conceal even by his boot. Another version of the story says, that the compact being out which the devil had made with some wicked youth, he had the power to seize him, even in the church, if he there found him sleeping. On his way through the churchyard, the Evil One overturned some boys he found playing at marbles upon the graves; and finding his victim as he expected sleeping in the pew, he caught him up by the hair, flew with him through one of the windows, and in his flight knocked down the pinnacle that did so much mischief. There are many other adventures told concerning the devil in this exploit; but these are the principal. Bishop Hall, in his admirable sermon *Of the Invisible World*, ascribes many storms to the agency of wicked spirits; and mentions that of Widdecombe as an instance.

I have seen it mentioned in the *Quarterly Review*, that the Ettrick Shepherd, in one of his tales, makes the devil be discovered by the wine hissing down his throat whilst drinking. This is a very remarkable coincidence with our Dartmoor tradition; which is not, I will venture to say, known beyond this neighbourhood.

Of England's psalmody upswelled, and all,
With lip and heart united, loudly sang
The praises of the Highest.   But anon,
Harsh mingling with that minstrelsy, was heard
The fitful blast;—the pictured windows shook,—
Around the aged tower the rising gale
Shrill whistled ; and the ancient massive doors
Swung on their jarring hinges.   Then—at once—
Fell an unnatural calm, and with it came
A fearful gloom, deep'ning and deep'ning, till
'Twas dark as night's meridian ; for the cloud,
Descending, had within its bosom wrapt
The fated dome.   At first a herald flash
Just chased the darkness, and the thunder spoke,
Breaking the strange tranquillity.   But soon
Pale horror reigned,—the mighty tempest burst
In wrath appalling ;—forth the lightning sprang,
And death came with it, and the living writhed
In that dread flame-sheet.
                    " Clasped by liquid fire—
Bereft of Hope, they madly said the hour
Of final doom was nigh, and soul and sense
Wild reeled ; and, shrieking, on the sculptured floor
Some helpless sank ; and others watched each flash
With haggard look and frenzied eye, and cowered
At every thunder-stroke.   Again a power
Unseen dealt death around !   In speechless awe
The boldest stood ; and when the sunny ray,
Glancing again on river, field, and wood,
Had chased the tempest, and they drank once more
The balmy air, and saw the bow of God,
His token to the nations, throwing wide
Its arch of mercy o'er the freshen'd earth,
How welcome was that light—that breeze—that bow !
And oh how deep the feeling that awoke
To Heaven the hymn of thankfulness and joy !"

Though storms attended with thunder and lightning are by no means common on the Moor, yet
when they do occur they are of a nature so terrific,
that every one must acknowledge the mercy of Divine

Providence in not suffering them to be more frequent. Were I to repeat to you the notices of such storms given by various writers, no spot of like extent in this kingdom could perhaps claim so fearful a record as the Forest of Dartmoor. The towers of the churches in this neighbourhood are by no means lofty, and spires are unknown. Possibly this circumstance may be the result of design; the wisdom of our ancestors might have suggested the necessity of erecting low towers in a region of high lands and mountainous tors, where any very elevated buildings perched upon them would have become as points of attraction to the clouds surcharged with the electric fluid. This, however, is a subject I leave to be discussed by those who are much better acquainted with it than myself.

It is not my intention in these letters to say any thing concerning the botany of the Moor. I am too ignorant of the subject to write about it, and even if I possessed the knowledge that is requisite for such a task, it would be unnecessary; since Mr. Polwhele, in his *Devon*, has given a most copious account of all its plants, both common and rare. Another consideration, also, makes me less anxious on this point. It is that you have truly observed in your *Colloquies*, that botanical books are only of interest to botanists. You are not I believe particularly partial to that science; and few readers are so. Should these letters, therefore, ever go farther than Keswick—should they go into the hands of any one who might be curious on such a point, I have stated where that curiosity may be most amply satisfied. The few remarks I have to offer respecting the wild products of the soil are such as would strike any one who has been fond of the pencil; and who consequently acquires a feeling, or as artists term it an eye, for the picturesque; an eye which becomes the inlet to one of the most innocent, delightful, and lasting pleasures of human life; a pleasure that fills the whole heart with the best and the most grateful feelings towards that Divine Providence, which has everywhere spread around us such a world of beauty and variety, for the solace, the delight, and the service of his creatures.

It is on this account, therefore, that even the slightest knowledge of drawing becomes so valuable; since it teaches the young student to see a thousand minute beauties of light, shadow, form, and colour, that would escape an uncultivated observer. And this is the reason why I would have all young persons taught to draw, as they are taught to write; since, though it requires talent to make a good artist, and genius to form a great one, yet I am persuaded that there are few, if any, so dull, but that they may be taught to imitate the forms they see before their eyes, even as they learn to write the alphabet; and when I add that on venturing to make this observation to Mr. Stothard, senior, the historical painter, he concurred in such opinion, it will be found not unsupported by a very high authority.

During the spring in our neighbourhood, and, I believe, in most parts of Devon, nothing can exceed the gorgeous display made by the golden blossom of our furze. It is said that when Linnæus was in England, he was more struck with the magnificent appearance of this wild furze than with any other of our native plants. It grows most abundantly on tracts of waste land, by the side of roads, and on certain portions of Dartmoor. Near Moreton Hampstead it is seen so thick and splendid, that it might be compared to an embroidery of gold on velvet of the richest green. I have seen this furze, when skilfully managed by a tasteful artist, introduced with good effect in foregrounds; where, like the rich opposition of colour in the pictures of Titian, it contrasts finely with the deep and ultramarine tints of the sky and the distant tors. Our May blossoms too, growing on the thorns in the hedges, are exceedingly luxuriant, and beautifully clustered. And scarcely does the yellow blossom of the furze disappear, when there comes forth in such abundance as I have never seen in any other county, that most elegant of all wild flowers, and most delicately painted in its bell, the digitalis, or foxglove; or, as the peasantry here call it, the 'flop-a-dock.' The height to which these plants grow in Devon is extraordinary. I have seen many hills so covered with them, that viewed in combination they have produced an effect truly magnificent; especially where some of our noble ferns interposed to add that variety of form and colour so essential to the picturesque. The white foxglove is an exceedingly rare plant even here, where I have always understood botanists find so choice a field for their pursuits: it is found on Dartmoor. In Somerset and Devon, the common people use a decoction of it as a most powerful emetic; too powerful, I should think, to be taken with safety.

Whortleberries are both fine and plentiful on some parts of the Moor. They are delicious (somewhat resembling in flavour the American cranberry) when made into tarts and eaten with that luxury of all luxuries, the clouted, or as we call it scalded, cream of our delightful county. The heath-polt principally feeds on the whortleberry that grows wild on the Moors. Round the tors of the Forest the finest white clover springs up spontaneously; and no doubt this in a great degree renders the Moor so excellent in the pasture it affords the sheep.

Though I have confessed my entire ignorance of botanical subjects, which I regret, I can tell, nevertheless, many of our wild flowers by the names that are prevalent among the peasantry. Some of these it may be as well to mention, since they are of antique date. And who would do other than look with an eye of interest on the pretty flowers that were chosen by Ophelia to form her 'fantastic garlands,' as she strayed by the 'glassy stream' under the willow that grew 'ascaunt the brook'?

> "There on the pendent boughs her coronet weeds
> Clambering to hang, an envious sliver broke;
> When down her weedy trophies, and herself,
> Fell in the weeping brook."

We have here crow-flowers, nettles, daisies, and 'long-purples,' and many other plants whose names are as ancient, as poetical, or as fantastic; for here, too, the 'long-purples' are called 'dead-men's fingers.' And poor Ophelia herself might have sung snatches of old tunes, as she formed garlands from flowers so wildly called as ours. We have the 'maiden hair,' a pretty pendent plant for her 'coronet;' and the 'lost-love' that would have reminded her of Hamlet; and the 'shepherd's calendar,' and the 'one o'clock,' the very dial of poetry; and the 'cuckoo-flower,' that opens its little pink buds at the time the bird from which it borrows its name does his note. And we have, too, the 'snapdragon,' as varied and as beautiful as any garden flower. And the 'thormantle,' excellent as a medicine in fevers; and the 'cat's-eyes,' that are as blue as ether, with a little white pupil in the centre; and 'bright-eye,' with its glossy leaves; and 'mother of millions,' with its numerous small drooping flowers; and 'honesty,' whose bells hang like open purses by the side of its stem. 'Milk-maidens' are little white flowers that grow in the meadows, or on the banks of running streams. And Love supplies many with his name; for we have a plant called 'seven years' love;' and 'love entangled,' a wild picturesque flower that grows on the tops of old houses; and 'love in a puzzle,' a delicate plant with leaves resembling in colour the wings of an early butterfly. We have also the blue 'hare-bell.' The harmless nettle is here called 'archangels.' And indeed we have a vast variety of others that speak in their very names the imaginative and poetic character of our forefathers in this lovely county.

As we have provincial names for the plants, so have we likewise for the birds. A grave naturalist would smile did he hear some of these. That beautifully-feathered bird, the yellow-hammer, which I can never meet without delight, as he spreads his wings and mounts and flutters aloft, is here known by no other name than the one which so truly expresses his character—the 'gladdy;' and it does indeed glad one's very eyes to see him. And then when I open the postern gate in the old Abbey walls at the end of the garden, and look out upon the foaming Tavy and its rocks, there I meet a pretty little fellow skimming over them, or dropping his wings and resting a moment, and constantly wagging his fan-tail of black and grey feathers over the old stones; an action which has procured for him the name of the 'dish-washer.' And we have, too, the 'mazed-finch,' a truly Devonian appellative, given to one species of this tribe in consequence of its wild and incessant motion. We have also, as the little boys here say,

> "The robin and the wren,
> God Almighty's cock and hen."

And then we have birds called by as compound epithets as if the good folks who gave them had studied Homer. For we have the 'ox-eyed titmouse,' a little bit of a bird not bigger than a wren, with a breast as white as snow. We have, likewise, the 'heck-mall,' a busy bird, and fond of making himself comfortable: a hole in an old apple tree, or a snug cell in the Abbey wall which some loosened stone has left for him, are to him as a palace; and there he lives as happy as a more ambitious bird amongst the loftiest rocks, even as

> "The lordly eagle sitting in his chair."

The 'hoop' is a bird of the same family, who makes more noise than he does work; and being somewhat choice in his dwelling, he selects an old hole that is well sheltered with ivy. The 'furze-chatterer,' it is probable, admires the golden bushes from which he takes his name as much as did Linnæus himself, since he regularly frequents them; and there, if he is not to be seen, he is constantly to be heard; and, like most great talkers, repeats the same note over and over again. We also have a bird called 'black-headed Bob,' a merry fellow; and well does he deserve his name; for whilst his bill is not idle in picking up what he can, his head bobs about from side to side, with a motion as perpetual as that of a Chinese joss. Part of his family are aristocratic, for the 'black-winged duke' is certainly of his kindred; but whereas Bob carries all his sable colours, like a black-plumed warrior, upon his head, the 'duke' displays his sables more like a mantle, about his back and wings. The 'stone-knocker' is the very mason of his tribe: he is fond of rivers and mountain streams, and will peck, peck, the very granite with his bill, till he finds a hole to his taste, and then he makes himself happy and brings home his love.   .

Knowing little about entomology, I have had recourse to Mr. Polwhele, to see what help he could give me; and as common insects are not grand enough to be named after such a catalogue as Bob and his kindred have afforded in the feathered tribe, I shall only say that Mr. Polwhele declares of insects that he is acquainted with none here which are not common to other counties, unless it be the stag beetle, and the mole cricket. He gives a very full and a curious account of both these insects. And here I may observe that the cricket's cry, which I believe in all other counties is considered a cheerful and a welcome note, the harbinger of joy, is deemed by our peasantry ominous of sorrow and evil. The *phalæna pavonia,* or 'emperor moth,' has been seen sporting and showing his magnificent wings on the boundary walls of the Abbey in our garden.[7]

---

[7] A beetle of the most rare kind has lately been discovered in the woods of Walreddon, about two miles from Tavistock. It is said to be the only specimen of this peculiar sort that has ever been found in England. I made a note of its name, but have mislaid it.

I must not venture upon any account of the finny tribes; for so little did I know about them that till I read Walton's *Angler* (which almost made me long to go a-fishing myself in our streams) I scarcely knew what kind of fish inhabit rivers only, and not the seas. And having no taste for fish, it is merely by the report of others that I can assure you our trout are as fine as trout can be; and that the rivers on the Moor abound with them in such plenty, that good old Izaak, or your friend Sir Humphry Davy, would have delighted to throw a fly along their banks. We have too salmon in abundance; and we have likewise the old story, common to all salmon countries, that the ''prentices' in former times used to make it a part of the bargain in their indentures not to be obliged to dine off salmon more than five times a week.

Our reptiles, saving one, are known by their general names, none having provincial ones, excepting the snake, and he is called the 'long-cripple;'[8] but why or wherefore is more than I know. Toads we have in abundance; they principally frequent the pools in this county. I remember a fine fat one, that was long an inhabitant of a hole under the ancient still-house of the Abbey in our garden; and so fearless was he, that in my favourite walk to this spot he would pop out of his hole, squat himself down in the middle of the path, and look at me as if he were a sentinel keeping watch before the old tower. He had very large bright eyes; and was, I can vouch from long acquaintance, as beautiful and as civil as a toad could be. Mr. Bray once observed one of these reptiles under a hedge with a monstrous snake coiled round

[8] Perhaps from long creeper.

him, but whether to exert his powers of fascination upon the poor toad, or to do battle with him, Mr. Bray could not determine. Mr. Polwhele gives a curious account of a toad that inhabited a hole before the hall door of a Mr. Arscott of Tetcott, in this county, which, during the space of thirty years, was a familiar friend with that gentleman, and would feed from his hand.

We have several species of lizards. The eft and the long cripple are also common here; and as to vipers, only take a ramble on Dartmoor on a very hot day, and you will see more of such reptiles than, I will venture to say, you have ever seen before or would wish to see again. I never venture there without putting on a good pair of stout boots; and I would advise all my female friends who may be enthusiastic in search of the picturesque to follow my example; since the finest scenery of the Moor is to be found amidst the wild and hidden valleys and the broken rocks, where vipers most abound. To go among them as guarded as possible against being bitten will be found a necessary precaution.[9]

I have now, I believe, named our principal reptiles. Under what class the bat is to be ranked I do not know; for though it has wings it is not a bird; and as it does not crawl it can hardly be called a reptile. But I mention it here because the remains of the Abbey, beautifully hung with ivy, abound with the finest bats I have ever seen. They sometimes come into our house. One, with a noble pair of horns, (that reminded me of the horned-head dress worn by the ladies in the time of Henry IV., when they were obliged to heighten the doors at court to give them

---

[9] The labourers on the Moor, particularly the peat-cutters, swathe their legs with ropes of straw to guard against the vipers.

free passage) we caught at night; and as I wished more particularly to examine it by daylight, I put my prisoner into the warming-pan, to secure him for that purpose. Next morning, when I gently raised the lid, no bat was to be found; and as nobody knew anything about the matter, it was settled by universal consent in our kitchen, that either a '*pisgy*' had let him out, or that with his horns he had pushed up the lid and effected his own escape.

LETTER XVIII.

TO ROBERT SOUTHEY, ESQ.

Vicarage, Tavistock, June 9th, 1832.

I PURPOSE giving you in this letter some slight account of the few vestiges of those ancient customs which still linger in their decay, not only on Dartmoor, but throughout this neighbourhood. My reason for introducing them here is that I consider they derive their origin from British times.

Many of the sacred solemnities of the Druids were

observed on particular days. Amongst these was the
festival of the god Belus, or Bel, on the first of May.
I have before noticed that on the Moor we have Bel
Tor, commonly pronounced by the peasantry Bellé
Tor; thus adding the vowel to the termination of the
word, as they do in the name of the Forest itself,
which they often call Dartémoor. It is, perhaps, the
ancient pronunciation; for we find Chaucer accents
the *e.* When speaking of a native of a Devonshire
town, he says—

> "For wel I wot he was of Dartémouth."

I have no doubt that on Mayday, sacred to Bel, or
the Sun, his tor on Dartmoor exhibited all the rites
and ceremonies due to the worship of that god.
There on its summit in all probability the cairn fires
were kindled, as victims were immolated, and the
earliest fruits and blossoms of the earth received the
benediction of the priest. It is not improbable that
the spring season of the year was chosen for the high
festival of the Sun, in order to celebrate his renewed
power, since he might then be considered as beginning
to dispense his warmer beams to raise the seeds of
the ground in promise of the future harvest. Many
august ceremonies were likewise observed on Mayday-
eve. Toland gives a very curious account of the
'Beltan fires' that in his time were still kindled on a
heap of stones, called a cairn in many parts of Ireland,
whilst the peasantry danced and sang round the
flames.

In the counties of Cornwall and Devon, 'May fires'
were long numbered amongst the sports of Mayday,
though I believe in *our* county they are now fallen
into total oblivion. So likewise is that very ancient

custom with the peasantry of the Moor, to collect
together a quantity of straw, to pile it up on one of
the heaps of stone, and then setting fire to it to force
their cows to pass over the expiring embers, in order
to make them fruitful in milk, and to preserve them
from disease during the rest of the year. As nothing
has been heard of this custom of late years I conclude
it is extinct ; but can there be a doubt that it was a
vestige of the sacrificial rites to the god Bel ? And
this opinion is confirmed by the circumstance of the
Druids sacrificing on Mayday-eve a spotted cow.
" It was the season in which British mythology commemorated the egress from the ark ; the place where
this cow was sacrificed afforded rest to the deified
patriarch, who is here styled Ysadawn, the consumer." [1]

The cuckoo's note was hailed by the British priesthood as the harbinger of the sacrifices of Mayday-
eve. With the Devonians the cuckoo is still an
ominous bird ; since to hear him for the first time on
the left hand—as I did this year—is considered a
marvellous sign of ill luck. Some unlettered muse
of our county has thus, truly enough, expressed his
peculiarities in rhyme—

> " In the month of April,
> He opens his bill ;
> In the month of May,
> He singeth all day ;
> In the month of June,
> He alters his tune ;
> In the month of July,
> Away he doth fly."

Mayday is still celebrated in the West of England,
though not so gaily as it used to be some years ago,
when I have heard my husband say the milkmaids of

[1] DAVIES's *British Mythology.*

this place would borrow plate of the gentry to hang upon their milk-pails, intermixed with bunches of ribands and crowns of flowers. It is, I believe, universally allowed that no custom has a higher claim to heathen antiquity than the erection of a May-pole, garlanded with flowers, as the signal-post of mirth and rejoicing for the day. These May-poles have, I believe, of late years, experienced some change; in former times they were often stationary; now, we generally see only the verdant pyramid crowned with flowers. This pyramid joins the procession, and sometimes even the dance; it receives its motion from having concealed within it a good stout fellow, strong and tall enough to perform the part for the day. 'Jack-in-the-bush' is his name; and he has existed (so am I told) as long as the May-pole itself.

Robin Hood, St. George and the Dragon, Maid Marian, the Hobby-horse and the ladle, have long been forgotten with us, though once so famous in the West. Yet I cannot pass the mention of the Hobby without venturing a conjecture of my own respecting his origin, which differs from the generally-received opinion. The antique Hobby, like the present May-pole, was formed by a man being dressed up, so as to disguise his humanity, with a pasteboard head resembling that of a horse, decorated with a real mane, and the performer could also boast a real tail. He was in fact made to look as much like a four-footed animal as a biped could possibly be made to do. Ribands, gilt paper, and gaudy flowers were disposed about him by way of decoration, and the ladle stuck in the mouth of the horse received the donation pennies of the boys and girls, to be spent in keeping up the sports. This Hobby was very gay and gorgeous, and hence have we, in all probability, the common saying of 'as fine as the horse,' to express extravagant decoration in the dress of an individual. This is the grotesque figure to which Hamlet alludes when he exclaims, "Heigho! the Hobby-horse is forgot;" and well might he do so, for it was falling into neglect even in the days of Elizabeth, though it survived in the West longer than in any other part of the kingdom.

Now this Mayday Hobby, with all submission to the learned, I cannot help thinking has a claim to much higher antiquity in its origin than they are pleased to assign to it; and that it is nothing less than a vestige, or figure rather, of the *sacred horse*, dedicated to Bel, the god of the Sun, on the first of May, by the British Druids. The custom, no doubt, came from the East, as did most customs of the Celtic nations. Dedicating horses to the Sun is spoken of even in the Bible; where we are told that the good King Josiah, who destroyed the groves of the idolatrous priests, took away the *horses they had dedicated to the Sun.* Tacitus also, in describing the manners of the ancient Germans, mentions the neighing of the *sacred horses*, as being consulted for the purposes of divination by priests and kings. The Saxons, before their conversion to Christianity, devoted horses to Odin, as a more noble offering than that of pigs sacrificed to Frea his wife. And, however impatient the Roman Catholics may be at the mention of it, there is nothing more certain than that many of the customs and ceremonies of their church were borrowed from the idolatrous rites of the ancient heathens. That custom, so frequent in the ages of chivalry, of

offering at the altar the horse of the victor, in all
probability derived its origin from pagan antiquity.
Many instances of such offerings might be cited;
one or two will here suffice.

There must have been something very noble in
such sights as were presented by the offerings in
question: when Philippe de Valois, for instance,
after a great victory, entered the cathedral of Notre
Dame fully armed and mounted on his war-horse,
as he moved slowly on, surrounded by the solemn
assembly of priests and warriors, whilst emblazoned
banners waved above his head, and the flame of a
thousand tapers glanced amidst column and fretted
arch, to offer up his arms and his horse to 'Our Lady
of Victory.'   So likewise at the funeral of the valiant
Gaston Phœbus Count de Foix, his horse and arms
were solemnly offered at the altar of Orthes, and
were afterwards redeemed for a large sum in gold.

To return to the Druidical festivals of the West.
That we have still some vestiges of that sacred to
Godo, the British Ceres, (so frequently mentioned in
the ancient poems of the bards) whose rites were
observed at *the time of harvest*, cannot I think be
doubted.   And as I have myself witnessed these, I
can speak with more confidence on the subject.
The few following particulars will be found not unworthy the notice of the antiquary.

One evening, about the end of harvest, I was
riding out on my pony, attended by a servant who
was born and bred a Devonian. We were passing
near a field on the borders of Dartmoor, where the
reapers were assembled. In a moment the pony
started nearly from one side of the way to the other,
so sudden came a shout from the field which gave

him this alarm.   On my stopping to ask my servant
what all that noise was about, he seemed surprised
by the question, and said, "It was only the people
making their games, as they always did, to the *spirit
of the harvest.*"   Such a reply was quite sufficient to
induce me to stop immediately, as I felt certain here
was to be observed some curious vestige of a most
ancient superstition ; and I soon gained all the information I could wish to obtain upon the subject.
The offering to the 'spirit of the harvest' is thus
made.

When the reaping is finished, toward evening the
labourers select some of the best ears of corn from
the sheaves ; these they tie together, and it is called .
the *nack.*   Sometimes, as it was when I witnessed
the custom, this nack is decorated with flowers,
twisted in with the reed, which gives it a gay and
fantastic appearance.   The reapers then proceed to
a *high place* (such, in fact, was the field on the side
of a steep hill where I saw them) and there they go,
to use their own words, to 'holla the nack.'   The
man who bears this offering stands in the midst,
elevates it, whilst all the other labourers form themselves into a *circle* about him ; each holds aloft his
hook, and in a moment they all shout, as loud as
they possibly can, these words, which I spell as I
heard them pronounced, and I presume they are
not to be found in any written record. 'Arnack,
arnack, arnack, we*h*aven, we*h*aven, we*h*aven.'²   This

----

² "*A knack*," says Fosbroke, "is a curious kind of figure, hung
up and kept till the next year." Thus we have in Shakspere—"A
knack, a toy, a trick, a baby's cap." I venture, also, to consider that
'*wehaven*' is a corruption of *wee ane,* 'a little one,' or child.—See
JOHNSON's *Dict.,* *wee.* For this note and the following I am indebted
to Mr. Bray. He suggests that *Pixy* may be derived either from *pix*

is repeated three several times; and the firkin is handed round between each shout, by way I conclude of libation. When the weather is fine, different parties of reapers, each stationed on some height, may be heard for miles round, shouting as it were in answer to each other.

The evening I witnessed this ceremony, many women and children, some carrying boughs, and others having flowers in their caps or in their hands or in their bonnets, were seen, some dancing, others singing, whilst the men (whose exclamations so startled my pony) practised the above rites in a ring. When we recollect that in order to do so the reapers invariably assemble on some *high place*, that they form themselves into a *circle*, whilst one of their party holds the offering of the finest ears of corn in the middle of the ring, can we for a moment doubt this custom is a vestige of Druidism? The man so elevating the offering is, in all probability, no other than the successor of the priest, whose duty it was to offer up the first and best fruits of the harvest to the goddess who fostered its increase, as his brother priests formed about him that *circle* which was held sacred in the forms and offices of religion; and I cannot but conclude that we have not throughout the whole kingdom a more curious rite derived from Pagan antiquity, than the one just mentioned on the borders of Dartmoor.

or *pax*, possibly both, as these words have been confounded by no less a lexicographer than Johnson. *Pix* signifies "a little chest or box, in which the consecrated host is kept in Roman Catholic countries;" and *Pax* "a sort of little image, a piece of bread, having the image of Christ upon the cross on it; which the people, before the Reformation, used to kiss after the service was ended, that ceremony being considered as a *kiss of peace*. 'Kiss the *pax*, and be quiet with your neighbours.' CHAPMAN'S *Comedy of May Day* (1611)."

I do not here allude to the mode of charming adders with the ashen bough or wand, still practised on the Moor, because I have before spoken at large on that subject. A few other customs though less striking in their character merit some attention, as they all help to throw light on that obscurity which involves the earliest ages in the history of this part of England.

We know from ancient writers that the British priesthood held sacred many plants, herbs, and trees. Their reverence for the all-heal or mistletoe is too universally known to require being noticed here. But it is not a little remarkable that the common people of Dartmoor, and indeed throughout all this neighbourhood, hold in great reverence many herbs, which they use to cure divers diseases, accompanying their applications, even as did the Druids, with sundry mystical charms in barbarous verse. Nothing can be more barbarous than the rhymes that compose them; and these are used over many of their decoctions from herbs that are really medicinal. The names by which such decoctions and herbs are known would puzzle a better botanist than I shall ever be; since who, for instance, would ever guess what was meant by 'organs tea,' an excellent potation for a cold, and here much in request. Other names equally strange could I repeat, if by any possibility I could guess what letters of the alphabet when put together would produce any word to express similar uncouth sounds.

I have been charmed myself, though against my will, by the good-natured assiduity of an old servant, who when I was suffering from inflammation in the eyes determined to cure me by one of these heathenish rites. Mr. Courtenay, of Walreddon House, in this neighbourhood, was also charmed for the same complaint by an old woman who exercised her skill upon him without his permission; and as he has never since been troubled with his old disorder, the cure is duly ascribed to successful magic by the vulgar.

Divested of their superstitions we have, indeed, in this town and neighbourhood many useful elderly women, who act not only as charmers but as nurses; and who, with a little more instruction, might become as serviceable as that most praiseworthy and respectable of all the religious orders of the Church of Rome—the Nuns of Charity. The charms which they hold in such estimation are carefully handed down from one generation to another. This is done by a woman communicating the secret of these mysteries to a man, or a man to a woman, as the most likely means of preserving them in their full efficacy; now and then, however, they tell the secret to one of their own sex. Here is a barbarous string of rhymes to stop an effusion of blood:

> " Jesus was born in Bethlehem,
> Baptized in river Jordan, when
> The water was wild in the wood,
> The person was just and good,
> God spake, and the water stood,
> And so shall now thy blood—
> ' In the name of the Father, Son,' &c."

If a man or woman has been injured by a scald or burn, then shall the charmer place her hand gently on the hurt, and in a soft voice shall say—

> " Three angels came from the north, east, and west,
> One brought fire, another brought ice,
> And the third brought the Holy Ghost,
> So out fire and in frost.
> ' In the name,' &c."

But these are Christian charms, grafted no doubt on heathenish superstitions. There are others, however, more decidedly of Pagan origin.

The apple-tree, brought into this country by the Romans, was soon held in almost sacred estimation by the Britons; it is frequently referred to as symbolical by the Welsh bards.[3] Probably the reverence that was paid to it might have arisen from the mistletoe being found to grow upon it as well as upon the oak.[4] On Christmas eve the farmers and their men in this part of the world often take a large bowl of cider with toast in it, and carrying it in state to the orchard, salute the apple-trees with much ceremony, in order to make them bear well the next season. This salutation consists in throwing some of the cider about the roots of the trees, placing bits of the toast on the branches; and then forming themselves into a ring, they, like the bards of old, set up their voices and sing a song, which may be found in Brand's *Popular Antiquities*.[5]

[3] " Hywell, the son of Owen, thus sings :—' I love in the summer season the prancing steeds of the placid-smiling chiefs; in the presence of the gallant Lord who rules the foam-covered nimbly-moving wave.' But another has won the token of the *apple-spray*, and Gwalchmai thus sings :—' The point of the *apple-tree* supporting blossoms, proud covering of the wood, declares—everyone's desire tends to the place of his affections.'"—DAVIES's *Bards*.

[4] On reading this letter, Mr. Southey made the following note:

" Mistletoe is so rare upon the oak, that a reward was offered for discovering it there some five or six and thirty years ago, by the Society of the Adelphi, I believe. It was found (and the prize obtained for it) at a place called the Boyse, in Gloucestershire, on the borders of Herefordshire, and there I saw it."

[5] Brand mentions the custom of saluting the apples as still practised in Cornwall and Devon. He gives two of the songs thus :—

" Here's to thee, old apple-tree,
Whence thou may'st bud, and whence thou may'st blow !
And whence thou may'st bear apples enow !

The last of October was, however, the principal, and indeed the most terrific day of all Druidical festivals: and truly may it also be called one of craft; since on that day every person was compelled to extinguish all fire in his house, and come to the priest, in order to obtain from him a consecrated brand, taken from the altar, to renew it. But if any begged this without having previously paid whatever might be due to the priest, it was denied to him, and the terrific sentence of excommunication pronounced. This sentence consigned the miserable defaulter to a lingering death from cold and hunger. His cattle were seized; he had no fire to cheer his home or to dress food for his subsistence, or to warm him in the depth of winter, whilst surrounded by frosts and snows. No friend, kindred, or neighbour, was allowed to supply him with fire, under pain of incurring the like cruel sentence. Never surely did an idolatrous priesthood invent a more certain or more cruel means of enforcing their extortions.

To beg fire at the doors of the rich on the last day of October, when the gift was generally accompanied by some trifling donation in money, I have somewhere read, was with the poor formerly a custom in the western parts of England, as well as in Wales. It is now, I believe, wholly extinct. But on old Midsummer-day, the farmers of the Moor ride about,

> Hats full! caps full!
> Bushel—bushel—sacks full,
> And my pockets full too! Huzza!"

The other song runs thus:—

> "Health to thee, good apple-tree
> Well to bear, pocket-fulls, hat-fulls,
> Peck-fulls, bushel-bag-fulls."

This last is, I understand, the song of this neighbourhood on observing the custom.

and lay hands on all the stray cattle or sheep they can find; these are consigned to the Pound; and they receive so much per head for all thus found.

The decay of ancient customs on Dartmoor is mainly to be attributed to what are considered its improvements. The chief amongst these was the erection of the French Prison. I have been told it was calculated to contain ten thousand prisoners; if this statement is correct or not I cannot say. The building also of Prince Town, Tor Royal, the mansion of Sir Thomas Tyrwhitt, and other habitations belonging to persons of property and influence, are all things that have helped to civilize the peasantry of the Moor, and to root out in a great degree their ancient superstitions; though, I believe, in no part of England has the march of intellect been at a slower pace than on the Moor. Many of its inhabitants cannot read; they speak the broadest Devonshire; but are in their general character a simple and honest race, and as hardy as the aboriginal inhabitants of the soil.

Since writing the above, I have been favoured with some few particulars respecting our animals in this neighbourhood, from a friend who is well known amongst us on account of his talents and worth—the Rev. Thomas Johnes, Rector of Bradstone, Devon. This gentleman, for whom we entertain a very high regard, to the pursuits of a scholar unites those of a naturalist, and has a feeling command of his pencil in the delineation of our scenery. Whenever you honour us with a visit at Tavistock, we hope to take you to see his beautiful collection of birds. These he stuffed himself, and in a manner superior to any I ever yet saw elsewhere; for he has been most happy in giving such a position to each as best to convey an idea of the action of the bird. Many of them are very beautiful; one hawk I particularly remember, with its prey; it looks as if it had at the instant darted upon it and grasped it in its talons.

Mr. Johnes thus begins his letter to me:—"At last I have summoned resolution to send you the long-promised account of the animals of this county. I anxiously hope that you will not be disappointed; and I am sure you will treat me with all due consideration when you reflect how confined and hackneyed is the subject which I have handled. . . . . The different species of four-footed animals, natives of this country, are so few in number, and for the most part so familiar to the sight, that a particular description of each, or a lengthened detail of their habits and manners, would be superfluous.

"The effect of that variety of soil and climate, which is a striking peculiarity of the district you have undertaken to describe, is most conspicuous in the breeds of domesticated quadrupeds: the wild sorts preserve their distinctions of size and form pretty constantly wherever they are found in this kingdom. Having first noticed the few varieties of domestic quadrupeds which are the produce of this district, I shall add such remarks on the others as are furnished by my own observations and the experience of credible friends.

"The Dartmoor pony is usually about twelve hands and a half in height, coarse in its form, but surprisingly spirited and hardy. The late Edward Bray, Esq., of Tavistock, reared great numbers of these horses, which were disposed of at an annual sale held on the Moor. Since the death of that gentleman the breed is become almost extinct.

"The North Devon breed of oxen, in great purity, is the common neat stock of this country. Its excellence consists in the superiority of its fatting quality. Heifers or cows of three and four years old are preferred for feeding; and they are fit for the market in the short period of twenty weeks. They are not much esteemed for the dairy, yielding but a small quantity of milk, and not of the richest quality. There is great symmetry in their form, and an appearance of high breed, but they are apt to be too long in the legs, and too flat in the ribs.

"The Dartmoor sheep, which produces the well-known Okehampton mutton, is a small breed weighing about fourteen pounds per quarter. They are kept on the Moor during the summer, and the cheapness of their feed, which amounts to twenty pence a score for that season, and from seven to nine pence for the winter, makes it profitable to the farmer to keep large flocks of them, principally for the sake of their wool, which averages seven pounds a fleece. Their superior flavour may be ascribed principally to the nature of the animal, and partly to the circumstance of their being killed at a more mature age than is usual in other places. By no means can it be attributed to the herbage of the Moor, which is exceedingly coarse and deficient in nourishment.

"The red deer, called in Devonshire the forester, or forest deer, was once abundant in the extensive woods on the banks of the Tavy and the Tamar, and many packs of stag-hounds were kept in the neighbourhood.[6] The hall in the manor-house of Bradstone

---

[6] So numerous were the red deer in this immediate neighbourhood, that the late Mr. Bray often mentioned that he could recollect, in the time of the then Duke of Bedford's grandfather, the farmers petitioning

is still adorned with the trophies of this glorious chase, the skulls and horns of the forester forming an appropriate series of metopes round that ancient room. But it is long ago extinct. A solitary straggler now and then visits us from the North of Devon: one was seen in the woods of Hornacott Manor, on the banks of the Tamar, in the spring and summer of 1831.

"The otter is an inhabitant of all the rivers in this neighbourhood. The river Ottery, or Ottry, which rises in the parish of Otterham, and falls into the Tamar at Werrington, is supposed to derive its name from the numbers of these animals formerly found in it. The hunting of the otter is hereabouts a favourite and agreeable summer sport. It is necessary to commence at or before day-break, as the animal seldom moves in the day-time, and the heat of the sun quickly exhales the scent. It is a hardy and wary creature, very tenacious of life; and success in this sport can only be insured by men and dogs who have been long and well trained to it. Its couch is formed in the bank of a stream, and the access to it is under water: there is a vent-hole for air at some distance on the top of the bank; here it deposits its young, four or five in number. It weighs from eighteen to twenty pounds, though some have been killed weighing thirty pounds. The North Teign is at present the favourite resort of the otter, simply because it abounds in fish, which are not hindered from coming up from the sea by weirs, as is the case in most other of our rivers.

his Grace to get rid of them, on account of the injury they did to the crops. The Duke sent down his stag-hounds from Woburn, the finest chases took place, and the deer were extirpated. So glutted was the town with venison at the time, that only the haunches were saved, and the rest given to the dogs.

"The polecat, foumart, or fitch, is found everywhere hereabouts, but particularly in the neighbourhood of the large marshes, or, as they are very properly called, 'mires,' of Dartmoor: where, besides rabbits, rats, and birds, it preys on frogs and lizards; and even the remains of fish have been found in its lair. This was first noticed by Bewick, and it was confirmed by an old gamekeeper on the Moor, who thought this curious circumstance was first remarked by himself. All the animals of this tribe, from the stoat to the weasel, are fond of the neighbourhood of water; the sable is known to be amphibious, and a variety of this species, an inhabitant of North America, mentioned by Pennant, has obtained the name of 'the fisher.'

"Since the preservation of game has been attended to in this neighbourhood, the martin cat and others of its kin have become scarce. This weasel is of a dark brown colour, and the throat and belly are white, which distinguishes it from the pine weasel, whose breast is yellow. The latter animal, though rare in this kingdom, was not uncommon a few years ago in the plantations of Mr. Carpenter, in the parish of Milton Abbot.

"The stoat, vair, or vairy, is the commonest of the weasel tribe. The most remarkable circumstance concerning it is its winter change of garb from brown to white, when it is called the ermine. This change is not universal in our latitude, as brown stoats are found in the winter, and others with various degrees of white. The change commences at the lower part of the sides; and the last part which turns white is the forehead. It is singular enough that the males are most subject to this

change, a female white stoat, or ermine, being considered a rarity by the warreners.

"There is a pretty variety of the squirrel found
hereabouts, which differs from the common sort in
having the tail or brush and the pencils of the ears
of a yellowish white. I hear they are common about
Kingston Hall, in Dorsetshire.

"Of the fox there are two sorts natives of this
country—the greyhound fox and the cur fox. The
greyhound fox is found on Dartmoor, where it is
known by the name of the wolf fox, and has sometimes been met with of an extraordinary size. One
killed there a few years since, when stretched out
measured five feet from the middle claw of the fore
foot to the tip of the middle hind claw. A friend of
mine in this neighbourhood had a tame vixen fox
of the cur sort chained up about a hundred yards
from his house. During the first spring of her con-
finement she was visited by a dog-fox, and in due
season brought forth six cubs. The male appeared
fully sensible of the captivity of his mate, and with
very substantial gallantry supplied her with abundance of food, as the items of her larder for one
night will show.

> One full-grown hare;
> Eight young rabbits;
> Six moles.

What a supper! He seems never to have meddled
with feathered game, though the neighbouring covers
abounded in pheasants. The same thing was repeated
in the following spring.

"The badger is common, and used here for the
cruel sport of baiting. Its skin is exceedingly thick
and tough. I once dissected a badger which had

been baited for three days, during which it killed several dogs, and was at last itself killed by a large mastiff; yet I could not detect a single perforation of the skin, though there was a great deal of extravasated blood, pointing out the parts which had suffered most from dogs. Its stomach contained only moles' fur. The badger is the fox's pioneer— the latter seldom, perhaps never, digging a hole for himself. When pressed for a habitation, the fox fixes on the hole of a badger, and ejects the owner by a certain nameless process, most offensive to the delicate senses and cleanly habits of the badger. A keen sportsman of this neighbourhood has made an ingenious use of the instincts of these two animals in order to stock his preserves with foxes. He tethers a badger to a suitable spot in his plantations, where it soon digs a convenient domicile, the badger is then removed, and a young fox put in full possession of the kennel.

"We have two kind of rats, the water-rat and the brown Norway rat. It was remarked more than two hundred years ago by an historian of the adjoining county[7] that, 'of all manner of vermine, Cornish houses are most pestered with rats; a brood very hurtful for devouring of meat, clothes, and writings by day; and alike cumbersome through their crying and rattling while they daunce their gallop gallyards in the roofe at night.' This was said of the black rat, which has been exterminated by the brown or Norway rat, of which we may truly say that it comes not a whit behind its predecessor either in daily rapine, or in the provoking cumbersomeness of its gallyarding by night.

7 CAREW, *Survey of Cornwall.*

"We have mice—the dormouse, the house mouse, the shrew, called here the *screw*, the field-mouse, and the short-tailed field-mouse.

"I have noticed three species of bats; the short-eared bat, which is greyish dun; the long-eared bat; and a small bat with black nose and legs, and the fur of a reddish cast.

"The hedgehog is common. It is the same calumniated and ill-used animal here as in other places. And thus much for the quadrupeds of this district. The birds are more in number, and of greater variety and rarity. They will form the subject of my next communication."

So concludes Mr. Johnes; and as I have a short notice to add, from Mr. Bray's Journal of this year, respecting a few vestiges not hitherto mentioned on the Moor, I propose to send them with the copy of the bird letter, above promised, at some future opportunity.

LETTER XIX.

TO ROBERT SOUTHEY, ESQ.

The Birds of Dartmoor.

I HAVE great pleasure in now being able to convey to you. the following interesting letter, which I have just received from the Rev. T. Johnes, on the birds of this district.

" The Tors of Dartmoor, lofty though they be and desolate, are yet too accessible to afford shelter to the eagle or its eyrie. Dr. E. Moore, of Plymouth, indeed, mentions a pair which built some years since on Dewerstone Rock, near Bickleigh Vale, but he speaks from report only. The osprey, or bald-buzzard, is the only bird of this tribe known in Devonshire, where it is supposed by good ornithologists to be more frequently met with than in any other part of England. The common buzzard frequents the sea-coast in great numbers, where it breeds in the cliffs. The honey-buzzard occurs but rarely ; it has, however, been noticed on Dartmoor. The moor-buzzard is not uncommon. About August they are frequently found hawking about the cultivated lands, and near farm-houses. It is affirmed that kites were common in this district forty or fifty years ago. At present they are so rare that I have never seen one alive ; and but one, a very beautiful specimen, in the collec-

tion of the late W. Baron, Esq., at Tregear.[1] I was
told that they were frequently found in that neighbourhood. The goshawk is admitted into the fauna
of Devon on the authority of Dr. Tucker, of Ashburton, who says it has been found on Dartmoor.
The sparrow-hawk is one of the few hawks which do
not migrate, but stay here all the year. I have not
noticed the hen-harrier, or the ring-tail (its female) in
the winter months. The country people call it the
'furze-kite.'

"The kestrel, called here the 'wind-fanner' and
'windhover,' from its motion when hovering over the
same spot in search of its quarry, comes in great
numbers in the spring to breed in the lofty rocks of
Morwell and Carthamartha. In the latter place more
than fifty have been shot during one summer. Some
few remain all the year. I have dissected many, and
have never found any thing in the stomach but a
small green lizard, which I have not been able to
find alive. The hobby, called in falconry 'the lady's
hawk,' comes here in the spring, and builds in our
woods on the tops of high trees, but is not common.
This bird is a great destroyer of the lark, as noticed
by Willoughby. In the stomachs of two I found

[1] Mr. Bray, however, tells me that about thirty years ago a kite,
having one of its wings clipped, was kept for several years in his
father's garden. It was fond of placing itself on the steps of the
portico of the house, and not unfrequently, by pecking at their feet,
alarmed such strangers as would enter it. The feathers of its wing
having through neglect been suffered to grow, the bird was accustomed
to mount the walls of the garden, and thence to dart at those who
were in it: for some time no greater injury had been effected, but at
last, when Mr. Bray himself entered the garden, having perhaps
become more daring from impunity, it took a lower flight, and would
probably have struck him in the face had he not prevented it by
knocking it down with his stick.

nothing but the remains of that bird. Hence it was called by Johnson *accipiter alaudarius.* The merlin is sometimes seen here in October, but rarely. It probably escapes our notice by its small size and quickness of motion.

"Of owls we have four sorts, one of which is migratory, namely, the short-eared owl ; though I have found the long-eared owl only in the autumn and winter, and in the neighbourhood of moors. But Col. Montagu says they have been killed in summer. Of the short-eared owl I possess two specimens, a male and a female. The male is smaller than the female. They are found, I believe invariably, on the ground in long grass, and young fir plantations. I believe they migrate to England only occasionally, and then in considerable numbers. I have neither seen nor heard of one for several years. It is called also the woodcock-owl, from the time of its appearance. The brown owl is found in woods, and especially among rocks covered with ivy. It is common. The beautiful white owl, or barn owl, is common, and a useful friend to the farmer, by whom they are usually protected. They fly in the day-time, and in the breeding season the quantity of mice they destroy is prodigious. They prey three hours in the morning, and three in the evening, during which time each bird brings to its young, at the very lowest calculation, twenty-four mice, making the sum of three hundred and thirty-six in the course of one week, besides what it destroys for its own food. This bird, as well as the brown owl, hoots. This fact is clearly ascertained.

"The ash-coloured shrike is so very seldom seen in England, that it scarcely deserves to be called a British bird, but the red-backed shrike is common

enough in the summer.   It builds in hedges, frequently near a public road, and leaves us in autumn.

"Ravens, crows, daws, jays, magpies, and rooks,
are abundant in their several localities.   The latter,
though doubtless a useful bird to the farmer in general,
yet in dry springs is quite a nuisance.   Last year
they almost destroyed the potato crops in the neighbourhood of a large rookery, by digging up the seed,
which the looseness of the earth permitted them to
do with ease.   The Royston crow is found on the
sea-coast in the winter.

"Starlings come here in September, and are found
in company with the rooks in the beginning of the
season.   In December and January they are in vast
numbers about the grass fields, but leave us in the
latter end of January or the beginning of February.
They do not breed hereabouts.

"The ring-ouzel visits Dartmoor in April, where it
breeds, and departs in the beginning of November.
The cock is a very restless and wary bird.   His
spring call, which consists of two notes repeated four
times with a short pause, is incessant ; while the hen
is sitting he sings mornings and evenings delightfully,
and is then very daring.   The nest is frequently
found in the side of a 'turf tye,' that is, a pit from
which they dig turf for fuel.

"The missel-thrush is common, and in August they
are seen in flocks of from twenty to thirty in the
fields where the 'beat' (that is, the slight layer of turf
which is spaded off the land) is burnt, preparatory to
ploughing for wheat.   It is singular that so shy a
bird should build its nest in such open and frequented
places.   April 13, 1830, I found the nest of a missel-
thrush in the fork of a young apple-tree, about two

feet from the ground, in an exposed situation near the road leading to the house. It was composed on the outside of the stems of couch and other grasses, a mixture of clay, a little moss of the apple-tree, and lined with hay. It then contained one egg. The bird continued to lay every day regularly between nine and ten in the morning until Friday, April 18, and immediately began to sit. On that day and the following it was restless, and easily frightened from the nest, but afterwards sat very close until that day fortnight, May 2, when four young birds were produced. I could not discover what became of the other two eggs, though I searched the nest and the ground round the tree very closely. On the 9th of May they opened their eyes. The rapidity of their growth was amazing; the four quite filled the nest. Their feathers also grew so fast that they were completely flushed on Sunday, May 11, a small space under the pinions excepted. On the following day they left the nest. Thus the number of days occupied from the commencement of laying to the perfecting the young amounted to only thirty. I once saw a song-thrush which had been taken from the nest and kept in a cage for sixteen years; it then died. It was very grey about the head and back, and apparently died of old age.

"The wryneck is a rare bird here, but is found in sequestered spots near the Cornish moors, where there are large timber trees: this bird and the nuthatch are similar in their habits, but the latter does not migrate.

"I have been able to detect but two species of the woodpecker: the green, and the greater spotted; the first is common, but the other very rare.

"The hoopoe is sometimes met with in the autumn, but may be considered as a very rare wanderer: yet I have heard a gentleman of great respectability, and very observing, say that he many years ago saw the nest of this bird with four young ones, which was taken in the wood close to the house at Morwell, in the parish of Tavistock.

"The crossbill I believe to be very rare; for though we have many orchards, I have never heard of one in this neighbourhood; and yet in the eastern part of Cornwall, about Egloskerry, where orchards are scarce, it has been occasionally found in old fir plantations. The grosbeak is also rare: I have seen but one specimen, killed in November, 1828.

"The cirl-bunting is found, but always near the sea-coast; there it remains all the year, and changes its plumage in the autumn, so as to become more like the yellow-hammer. Some, however, come over from the Continent in the spring, as they are then found in greater numbers than in the winter.

"Linnets, buntings, and bullfinches are common, except the reed-sparrow, which is found on the reedy banks of the Tamar, below Morwell Rocks. The mountain-finch has been taken here, but only in severe winters. The rest of the tribe are common, except the siskin.

"The pied wagtail remains here during the winter. I have seen the grey wagtail on the Tamar in June; no doubt it breeds there. The redstart is uncommon; but there are certain spots where a pair is found every year. Some specimens are almost black on the back: the country folks call them 'fire-tails.'

"Sand-martins build on the Tamar in great numbers; I have seen them on the river Cary, in the early part of March. The latest swallow I have observed was on the first of December; it was apparently a young one, but very vigorous.

"The night-jar is not uncommon here; but I have nothing to record concerning it, except that I have never been able to find its nest.

"Ring-doves are very common. The turtle-dove is seen but rarely in the autumn, solitary. I have occasionally seen flocks of a middle-sized dark blue pigeon, amounting to.many hundreds, flying about the valley of the Tamar, in the latter end of autumn, the weather mild, but have never been able to procure one of them. They appear to be always on the wing in the day-time, flying very high in the air. ..

"Domestic poultry of every sort are most abundant, and very cheap; I have seen a goose, weighing nine pounds, sold in Launceston market for half-a-crown. Cart-loads are taken every week from Launceston to Devonport and Plymouth by the regraters.

"The pheasant has been introduced of late years by the Duke of Bedford, and Sir W. P. Call. The ring-necked variety is the most common. We have some partridges, and the quail is sometimes met with in the summer.

"Of the black grouse, some few still remain on Dartmoor, where they breed in the 'turf tyes.' All attempts to preserve this beautiful bird are unsuccessful. The great extent of the Moor, while it is the sole protection of a few individuals, renders it impossible to defend them from the depredations of the miners and turf-cutters who frequent the Moor.

"Of the great Norfolk plover (*edienemus*) a specimen was killed on Dartmoor, October 5, 1831, by F. Scoble Willesford, Esq.: it weighed seventeen ounces. This bird was a female. In the stomach we found the elytra and legs of a small black beetle. It is seldom met with so far west, and was not known to the moor men. By the description given us, another had been shot a few days before at Widdecombe-in-the-Moor, probably the male of this.

"The lapwing and golden plover are common enough in the cultivated lands during the severity of winter: the former breeds in great numbers on all our moors; and the natives assured me that the golden plover bred in Fox Tor Mire, which is a vast and dismal swamp on Dartmoor.

"Ring dotterels are found in large flocks, in company with stints, &c., on the sea-coast, and in the estuary of the Tamar. The sandpiper retires in pairs to the interior, in the latter end of April, and is found on all the rivers of this country during the breeding season.

"The oyster-catcher is rather a scarce bird; but a few pairs are found, especially on the north coast, in the summer and autumn.

"The water-crake I have never seen; but the water-rail is very common, as is also the water-ouzel, which is found on all our rocky streams. Dr. Turner, as quoted by Ray, says that the rail he never saw nor heard of but in Northumberland. Hereabout it is not uncommon, and in the neighbourhood of Ivy-bridge three couple have been shot in one day by a single sportsman.

"The kingfisher is found in greatest numbers near the sea; they are rather uncommon far inland.

"I once saw a specimen of the spoonbill, which was taken in one of the creeks which communicates with Hakeavre.

"The bittern is very rare, and only met with in severe winters, such as that of 1831–32, when a great number were killed in this district. The curlew breeds on all our moors, and is found on our coast during the winter months. The whimbrel is not so common.

"I know but one heronry in this immediate neighbourhood, which is at Warleigh, the seat of the Rev. W. Radcliffe. In January, 1832, a waggoner passing over Whitchurch Down saw a large bird rise from the roadside close to him; he struck it down with his whip, and it was presented to me by C. Willesford, Esq., of Tavistock. The bird was evidently exhausted by fatigue and hunger. The following is its description:—Length two feet nine inches, breadth three feet six inches; bill six and a half inches, leg five and a half; middle toe, which is pectinated, five and a half; tail-feathers twelve; fore part of the head black; hind part of ditto rufous, the feathers forming a small crest. Back part of the neck rusty ash colour, front part of ditto white streaked with black, the streaks growing larger as they descend to the breast, where they are long and loose; these spots are formed by the feathers of the fore part of the neck having their inner webs black, the outer webs being white. The back is brown, each feather being edged with rust colour, as are also the greater and less wing-coverts. Quill feathers black, fading into rust colour on the inner web. Two inside toes webbed to the first joint. I find no description of heron with which this agrees so well as the purple heron (*Ardea purpurea*, Lin.) of which Montagu says, 'that not more than two of this species have been met with in this country.' It may, therefore, be considered as one of our rarest stragglers.

"A woodcock, weighing only seven ounces, was shot at Trebartha, in the year 1833: it was in very perfect plumage, and excellent condition. The common snipe and the dunlin breed on Dartmoor, but the jack snipe leaves us in the spring.

"Of what are usually called fen birds we have but few, and they are only met with occasionally, driven most probably out of their course, during their migration, by adverse winds. The water-hen is common on the Tamar; but the coot seldom visits us.

"The grey phalarope. This bird is very rare in the North of England, according to Bewick. Scarcely an autumn passes but I have a specimen or two sent me. Mr. Jackson, of East Looe, informs me that on October 27–28, 1831, heavy gale S.S.W., great numbers of the grey phalarope appeared on the coast, in flocks of about fifty each. They invariably alighted on the sea and swam with ease and elegance among the breakers, and darted to and fro after maggots and chrysalides. They were by no means shy, but appeared lean and fatigued.

"Baron-bills (called in Cornwall murres), guillemots, and puffins, or naths, abound on the north coast of Cornwall, about Boscastle and in the parish of St. Gennys. I saw a specimen of the great northern diver alive, in full plumage, at Plymouth, in the month of July, about twelve years ago. It was taken at sea by some fishermen, who were carrying it about as a curiosity. I do not recollect on what they fed it.

"The great imber is often seen on the coast in Whitsand Bay in the summer, and very high up the Tamar in winter. Terns are often found on the sea-coast, and they have been killed on the Tamar.

"Of gulls, the great gull is rare. Out of the stomach

of one, answering to the description of the wagel, which Linnæus and Pennant treated as a distinct species, I took an entire redwing; an evidence of its indiscriminate voracity.

"*Larus canus*, the common gull. We have a curious emigration of these birds in the spring; they leave the sea-coast and appear in the grass lands in flocks of five, ten, or fifteen, in search of the caterpillars of beetles, which at that time are produced under the surface. The time of their appearance varies from February till March, and they disappear the beginning of May. It is to us the first harbinger of spring. It is called in some parts hereabouts the barley bird, from the time of its appearance at barley sowing, I suppose, as I never observed them alight anywhere but in the pastures.

"The goosander. This is so rare a bird, that Montagu, during the long period which he devoted to the study of ornithology in this county, 'never had the good fortune to dissect a single specimen.' Feb. 5, 1830, I dissected a male goosander, shot on the Tamar. I have the trachea in my possession; it corresponds with the description given by Willoughby. And on the 9th I dissected another, which resembled the former in every respect. At the same time I dissected a dundiver: it was a female: there was nothing remarkable in the trachea, excepting perhaps that it was a little wider and flatter at the upper part than at the divarication of the bronchia. These two last were killed at one shot by Mr. Walter Weeks, of Bradstone, out of a flock of seven goosanders and dundivers. The dundiver is found here, a single specimen or so, every winter.

There is still much obscurity concerning the history

Trachea of the Goosander.

Trachea of the Dundiver.

1 inch 8-10ths.

1 inch 6-10ths.

1 inch 4-10ths.

Length, 1 foot 6 inches.

Length, 1 foot 2½ inches.

of these birds; some contending that the dundiver
is the female of the goosander, others that they are
of distinct species. In the year 1832 I dissected a
bird in the plumage of the dundiver. The trachea
(of which I have given a drawing) is so very different
from that of the goosander, that I cannot believe this
bird to be a young goosander in its immature plumage.
Still, however, we want the female of the goosander.
I am inclined to think, from the number of specimens
I have examined, that there are two sorts of birds with
the plumage of the dundiver, one very much larger than
the other, and of which I possess a specimen: this may
be the female of the goosander. The male of the
smaller species may continue in the same plumage
of the female without changing when at maturity.

"Of the smew or white nun, and the red-headed
smew or weasel-headed coot, I have seen specimens
shot on the Tamar far inland.

"In January, 1830, many wild swans were killed
in this district. In this severe season the common
wild goose was seen only at the beginning of winter.
When the frost set in severely, this bird, together
with the widgeon and others of the duck tribe, which
usually remain with us during the winter, retired
most probably further to the south, and were succeeded by the wild swan, the white-fronted or laughing
goose, the scaup, goosander, and the dundiver, birds
seldom seen in this latitude.

"The cormorant is not rare, but not so common as
the shag, which is numerous on the north as well as
the south coast. The gannet is sometimes taken by
the fishermen during the summer. Ray calls it a
Cornish bird."

So concludes Mr. Johnes's account of our birds.

LETTER XX.

TO ROBERT SOUTHEY, ESQ.

THE following letter, on a subject that I think you
will find of considerable interest, was addressed by
Mr. Bray to myself; and as I deem it better to send
it to you entire, instead of making any extracts from
it, I now therefore enclose it in this packet.

"TO MRS. BRAY.

" *Vicarage, Tavistock, March* 10, 1834.

"MY DEAREST ELIZA,—I fear that you almost suspected I should never fulfil my promise of giving you
some account of the inscribed stones connected with
this neighbourhood; and I fear yet more that the

account will rather *suffer* than *improve* by the delay. But such as it is I now present you with it, and leave you to present it to whom you may.

"Of the lettered obelisk I have lately erected in our garden, I have often heard you say, 'I wish it would speak, and tell me all the things it has either seen or heard, that I might note them down.' My reply has been, that were it to open its mouth it would but frighten you, and not only make you more nervous than you frequently are in your *speech*, but also in your *writing*. It certainly has been the silent witness of many pleasant conversations I have shared with you whilst walking in the garden; and thus much am I disposed to personify both it and its companions as to give some account (as far as I know) of their history, I had almost said of their biography.

"I will begin then with the stone last mentioned. And first, as I have transplanted it into my garden, and from no small distance, lest it should be thought indigenous to the soil, I will notice what I think I have heard botanists call its *habitat*, or place of its natural and possibly native abode; for as soon could I believe that Deucalion converted stones into men by throwing them behind him, as that any one previous to myself had incurred either the trouble or expense to convey such a cargo of stone-crop into his garden, without too the least prospect of being productive.

"Having learnt from Polwhele's *History of Cornwall* (for I had not then seen his *History of Devon*) that an inscribed stone existed at Buckland Monachorum, distant from Tavistock about four miles, I went thither on the 28th of September, 1804, with no other clue to its discovery than that it was 'close to the churchyard.' On my arrival at the village I inquired for the sexton, thinking that he was the most likely person to give me information. He could hardly, however, be convinced that the object of my search could be other than the monument then but lately erected in the church to the memory of the brave defender of Gibraltar, General Lord Heathfield; considered by some one of Bacon's best productions. And on my correcting him in this particular, he still perversely conjectured, from my asking about an inscription, that I sought from him a description of the church. But on using more familiar language, and describing it as a stone post with letters upon it, he smiled, and said, 'I suppose, Sir, that must be it behind your back.' · I turned round, and perceived the subject of my inquiry within a few paces from me. It served as a coigne to a blacksmith's shop, adjoining the entrance to the churchyard.

"In the course of the year 1831, (for I have mislaid my memorandum of it) on again visiting Buckland, I found that the blacksmith's shop had recently been taken down, and that the stone in question was lying with its inscription exposed towards the street, with the possibility of its being worn, if not obliterated, by every passing wheel. On applying to Sir Ralph Lopes, as lord of the manor, (intimating that I had already in my possession a stone of probably the same era) he most kindly made me a present of it. I sent therefore a waggon with three horses, together with what is here called a jack, an engine for lifting it. But I nearly ran the risk of sending them in vain; for the tenants then assembled at the Court Baron refused to let my servant touch it till, fortunately, the lord himself arrived, and removed the embargo.

It was brought by a circuitous route of more than five miles to avoid some precipitous hills, and erected, as before noticed, in my garden.

"It is a rude and rough pillar of granite, but certainly more picturesque than were it a more regular column. Besides, it is not only the more interesting from its resemblance to the consecrated stones or idols of our pagan ancestors, but also from its resemblance, by rising in a gently-sweeping line from the ground, and somewhat tapering at the top, to the trunk of a stately tree. The inscription also strengthens the similitude; as it may well be compared to those rustic letters carved, more with feeling than with art, on the bark of some venerable beech. Polwhele is of opinion that (as well as many others of the same description) it originally stood within the precincts of a pagan temple, where, in consequence of the reputed sanctity of the spot, was subsequently erected a Christian church. I hope, however, that I may not be accused of the guilt of sacrilege in removing it; for it certainly deserves a better fate than to be applied to such 'base uses' as to be a 'buttress,' or 'coigne of vantage' to the 'castle' of any modern Mulciber; nay, what is worse, than to be laid prostrate in the street. It might even at best have been appropriated to the purpose of a gate-post, as is actually the case with another inscribed stone in the neighbourhood; and indeed (of which more hereafter) this, or something of a similar description, seems to have been its original destination: for even in the midst of the inscription is a cavity, in the form of an oblong square, which possibly may have been cut for the reception of a latch or bar. Its obelisk form is more apparent when viewed laterally ; as at the back, which is of a smoother and blacker surface, (probably caused by the contact of a contiguous stratum) it is rather acutely gathered to a point ; seemingly however more by Nature than by art.

"Polwhele, even in his *Devon*, presents us only with some few particulars as to the nature and dimensions of the stone, but not with the inscription. As he is not quite exact in the dimensions, I here give them. Its height, as it at present stands, is seven feet two and a half inches. Its breadth at the bottom is seventeen, at the top fourteen inches. From the top to the beginning of the inscription are two feet one and a half inch. And the cavity is eight inches long and two and a half deep.

"This and other similar monuments he imagines to have been Romano-British, and to have been erected to the memory of a 'Christianized Roman.' I should rather consider it as the memorial of a Romanized Briton, previous perhaps to the introduction of Christianity into this island. There is no cross, nor any request to pray for the soul of the departed, which are so commonly found on the sepulchral monuments of the early, or rather Romanized, Christians.

"The inscription may be read (*Sepulchrum, sive memoriæ*) SABINI FILII MACCODECHETII. Of which the translation, I conceive, may be '(The grave, the gravestone, or to the memory) of Sabinus the son of Maccodechetius.' The Romans we know had usually three names—the *prænomen*, the *nomen*, and the *cognomen*. The *prænomen*, answering to our *Christian* or *proper* name, marked the *individual ;* the *nomen* marked the *gens* or *clan*, consisting of several families ; the *cognomen* marked the *familia* or immediate family.

Thus in Publius Cornelius Scipio, Publius is the *prænomen*, Cornelius the *nomen*, and Scipio the *cog-*

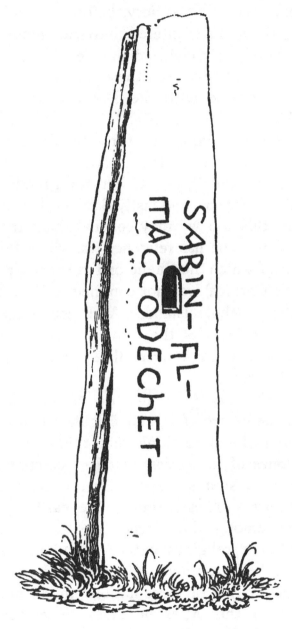

nomen. Sometimes there was also a fourth name, called the *agnomen*, added from some illustrious action or remarkable event. The Britons (as indeed the

Romans themselves) originally had but one name.
We may suppose, therefore, that this was erected at
a very early stage of society, before the Britons, in
imitating them, had entered into the more refined
distinctions of their civilized invaders. At the same
time it is evident that even these barbarians, previous
to any intercourse with the Romans, felt in some
degree the pride of ancestry : for in this very inscription, though containing but three words, are noticed
as many generations. Mac (as still in Scotch), signifying son, we have first Codechet, the grandsire, then
Maccodechet, his son, and lastly Sabinus, his grandson.
And from this too we may conclude that the period
to which this stone has reference was when the Celtic
language (of which the Gaelic or Erse is but a dialect,
as also the Cornish) was not confined to Scotland, but
pervaded the whole island. And, according to the
opinion of antiquaries, the Celtic, at the time of the
Roman invasion, was universally spoken all over the
West of Europe.

"From the cavity or mortise above alluded to,
nearly in the centre of it, and calculated to receive a
bar, I am inclined to think that this might be one
of the stones of an ancient barrier; erected not improbably at a spot set apart for the celebration of
public games. These, among the earliest nations,
and even among the Greeks and Romans, were
generally of a religious nature. And as the Celts
are now, I believe, universally admitted to be more
ancient than either of these nations, might not, I ask,
the circus of the latter be taken from the Celtic
circle, and their *stadium* or *cursus* from the Celtic
avenue or parallelitha ?

"We first hear of this stone, where perhaps it was

originally placed, at Buckland Monachorum, or Monks'
Buckland, and close to the churchyard. Now we
know that in the early ages of Christianity spots
already sacred were generally chosen on which to
erect a church, that the heathen might thus be the
better conciliated to a change of religion.

"Whether for the purpose of showing him greater
honour, or because it was at hand, and on that
account made use of, it is not unlikely that the
Romanized Britons dedicated this stone, at his death,
to the memory of one who was descended from those
their Celtic ancestors, by whom it had originally been
erected. It is evident, I think, that it could not have
been converted to the purpose of a gate-post (as is
another stone in that neighbourhood) subsequent to
the inscription; as the letters, by being lessened in
size, have been made to accommodate themselves to
the interruption occasioned by the cavity. Nor is it
likely that so large and lofty a stone would originally
have been selected for a common gate-post, whilst, on
the other hand, its size and height would naturally
have recommended it in constructing a grand barrier
by which to regulate the public games.

"There is a stone, probably of about the same era
as the preceding, which may be found by following
the lane leading from the Rock on Roborough Down
to Buckland Monachorum, till you come to a turning
on the right hand that will bring you to a field of
which it forms the gate-post. I am thus particular in
my directions, as in searching for it myself I rambled
without success for miles, and that too for several
days, having received no other information than that
it was a stone in a hedge near Roborough Down.

"The inscription contains three names; but it may

be doubted whether they all are the names of individual persons, or whether one may not be of a professional, and another of a national description.

"Various interpretations have suggested themselves.

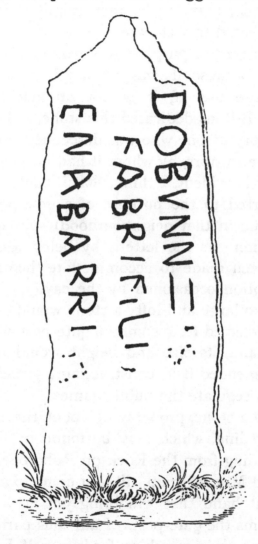

Some of these I shall mention, and leave the reader to determine for himself.

"The gravestone—'Of Dobunnius Faber, the son of Enabarrus.'

"'Of Dobunnius the smith,' &c.

"'Of Faber, one of the Dobuni,' &c.

"Faber, in later ages, was no uncommon name. But I am not aware of any nearer approximation to it among the Romans themselves than Fabricius. A skilful workman in any art (and more particularly in metal, for *faber* has more especial reference to a smith or worker of iron) would be of such paramount importance in barbarous ages, that his trade or occupation would naturally become not only an addition to, but in itself a proper name. And probably it is so in the present instance. Indeed there is still no name more common than Smith in our own language. And it is no less probable that the first name in the inscription is that of his people; as Dobunnius alone, without adding 'the smith,' would be a sufficient designation, particularly as he is also stated to be the son of Enabarrus; and few persons it may be supposed, unless they were chieftains themselves or the sons of chieftains, would be honoured with any monument at all. Nor is it likely that, were there two names, the first would have been British and the second Roman, but *vice versâ*, out of compliment to their masters. And here I must be allowed to add—as possibly throwing some light on the date and perhaps also connexion of these stones in point of time, as they certainly were in regard to place—that Sabinus, to whom the former was erected, might have been so called in compliment to a Roman officer of that name, the brother of Vespasian, who was afterwards emperor. These, with others under Aulus Plautius, commanded the army consisting of four complete legions, with their auxiliaries and cavalry, making about fifty thousand men, which was sent, A.D. 43, by Claudius into Britain.[1]

[1] See HENRY, vol. i. p. 30.

"If, instead of being a variety in spelling, the redu-
plication of N signifies the genitive plural, namely
Duboniorum, the figure ⊏⊐ might purposely be used
for two instead of II., lest the latter should be taken
for the genitive singular of a person. As there seems
to be some trace of letters at the end of the first line,
these might indicate that he was of the second cohort
of the Dobuni. Cohort we know was often used in-
definitely for a band or company of any number of
men.

"Henry (p. 32) tells us that 'a part of the Dobuni
submitted to the Romans. These were probably the
subjects of Cogidunus, who became so great a favourite
of Claudius and succeeding emperors, for his early
submission and steady adherence to their interest.'
Also (vol. ii. p. 459 app.) : 'The second legion,
which was surnamed Augusta, or the August, came
into Britain A.D. 43, in the reign of Claudius, under
the command of Vespasian (who was afterwards
emperor) and continued here near four hundred years
to the final departure of the Romans. It was on this
account that this legion was also called Britannica, or
the British.' Camden says that 'The Cassii had
conquered the Dobuni before the arrival of Cæsar,
who made the prince of this country commander-in-
chief of the forces of the whole island.' Also—'The
Dobuni inhabited Gloucestershire and Oxfordshire.
Their name seems to be derived from *Duffen*, a British
word signifying deep or low, because inhabiting for
the most part a plain, and valleys encompassed with
hills. And I am the more induced to be of this
opinion, because I find that *Dion* calls these people
by a word of the same signification, *Bodunni*, if there
is not a transposition of the letters. For *Bodo*, or

Bodun, in the antient language of the Gauls, as Pliny informs us, doth signify *Deep*.'

"Whether therefore the name on this stone be that of an individual or of a nation, it certainly is of British origin. It is by no means improbable that the spot near which it stands (in the vicinity of Roborough Rock) might have been a military station for the Romans or their auxiliaries and allies, as from its elevation it commands an extensive horizon, including the beacons of Brent Tor and other tors on Dartmoor, and is also within a few miles of Tamerton, probably the ancient Tamare.

"The reader may possibly lament that he has wasted a few minutes in reading these observations; but let him know for his comfort that I have wasted many hours, not only in attempting to interpret, but even to decipher the inscription. In order to get what I believe is technically called 'a rubbing,' I have gone over and over again to the spot where the stone is situated, amply provided with silver paper, (it ought I am told to have been tea-paper) black-lead, and brushes of various kinds. But sometimes owing to the wind, and sometimes to the rain, I was never able to take any thing like an impression, and was forced, therefore, to content myself with different sketches in pencil, of which I have tried to select the best.

"With a hope of succeeding better at my leisure, and perhaps also with the assistance of the sun, when at a certain point in its course it would illumine only the surface, and throw the letters into shade, (as the inscription on Pompey's Pillar, in Egypt, which had so puzzled the French *sçavans*, was at last thus deciphered by some officers of our army) I set on foot a negociation for its transfer to my garden, as a companion to my two other stones. But though antiquarian covetousness was seconded by beauty, in the person of one of the daughters of Sir Anthony Buller, who resides near the spot, the farmer was inexorable, and it there remains as a gate-post to his field.

"I must be allowed to state that on the reverse of the inscription may be seen G. C. It will add but little to the presumption of my former conjectures if I venture to suggest whether this may not stand for Galba Cæsare. Servius Sulpicius, the seventh of the twelve Cæsars, was surnamed Galba, from the smallness of his stature. The word signifies 'a mite or maggot;' but according to some it implies, in the language of Gaul, 'fatness,' for which the founder of the Sulpitian family was remarkable. Galba was next succeeding emperor but one to Claudius, who will be found mentioned in the following extract from Henry (vol. i. p. 260): 'Cogidunus, who was at that time, as his name imports, prince of the Dobuni, recommended himself so effectually to the favour of the Emperor Claudius, by his ready submission, and other means, that he was not only continued in the government of his own territories, but had some other states put under his authority. This prince lived so long, and remained so steady a friend and ally to the Romans, that his subjects, being habituated to their obedience in his time, never revolted, nor stood in need of many forts or forces to keep them in subjection.' Perhaps the reader will good-naturedly admit, and be thankful for, the following lines of Shakspere by way of apology for this whimsical digression :—

"' Figures pedantical, these summer flies
Have blown me full of *maggot* ostentation :
I do forswear them.'

"My mind being not a little occupied with the inscription I had seen at Buckland, (not then even surmising that there was another near it, namely, the one last noticed) I asked my father, who was born and lived at Tavistock, if he had ever heard of any inscribed stone in our immediate neighbourhood. He said that about twenty years ago, presentment was made at the Court Leet of the Duke of Bedford, of a large stone forming part of the pavement of West Street, as a nuisance ; it having become so worn and slippery as to be dangerous to horses. As his Grace's agent, therefore, he had ordered it to be taken up, when, if his memory failed not, he thought he had seen letters on the under part of it. The stone, he added, had afterwards been placed as a bridge over the mill-leat near Head-weir. This weir is about half a mile distant from Tavistock, and crosses the river Tavy for the purpose of conveying a stream of water, here called a leat, to the parish mills.

"On visiting the spot I found the stone. Its smooth surface was still uppermost, and the bottom of it so close to the stream, that I could only get my hand under it, and on doing so, fancied that I felt letters. On the strength of this I caused it to be taken up, and found I had conjectured rightly. The letters, fortunately, had been twice preserved ; first from the friction of wheels and the tread of horses and passengers in the street ; and secondly, from the slower but scarcely less certain erosion of the passing waters. I resolved therefore to bring it to a place of greater safety ; and on October 22,

1804, about a month after I first visited the stone at Buckland, had it removed and placed by the side of the arch, then within the grounds of the Abbey house, and now within the precincts of the churchyard. This I the more particularly notice, as an engraving of it in this situation, has, I believe, appeared in a little topographical work called the *Antiquarian Cabinet.*

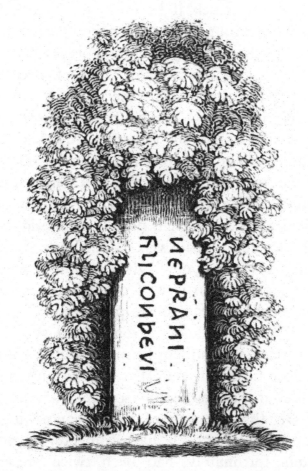

" On my quitting the Abbey house for the Vicarage, I brought it hither and placed it where now it stands, near the drawing-room window. Some of my friends, perhaps thinking it out of place, compared it to a sentinel. In some degree to obviate this, and to hide a defect not much in character with a soldier, namely what might be called a hunch back, (for the wheels, I suppose, had worn it into this shape) I planted at its foot some Irish ivy. This has so wonderfully increased, particularly at the top, that on cutting part of it away in front to render the inscription legible, it has assumed, curiously enough, the form of a sentry box. I felt loth, I confess, to cut away more of the ivy than was absolutely necessary for this purpose, from the circumstance that for many years a couple of blackbirds have built their nest there or frequented it; which is the more remarkable from their general shyness, and, seemingly at least, their aversion to the haunts of men.

"The inscription, as the first already noticed, contains the names of father and son; viz., 'Nepranus, the son of Condevus.' Some, perhaps, may be inclined to read Con*b*evus, as the fourth letter is more like our small b than D. The rudeness of the sculpture, however, may account for this. And indeed Mr. Samuel Lysons, in his *History of Devonshire*, has not hesitated in a wood-cut to represent it completely formed as the latter. I am not much surprised at this inaccuracy, from the hasty sketch he made, in my presence, when I first directed his attention to the stone in question several years ago; and only mention it now that the reading proposed may be supported by the opinion of so great an antiquary. With respect to Condé, in Latin Condate, (and to which perhaps we may trace Condevus) there are several towns of this name in France. It is an appellation in antient geography, probably of Celtic origin, bearing relation to the idea of *confluent*, and means a place built on the spot where two rivers meet.

There was a Roman station, also, of the name of Condate, in this island, as appears from the second *iter*
of Antoninus.[2]　 The person here commemorated,
therefore, may have taken his name from one of
these towns, as does one of the branches of the
Bourbon family in France.　At any rate the name
is of British or Celtic origin.

"Of the stones which I now propose to notice, my
earliest remembrance is that when I was a boy they
were lying in a little plot of garden-ground over the
gateway of the Abbey, commonly known by the name
of Betsy Grimbal's Tower.　I thence, several years
ago, removed and placed them as on a kind of shrine
in front of the arch before mentioned.

"On exchanging my residence for the Vicarage, I
restored them pretty nearly to their former situation,
by placing them beneath instead of on the top of the
gateway.　They were there more accessible, and as
I imagined equally safe.　In this respect, however,
I was unfortunately mistaken : for, two or three
years since, on going to show them to a friend, the
stone marked No. 2 was nowhere to be found.　I was
the more provoked at the loss, as I am not without
suspicion that I myself, though altogether unintention-
ally, was in some degree accessory to the theft : for
only a few weeks before, having but just mounted my
horse, it shied at the noise or motion of a mason who
was working near the gate, and I sent back my servant to tell him that it was a very improper place for
him thus to be cutting a stone, and begged he would
remove it.　I have reason to think that it was the very
stone in question, and that he had no other view in
purloining it than to convert it into a pig's trough.

[2] REES's *Cyclopædia*, and HENRY's *History*.

"The other stone I have placed, for shelter as well as security, beneath the trellised shed before the door of my house. I am not without suspicion, however, that not only masons but antiquaries have little fear either of lares or penates; though at the feet of the former there should be the figure of a dog barking, (with the words *cave canem*) and though the latter be placed in the inmost and most secret parts of the house. Indeed it may be apprehended that too many might be tempted to steal even the household gods themselves.

"Whether these stones were but parts of one and the same, it is difficult to determine. If they were, it is probable that there existed an intermediate portion. Certain it is that they were of the same

I

description of freestone, were of the same thickness, and had upon them letters of precisely the same form and workmanship. By no greater stretch of imagination than antiquaries are sometimes known to indulge in, and perhaps with not much greater credulity than they frequently possess, one if not both these stones

might plausibly enough be considered as commemora-
tive of Alfred the Great. There are parts of two
words, one immediately below the other, the former
ending in FRIDUS, the other in NUS. May they not,
therefore, be ALFRIDUS MAGNUS? The orthography,
at least in early times, was far from being settled.
'Anglo-Saxon writers, and among these the king
himself, commonly write his name Ælfred, and this
orthography is frequently followed on ancient coins;
in some instances, however, as on a coin in the
British Museum, the name is written Aelfred: in
other writers, and indeed on some coins too, we find
Elfred.'[3] Nay, it was not only written Alfredus but
also Aluredus.[4] But this respects only the beginning
of the word. We may naturally infer, however, that
there was some degree of uncertainty in regard to the
termination also. In Smith, *De Republica Anglorum*,
we find our Alfred, the son of Ethelwolf, written Alfredus; but Alfred, the son of Oswy, he spells Alfr*i*dus;
whilst Rapin and Hume call them both Alfred.

"A pretty strong objection however to this hypo-
thesis is, that Alfred died A.D. 901, and the Abbey
was not begun till 961! I might say it was his
cenotaph, or that it was removed from the place of
his sepulture. However much disposed the monks
might be to avail themselves of his name, either as a
king on earth or as a saint in heaven, the expression
situs est hic is too strong for a cenotaph, and would
accord better with his relics, which we might easier
believe they would pretend to have, rather than that
they carried away his gravestone. It is, however, not
a little remarkable, that his remains were transported
more than once from the place of their original inter-

[3] *Penny Cyclopædia.*   [4] AINSWORTH, &c.

ment. 'His body,' says Rapin, 'was buried first at *Winchester*, next removed into the church of the *New Monastery;* and lastly, his body, monument, church and monastery were all removed (about two hundred years after) without the north gate of the city, since called the *Hide.*' Nor indeed is it perhaps less remarkable that CONDITOR A, on the other stone, may mean *conditor Angliæ legum*, as well as *conditor Abbatiæ.* 'And Alfred,' says Blackstone,[5] is generally styled by the same historians the *legum Anglicanarum conditor*, as Edward the Confessor is the *restitutor.*' And possibly, after all, it will be considered not the least remarkable of these coincidences, that there were no less than three monks of Winchester who became Abbots of Tavistock; namely, Livingus, who died in 1038; Aldred, his successor, who died in 1069; and Philip Trentheful, who was confirmed as Abbot in 1259. Is it altogether improbable that one of these, from the veneration he may naturally be supposed to feel for the name of Alfred, might have placed this memorial of him in a spot to which he had been himself translated, when he remembered that the removal of the very remains of this great monarch had taken place either for their greater safety or greater honour? Or the mere estimation in which he was held by the fraternity at large, which is sufficiently proved by his translation of *Boethius de Consolatione Philosophiæ* being printed at their press, may account for their pretending to possess either his grave-stone or his relics, though each might be equally supposititious.[6]

[5] Vol. i. p. 66.

[6] I probably was led into this error of confounding together two separate works, from having somewhere seen it noticed that an Anglo-Saxon grammar was published here; and knowing that Alfred had translated Boethius into Anglo-Saxon. This translation, however, was

" The monastery called the 'Newen Mynstre,' and afterwards Hyde Abbey, which was founded by Alfred, and completed by his son Edward, being in an unhealthy and inconvenient situation, 'a new and magnificent church and monastery were erected just without the north wall of the city, on the spot called Hyde-meadow, to which the monks removed in 1110, carrying with them the remains of several illustrious personages who had been buried in the former abbey, among which were those of Alfred himself, and some of his descendants.   The church and monastery were soon afterwards demolished, and even the tombs of Alfred and other eminent persons were despoiled. Precisely on the space occupied by the abbey church was some time ago erected a bridewell, or house of correction, on the plan of the benevolent Howard.' And 'between fifty and sixty years ago,' (I extract this from Rees's *Cyclopædia*) 'among the remains of the buildings was found a stone with this inscription in Saxon characters, " Alfred Rex DCCCLXXXI." '

" This date is twenty years before his death.   It might otherwise have been taken for his gravestone. Some mystery we find even here is connected with the memory of this illustrious personage.

" With respect to the stone marked No. 2, (if it be not connected with the preceding) many conjectures present themselves ; but I shall offer only two, as requiring the least addition ; namely,

INDOLEM . . . .
CONDITOR (abbatiæ)
PRÆSTET AMŒNAM :

not printed, I believe, till 1698, at Oxford.   But perhaps I may be indulged in the conjecture that the monks possessed this work in MS., and might attach such value to a more recent version as to commit it to the press, from knowing that the original had previously been translated by so renowned a prince.

which we may suppose a prayer that the founder (for
'*O Thou that hearest prayer*' is not, be it remembered,
confined by Romanists to God) might continue his
favourable disposition to the Abbey; or, if we imagine
the sentence to refer to the person to whose memory
the stone was inscribed, we may complete the inscription in some such form as the following :—

        (Oramus ut ille)
        INDOLEM (eandem quam)
        CONDITOR (abbatiæ nostræ)
        PRÆSTET. AMEN. AMEN.

'Let us pray that he may show the same disposition
as did the founder of our Abbey. Amen. Amen.'

2

  "There can be no doubt, however, that the lateral
sentence may be thus completed—(*In spe resurge*)
NDI SUB JACET INTUS. And from the word *intus*
we may at once conclude that the stone formed the
cover of the stone coffin or sarcophagus.

"Some years since, previous to placing the painted glass in the window of his dining-room at Endsleigh, the Duke of Bedford applied to me for a sketch of the arms of the Abbey of Tavistock; and I ventured to emblazon them from the description contained in Prince's *Worthies of Devon.*

"I find however, from a fragment of Beer-stone sent to me in September, 1833, by Mr. Rundle, builder, who met with it among other pieces of sculpture in taking down part of the brewery here, that there is a want of correctness, not only in myself, but even in Prince. He describes the arms as 'Gules, two crosiers saltireways between two martlets or, in a chief argent three mullets sable.'

"I instantly recognized the mullets, but I was at a loss respecting the crosiers; the martlets, also, must have been four instead of two. I was satisfied, however, that it is a fragment of the arms of the Abbey, when I found crosiers thus described in Fosbroke's *Encyclopædia of Antiquities*: 'They were sometimes barely curled, sometimes like beadles' staves,—more like maces than crosiers.'

"From two hands that still remain at the top and

side, it is evident that the shield was supported by two angels, one on the dexter, and the other on the sinister side.

"On the 30th October, 1833, Mr. Rundle sent me also another stone, with an inscription in black-letter painted on a white fillet, being a kind of upper border to the same, the ground of which was vermilion. The words are REGINA CELI (cæli) LETARE (lætare) A——probably Alleluia. 'Rejoice, O Queen of heaven—Hallelujah.' Of course they are addressed to the Virgin Mary, and possibly were placed on her altar.

"In November, 1833, Mr. Rundle also sent me two other stones. One seemed to be a kind of plinth, on which, in red characters, was painted what I take to be the contraction of *Jesu*,[7] which is followed by FILI DEI MISERERE ... O ... probably NOSTRI. The other was the capital of a column or pilaster, having at the top gilt quatrefoils, whilst at the bottom are bunches of grapes painted red. Between them is the inscription (as far as I am able to decipher it) ORATE PRO DIVO E ..... The latter word, perhaps, might have been Eustachio, to whom the parish church was dedicated; so that it is difficult to decide whether these sculptured remains were taken from the conventual or the parochial church, possibly from both, when the former was pulled down, and the latter freed from its idolatries (for there stood in it the altar of St. Eustace) at the time of the Reformation. It is probable that they were not removed for

---

[7] I am indebted to Mr. Kempe for the information that iþu stansp for Jesu: an adoption of the *h* for the great eta. "Jesus is written I.H.S. (in antient MSS.) which is the Greek IHΣ, or ιης, an abbreviation of Iησους."—CASLEY'S *Catalogue of the Royal Library*, pref., p. xxiii.

preservation, but used when wanted as mere materials for other buildings.

"Thus, my dearest Eliza, have I endeavoured to fulfil my promise of contributing towards your work by giving some account of the inscribed stones, &c., connected with this neighbourhood, and remain,

"Your faithful and affectionate husband,

"E. A. BRAY."

Before I make up this packet for Keswick I shall add the following extracts from Mr. Bray's Journal respecting an

EXCURSION ON DARTMOOR TO OVER TOR.

"August 8th, 1832.—Having seen but the basins on Pew Tor, and from their elevation being unable to reach them, Mrs. Bray playfully expressed a wish to wash her hands in one of those that were the most accessible on Dartmoor. The basin called Mis Tor Pan being the largest, and if I recollected rightly not difficult of access, we got out of the carriage, near the Merrivale circles, with the intention of paying it a visit. But it was at no small distance, with a considerable ascent all the way, principally amid rocks, the weather was extremely warm, and my companion very weak from illness. We gave up, therefore, our original design, and resolved to content ourselves with exploring a neighbouring tor, which we afterwards learnt was called Over Tor. I was the more induced to do so from never having visited it before; and probably for the same reason that, had it not been for what I have above stated, we should not have visited it now; namely, because it seemed but insignificant in itself, and because my mind was occupied with a far more important undertaking, that of reaching Mis Tor.

"But Over Tor, though of no great magnitude, most amply repaid us for the visit. Probably from not being so elevated, and therefore less exposed to 'the pelting of the pitiless storm,' it is less bare and denuded than most others. Indeed it is almost covered with lichen and pendent moss : so much so, that it forcibly reminded me of grotto-work; to which the cavities, that are here more numerous than usual, not a little contributed. Even some of the incumbent strata, possibly from being thin, and little else than laminæ, when I struck them with my umbrella sounded hollow. A flower, also, in the shape of a white pointed star, glittered amid the dark verdure of the moss, and might well be compared to the sparkling shells with which these artificial structures are generally decorated. That art, too, had been used even here is evident; for Mrs. Bray had the pleasure of herself discovering a rock-basin. And as we have not only the classic, or at least far-fetched authority of 'Venus's Looking-glass,' but the nearer one of 'Lady Lopes's Hat,' (being no other than the covering of an old lime-kiln) I may be allowed, perhaps, to designate this as 'Mrs. Bray's Washhand Basin.' It had water in it at the time ; though not enough for the purpose above stated. The basin, I should think, is about a foot in diameter at the bottom [8]. The exterior brim stands boldly prominent, thin, and somewhat curved (at least on its upper surface) like the cup of a convolvulus. Standing, or perhaps seated beside it, the Druid might scatter his lustrations on

---

[8] I subsequently found it by admeasurement fourteen inches ; and one foot and a half above.

his votaries below; whether they were the multitude
generally at the base of the rock, or such select few
as might be admitted nearer for initiation on a kind
of natural platform, about five feet below, composed
of the rock itself.

"Mrs. Bray was fortunate also in making two other
discoveries; namely, a fallen rock on which were two
basins, and a fallen tolmen. I already have alluded
to some young men, who, on one of them coming of
age, or rather on the expiration of his apprenticeship,
which was probably simultaneous, celebrated this most
important era by throwing down some rocks on Dartmoor. I never could learn the exact spot, but had
reason to imagine that it was on or near Mis Tor. I
now am satisfied that it could be no other than Over
Tor; and except, perhaps, the overthrow of the cromlech at the *cursus*, they did no further mischief. This
no doubt was enough, and more than enough; and
well would they have deserved the same sentence,
could it have been put in execution, that was passed
on and undergone by that lieutenant in the navy who
threw down the Logan Rock in Cornwall, and was
forced to put it up again. Were it not for this latter
circumstance, I should hardly have attributed the
violence so visible on this Tor to human agency,
but to an earthquake or some convulsion of nature.
But the power of the wedge, though perhaps the
simplest, is almost incalculable. The rock itself, as
I should conceive, afforded materials for its own destruction.

"The basins are generally to be found on the
upper lamina; between which and the next a stone
may easily be inserted, and being struck and forced
inward by another, and that by a third, one end of

this thin mass is elevated, till by a corresponding depression the other end preponderates, and the summit of this lofty structure, which had defied a thousand storms, not only falls below but carries ruin and destruction far around. Indeed, I cannot but think that the very name of Over Tor is owing to this overthrow of the rocks, which, whether natural or artificial, must strike the most inattentive observer. At any rate the etymology is not so far-fetched as St. Mary Overy, a name given to a church in Southwark, as I was informed by a learned antiquary, from the circumstance that near it people were accustomed to go 'over the ferry' to the city. Certain it is that you can trace this cataract of rocks, as you might fancy a cataract of water suddenly arrested and fixed by ice.

"The rock on which this elevated pile was poised is still as horizontal as the base itself beneath it. The second rock has slid from it, but finding a *point d'appui* on a kind of platform which is itself of considerable elevation, remains only in an oblique position. The third rock is completely pendent from the platform, but is prevented falling by the fourth, that has found a base on some rocks below, and thus completes this accidental bridge : for a chasm of no small dimensions is formed by it, and an ox we saw had retired to it for shade and shelter. The fifth, on which are the basins, is perpendicular. Contiguous to this, and thrown I think out of their position by its falling against them, are two rocks, which we ventured to consider were tolmens. They rest on a rock whose face is as smooth and perpendicular as a wall, thirteen feet and a half in length, and seven feet in height. There seems to have been a semicircular inclosure of stones in front of it; and, from the upper edge of this wall, one of the two rocks projects three feet and a half, like the sounding-board of a pulpit. Three or four stones, somewhat similar to that which supports the tolmen at Staple Tor, are lying under them, and were probably applied to that purpose here. Were this the case, there is reason to conclude that these tolmens, which seem to have been parallel, if not resting against one another, were overthrown by the shock occasioned by the fall of the rock on which are the basins; for it seems to have struck them near their point of conjunction, and, causing them to open to the right and left, deranged their supports and destroyed their equilibrium. The fallen basins are of an oblong shape, two feet by one, and about four inches and a half deep. The view from behind this Tor (itself forming the foreground, rich in colour and every possible variety of outline) is truly magnificent. Its more elevated points afford a bold contrast both in shape and shadow to the faint and sweeping undulations of the distant horizon. Plymouth Sound, Mount Edgcumbe, and Hamoaze are conspicuous and attractive objects. Walkhampton Tower (or possibly that of Sampford Spiney) glitters in the view, whilst the bold mass of Vixen Tor, and the crowned summit of Pew Tor beyond it, form a broad and sombre background for Merrivale Bridge, and the sparkling river Walkham that winds beneath.

"I here may mention that on approaching this Tor we found several mounds of earth, from about five and twenty to thirty paces in circumference. They are not in the usual shape of barrows, being of an oblong square, whilst the latter are generally round or oval.   From their proximity to the circles, the *cursus*, and the Tor, which, from its basins, &c., we have thus connected with Druidism, one might be tempted to imagine that these were places of sepulture for persons of that order; but on my afterwards asking Hannaford, the farmer, if he knew anything about them, he said they were rabbits' burrows; and I am inclined to think he is perfectly right.

THE WALKHAM.[9]

" Close to Merrivale Bridge I was shocked, for I can use no milder expression, to see in the bed of this truly romantic river some of the largest rocks split with wedges, and, instead of presenting their usual flowing outline and their dark natural colour enriched with moss and lichen, obtruding themselves on the eye, not only bare but in straight and angular deformity. It is to be hoped, however, that they will soon be removed. I am sorry to observe that they have begun to take stones for the roads from the bed of our own beautiful Tavy. But such is the march of intellect and improve-ment.   As a further proof of its progressing even on the Moor, I soon afterwards remarked a hand-bill pasted on one of the rocks near the side of the road. I could not help thinking that my inscriptions were more in character. But even these, I found, when I reached Bair-down, were beginning to be illegible. Indeed, when looking from the bridge for the name of a poet to whom I had consecrated one of the rocks beneath, we could only see some faint traces of the

[9] In our excursion of this day, I observed that among the various forms that Vixen Tor assumes, this lofty mass of rock has one which I have omitted when elsewhere describing them ; but which now forcibly im-pressed itself on my fancy ; namely, that of a lion sucking his paw.

letters when the sun shone out. It was about two o'clock, and perhaps (from the spot where we stood) it might be wholly undistinguishable at any other hour. This vanishing and reappearing excited some degree of interest, and reminded me of the effect of the diorama. The loudest roar that then ascended from the Cowsick was occasioned by the rush of water over the rock that crosses the river, which I learnt from Hannaford is fifty-nine feet in length—it is perfectly straight: this they once talked of converting into an obelisk."

EXCURSION ON DARTMOOR. KISTVAEN, &c., ON BAIR-DOWN.

"11th Sept. 1832.—About two or three minutes' walk from the house, in a north-east direction, are the remains of a kistvaen which we had long proposed to open. ʿThree stones, about six or eight inches high, forming three sides of an oblong square, were all that was visible. On removing some turf and rushes, we found a rough pavement around them to the extent of three or four feet. The stone at the western end (for they face pretty nearly the cardinal points) is two feet eight inches long. The northern stone is three feet ten inches ; the southern about the same dimensions, and the eastern stone is wanting.

"We opened the centre, about two feet and a half ; and there came to the natural substratum, a hard gravel. The stones of inclosure reached to the same depth. Hannaford, who is somewhat acquainted with what he calls these *caves*, in procuring stones for walls, &c., was of opinion that it had been opened before, and that the stone at the east, together with the covering stone, had been removed for similar purposes. I had reason afterwards fully to agree with him, for we found nothing amid the peat earth that filled the cavity but a small fragment of earthenware. It was of the very coarsest texture, somewhat smooth on one side, and extremely rough on the other. The surfaces were reddish, but the centre of a deep brown. It probably was the only remaining portion of an urn that had been broken and taken away with its contents, whatever they might be, by some previous and more fortunate explorer; though it is likely enough that the discovery gratified no other feeling than that of mere curiosity. An antiquary, perhaps, had he been present, might have decided, I will not say with what certainty, whether it was or was not the sepulchre of some chieftain or Arch-Druid on the hill of bards. About a quarter of a mile distant, immediately outside the present boundary of Bair-down, (for my father gave it up for the purpose, I believe, of building a chapel which was never erected) and nearly opposite the road that leads to Plymouth, I was informed by Hannaford that a person named John Kerton, among what he called 'burrows and buildings,' found some human bones; and that he told him he could not rest till he buried them again.

"I learnt from the same authority, having previously requested him to measure it, that the erect stone or obelisk, called Bair-down Man, (probably corrupted from *mên*, a stone) is eleven feet high, and eight feet round."

The length of these extracts from Mr. Bray's Journal prevents my at present adding more.

LETTER XXI.

TO ROBERT SOUTHEY, ESQ.

Vicarage, Tavistock, June 16th, 1832.

HAVING now led you through the western limits of Dartmoor, whence the river Tavy takes its rise, I purpose in this letter commencing my account of the town to which that river gives name: a town of very high antiquity, and possessing many interesting claims on our attention, not only in a general but individual point of view; since it has given birth to many whose names have become illustrious in the history or literature of this kingdom.

Tavistock is situated on the banks of the Tavy, on the western side of the Forest of Dartmoor, and not very far distant from the river Tamar, which divides the counties of Cornwall and Devon. It lies thirty-two miles west from the city of Exeter; sixteen south from Okehampton; and fourteen north from the good town of Plymouth. Few places in England, perhaps, have been more blest with local attractions by the bounties of a gracious Providence. •

The town lies in a valley surrounded by hills, whose verdure is perpetual. The river is here peculiarly beautiful: it runs, with great rapidity, over vast portions of rock that form its bed. The whole parish abounds with springs and rivulets of the purest water. The woods (where they are suffered to remain, for the love of lopping a· tree in every hedge is the sin of this neighbourhood) are exceedingly luxuriant: the oak is common, and the most wooded parts lie westward in the parish. The soil is, generally speaking, of a deep brown, here and there tinged with red; it is exceedingly rich and fertile; and strata of alluvial deposit may be observed in many of the valleys. Our pasturage is abundant; and we are celebrated, like most parts of Devon, for the excellence of that luxury, our *scalded* or *clouted* cream. This has been honoured by the notice of a poet whose verse captivates the fancy, and raises even to ecstasy the spirit of every reader whose heart and eye are sensible to the charms of Nature, in all the varied productions of her hand. Spenser thus alludes to our cream in his delightful poem, the *Shepherd's*

Calendar; where Colin recites to Thenot the graces
and courtesy of a deceased shepherdess :

> " Ne would she scorne the simple shepheard swaine ;
> For she would call him often heme,
> And give him curds and clouted cream."

We have another delicious preparation from our
milk, called *junket,* which has also been noticed by a
great poet ; for Milton writes in his *L'Allegro,*

> " And fairy Mab the *junkets* ate."

Indeed we are so celebrated for our cream, and have
been in all ages, that I doubt not of this was made
the very sort of butter, in the western parts of Britain,
so much esteemed by the Romans : the wicker-worked
baskets, and the butter of the Britons, being alluded
to by one or more of their most famous writers.[1]
This luxury, no doubt, continued to be held in
estimation in the times of the Anglo-Saxons, when
the western part of the island became more than
ever valuable on account of its flocks and herds.

Respecting the name of our town, I here insert
an extract from my brother Alfred John Kempe's
historical notices of Tavistock Abbey, that appeared
in the *Gentleman's Magazine,* to which, on almost all
subjects connected with antiquity, he was for many
years a constant and valuable contributor.

"The etymology of the name Tavistock does not
appear to be of difficult solution. 'The place on the
Tavy' is evidently implied by the compound ; but it
may be observed that, by early writers of the monkish
age, the Tavy is called the *Tau,* and that the *Taw,*
the *Towy,* the *Tay,* and the *Taf,* are common appel-
latives of many British rivers. The Tavy discharges
itself into the Tamar, a few miles above Plymouth ;

[1] Martial mentions the baskets, Pliny the butter, of the barbarians.

of which last-mentioned river it may be accounted a branch. There can be little doubt, therefore, that the Tavy is an abbreviation of the British words *Tau-vechan*, or the 'little Tau,' thus distinguishing the tributary branch from the *Tau-mawr*, (afterwards Tamar) the 'great Tau.' When the Saxons established this town and monastery on the banks of the *Tau-vechan*, they were content to affix a short adjunct from their own language to the original British words, and the abbreviated form, so much sought by common parlance, easily moulded *Tau-vechan-stoke* into Tavistock. The *Saxon Chronicle* indeed strongly countenances this opinion; in that venerable record it is called 'Ætefingstoke,' which, without any distortion, may be read At-tavingstoke.[2]

I confess, that in describing my beloved town, I shall find some difficulty in speaking with other than the most partial feelings; since so much cause have I to give it a good name; so much do I delight in the scenery that everywhere surrounds us; so much pleasure do I feel in the tranquil retirement of the Vicarage, (situated as it is in a beautiful garden,

[2] Respecting the etymology of Tavistock, I also copy the following passage from the works of Browne, the poet, who was born in that town. "Tavie is a river, having his head in Dertmoor, in Devon, some few miles from Marie-Tavy, and falls southward into Tamar: out of the same Moore riseth, running northward, another, called *Tau*: which by the way the rather I speak of, because in the printed *Malmes-burie de Gest. Pontific.* lib. 2, fol. 146, you reade: 'Est in Damnonia cœnobium Monachorum juxta Tau fluvium, quod Tavistock vocatur:' whereas upon Tau stands (neere the north side of the shire) Taustocke, being no remnants of a monasterie; so that you must there reade, 'juxta *Taiv* fluvium,' as in a *Manuscript* Copie of Malmesburie's time (the form of the hand assuring Malmesburie's time) belonging to the Abbey of Saint Augustine, in Canterburie, I have seen in the hands of my very learned friend M. Selden." Indeed Tawstock and Tavistock are still very frequently confounded.

where the venerable walls of the Abbey form the
boundary of our little domain) that I fancy no spot
so delightful as my own home. Many I dare say
would smile at hearing such an assertion; but if it
be a prejudice, it is not only a very harmless one,
but such as may be encouraged and turned to good
account; a grateful contentment with that lot given
to us as our portion by the goodness of Providence,
being one of those duties that carry with them their
reward—a constant enjoyment of the things that are
our own. Here, indeed, may we say, "the lines have
fallen to us in pleasant places." And if it be true,
(which surely no considerate mind will deny) that next
to the blessing of dear kindred and friends, there are
no temporal blessings to be compared to a quiet
home situated in a picturesque country, with plenty
of books and leisure to read them, we have every
cause to feel that we are blest; and to entertain that
kindly spirit even towards the inanimate things of
this neighbourhood, which can only be truly felt
where there is content at home to receive it. A mind
distracted with worldly cares and desires, the gratification of which arises from without, and is dependent
on the will of others, on casualty, or caprice, can never
be sufficiently disengaged to admit that fellowship of
feeling which associates its own tranquillity with the
beauty and harmony of Nature. There must be rest
in the soul to enjoy it in the fields; and there it will
be found, like "that peace of mind which passeth all
understanding, which the world can neither give nor
take away," a constant source of the most enduring
pleasures.

Browne the poet was fully alive to this feeling,
when he celebrated, in the numbers of pure English

verse, the pastoral delights of his 'native Tavy,' as he calls the river that watered the town where he first drew breath. The associations created by poetry never die : they are like the immortal spirit to whose aspirations they owe their birth, above the things of this life, and are neither liable to the chances nor changes of fortune. To live in a neighbourhood that has given birth to a poet, that has seen him in his infancy sporting amidst its hills and valleys, and receiving by its 'voiceful streams' those early impressions which in after and maturer years become the theme of his song, is a circumstance in itself enough to inspire even a common mind with some of those better feelings that have no part with the world, or the world's law. On this account, had Tavistock no other claim to veneration—as the birthplace of Browne, the author of *Britannia's Pastorals*, it would stand eminent amongst towns. With what feelings its picturesque situation inspired the youthful poet, even these simple lines (which more by chance than design have just met my eye, in turning over the pages of his works) may serve to tell.

> "As (woo'd by Maye's delights) I have been borne
> To take the kind ayre of a wistfull morne
> Neere Tavie's voyceful streame (to whom I owe
> More straines than from my pipe can ever flowe ;)
> Here have I heard a sweet bird never lin
> To chide the river for his clam'rous din ;
> There seem'd another in his song to tell,
> That what the fayre streame did he liked well ;
> And going further heard another too
> All varying still in what the others doe ;
> A little thence, a fourth with little paine
> Con'd all their lessons and then sung againe ;
> So numberlesse the songsters are that sing
> In the sweet groves of the too careless spring,

> That I no sooner could the hearing lose
> Of one of them, but straight another rose
> And perching deftly on a quaking spray,
> Nye tired herself to make her hearer stay,
> Whilst in the bush two nightingales together
> Show'd the best skill they had to draw me thither."

Browne's allusion to the nightingale, in these lines, must either have been a poetical licence, or some change must have taken place in the natural history of Devon since his day; as that bird is now unknown in our county. White attributes the failure of it with us not to want of warmth, as the West is the mildest part of the whole island; but considers it a presumptive argument that this bird crosses over from the Continent at the narrowest passage, and strolls not so far westward. Some naturalists, however, conclude that we are wanting in the peculiar kind of food on which the nightingale delights to feed.

I shall not enter here upon any individual local descriptions; because, as in the letters about Dartmoor, it will, I think, be more amusing to blend all such accounts with the historical and antiquarian notices, as they may occur. Thus, for instance, when I shall have occasion to speak of the great Sir Francis Drake, it will be time enough to mention the beautiful spot in which he was born, about a mile from our town. Something must previously be said of the early history of this place; and the British period having already occupied many letters in relation to the Moor, the Saxon comes next in succession; as very little is known of the Roman era in this part of England.

Indeed Tavistock is intimately connected with the Anglo-Saxon times, since not only to a Saxon noble was the town indebted for its costly Abbey, but here also was that language studied and taught after it had become obsolete in every other part of the kingdom. Here, too, the daughter of the founder of that Abbey—the unworthy wife of Ethelwold, the queen of Edgar, the cruel step-mother of his son— the beautiful Elfrida, first drew breath ; and here was acted the scene of that interview, which awakened in the heart of the young king a guilty passion that prompted him to commit the crimes of treachery and murder.

The foundation of the Abbey of Tavistock was a thing of so much importance, not only to the town, but in the ecclesiastical history of the county, that it becomes necessary to offer a few brief remarks on the progress of Christianity in the West, which inspired the kings of Wessex and the earls of Devon with that piety and zeal for the Church, so beneficial in its day, and so productive of good, before those corruptions gradually crept in which rendered the Reformation absolutely necessary, to restore the ceremonies, as well as the doctrines of our religion, to their primitive purity and spirit.

At what period Christianity was first propagated in Damnonia, or by whom, is not I believe known with any degree of certainty : but, from the circumstance of the ancient Britons making Cornwall one of the strongholds of their retreat, it is probable, as the remnant of the bards and Druids still lingered with that people, that paganism might have maintained its sway in the West, when it was no longer to be found · in the Midlands or other parts of Britain[3].

[3] A few days after the above passage was written, a letter from Mr. Southey confirmed the opinion here expressed. That gentleman says : " Perhaps the Western Britons were less disturbed by wars than any

It seems doubtful if Christianity was here propagated previous to the Saxon Conquest; though it is highly probable the natives of Devon benefited in civilization after the Roman power was established in these kingdoms. The Romans were stern foes, but generous conquerors; and the nations they subdued were not left by them, as by the barbarous hordes of the North in their achievements, with no other mark than that of destruction to witness their victories. The useful and even the elegant arts of life came with them: the very ensign they bore—the eagle—a noble and a royal bird, as truly denoted the high character of their conquests, as did the banner of the raven, that dark bird of prey, prefigure the destructive victories of the cruel Danes.

Though the Damnonii cannot be supposed to have acquired that degree of civilization which would have rendered them equal to their Roman victors in the general refinement of their manners, yet the discountenance, and, as far as it could be effected, the extirpation of the rites of Druidism, answered a good end, by lessening the frequency of human sacrifices. The people, who had been accustomed to witness this wanton immolation of their fellow-creatures, became less barbarous: murder ceased to be a spectacle; the keen relish for human blood, which in all nations such savage rites never fail to create, died away; and the

other people in the island, during the whole time of the Heptarchy. They bordered only upon Wessex, which was generally the best governed of the Anglo-Saxon kingdoms; which was strong enough, for the most part, to make them quiet neighbours; and was too much occupied on other sides to think of molesting them. Exeter continued long to be a half Welsh town, just as Freiburg, in Switzerland, is still divided between the two languages. During such a state of things, the bards had leisure to keep up the old religion in all its forms, and make the last stand against Christianity."

first noisome weed that would have impeded the growth of the good seed being thus cast out, the ground was gradually prepared to receive the future blessings of the tree of life.

However much of superstition or of fraud there might have been in the Church at a very early period, yet, even in its corrupt state, its benefits were incalculably great to a land that had so long been buried in the darkness and cruelties of paganism. Christianity, in every country where it takes root, as its first-fruits improves the wretched estate of the slave, the poor, and by teaching man that he is a responsible being, makes him become a reasonable one. How great must have been the change in Britain produced by planting the doctrines of Christ in lieu of those which were said to be derived from Odin or from Belus, which, like those of their eastern ancestors, were

> "Abominations ! and with cursed things
>   His holy rites and solemn feasts profaned,
>   And with their darkness durst affront his light,
>   First Moloch, horrid king, besmeared with blood—
>   Of human sacrifice and parents' tears !"

The barbarisms too of divination, of consulting the entrails of human beings and of animals, whilst they were yet panting under the knife, were abolished. With no people was this custom more apparent than with the ancient Britons, who undertook no wars, or actions of any import, without consulting the lots or augury of the priests.

To draw a comparison between sacred and profane things, it might be said of the early Christian missionary in his overthrow of augury, and preaching the glad tidings of the gospel in its stead, that like Prometheus, as he is made to recite his acts by the poet Æschylus, he took from man the power of searching out his future destiny, but gave him a far better boon—even Hope—in its stead. Surely this was a very just and beautiful allegory in the Greek dramatist; since, could men know the miseries they will suffer in their progress through life, the source of honourable or necessary exertion would become dried and barren ; but Hope, as a perennial fountain, plays on, and affords her refreshing draughts to the pilgrim of the world, even to the last and closing hour of his weary journey towards the tomb.

After the Anglo-Saxons were settled in this part of the island, Christianity was first propagated in the kingdom of Wessex, during the reign of Cynegils, by Byrinus (A.D. 634) who, finding the people idolators, undertook their conversion, with the sanction of Pope Honorius. The first episcopal see was in the city of Dorcester, not the Roman station, but, according to Fuller, an old city in Oxfordshire, where a church was erected. On the death of Byrinus, the kingdom in which he had planted the good seed was cruelly torn and divided; for that fierce idolator Penda, king of Mercia, invaded and conquered it; and not till the rightful and Christian heir of the crown was restored did Wessex again taste the blessings of peace and of the gospel. Several worthy ecclesiastics were now favoured by the prince, and received by the people ; and the Spirit of God, 'mighty in word and works,' was everywhere spread abroad with the happiest effects. Many churches were built, and that magnificent structure, Winchester Cathedral, was first commenced by Cenowalch, who there fixed Wina as its bishop.

The civil wars which succeeded the death of the king, though they might for a while impede the growth, did not extirpate the fruits of Christianity; and soon after, the kingdom being divided into two dioceses, Winchester and Sherborne, Devonshire, in ecclesiastical matters, came under the jurisdiction of the latter. Good Bishop Aldhelm then filled the see, and ruled with great prudence, learning, and piety. In process of time Devonshire had bishops of its own, who were stationed at Tawton, Crediton, and Exeter. The first Bishops—Werstanus and Putta—were appointed about the beginning of the tenth century; the last-named met with a violent death; since, on visiting at Crediton an officer of the royal household, from some unknown cause he was slain by one of Uffa's men. Putta was succeeded by Eadulphus, Ethelgarus, and Algarus. The last having sat ten years, gave up his see to Alfnodus, in consequence of the strenuous exertions of the famous St. Dunstan. This occurred about the year 962. He was succeeded in 970 by Alfwolgus. It must, therefore, have been during the time of Bishop Algarus, and of Edgar, King of Wessex, that Tavistock Abbey was first founded by Orgar, Earl, or Heretoge of Devon.

. That once magnificent Abbey is now in ruins;— the writer of this letter dwells within the boundary of its venerable walls; nor is that dwelling, though become familiar by long use, unassociated with those recollections which render such a habitation replete with local interest and feeling. The grey walls; the mouldering tower with its ruined windows, once gorgeous in the glowing hues of their stained glass, through whose empty space the wind now whistles

in melancholy cadence; the ivy-mantled arch; the
winding steps; the entry, strewn with fragments of
those columns which once upheld the stately roof,
where now the bat waves her dusky wing, and all of
former times is silent or forgotten, saving the whis-
perings of superstition that have peopled even this
poor archway with the ghosts of the dead!—all are
objects that cannot be contemplated without some
thoughts that lead us to dwell on the rapid flight of
time; the mutability of governments; the passions
of men, and their violence even in a just cause—for
the greater part of the ruin before our eyes was the
work of the Reformation. Who but would lament
this, when he reflects how much there is of evil that
mingles itself with human actions, however good may
be their aim! We see the effects of those passions
which exceeded the limits of reason or necessity, and
but hastened that decay which is the final doom of
all things here on earth. This is a lesson that may
be taught even by such speechless monitors as these
old Abbey walls. We look on the last fragment
now left of the Abbey Church itself,[4] and call up
the remembrance of what it was in the strength and
beauty of its early days — a holy fane stately in
every proportion, decorated with every ornament the
sculptor's art could supply, and hung with jewelled
pomp bestowed by nobles and kings to render it a
temple fitted, in outward splendour, to the worship of
Him in whose keeping are the hearts of kings, and
from whose hand the royal crown is placed upon their
brows.

. Orgar, to whose munificence the Western Church
was indebted for the Abbey, which, no doubt, gave

[4] The archway, said to be Orgar's tomb.

rise to the wealth and importance of the town, was
born in or near Tavistock, and held the rank and
office of earl, or alderman, of Devon. The court in
which an earl presided met twice a year, after
Michaelmas and Easter; it was composed of the
freeholders of the shire, who had a voice in the
decisions. The bishop also presided in it with the
earl, (so early was the spiritual combined with the
civil authorities in this kingdom) whose rank was the
highest in the order of thanes. Before the time of
Alfred the Great this nobleman ruled in the county
with the power of a petty king, since all affairs, civil
as well as military, were within his absolute control.
Such power Alfred, with that wisdom which distinguished all his actions and his laws, considered
too much to be vested in the person of any subject;
and as some counterpoise he appointed a sheriff
in each shire, who in all matters of jurisprudence
should have an equal authority, and should guard
the dues of the crown from any abuses or misappro-
priation.

During the early periods of the Heptarchy the
sovereign might nominate the earl of a county, and
could deprive him of his rank, if he wilfully suffered
a notorious robber to escape justice; but in process
of time he was more frequently elected at the shiregemot, a general court, by the voice of the freeholders
of land; and Alfred, who was so true a friend to liberty
that he left it recorded in his will, that a native of
England "should be free as his own thoughts," was
nevertheless too wise to fancy that real liberty could be
long maintained if it degenerated into licentiousness.
He supported, therefore, the full power vested in the
freeholder of land, who had a stake in the country;

but never did he suffer power to fall into the hands of
the mob, certain that the base in spirit will ever be
the turbulent in action ; and therefore, even for their
own sakes, to be held in subjection.

The office of earl was not at first hereditary, though
in process of years it became such by the increasing
fitness, learning, and wealth of the aristocracy.   In
times of war the earl assumed the title of duke, or
heretoge, a title which signified 'a leader.'   He was
a member also of the Witenagemot, or 'assembly
of wise men,' the parliament of the Anglo-Saxons.
Such was the rank and office of Orgar, the founder
of our Abbey, the father of Elfrida ; and ere we turn
to the history of that monastic building, it will be
proper to say something respecting that of the earl
and his celebrated daughter.

Indeed, the story of Elfrida forms so striking a
feature in the history of this place, and as *one particular event* connected with it has been a subject of
discussion with antiquaries, there needs no apology
for here reverting even to those very circumstances
which are already so well known.

The daughter of Orgar, Earl of Devon, had
acquired such reputation for her charms, that it
excited the curiosity and interest of the king, whose
passionate admiration of beauty had already induced
him to commit many immoral actions, which Dunstan
(then Archbishop of Canterbury, and the keeper of
his conscience) let pass on terms of easy reprehension ;
though for a marriage contracted within what the
Church of Rome pleased to consider a prohibited
degree, he had, in the former reign, persecuted with
the utmost bitterness the youthful and royal pair,
Edwy and Elgiva.   But Edgar was more friendly to

the views of the primate, and to the monks; and was, also, as hard upon the married clergy as Dunstan could desire he should be. To treat, therefore, his amours with lenity, or to absolve them on the easiest possible penance, might have been considered as a grateful return for obligations such as these.

In order to satisfy his curiosity, Edgar deputed his friend and favourite, Earl Ethelwold, to visit Elfrida at her father's palace, which was situated in or near Tavistock; and Ethelwold, as we shall presently find, being considerably older than the young lady, perhaps there was not so much imprudence in the act as on the first view might be suspected. The object of the favourite's journey was to ascertain if she was really possessed of that surpassing beauty which fame had ascribed to her, and if so to offer her, on the part of the king, a crown as queen and consort of England. We see by this that Edgar must have entertained a very good opinion of his friend's taste; and we also see that he acted quite in character, and evinced no other desire in taking a wife than that of finding her very handsome. Such a motive, when it stands alone, has nothing in it of that delicacy which gives grace and dignity to the youthful passion of love; and we hear nothing of Edgar's being anxious to ascertain if she were good as well as fair.

Ethelwold, no doubt, set off with every intention to execute his charge honestly towards the king; but the poet writes—

> " Friendship is constant in all other things,
> Save in the office and affairs of love :
> Therefore all hearts in love use their own tongues.
> Let every eye negotiate for itself,
> And trust no agent ; for beauty is a witch
> Against whose charms faith melteth into blood."

Edgar had yet to learn this lesson, and Shakspere
was not then born to teach it.

The court of Orgar, equal in splendour to that of
many of the Saxon princes, received its greatest lustre
from the personal character of its lord.   Munificent
and courteous, zealous for the Church, brave and
noble, Orgar indeed was a man whose alliance might
be sought by Edgar as one of the most honourable
the age and the kingdom could afford.   Nor was he
at this period less happy in his domestic than in
his public fortunes.   His son Ordulph, of gigantic
stature and strength,[5] possessed a courage not inferior
in proportion to those extraordinary physical powers
with which it was combined.   He was also of such
eminent piety that, according to the monkish historians, Heaven deigned to visit him with visions
and dreams; to one of which, hereafter to be told,
we are indebted for the foundation of our Abbey on
the banks of his native Tavy.

Elfrida was the only daughter of this illustrious
earl.   Young, lovely, and living in comparative
seclusion under Orgar's care, amidst the shadowy
groves and sweet retirement of Devon, she had not
yet known the temptations which in after years,
awaking in her bosom the passions of pride, self-
will, and ambition, led her step by step to the commission of those foul crimes that, however much her
outward form might resemble a spirit of light, cast
over her soul a darkness which rendered it fit for those
regions where hope never enters.

At the time Ethelwold first beheld her, it is most
likely he saw nothing in her that could lead him to
suspect she was less amiable than beautiful.   He saw

[5] The thigh bone of Ordulph is still preserved in Tavistock Church.

and loved her for her surpassing fairness. Beauty is
considered by moralists and divines as a dangerous
gift: no doubt it is so unless it is governed by those
precepts of virtue and religion which render it harmless. Yet, when thus governed, surely as the gift of
God it must be numbered amongst his blessings.
There is a law to regulate all things of the earth
and of the spirit. The 'heavenly arch' that hangs
above our heads, and compasses the whole celestial
sphere, is beautiful with order and with light, and, as
the stay of all creation, is obedient to the Hand that
raised it. That 'heavenly arch' exalts not itself, but
its Maker. So should it be with human beauty; and,
when so considered, to condemn the fair gift of an
infinite and wise Disposer of all gifts, is as great a
folly as it would be to censure or to look with indifference on a delightful landscape, or to prefer the
hard and barren ground to mountain and valley
clothed with wood, and lovely in the mantle of its
verdure and its flowers.

Ethelwold thus captivated by her charms, unmind-
ful of his honour and unfaithful to his trust, demanded
her hand, not for Edgar but himself. Orgar, ignorant
of the more elevated fortune to which his daughter
was justly entitled by the intentions of the king, and
in all probability deeming the favourite an advantageous match for her, consented, provided Ethelwold
might gain Edgar's approval of the marriage. Besides
the respect which Orgar wished to show the king,
there might be some policy in thus referring to him
to sanction the proposal of the favourite; since the
time had not yet arrived that rendered a Saxon earl
of a shire in a great measure independent of any
authority higher than his own. The king had then

the power to nominate the alderman of a county; the office was not yet hereditary in its succession; so that the reigning prince might become troublesome should he take offence at any act that bordered on too much independence of his will.

To obtain Edgar's consent to marry the very woman Ethelwold had been deputed to visit on his account, must have been a difficulty which none but a crafty man would have attempted; as, by a fair statement of the case, the enamoured earl must have been certain such consent would be withheld. Despairing of success by honest means Ethelwold had recourse to artifice: and as such schemes generally end in open shame or misery, even so was it in this instance; since in obtaining his object by falsehood, he did but eventually "commend the poisoned chalice to his own lips." He now abused the king's ear with the report that though Elfrida was fair, her beauty was not equal to the celebrity it had acquired; no doubt her rank and fortune had been the cause of her personal attractions being thus magnified by the common voice of fame. And he took occasion to intimate, that though such advantages could be of no value to the king, they would be of great benefit to a nobleman of his court, and finally requested permission to marry her himself, as a means of raising his fortune. The king suspecting no deceit consented, and the marriage was solemnized; but Ethelwold, fearful of the consequences, held his bride in the utmost seclusion in Devon, lest, meeting the eye of Edgar, her fair face should at once betray the artifice by which he had made her his own.

But however much he might labour to hide it, Ethelwold's falsehood could not long be concealed.

No sooner had Edgar received the intimation that his confidence had been abused, than he resolved to discover the truth.   For this purpose he went to Exeter; and thence sent word to the Earl of Devon, with whom Elfrida and her husband were residing, that he designed speedily to be with him, to hunt in the Forest of Dartmoor adjoining.   The guilty Ethelwold, suspecting the true cause of the royal visit, now found that confidence which had enabled him to act with such duplicity, in a moment forsake him : he had no resource left; but acquainting his wife with the truth, entreated her by the plainness of her dress to conceal her charms as much as possible, from the eyes of a monarch whose susceptible and light disposition would so little enable him to resist them.

Elfrida promised compliance ; but, prompted by vanity and by resentment towards her husband for having been the means to deprive her of a crown, she used every art to set forth her beauty to the greatest advantage, and inflamed the king with so violent a passion, that he resolved to revenge himself on his perfidious favourite.   On the following morning, whilst they were hunting, he watched an opportunity, and taking Ethelwold at an advantage slew him ; and at a place in Dartmoor Forest called Wilverley, since Warlwood, the earl was found slain with an arrow, or, according to William of Malmesbury, run through the body with a javelin.

That historian also states that the illegitimate son of Ethelwold approached the king immediately after the commission of his father's murder, and on Edgar's asking him " How he liked that kind of game ?" barbarously and servilely replied, " Well, my sovereign

liege ; I ought not to be displeased with that which
pleases you." The king who could be brutal enough
to put such a question at such a moment to a son,
was quite capable of being pleased with the unnatural answer; and the young man from that hour
succeeded to his father's place in the royal favour,
which he held till the death of that monarch. From
the circumstance of this illegitimate son being a
man grown at the time of his father's death, we may
gather that Ethelwold must have been much older
than his wife, or his murderer ; since Edgar, who soon
after married Elfrida (probably younger than himself)
lived with her some years, and died at the early age
of thirty-two.

Edward, the child of his first marriage, succeeded
to the throne ; but Elfrida was anxious that her son
Ethelred should be king. In consequence of this
determination, about four years after Edgar's death,
she took an opportunity of ridding Ethelred of the
only impediment that stood between him and the
'golden round' that she longed to see glitter upon his
brow. For her step-son, Edward, chancing one day
to call at her castle gate, she hastened to receive him ;
and though the young king refused to alight from his
horse, he accepted the stirrup-cup she offered as the
customary mark of hospitality. Whilst engaged in
drinking, the unfortunate Edward was, by her order,
stabbed in the back by the hand of a ruffian. He rode
off immediately, mortally wounded ; and at length
dropped dead from his horse, near the door of a poor
blind cottager; where the body was found by Elfrida's
people, who had pursued Edward by tracking his
blood. Thinking to conceal so foul a crime, the cruel
step-mother caused the corpse to be thrown into a

well; but a few days after it was discovered and buried.

Such was the guilt of this miserable woman. It does not appear, however, that she was accessory to the death of Ethelwold. I am aware that the place where he fell has become a subject of doubt. I shall here, therefore, give the different opinions that may be cited, and leave you to determine which approaches nearest to the truth. Prince, in his curious work, the *Worthies of Devon*, expressly says that Earl Ethelwold was killed at *Wilverley*, since Warlwood, in the Forest of Dartmoor. There is a place near Dartmoor to this day called *Willsworthy;* and Prince makes this assertion on the authority of Risdon's *Manuscript Survey of Devon*. Risdon's reputation stands so deservedly high, as an antiquary who in his day had examined many ancient records, that from whatever source *he* derived his opinion it is worthy attention.

William of Malmesbury, on the contrary, says that Ethelwold was slain by Edgar whilst hunting "in a wood at *Warewelle*, or *Harewood*, in Dorsetshire." But Browne the poet has proved, in the instance of the river Tavy being printed the river Tau, that the printed copies of Malmesbury differed in that point from the manuscript one of '*Malmesbury's time*,' in the possession of his 'learned friend Mr. Selden.' No doubt this error arose from the carelessness of transcribers; and if the name of one place might be thus erroneously stated, even so might be that of another.

Some antiquaries, unacquainted with the localities of Earl Orgar's territory, and never suspecting that any printed copy of Malmesbury could be incorrect,

overlooked his error about the county, and determining to keep as close as possible to *Devon*, placed
the scene of Ethelwold's death on the opposite side
of the river Tamar, at *Harewood* in *Cornwall!* This,
I do not hesitate to say, is a most improbable conjecture; since in order to reach it Edgar must have
encountered the most formidable difficulties; those
of riding many miles about, through forests vast and
intricate, and rendered dangerous of access by a river
so broad and deep as the Tamar; for no bridge
could at any time have existed nearer than New
Bridge, a structure of a much later period: whilst on
the other hand, the Forest of Dartmoor lay contiguous
to Tavistock, where Orgar, the father of Elfrida, had
a palace; and where Ethelwold and his beautiful
wife were residing with him, when Edgar surprised
them by that visit which ended so fatally for the
husband.

Some have supposed the woods of Warleigh—and
certainly with much better reason than those of
Harewood—to have been the scene of the murder.
To reach those woods no river intervened, to render
access to them either difficult or dangerous. Besides,
they were in all respects fitted for the pleasures of
the chase. And if it was improbable that Edgar
should cross the river into Cornwall to commit the
murder, still less likely is it that (as some antiquaries
aver) he should ride so far as into Dorsetshire for that
purpose. William of Malmesbury might possibly
have been mistaken when he says that Elfrida built
a nunnery at Warewelle, or Harewood in *Dorset*, on
the spot where her *husband* was slain. After the
death of her second husband (the king who killed
her first) she retired to Corfe Castle, where she caused

his unfortunate son to be stabbed at her gate. He rode off, but his body was found in a wood in *Dorsetshire*. Might it not therefore have been in consequence of this circumstance that, after she was awakened to remorse, she erected the nunnery in expiation of so atrocious a crime? The death of Ethelwold probably cost her no remorse, since there is no evidence that she had any share in that murder.[6]

As a strong confirmation of this opinion, I shall here cite the following passage from the *Saxon Chronicle*: "This year" (978) "King Edward was slain at Corfes-geat (Corfe Castle) in the evening of the 15th of the Calends of April, and he was buried at *Wareham* without any royal honours. No worse deed than this had been committed amongst the people of the Angles since they first came to the land of Britain."[7] Now, when we recollect that William of Malmesbury says Elfrida built her nunnery at Warewelle, in Dorsetshire; and that Edward dropped dead from his horse in a wood, and was buried as above stated; I cannot help thinking that *Warewelle* and *Wareham* were contiguous, and that the nunnery was erected on the spot where *his* body was found, and not Ethelwold's.[8] It is absolutely necessary in all doubtful points to compare one fact with another, as the most careful chronicler will sometimes fall into an error; or mistakes (as Browne discovered

[6] Rapin says Elfrida founded *two* nunneries as an atonement for her crimes; one at Ambresbury in Wilts, and the other at Warewelle or Whorwel in Dorset.

[7] Miss Gurney's translation.

[8] Though Edward the Martyr was buried at *Wareham*, he did not long rest there; for, in 980, the *Saxon Chronicle* states that "St. Dunstan and the Alderman Ælfhere fetched the body of the holy King St. Edward from Wareham, and brought it with great pomp to Shaftesbury."

in William of Malmesbury) may have been committed for him in transcription. Whilst in Britanny, by an attentive examination of the localities of Auray, we discovered an error made even by Froissart, respecting the spot where the great battle was fought between De Blois and De Montford. For want of collating, even Hume committed a mistake about Elfrida; for when speaking of her marriage he says she was the daughter and *heir* of the Earl of Devon; this could not have been the case, as her brother Ordulph was then living.

Elfrida, about the time she built the nunnery at *Warewelle*, was not only held in execration by the people of England, but became a prey to a state of remorse bordering on despair. Her alarmed conscience represented to her imagination a fiend that was ever present before her eyes, on the watch to seize her soul to convey it to a place of torture. Her days and nights became horrible; and she was heard to shriek and wail as if endeavouring to escape the grasp of this imaginary phantom. She clothed herself with such armour as was then considered invulnerable to the shafts of infernal malice—a robe covered with crosses: and giving herself up to the rigours and seclusion of her nunnery, she there died a miserable but striking example of the retributive justice of Heaven, which thus visited her crimes by the bitter and enduring agonies of remorse.

Before I quit the subject of Edward's murder, I cannot resist giving the following passage from the *Saxon Chronicle*, as it serves to show with what just indignation the crime was considered. In speaking of his death that venerable record says—" His mortal kinsman would not avenge him, but his Heavenly

Father hath avenged him greatly. His earthly murderers would have blotted out his memory from the world, but the Avenger who is above, hath widely extended his fame in heaven and earth: and whereas they formerly would not bow down before his living body, now they piteously bend their knees to his dead bones."

So universal was the consternation with which all were seized on hearing of this event, that no man, after such an example of treachery, held his life to be safe. The murder, too, had been committed in violation of the common laws of hospitality, hitherto considered sacred. Deep drinking, the vice of the age, which both the Saxons and the Danish marauders had contributed to render familiar, was for awhile discontinued; since no one would trust himself in the unguarded posture of partaking of the social cup, for fear it should be followed by the blow of an assassin. Hence, as we are told by William of Malmesbury, each man before he tasted of the 'wassail bowl' required a pledge from his companion that he would watch over and protect him whilst engaged in the act. By all antiquaries this is considered the origin of the familiar expression of pledging, or desiring another to partake first of the cup.

I have already alluded to Mason's *Elfrida;* and that, following the popular error, he had laid the scene of his drama in Harewood forest, in Cornwall. This, however, is a trifling mistake compared to Miss Seward's; who, in one of her letters on visiting Gawthorpe Hall, the seat of Lord Harewood, in *Yorkshire*, talks about 'the poignancy of her sensations,' 'Harewood's glassy waters' shining through 'tangled brakes in the glens,' 'expanding into lakes' and 'sleeping on lawns,' whilst all the charm of these delights she experienced on this 'classic ground' (situated in Yorkshire) was conveyed by its connexion with the story and the drama of Elfrida! Mason took liberties enough with that story to destroy almost all historical truth; and Miss Seward goes a step beyond him: for she, something like Mr. Bayes's prologue, where the sun, moon, and earth 'dance the hays,' makes Yorkshire take the place of Devonshire with no more ado than the flourish of a pen. I notice this out of no motive of disparagement to Miss Seward, of whose writings (excepting this letter about Harewood) I know very little. But she has reputation: and therefore so gross an error ought to be remarked, lest it should mislead those who, being under the dominion of 'a name,' may think what such a lady as Miss Seward asserts must be true.

Wishing to refresh my memory respecting what Mason had made of the story of Elfrida, I last night read his drama, and his letters on the subject of his composing it on the Greek model; and though his play contains some very beautiful poetry, as I closed the book I could not help feeling the truth of what was so long ago said by Horace—'*Incredulus odi.*' Poems, dramas, and romances, though each when founded on historical subjects affords the greatest delight, should I think, if I may venture to give any opinion, be always made subservient to some useful purpose; and should never falsify the truth of history in any really important point. In many works, as the historical plays of Shakspere, and the historical novels of Sir Walter Scott, information and instruc-

tion accompany delight.   Who, for instance, has ever
read *Coriolanus* or *Julius Cæsar*, without becoming
familiarly acquainted with some of the most interesting characters and events of the Roman history? or
Henry IV. and *Henry VIII.*, without feeling as if he
were living in the very days of those Princes?   And
who has ever read *Old Mortality*, and many other of
those masterly and lively fictions, without becoming
familiar with the spirit of the times therein described,
and fancying himself carried back to the very scenes
in which the characters of the story bore so prominent
a part?

But this praise can scarcely be given to Mason,
who in his drama of *Elfrida* preserved little more of
truth in his historical characters than their names;
and has consequently perverted facts.   He tells us in
his letters, that a Chorus ought to be introduced in
every tragedy, "to advance the cause of honesty and
of truth," and that for want of this an audience will
often go from a play with very false impressions.
To follow the rule he has thus laid down, he ought
to have made his own Chorus in *Elfrida* have but
one burthen to their songs, and it should have been—
'This story is all false;' then neither audience nor
reader could have mistaken the matter.   For if truth
be in *historical* fiction what the soul is to the body—
the cause of its usefulness, its vitality, and its interest
in a moral view, we may say, comparatively, of the
flowers of poetry which Mason has so abundantly
scattered throughout his *Elfrida*, that they are but as
flowers scattered upon a corpse.

No female character throughout the whole history
of this country is stained with a worse crime than
that of Elfrida: yet Mason represents her as if she

had been as gentle and as amiable as a Lady Jane
Grey; and as constant and as virtuous in her love to
her husband Ethelwold, as a Lady Rachel Russell.
Though Elfrida had purposely set off her charms
with art to allure the king, and became immediately
after her husband's death the wife of his murderer,
yet the poet ends the play by making her swear to
die a widow for Ethelwold's sake! and the vow is
echoed by the Chorus, stationed on the scene to
'advance the cause of truth' with the reader or
spectator. It may also be remarked that the poet
has gained nothing by thus falsifying historical facts,
since the true story is more suited to the muse of
tragedy, whose emblems, the dagger and the poisoned
bowl, proclaim her to be the queen of terror. It is
also more replete with dramatic interest than his
alterations; and if he wanted fiction he might have
resorted to it without the change of a single event.
The monastic character of the times would have
opened to him a fine field; and the superstitious legends
then so generally credited would have furnished him
with a sufficient apology, had he introduced an old
monk, with a black cowl and a long beard, who like
the Chorus might have been made a sort of monitor
to the passions of the scene; and who, in his prophetic character, (for prophecy and visions were
common with the monks) might have warned or
foretold Elfrida the miseries that would follow as
the consequences of her pride, her cruelty, and her
ambition.

But I have done; for though a little angry with
Mason for altering and perverting the story of our
Tavistock heroine, no one admires him more than
I do; and if he had never written anything else,

such noble poetry as we find in his *Caractacus* would have placed him in the first rank of modern bards.

This letter having extended much farther than I designed it should when I took up the pen, I must defer the account of the Abbey till another opportunity.

TO ROBERT SOUTHEY, ESQ.

Vicarage, Tavistock, June 11th, 1832.

BEFORE entering upon the history of our Abbey, in
its foundation, its prosperity, and its overthrow, I may
perhaps be pardoned if I still endeavour, by a few
prefatory remarks, to keep in view the general state
of morals and religion, since abbeys and towns, like
the fortunes of individuals, are in a very great degree
indebted for their prosperity or their decline to the
state of the country in which they exist.

All nations throughout the world, more or less,
take their character from their religion ; and it fol-

lows as a necessary consequence, that where true religion is best practised and understood, there will men become the best and the most enlightened. The gods of barbarous nations are represented as fierce and bloody, and the barbarian is both. Those of Greece and Rome were warlike and luxurious, and the people were remarkable for war and luxury. And though they had amongst them a few such admirable persons as Socrates and Marcus Aurelius, yet the general character of their greatest and their best men was essentially different from that of the Christian philosopher.

The gentler virtues, the self-subduing spirit, inculcated by Christianity, which makes forgiveness of an enemy and the returning good for evil duties of the noblest kind, were unknown; and we therefore find no such men amongst the heathen worthies as our good Bishop Andrews, our Hooker, our Jeremy Taylor, or those humble and devout martyrs who, with a courage that equalled any ever displayed by the heroes of antiquity, had yet the meekness and the tenderness of the dove, the beautiful emblem of that Holy Spirit which dwelt within and sanctified both their hearts and minds.

The introduction of Christianity was therefore in every way a blessing; and notwithstanding the setting up traditions and inventions of men, as even of more import than the written word of God, rendered it both corrupt and superstitious, yet the history of this country will serve to show how powerfully and how happily, even in this state, Christianity acted on society at large. It was as the dawn of day after a long and black night. But it was reserved for the Reformation to dispel every noxious vapour of human

opinion, and to go forth with the splendour of an unclouded sun, when there was 'perfect day.'

It was the observation of Cicero in censure of the
poet, that instead of raising men to live ·after the
manner of the gods, Homer brought heaven down to
earth, and made the gods live after the manner of
men.　The same kind of censure may be passed on
the inventors of the Romish frauds and traditions;
for the things they added to the truth were more of
earth than of the spirit.

That monasteries in former ages were eminently
useful cannot be denied.　In those early times, when
the art of printing was unknown, all learning was
found within the cloister.　The regularity, the repose,
and the leisure of a monastic life were absolutely
necessary to the preservation and the culture of
letters.　Every monastery also had its school, and
the novices were in many instances scholars.　The
sons of princes and nobles were generally educated
within the walls ; and no rank or station was held to
be above obedience to the Church.　There youth was
instructed, and those habits of submission, so salutary
in themselves, so necessary for individual happiness,
(since it is by obeying others that men learn to master
their own passions) were inculcated as an essential
duty.　And age, as in the patriarchal state, was
looked up to with that deference and respect which
wisdom, derived from experience—its most certain
source—is ever entitled to command.　There is something beautiful in the picture of a young man, with
all his ardour, his golden hopes and airy imaginings,
standing silent with modesty in the presence of the
aged, and listening to those counsels which are to
guide his future course.

Regularity, without which there is little profit in study, was rigidly enforced by those minute rules that gave to each hour its appropriate task, its duties, and its relaxations. There was then little or no infidelity: for the student did not doubt those sacred truths which were above his capacity or his years; nor did he presume to fix bounds and limits to the all-wise providence of God, or to make the greatest things the least, by measuring them after the standard of his own faculties. Singularity was not then mistaken for superiority; consequently it did not raise a false ambition in the weak and the vain to become singular, or to show their own folly in the effort to be wise beyond that which was written for their learning.

Obedience to rulers, governors, and parents, was with them the promise in the spring-time of their days; and honour and wisdom became their summer fruits. How beautiful an example have we of this in the life of the great Sir Thomas More, who always, on first seeing his father for the day, knelt down and reverently begged his blessing. "*Train up a child in the way he should go*," says Solomon, "*and when he is old he will not depart from it.*" This was done, according to the religion of the times, and the child from early habit found submission no state of bondage.

Nothwithstanding the faults and superstitions of a monastic education, this early habit of obedience as a religious duty was to it as the salt of the whole; and the heroes of chivalry were thus prepared to follow without a murmur, through pain, toil, and death, wherever the call of duty—even though its object might sometimes be mistaken—should summon them to appear. The knights who, amid the arid and

burning sands of Syria, rescued from infidels at the
call of a hermit the sacred sepulchre of Jerusalem,
afford a striking instance of that devoted spirit of
obedience which men in those times thought it their
chief glory to pay to their religion.

In the cloister, too, the sage, whose learned toils
had no earthly praise for their object, and no reward
but that with which such labours repay themselves,
felt, as he contemplated the emblems of the sacred
sufferings before his eyes, that all human knowledge
in whatever path pursued has but one desired end—
to know 'Jesus Christ and him crucified' for the sins
of the whole world. Kings 'worn with the cares of
state,' sometimes came to end their days, and 'lay
their bones' within these monastic walls, and cast
down their crowns at the foot of Him whose diadem
was one of thorns. The poor, the abject, the despised,
the very beggar who took his alms and left his benison
at the convent door, as he lay prostrate before the cross
felt how ennobling was the humility of a Christian—
a humility that raised him from earth to heaven.

Such perhaps is the fair side of the picture, in the
earliest and the best state of monachism, before those
gross superstitions and frauds which gradually crept
in, produced its ruin in this country; and but for such
crimes these institutions might even to this day have
been spared, in a limited degree, as a refuge and a
blessing to the old, the learned, the pious, and the
friendless.

"Hermits," says Sir Thomas More, "as well as
monks, Montesinos, have been useful in their day.
Your state of society is not the better because it
provides no places of religious retirement for those
who desire and need it."

"Certainly not," replies Montesinos, "I consider the dissolution of the religious houses as the greatest evil that accompanied the Reformation."

"Take from such communities," says Sir Thomas More, "their irrevocable vows, their onerous laws, their ascetic practices; cast away their mythology, and with it the frauds and follies connected therewith, and how beneficial would they then be found! What opportunities would they afford to literature, what aid to devotion, what refuge to affliction, what consolation to humanity."[1]

Certain it is that a state of seclusion never was, and never will be, suited to all tempers and minds. The great evil of monachism was its want of discrimination in this respect. If temporary disgust, some present care, or some worldly interest, had been the cause of consigning a human being to the convent walls, and, on those circumstances passing away forgotten or reconciled, he grew tired of his retreat, and would gladly have returned again to take a part more congenial to his natural character in active life, his 'irrevocable vows' became to him a chain of adamant, that held him like Prometheus bound to a rock, whilst discontent as a vulture preyed upon his heart. Thus was his retreat a state of slavery, not of profit or of devotion; and he was as worthless to others as he was miserable to himself; since a large degree of mental ease, of comparative happiness, is necessary to render men useful in society: a despairing can never be an active mind, for a withered tree bears no fruit.

But perhaps the greatest dangers of a state of seclusion were experienced by those who, possessing

---

[1] See *Colloquies on the Progress and Prospects of Society.* Vol. i, page 338.

a vivid imagination, would not confine its exercise
to the right objects of faith, but lavished it upon
those mysteries of God which are beyond 'this
visible diurnal sphere.' Imagination is like wine,
a draught to sweeten life or to drown reason—all
depending on the measure of indulgence. To speak
of this high faculty in a figurative manner, her
power is regal, and the passions stand as servants
around her, in due subjection to her will; but if
once she permits them to exceed the bounds of
reason, they will hurry her along with them in their
wild career; madness or superstition seizing upon her
as a slave.

The wanderings, the perversions of the mind, no
doubt produced many of those extravagances and
disorders which have taken place in the worship of
that Being who is the life and soul of order; and who
shows forth the greatness of His power in His calm
but irresistible course. Yet how miserably was the
nature of God mistaken by those ascetic devotees
who fancied, in the darkness of their credulity, that
voluntary misery could be pleasing to Him; and
who, in the melancholy or the madness of their own
mood, dwelt on the visions of a distempered imagination, and gave them forth as the immediate
revelations of Heaven! To some such causes may
be attributed those false visions and miracles, that
render the pages of the monkish chroniclers in many
instances not much better than a garden, so en-
cumbered with weeds as to make it difficult to
separate from them whatever is of a useful or a
wholesome kind.

But though during the early ages it was the general
practice to ascribe remarkable events to some super-

natural cause, we must not hastily conclude that *all* records of such a nature were fictions.

It was the character of former ages to believe too much; our own believes too little: their vice was that of credulity; ours is too often that of infidelity: and what is above reason too many deem contrary to it. Yet so little do we really know concerning our own faculties, and of those things which we have no power to penetrate, that it should make us cautious how we judge the ways of God. There are spirits who walk the air as we do the earth; there are intelligences everywhere about us that, as winged messengers of God, perform His will, and yet we neither see nor understand them.

But what say the good and the wise, those who are wise because they are humble, and are as little children before their father? "I doubt not," says Addison, "that dreams, though known liars, sometimes speak the truth." And Bishop Bull (who combated superstition, and was the adversary of the learned and eloquent Bossuet) thus writes:—"I am no doter on dreams, yet I verily believe that some dreams are *monitory*, above the power of fancy, and impressed on us by some superior influence. Nor shall I so value the laughter of sceptics, and the scoffs of Epicureans, as to be ashamed to profess that I myself have had some convincing experiments of such impressions. Now it is no enthusiasm; but the best account that can be given of them is, to ascribe these things to the ministry of those invisible instruments of God's Providence that guide and govern our affairs and concerns—the angels of God."

The remarks here ventured arose from my thoughts having been turned on the subject of dreams, by

finding how much an attention to them was the
characteristic of the times about which I am now to
write; for the foundation of our Abbey is ascribed,
according to the Cartulary of Tavistock, to a vision
or dream; though it is one of so. marvellous and
monkish a kind, that it most likely had its origin in
the customary practice and credulity of the chroniclers
of the age. Be this as it may, after consulting all
the authorities I can here command, and some
original notes and extracts from various writers
made by Mr. Bray, I now proceed to glean from the
whole the sum and substance of the following wonderful tale.

I must, however, first observe that Orgar, Earl of
Devon, died A.D. 971, and was interred in the Abbey
Church of Tavistock, where his tomb, and that of
his son Ordulph, William of Malmesbury states
were to be seen in his time. As the Abbey was
·commenced in 961, it should appear that, though the
idea of its erection originated with the son, yet as
Orgar was then alive, and indeed survived him ten
years, he was considered, and with good reason, its
co-founder.

Ordulph was a religious and devout man, and
rising one night, as was his custom, went out of
doors to offer up his prayers. There is something so
remarkable in this, (since many of the Druidical
temples, we know, were used as places of worship
with the early Christians, and on that account were
long afterwards held sacred) that it would almost
lead one to suspect that some vestige of this nature
was the favourite resort of Ordulph for the purposes
of his midnight devotion. Whilst engaged in the
act of prayer he beheld in a vision a glory that

seemed to reach from earth to heaven, surpassing the
brilliancy of the sun; and he thought on the goodness
of God, who appeared to Moses in the burning bush,
and who led forth the children of Israel by day with
the pillar of the cloud, and by night with that of fire.
Struck with awe at this miraculous appearance,
Ordulph again retired to rest, and after shedding
many tears sleep closed his eyes, and he beheld in a
dream a 'shadow like an angel,' whose countenance
was of exceeding brightness, and who accosted him
with the words—'*Ne timeas, vir Deo dilecte.*' The
spirit then commanded him to rise and erect an
oratory on the place where he had seen the glory,
and where he should find four rods fixed at right
angles, to the honour of the four evangelists, who
had, as on a four-wheeled chariot, spread the word
of the gospels throughout the world. On the fulfil-
ment of this command, the angelic messenger promised him the forgiveness of his sins.

Starting from sleep, Ordulph related the vision to
his wife, who affirmed that she had seen the like;
and after saying his prayers˙ devoutly on his knees,
he once more composed himself to rest. But the
same angelic figure appeared to each a second time,
and rebuked the husband for his delay; telling him
that to obey was better than sacrifice. And the
same visitation being a third time repeated on the
same night, Ordulph no longer hesitated. Rising
therefore early in the morning, and reverently making
the sign of the cross, he entered a neighbouring wood,
where he found the precise spot that had been re-
vealed to him, by the four rods. It was pleasant,
open, and every way suited for the purpose; and
there he soon raised an oratory, on the western side

of which he afterwards founded a very magnificent monastery to the honour of Mary, the mother of God, and St. Rumon, and so large as to receive a thousand men.   To this he added several other houses for the service of the monks, and at length he richly endowed it.[2]   This noble abbey completed, Prince, the author of the *Worthies of Devon*, says, "He filled it with Augustine friars, afterwards, from their *habit*, called *black* monks." In this, as we shall presently see, Prince must confound the Augustines, who first inhabited it, with the Benedictines who soon after took their place; since in the earliest times the former Order were distinguished by *white* habits, though a black mantle was long after allowed to them; whereas the Benedictines, from their very foundation, were clad entirely in *black*.

Ordulph is represented to have been of gigantic stature, and prodigious strength. Travelling towards Exeter with King Edward the Confessor, to whom he was related, when they came to the gates of the city they found them locked and barred, while the porter, knowing nothing of their coming, was absent. Upon this Ordulph, leaping off his horse, took the bars in his hands, and with great apparent ease broke them in pieces, at the same time pulling out part of the wall. Not content with this, he gave a second proof of his strength; for, breaking the hinges with his foot, he laid the gates open. Whilst those who witnessed this extraordinary feat could not suppress their admiration, the king, pretending to underrate

[2] With the manors of Tavistock, Midleton (now Milton), Hatherleigh, Borington, Leghe, Dunethem, Chuvelin, Linkinhorn; and his wife with the manors of Hame, Werelgete, Orlege, Auri, Rame, Savyoke, Pannaston, Tornbire, Colbroke, Lege, Wesithetun, and Clymesland.

his prowess, declared it must have been done by the sole power of the devil, and not by the strength of man. However wonderful this story may appear, it is not more so than what William of Malmesbury relates of him in another particular—that he was of such gigantic stature, that for his amusement he would often bestride a river, near his residence, of ten feet broad ; and with his knife would chop off the heads of such wild animals as were brought to him, and so cast them into the stream.

But notwithstanding the superiority of his strength and stature, Ordulph died in the flower of his age. He gave orders to be buried at his abbey at Herton, in Dorsetshire ; but was interred in or near the Abbey Church of Tavistock, where a mausoleum or tomb of vast dimensions was erected to his memory, which is represented to have been visited as a wonder. Prince, in his *Worthies of Devon*, says, " There is nothing now remaining of it but an arch, where, as tradition testifies, this mighty tomb stood."[3]

An arch still remains in tolerable preservation on the site of what, there is every reason to believe, had been part of the Abbey Church. It bears evidently

---

[3] " Browne Willis tells us, that in his time the sepulchral effigies of this Saxon giant, of great length, were still preserved by lying under an arch in the north side of the cloisters of the Abbey Church. This identical arch, as I apprehend, still remains a solitary remnant of the immediate appendages of the Abbey Church. The architecture of this recess is of the time of Henry III. And as there is no example extant which can lead us to conclude that sepulchral figures were placed over tombs in the middle ages, till the twelfth century, and as it was usual to re-edify and remodel the monuments of saints and remarkable persons, (of which custom the shrine of Edward the Confessor, now in Westminster Abbey, is a prominent example) Ordulph's tomb, per- haps, underwent a renovation about this period, and was supplied with a sepulchral effigy."—*Notices of Tavistock and its Abbey.* By A. J. KEMPE, F.S.A.

the appearance of a shrine, or sepulchral monument; consisting of a rich and highly-relieved moulding, supported by three short pillars at either extremity. It is pointed at the top, but spreading, and being closed, or built so as to form part of a wall, is crossed just above the capitals of the columns by a range of small arches, supported also themselves by a row of little pillars on a kind of plinth.

Though Mr. Bray is rather inclined to consider this the tomb of Ordulph, it is generally denominated Childe's tomb. And as the story of the latter person, if not true, is at least curious, I shall not scruple to introduce it here.

Having no children of his own, and being the last of his house, which was of ancient standing in the county, Childe of Plymstock is said to have made a will, wherein he devised his lands to that church in which he should happen to be buried. Some time after, whilst recreating himself with hunting in the Forest of Dartmoor, he lost both his way and his company, during an inclement season, in a very deep snow. Being surrounded by desolation, and seeing no possible means of escape, he began to think what was to be done to keep life and soul together; and as in his day the acts and miraculous adventures of the clergy and the saints were much talked of, it is not impossible he might have called to mind one recorded of Elsinus, the Saxon Bishop of Worcester, when crossing the Alps to receive his pall from the hands of the Pope. Be this as it may, he determined to take up the same kind of lodging the saint and bishop was said to have done; and so killing his horse, and embowelling him on the spot, old Childe crept into the body for the purpose of procuring a little warmth in his distress. But the expedient had not saved a saint, how then could it be expected to preserve a sinner? Finding his last hour approach, Childe, in order to confirm his will, took some of his own blood, (though one would have thought it was more likely to have been that of his horse) and made the following distich in writing; though how he procured pen or paper to do so this wonderful record has forgotten to tell:—

> " He that finds and brings me to my tomb,
> My land of Plymstock shall be his doom."[4]

Now whatever modern critics may think of the rhyme, it soon appeared that the monks of Tavistock found there was reason in it; and good reason, too, that they should constitute themselves the heirs of old Childe; for soon hearing that he was frozen to death somewhere near Crockern Tor, they set their wits and hands to work to give him as speedily as possible an honourable sepulchre.

But as the heirship was left thus vague and open to competition, there were others who thought themselves quite as much, if not more, entitled to succeed than the friars; and these were the good people of Plymstock, in whose parish the lands in question had their standing; and though not invited to the funeral, yet, out of respect to the old gentleman or more probably to his acres, they not only determined to invite themselves, but also to try how far club-law might settle

[4] Prince says, in the *Worthies*, "Now something in confirmation hereof I find, that there is a place in the Forest of Dartmoor, near Crockern Tor, which is still called Childe of Plymstock's tomb; whereon, we are informed, these verses were engraven, and heretofore seen, though not now:

> " 'They first that find, and bring me to my grave,
> My lands, which are at Plymstock, they shall have.'"

the heirship in their favour; and so, taking their post at a certain bridge over which they conceived the corpse must of necessity be carried, they came to the resolution to wrest the body out of the hands of the holy men by force, if no better settlement of the matter could be effected.

The friars, however, were men of peace, and had no mind, may be, to take up any weapon sharper than their wits; since, as Dr. Fuller says, when speaking of this adventure, "they must rise betimes, or rather not go to bed at all, that will overreach the monks in matters of profit;" for these cunning brothers, apprehensive of losing their precious relics, cast a slight bridge over the river at another place, and thus, crossing with the corpse, left the men of Plymstock the privilege of becoming, very sincerely, the chief mourners, whilst they interred old Childe in their own Abbey Church, and according to his last will took possession of his lands.

It is certain that the Abbot of Tavistock enjoyed considerable property at Plymstock, which is now in the possession of the Duke of Bedford; and Fuller states that, in memory of this successful stratagem on the part of the monks, the bridge raised in or near the spot in Tavistock bears the name of *Guile* Bridge to the present day. It is, however, now more commonly known by the name of the Abbey Bridge. Childe is supposed to have lived in the reign of Edward the Third.

The Abbey, with its church, was dedicated to St. Mary the Holy Virgin, and St. Rumon; the parish church, to St. Eustachius. The arms of the Abbey were gules, two crosiers saltire ways between two martlets or, in a chief argent three mullets sable.

The arms of Orgar were, according to one authority, verrey D. and arg., in chief or two mullets gules. According to another, verrey B. and arg., in chief arg. three mullets sable. This latter coat, impaled with the arms of the Abbey of Tavistock, was, in the time of Prince, painted in a glass window of the dining-room at the Bear Inn, Exeter. Though little of a herald, I am thus particular, as, in the groined ceiling to the porch of what was formerly the Abbot's hall (says Mr. Bray, from whose papers I have gleaned the above particulars) the latter arms, surrounded with a wreath, are still discernible, cut in granite, and forming one of the key-stones; while, on the other, in a lozenge, is represented a dove with a cross on its breast.

Respecting St. Rumon, to whom, with the Virgin, the Abbey Church was dedicated, I find the following notice in the account by my brother, Alfred Kempe, before mentioned.

" Leland found a MS. life of Rumon in Tavistock Abbey at the time of the suppression of monasteries. He appears by this work to have been one of many saints who emigrated from Ireland into Cornwall in the fifth or sixth century, for the purpose of enjoying the deepest seclusion, and to have erected for himself an oratory in what the author terms a Nemæan forest, formerly a most frequented haunt of wild beasts. This, according to the MS., was at Falmouth, where he died and was buried; but the fame of his sanctity still surviving, Ordulph, on completing the monastery at Tavistock, was induced to remove his bones from their resting-place, and to enshrine them in the Abbey Church, where they became an object of ignorant devotion. William of Malmesbury seems

to lament that the miracles of Rumon, in common
with those of many other saints, owing to the violent
hostility of subsequent times, remained unrecorded.
No doubt this hiatus was amply supplied in the
volume found by Leland, and the labours of one
who perhaps was really a zealous and fearless pro-
pagator of Christianity in the primitive times, were
converted into a series of ascetic mortifications,
degrading to reason, and worse than useless to
society, while his sanctity became attested by the
detail of miracles more absurd than the wildest of
the *Arabian Tales*. Of the reputed saints, however,
many were really such in their day; heroic soldiers,
like St. Paul, of Christ's church militant on earth,
in perils and persecutions; but the purity of their
doctrines becoming obscured during temporal convulsions, the monks issued from their *scriptoria*
new versions of their lives, which suited their own
purposes for the time, but have had the effect in these
enlightened days of clouding the memory of holy men
with much of doubt and incredulity."

The Abbey of Tavistock being thus finished,
dedicated, and endowed, in the year 981 King
Ethelred, the son of Elfrida, confirmed and granted
to it many considerable privileges, making it free
from all secular services excepting rates for military
expeditions, and the repair of bridges and castles.
"In the preamble to this instrument he laments
that certain persons, stained with infidelity, had
been allowed, without his consent, (he being, as it
might be said, in an infant and powerless state, not
more than twenty years of age) to drive the monks
of Tavistock from their sacred places and possessions.
This stain of infidelity was, I apprehend, nothing

more than a disbelief in the sanctity of monachism, and the expulsion of the monks from Church bene- fices, in which they were replaced by the much more deserving secular clergy." Such are my brother's remarks; but we shall hereafter see that, in all probability, the expulsion thus alluded to by Ethel- red had reference to the Augustine friars, who were so soon turned out of the very Abbey in which they had been placed by Orgar and Ordulph. What I have to say on the subject must, however, be reserved for another letter.

Ethelred's charter (witnessed by his mother, Queen Elfrida, and the Archbishop of Canterbury) em- powered our Tavistock monks to choose their own abbot, and contained the following severe penalty on any one who should presume to alienate any part of the privileges thus granted and confirmed.

"If any seduced with the madness of covetousness shall presume to infringe this our munificence, let him be driven from the communion of Christ's Church, and from any participation of the body and blood of the Son of God; let him stand at last with the traitor Judas on the left hand; and, unless he repents and makes satisfaction, let the vile apostate never be forgiven, either in this life, or in that to come; but let him be thrust down, with Ananias and Sapphira, to the bottom of hell, where let him be tormented for ever. Amen."

Almer, a Saxon, was chosen the first abbot; and I shall presently give a list of all the abbots, down to the Reformation. Something must now be said of the order of monks who were appointed to the Abbey about the time that Ethelred granted his charter.

LETTER XXIII.

TO ROBERT SOUTHEY, ESQ.

Vicarage, Tavistock, August 1st, 1832.

IT is not unworthy observation that about the time of the building of Tavistock Abbey, Dunstan, that crafty churchman of miracle-lying memory, by his exertions removed Algarus from the see of Crediton, after he had held it ten years, to make way for Alfodus, a friend of his own, who there remained bishop during seventeen years, when he died. What motive could have prompted Dunstan to desire the removal of Algarus is not ascertained; but it may, I think, be inferred with a nearer approach to certainty than generally accompanies conjecture.

The power which that ambitious primate had acquired over the mind of the licentious Edgar is too
well known to need much notice here ; the king was,
in fact, in all ecclesiastical matters, no more than an
instrument to forward the artful and grasping designs
of Dunstan.   Assured of royal countenance, he soon
put in execution the tyrannical schemes which he had
so long formed to establish celibacy as a law with the
clergy, to expel or convert them into monks, and to
render those monks Benedictines : a rule that was
dependent on himself, and would help to carry on
his plans throughout the kingdom.   Dunstan, moreover, had been the first abbot of Glastonbury, a
monastery built, endowed, and filled by him with
Benedictines; an order of which Fuller (in the spirit
of pleasantry he so constantly mingles with the most
excellent sense) says, " they now began to swarm in
England, more than maggots in a hot May, so
incredible was their increase."

No sooner had Edgar succeeded to the throne of
his unfortunate brother Edwy, than the primate procured Oswald and Ethelwald to be promoted to the
sees of Worcester and Winchester, as ecclesiastics
avowedly devoted to the grand object of forwarding
by every means the advancement of the Benedictine
rule ; and he hesitated not to remove or persecute any
of the clergy who offered the least resistance to his
will.   When we recollect these things, we need not
look far to find a very probable motive for the removal
of Algarus from the see of Crediton.   Nor can I
help fancying that, by inference at least, this motive
may be yet further developed, and that it was not
other than connected with the Order of monks in our
Abbey.

Orgar, Earl of Devon, in the very nature of his office could not but be in some measure acquainted with Algarus; since, as Bishop of Crediton, the latter must have taken his seat with the earl of the county in the Shiregemot Court. Now, at the time Orgar contemplated building and endowing his Abbey on the banks of the Tavy, might he not have consulted with Algarus respecting the *Order* of monks he should place in it? For if Prince be correct in his statement (and there is no reason to think he was otherwise, as he chiefly followed that excellent antiquary Risdon) our Abbey was at *first* peopled with *Augustine* canons:[1] though according to Dugdale such Order could not have been then of long continuance; for Tavistock Abbey was founded in 961, and Dugdale cites a charter of the reign of Ethelbert, dated 981, giving the monks therein power to choose their own abbot, in which they are expressly stated to be of the *Benedictine* rule. The same learned writer tells us, that Edgar in 964 made it his boast that he had endowed not less than forty-seven monasteries of that Order in his kingdom. Our Abbey, it will be recollected, was commenced three years before this; and was endowed by Orgar, *not* by Edgar.

When we consider the boast on the part of the king, we see how friendly he was to the monks whom Fuller compares to the 'maggots in a hot May.' And when we consider also Dunstan's determination to have all the monks Benedictines, the Augustine canons of Tavistock were tolerably sure of being turned out. And the removal of Algarus (in whose

[1] The Augustine Order seems to have been a favourite one with the family of the Earl of Devon; for his daughter, Queen Elfrida, peopled her convents of Warwelle and Amblesbury with Augustine Nuns.

diocese they were) by the interference of Dunstan, leads me to suspect that the bishop was, in some way or other, an obstacle to this change of the Order; or he might at first have prevailed with Orgar to make choice of the Augustines, which suited not with the plans and intrigues of Dunstan; for we cannot doubt that with his views, an abbey endowed on so large a scale as Tavistock (to hold a thousand men) and by so great a benefactor as Orgar, must have been a foundation worth intriguing for on the part of the primate, who sought to extend his own power by peopling, if it were possible, every monastery with those Benedictines who were so entirely subservient to his will.[2]

His character renders these conjectures (and they are only offered as conjectures) the more likely; since, with the exception of Wolsey, there is not, perhaps, in the ecclesiastical history of this country, so deeply designing, or so far-sighted a prelate as Dunstan. "Becket," says the *Book of the Church*, had a "daring spirit, a fiery temper, and a haughty heart," loved power, and pursued his ends by means suffi-

[2] The dislike which Queen Elfrida, and her son Ethelred, entertained for Dunstan is well known; and so far had it extended that, at one time, there was the queen's party, and the archbishop's, in the State. "Elfrida" (says Turner in his *History of the Anglo-Saxons*) "was as ambitious as Dunstan, and therefore became his rival. She joined the party of the clergy, and endeavoured to bias the minds of the great in favour of her son Ethelred." This was *before* he succeeded to the throne by her murder of Edward the Martyr. It is therefore the more probable that Ethelred's complaint, in the preamble of his charter, about the monks being turned out of their possessions in Tavistock Abbey, referred to the *previous* removal of the *Augustine* canons. Some years after this event, the Abbey being thus finished and endowed, King Ethelred, grandson of the founder, confirmed and granted to it many considerable privileges, making it free from all secular services, those before named excepted.

ciently proud and overbearing. But the high tone
with which he maintained the dignity of the priesthood, as, with his crosier in his hand, he met Henry
face to face,—presenting before him that pastoral
emblem of a servant of the Good Shepherd, as arms
placed in his hands by God Himself, to command
even the respect of kings—inspires a feeling of admiration which true magnanimity will always awaken
in a generous breast; and was far different from the
mean compliances with the king's vices, the frauds
and the hypocrisy, of Dunstan. Those mean compliances were apparent when he enjoined on Edgar a
mock penance for the flagrantly immoral actions of
his life: since his penances were no weightier than
that the king was not to wear his crown for a certain
space of time, and was to fast during certain days.
And most truly did he turn even the king's sins to
his own profit, when above all other things he recommended that the royal penitent, as an atonement for
them, should persecute the married clergy might and
main, expel them, and set up the Benedictine rule
throughout the land. Assuredly the acts of Dunstan
witness for him that his intercourse with the devil was
no fiction, though it may be questioned if it were
not in a more friendly way than that of taking him
by the nose.

However, to the praise of the Benedictines be it
spoken, their Order, from the earliest times to the
latest, was favourable to learning. And as any history of our Abbey would be very imperfect did it
not give some account of the rule which prevailed
in it for so many centuries, instead of offering any
excuses for here introducing it I should have to
apologize did I omit it: more especially as it will be

found, in the sequel, that our Tavistock monks have
the honour of being connected with the art of printing in its earliest age; and, indeed, as Benedictine
brothers, may be classed with those who assisted in
the preservation and revival of letters.

Though foreign wars have occasionally been the
means of spreading literature, or of bringing it with
profit home, yet nothing, it is universally allowed,
is so injurious to its immediate interests, as the
revolutions and civil brawls of political states. Very
different from the first position, however, was the
invasion of Italy; when Rome being sacked by the
Goths, in the time of Honorius, and the whole
country subsequently conquered by Odoacer, completed the ruin of that celebrated empire, second
only to Greece as the fertile mother of genius and
the nursery of learning.

Learning, though fearfully assailed and at last
overthrown in the empire of the West, was saved
from total extinction by the followers of the Christian
Church. It has been well remarked by an intelligent
but anonymous writer on the subject of its decay,
that whilst a 'Gothic tempest' would have swept from
Europe the arts and the written wisdom of antiquity,
one thing contributed to save them from total destruction, though that was in itself a bad thing—
'superstition.' For the barbarous hordes of the
North entertained so great a dread of their idolatrous
gods, that it inspired them with a fear and deference
for their priesthood; and this feeling in some measure
accompanied them even into foreign countries, and
was now and then evinced towards the ministers of a
foreign religion; so that the monastery (and would
that the Danes had done the same in England at

a subsequent period!) was sometimes spared, when palaces were sacked and committed to the flames.

In the primitive ages of Christianity, learning was alone cultivated by the Fathers of the Church; and the writings of such men as St. Chrysostom, Augustine, Gregory Nazianzen, Cyprian, and others, independent of the great truths they inculcate, were of that feeling and poetic order of eloquence which ranks them next to the prophets and the apostles, and shows that the writers were filled with a large portion of the Holy Spirit, so abundantly poured forth in the early ages of the Church. Their disciples followed in their path; and whilst the barbarities of the Northern conquerors had spread around a darkness which, to the human soul, was as 'thick night,' light was only to be found in the cell of the Christian scholar; whose lonely lamp, as it glimmered on the shores of some placid sea, was a guiding star to the weary and persecuted of the Church, where religion and learning, those twins of peace and love, reposed like the dove of David far away from the stormy winds and the tempest.

That not only the sacred writings, but such of the classics as have come down to us, were preserved in the monasteries, is a fact so universally known that nothing more than here to notice it need be said upon the subject. The Benedictines, from the seventh to the last century, were employed in those labours that have made the learned of all times their debtors. And amongst many excellent works, one of the most valuable sent by them into the world in modern days, is an edition of St. Chrysostom, edited by Montfaucon, with the assistance of other members of the same community.

The Benedictine Order had its origin with Benedict, an Italian, who, about the end of the fifth century, first attracted notice on account of his talents and his worth. He is generally considered to have been the son of a peasant, though some writers have affirmed that his father was of a noble house. Be this as it may, his zeal for religion and good morals proved that he was possessed of that true nobility of mind which, as an old writer says, "hath its patent from God Himself, and needeth no earthly addition." Benedict, on conversing with young men of his own age, felt so shocked at observing the licentiousness of their manners, that he retired from the world, and shut himself up in a cavern, where no one, saving an old monk, knew of his retreat. At length he was induced to converse with the monks belonging to the community of his friend; and so much were they edified by listening to his devout discourses, that they spread his fame far and near; and after a while he was requested to leave his cave, and become superior of a monastery in the neighbourhood.

Sacrificing his love of solitude for the hope of being useful to others, Benedict accepted the office, but resolved, should he be disappointed in his expectations, that the old cavern should once more become his home. The monks over whom he now presided in their religious exercises, fell far short of the ideas he had formed of devotional perfection; he liked not their manners, and they liked not his discipline, and so they speedily parted on less happy terms than they had met. According to those chroniclers who celebrated the lives of the saints, the power of working miracles was now added to all his other extraordinary endowments; and this power drew

around him a multitude of followers and disciples.
It is to be supposed they supplied him amply with
this world's goods; since, unless he did it by miracle,
Benedict erected by his own means many monasteries, and placed in them persons who were more
willing than the monks had been to follow his rule;
and even some of the nobles brought to him their
children, that they might receive such an education
as he should direct.

Imitating the manner of life practised by the holy
apostles, Benedict travelled into several kingdoms,
preaching the gospel, and confirming the truth of its
doctrine by many marvellous works. In the country
of the Samnites he overthrew the altar of Apollo,
destroyed the statue of that god, cut down his grove,
and erected an oratory in the place where the heathen
temple had stood; but so numerous were the persons
who wished to devote themselves to his way of life,
that he found it necessary to turn his oratory into a
monastery, of which he now became the chief, and
thus established on a more permanent footing that
rigid Order which ever after bore his name.

Benedict was not the only saint of his family; his
sister, to whom he was exceedingly attached, being
no less celebrated for piety than himself. She was a
nun, and one day only in the year did these near
relatives indulge themselves with any pleasure so
allied to earthly feelings as that of the interchange of
fraternal affection. During an interview of this description, whilst Benedict, attended by his disciples,
was about to retire, after having preached and prayed
from his cell, his sister threw herself on her knees
before him, and begged him to tarry another day;
but her brother told her that the rule of his Order did

not allow him to pass one night beyond the walls of
the monastery of which he was the chief. She then,
in a fit of passionate sorrow, supplicated God to grant
her patience and resignation, as she felt assured that
she should never more behold her most beloved friend.
Benedict endeavoured to console her; and though he
refused compliance with her request a sudden and
violent storm which ensued caused some delay in
his departure. At last he went: great however was
his grief when, soon after his return to the monastery, he received the information that his sister was
dead—so speedily had her own prediction been
fulfilled. He caused her body to be removed to
the tomb that he had prepared for himself, in order
that his ashes might hereafter mingle with hers in the
same grave.

Another striking story is recorded of Benedict, respecting his interview with the fierce Totila, King of
the Goths. So great was the reputation of the saint,
that the barbarian prince entertained a wish to see
him, and the more so as he understood that Benedict
possessed the gift of prophecy, and he hoped to learn
from him some intelligence of his future destiny. The
king was struck with awe on beholding the venerable
aspect of the saint, and he who had never before
humbled himself in the presence of mortal fell at the
feet of the recluse, who had nothing about him to
excite terror excepting that air of authority with
which, as a prophet of God, he looked upon the king
and reproached him for his cruel victories. Totila,
alarmed but not converted, struggled with feelings so
new to him and so embarrassing; and determining,
let what would be the event, he would inquire of this
man of God his future fate, received, in reply to those

inquires, the following brief prediction: "You will enter Rome; you will pass the sea; nine years a crown is yours, but the tenth that crown shall be given to death." This warning was said to be strictly fulfilled, for Totila died in the tenth year after he had entered the city of Rome. Many are the legends told of St. Benedict. No doubt he was a remarkable person; and the great object, both of his rule and of his life, was to bring into a more moral government the then existing orders of monachism. He had also the good sense to recommend the cultivation of letters to all who devoted themselves to religious retirement. Such was the man who founded the order of the Benedictines.

CROSS ON WHITCHURCH DOWN.

In this neighbourhood we often meet in our walks and rides, in many a solitary spot, a rude and ancient cross; some so ancient that we are inclined to consider them as having been set up by the earliest converts to Christianity in this part of England.

When we meet with a vestige of this description in the vast desolation of Dartmoor, or in the midst of the rural scenes of wood and water that abound in Devon, near the village or the antique church, how many delightful thoughts and feelings arise in the breast of him who views it in its relation to past times and holy men! Yes, those who reverence antiquity, who love knowledge as the friend of all that is noble and good—of all that makes life pleasant, and time as a field that if carefully cultivated will find its harvest in eternity, will look with an eye of deep interest on such venerable records of the past: even the rudest emblem of the cross will not be met with in vain.

Well would it have been with those who conducted the great Reformation had they been content to repair rather than to overturn. And how good it is to preserve temper in all things may be learned from the example of St. Paul, who, when he saw the altar dedicated by the Greeks to the 'Unknown God,' did not overthrow it, but Him whom they ignorantly worshipped truly taught them to understand; thus showing that a heathen altar, from which the false fires of idolatry had arisen, was as capable as the altar of Abraham of becoming a place of sacrifice to the Father of truth.

How often, as I have wandered under the Abbey walls, that now form the boundary of our own garden, and looked on the romantic and beautiful scene that was before me, have I fancied I could see it, animated with human beings, as it must have appeared in other times. These walls were spared during the general destruction; their massiveness and the roughness of their stone were not improbably their protection.

They are even now nearly perfect; and in the quarter towards the Abbey Bridge appear lofty and battlemented. A tower called the Still-house, in one part stands forward and breaks the uniformity of the long line of wall, so beautifully hung with ivy. A raised causeway lies between these walls and the river, and affords a walk so delightful, that it may truly be termed the Abbey terrace.

Immediately below this causeway flows the rapid Tavy, over vast masses of rock that here and there divide the current of the waters, and form them into many picturesque and low falls, white and dazzling

TAVISTOCK ABBEY WALLS.

with foam. On the opposite hill, beautifully diversified by trees, some of which droop their branches into the passing waters, once stood a cell, the Hermitage of St. John. Of this no memorial is now left, excepting a spring of the purest kind, but the spot is still called by its ancient name ; no doubt this was the sacred fountain dedicated to John the Baptist. There is a record, preserved with the parish documents, consisting of an old inventory of the treasury of Tavistock church, in which it appears that a hermit left his silver crucifix, inclosing a piece of the true cross, to our church. In all probability the recluse who made this bequest was the hermit of St. John.

As you have already read of *the Walk* (as it is called) under our Abbey walls, in *Fitzford*, I do not here enter upon more minute particulars, lest it should come to you as a tale twice told. I shall only therefore add that, looking to the east, the Guile Bridge and the distant heights of Dartmoor, intersected by some trees that grow at the foot of the hill beyond the bridge, close a scene of beauty seldom found so near a populous town in any part of England. As the walls I have mentioned formed the boundary of the Abbot's garden, and there was, and yet remains, a portal which stands near the Still-house, opening upon *the Walk*, I am disposed to think it might have been used by the holy brothers, whenever they wished to sally forth and enjoy the cool air from the river in their hours of recreation. The river alone separated them from the precincts of the Hermitage, a view of which they commanded from this walk.

I have often fancied, as I looked across the Tavy, that I could see the Gothic oratory as it once appeared about the spring ; the roof which formerly overarched it, the sculptured image of the Baptist, in his raiment of camel's hair, as he stood in a niche above, pointing with his hand to the holy well beneath, and holding in the other a staff with the banner

of the Agnus Dei.   The crucifix, the hour-glass, and
the skull appear on the rough-hewn table, and there
kneels the venerable hermit, engaged in the office of
his evening prayers; as the 'small birds' twitter on
the boughs around his cell, and seek their nest amid
a canopy of leaves, whilst the setting sun casts over
the whole scene a departing gleam that 'fires the
proud tops' of the Abbey towers and walls, or flashes
on the rushing waters in meteor rays of light.   The
stillness of evening settles on all around; not a human
sound breaks the universal repose: the masses of
rock, now seen only in their outline, assume a variety
of dark and fantastic forms, as the constant murmur
of the Tavy, that never ceases, seems to find its echo
in the 'listening heart,' till, slowly flinging its sounds
as the light of day withdraws over hill and vale and
water, I am awakened from these thoughts of other
times; as (in the language of the poet, who has thus
expressed it in a line of matchless beauty for its
euphony) I listen, and

> "Hear the bell from the tower, toll! toll! through the silence
> of evening."

These are 'thick coming fancies,' that steal upon
the mind in hours of poetry and of feeling—but the
reality is before me; there lies the once holy, and the
ever pure spring of St. John, unsheltered, open to the
sunshine or the storm; those just emblems of the
fortunes experienced by the departed guardians of
this fountain.   Oh! thoughts like these, how do ye
delight to pause on the shadowy or the mouldering
records of former years!   How do ye whisper to one
who welcomes you as sweet and pleasant friends! that
a few years more, and, over the name and the remem-

brance of that one, oblivion shall roll her dark and
rayless night, even as it is now falling, like a mantle,
on these once stately towers.. But there is a memory
in Heaven, and being a record of mercy, it can never
be blotted out.   Such is the comfort of all who feel
"the weight of time and of eternity upon the spirit."

LETTER XXIV.

TO ROBERT SOUTHEY, ESQ.

Abbey burnt by the Danes—Hengist-down—Scene of a great Battle—
Horse Bridge—Some conjectures concerning it—Wars during the
Saxon Era—Saxon Princes of the West—Arthur, his career—Saxons
and Danes—Their fierce contests near Tavistock—Adage respecting
one of their Battles—The Danes ravage Tavistock; destroy the Abbey
—It rises again—Its Benefactors—Livingus, its munificent Abbot
—Brief notice of his History—His Death; buried in the Abbey—
Lands, Deeds, Privileges, Benefactions, Charters, &c. &c., conferred
on the Abbey—Abbots grown rich; Parish Priest so poor as to
petition for a pair of Shoes—John Banham made a mitred Abbot—
Anglo-Saxon Monasteries, their simplicity and piety—Benedictines,
their Dress, &c.—Their Hospitality.

Vicarage, Tavistock, August, 1832.

AFTER having, in my former letters, traced the history
of our Abbey from its foundation to its completion
in the year 981, I have now to speak of the first
severe shock it experienced by a change of fortune,
for scarcely had this magnificent structure stood thirty
years, ere the Danes became its ruin.

The first appearance of those barbarians on our
shores was about the close of the eighth century,
when Brihtric reigned in Wessex. In the time of
Egbert they pillaged the Isle of Sheppey, and soon
after gained a great victory at Charmouth, in Dorsetshire; where they murdered two bishops, and
kept possession of their camp. But the greatest
incursion in this part of the West was in 835. The

Saxon Chronicle states, that a large fleet of these marauders came to the 'West Welsh'—the people of Cornwall—who united their forces with them, and made war on Egbert. The circumstance of the men of Cornwall thus joining heathens to carry arms into the territory of a Christian prince, may be considered a strong confirmation of the opinion that they still clung to the old superstitions of the ancient Britons, and were not yet converted to the truth. Egbert, when he heard of this alliance against him, " marched with an army" (says the same chronicle) "and fought with them at Hengist-dune, and there he put to flight both the Welsh and the Danes."

Hengest-dune (now called *Hengesdown*,[1] and sometimes Hingston) is in our neighbourhood ; and not very far distant from it is *Horse Bridge ;* and I cannot help entertaining the conjecture that the hill where Egbert thus beat the forces combined against him derived its name from some battle fought long *before* his time, in the days of Vortigern, the British prince. I shall here state the reasons which have induced me to venture this conjecture.

There is no record, that I am aware of, now in existence, by which we have any authority for saying that the Saxon brothers, Hengist and Horsa, when they visited this country and so cruelly massacred the Britons, were ever in *this* part of England. Yet

---

[1] There are several barrows on Hengist-down : one or two of which (says Mr. Carrington, jun., in the *Devonport Guide*) were opened a few years since. In one of them were found a human skull and several bones. A Druidical cell (corresponding in its appearance to those called by Davies 'arkite cells' of the bards) was also dug up on Hengist-down many years ago. Near Cothele, a narrow glen is still called *Danes Combe ;* the Danes having passed through it on their way to meet Egbert in battle.

the thing seems to me not improbable, nor impossible. The records of that time were very imperfect. The principal historian, Witichindus, a Saxon, might not have been acquainted with every minute circumstance of the period about which he wrote. And when we recollect how many monasteries in this country were afterwards burnt by the Danes, we cannot but conclude that some chronicles or documents, that would have thrown much light on our early history, were consumed in the flames.

It is so remarkable a circumstance that Hengist-down should lie not very far from Horse Bridge,[2] that it is a strong temptation to fancy those places derived their names from Hengist and Horsa. Let it also be remembered that Vortigern (who leagued with those chiefs, and by his base treachery and intrigues fixed the Saxon yoke on his countrymen) was earl or heretoge of *Cornwall*. The very station he held connected him more particularly with the Cornish Britons, and with the people of Devon: they were also numbered with those who made the longest and most vigorous resistance against the Saxon wolves; and though the greatest battle took place at Bampton, where the miserable Britons lost (according to the *Saxon Chronicle*) two thousand and forty-six of their bravest men, yet many battles were fought of less import, previous to that decisive engagement. Might it not then be possible that one of these 'many battles' was on the borders of Cornwall, where Vortigern, the base heretoge of that county, might even have guided Hengist and

---

[2] Horse Bridge is a beautiful object in a beautiful spot; it crosses the river Tamar, that divides Cornwall and Devon. It is noticed by Baretti in his delightful letters.

Horsa; and where each (the one on the hill, and the other at the pass of the river) might have achieved a minor victory; and so have left their names as memorials to those places?—names that have survived stone or brass, and still may point out to the local historian the scene of carnage and victory. How much light will even a name throw on a place, where it awakens a spirit of inquiry! How pleasant is it to sit at a desk and settle about the site of battles, and the tyrants who fought them, a thousand years ago! You will, I dare say, smile at my conjectures; but I will endeavour yet further to show that they are not so wild as they might at first be imagined.

That *this* part of England was the scene of many fierce engagements, long before the time of Egbert, is proved by historical facts. Encouraged by the success of Hengist, many Saxon adventurers crossed the seas, and eventually gained a footing in Britain. Amongst these was Cerdic, the founder of the West Saxon kingdom, who was opposed in his career by Aurelius Ambrosius, and the heroic Prince Arthur; whose virtues became so magnified by the bards, and his real actions so blended with those purely fabulous, that, like Hercules, he was rendered quite as much a god of mythology in Britain as that renowned and laborious hero was in Greece; and who, likewise, received his divinity from the poets.

That Arthur was an extraordinary prince, a light amidst darkness, cannot be doubted; the very extravagance of his fame had in all probability its foundation in the enthusiasm and admiration he inspired amongst his countrymen; for glory in a half-civilized nation is ever the result of actions which so far surpass the capabilities of the ordinary race of men who witness them, that they attribute such achievements to some power more than human vested in the person of their hero, who speedily becomes their god. Such almost was Arthur with the Britons; but whatever might have been his valour or his success, it appears he did not wholly subdue Cerdic, who after a struggle of several years conquered many of the *western* parts of this kingdom. His son Cynric succeeded to the throne of Wessex; and his grandson Ceaulin won a great battle over the Britons in Gloucestershire, which so enabled him to enlarge the extent of his kingdom, that he added to it those shires now called Somerset and Devon.

Though the Saxons had gained thus far a permanent footing in England, yet we have seen by a vast number of facts that the Britons were not wholly subdued; since Cornwall and the adjacent parts of Devon (in which no doubt Dartmoor on the borders of the latter was included) might still in a great measure be called their own. For many years a continual warfare had been kept up between the Britons and Saxons, till Egbert, who succeeded Brihtric on the throne of Wessex in 801, after devoting his first cares to the welfare of his people, attempted the difficult task of reducing the ancient British chieftains to his obedience; and the battle of Hengistdown was decisive, though he was not the aggressor in that contest.

That the Danes made great havoc in these parts at a subsequent period is well known. They burnt the cathedral and palace of Launceston[3] in Cornwall,

---

[3] Authorities differ, some stating that Launceston was the place so burnt, and others Bodmin.

twelve miles from this town, which caused the bishop's see to be removed to St. Germans; and the ancient Norman church there built still remains a beautiful object in the eye of the antiquary and the artist. Lydford (of which more hereafter) was also burnt and ravaged; and to this day in Tavistock we have the following tradition respecting the havoc they made here. After the Danes landed near Danescombe, and met with a repulse on Hengist-down, some of them escaped, crossed the Tamar, and surprised Tavistock, rushing into the town from a rugged hill by the side of the old Launceston road, in those days said to have been the only entrance from the West. The inhabitants, armed to a man, met them at the foot of the above-named hill; and a great battle ensued, which gave rise to the old adage—

> "The blood which flowed down West Street
> Would heave a stone a pound weight."

I am also informed (since I wrote my previous letters) that a tradition is still current in this place, which asserts that Okehampton Castle was a favourite residence with Orgar, Earl of Devon. Not having had an opportunity of acquainting myself with the history of that castle, (whose singular and romantic ruins I have seen with admiration) I cannot say how far this is likely to be false or true; though when that tradition adds, as it does, that Orgar was *residing* there at the period Tavistock Abbey was burnt by the Danes, we know by chronological records it must be incorrect; as *he* died twenty years before the con-flagration took place. Two or three forts at the mouth of the Tamar, nearly opposite Mount Edg-cumbe, I am assured are considered to have been very ancient constructions; and were most probably intended to protect the coast from the incursions of these foreign marauders.

It was in the year 997 that a Danish fleet, under the command of Sweyn, entered the Severn; and after numerous successful depredations, sailed round the Land's End, and finally turned its course up the Tamar. Though these invaders then burnt Lydford, they must have quitted their ships many miles distant from that most ancient town; since never at any period could the Tamar have been navigable higher than New Bridge, three miles from Tavistock. They carried fire and sword throughout the country; and our Abbey, but thirty-six years after its foundation, was plundered and burnt to the ground. The marauders soon returned to their ships, laden with the spoil they had accumulated.

Of the original building nothing perhaps remains, unless we except one portion of the boundary walls, (those of our garden) which must have been fire-proof, as there never was any lead or wood-work about them; and the blocks of stone of which they are composed are held together with a cement so hard and admirable, that it appears to be like that seen in the stupendous walls of Pevensey Castle, the old Roman fortress on the Sussex coast.

The Abbey, thus burnt and ravaged, though it remained for some time in ruins, was yet destined, like the fabled phœnix, to rise once more from its ashes. By whom it was rebuilt is not, I believe, exactly known; most probably not by an individual, but by many benefactors. Amongst these we may number Le Arcedekne, Vipont, Ferrars, Fitz-Bernard, Edgcumbe, and others. My brother considers that its re-erection was probably owing to the exertions and liberality of Livingus, who was nephew to Brith-wald, Bishop of St. Germans, in Cornwall. This prelate is, indeed, so connected with the history of our Abbey, that it may not here be amiss to offer some brief account of him.

Hooker and Prince reckon him amongst the illus-trious natives of this county; and the latter is care-ful in distinguishing him from Livingus, surnamed Elstanus, Archbishop of Canterbury, who crowned Canute king of England, and died in 1020.

Certain it is that the Abbey must have been re-erected in his time, and so far finished as to be capable of receiving the monks, since our Livingus was some time Abbot of Tavistock, and was advanced to the see of Devon in 1032. His palace stood at Crediton, and he was the last bishop who there resided during life. Canute valued him for his piety and wisdom; and so much was he in favour with that king, that he made choice of the Bishop of Devon-shire as the companion of his journey to the tomb of St. Peter and St. Paul at Rome. Returning in the same year, 1031, Livingus found his uncle, Brithwald, dead; upon which Canute, from the great love he bore to the companion of his pilgrimage, gave him his late uncle's see of St. Germans, in Cornwall, allowing him still to hold Crediton, and not long after added to these dignities by making him Bishop of Worcester.

It is not improbable that such a plurality of prelacies being heaped on the favourite excited discontent in those who aspired to church preferment, and who might think they were overlooked or neglected for the sake of one man, in their own opinion not more deserving than themselves. Hence might have arisen envy, the fertile mother of falsehood and slander; and the worthy character of the prelate proved to be no security against the shafts aimed at him by such enemies as these: for he was charged by Alfricus, Archbishop of York, as being accessory to the death of Alfred, the eldest son of King Ethelred; the archbishop having himself been removed from his own see but a short time before, on account of his busy temper in secular affairs.

Alfred's death had been brought about by many circumstances, that excited a general feeling of commiseration for the unfortunate young prince. Canute, though he had engaged with the Duke of Normandy that his issue by his marriage with Emma should become his successors, nevertheless named Harold, the son of a former union, his heir to the crown, to the great discontent of the English; who desired to see Hardicanute, a prince born among them, succeed to the throne. The jealousies of these contending parties ran so high, that a civil war was likely to be the result, when a present peace was secured by compromise. The terms were, that Harold should hold the provinces north of the Thames, and Hardicanute keep those on the south, and during the absence of the last-named prince, his mother Emma assumed the regal authority in the place of her son.

But however secure Harold might appear to be in his possessions, he thought himself not so whilst the sons of Emma by her former husband, Ethelred the Saxon, were in existence. Earl Godwin, from motives of ambition, had espoused the interests of Harold, and was kept firm to them by a hope being held out that his daughter should become the wife of that tyrant.

He did not hesitate, therefore, to join in the cruel plan now framed for the destruction of the young Saxon princes, who at this time were with their mother, Queen Emma, at Winchester; and as some said with a view to attempt making good their pretensions to the crown. If Harold knew or only suspected their intentions is a matter of doubt; but certain it is he invited Alfred, the elder brother, to London, with every promise of an honourable reception. Thus was he deceived; and setting forward on his way, attended by many followers, had not proceeded farther than Guildford, in Surrey, when he was surprised by the treacherous Earl Godwin, his people slain, and himself, cruelly deprived of sight, committed as a prisoner to the monastery of Ely, where it pleased God to end his sufferings by a speedy death.

This cruel deed appears to have excited a general feeling of indignation; and it is not improbable that Alfricus might seek to gain his own restoration to the see of York, by paying court to the popular feeling; and to Harold, in the endeavour to fasten the guilt of the murder on another man, when the king was grievously suspected of being concerned in the act. A bishop who held three sees in his own person was not perhaps, he considered, the worst object he could fasten upon to make him appear criminal; and the worthy Livingus was accordingly vehemently accused by the deposed archbishop. The affair must have been unusually prolonged, as not till the reign of Hardicanute did the artful Alfricus so far succeed as to obtain the dismissal of the innocent bishop from his preferments in the Church. This deprivation did not, however, last long. It is most probable that Livingus owed his

restoration not so much to his want of guilt, for that
was a poor plea against tyranny, as to the cunning
and the contemptible conduct of the king; for Hardicanute, notwithstanding his wrath towards the
murderers of his half-brother, was mean and base
enough to accept a bribe (a gilded galley manned by
rowers decorated with bracelets of gold) from Earl
Godwin, who thus found an easy way to escape
justice. In order to let him appear guilty, it was
necessary to acquit Livingus, who had been so falsely
accused as his accomplice in the crime.

These circumstances form the most probable solution of the cause that procured the restoration of the
Bishop of Devonshire to all his honours; no small
instance of good fortune in the reign of such a
tyrant; and this event seems to be the last of any
public import in the life of Livingus. His latter
days were spent in peace, in the regular discharge of
his episcopal duties, and in the innocent and delightful pursuits of letters. He composed during his
retirement a work which, could it now be recovered,
would form indeed one of the curiosities of literature;
according to Prince's translation its title was *Canute's
Pilgrimage, and his own Doings.*

Livingus, notwithstanding all his troubles, lived
through the reigns of four kings; a thing not very
common with one so eminent, who had been assailed
by the envy and jealousy of others in times so
marked by violence and injustice. Historians and
antiquaries differ as to the place of his death; but
Hooker is of opinion that it occurred at his favourite
monastery of Tavistock; of which he had been
chosen the first abbot after its rebuilding, and
where his munificence had been so largely displayed.

However his mind might be at rest at the time of his dissolution, he could hardly be said to depart in peace; since the monks have recorded that, at the very hour of his decease, the greatest storm shook all England that had been felt for many years.— "*Horrisonus crepitus per totam Angliam auditus, ut ruina et finis totius putareter orbis.*" Prince, however, is of opinion that this "horrible crack of thunder," as he calls it, "did rather prognosticate the ruin which threatened the liberties of England" on that great change which so speedily succeeded, in the invasion of our island by William the Conqueror. Be this as it may, Livingus died as the worthy would wish to die, in a good old age, in favour with God and man. He was buried in the Abbey Church of Tavistock. Hooker says he departed this life on the 23rd of March, 1049; but the *Saxon Chronicle* fixes that event in 1044, when it simply states, "This year Living, Bishop of Devonshire, died, and the king's priest Leofric succeeded him."

Another remarkable person also ended his days in our Abbey in these early times; Edwy Atheling, a son of King Ethelred, grandson of Elfrida, and great grandson of Orgar, the founder. Alarmed by the jealousy of Canute, who, like his son Harold, looked with an eye of suspicion on the princes of the Saxon line, Edwy sought a refuge in the Abbey: he did not very long survive, and was buried in the church: no vestige remains of his tomb.

Many noble persons were munificent patrons of the monastic foundation of Tavistock. William Rufus, in the year 1096, confirmed to the monks a mansion called Walsinton, which they made it appear they had a right to consider their own, time out of mind, though

some busy men on the part of the crown would have
deprived them of that possession.

The grant of Walsinton was confirmed to Tavistock
in the presence of Walchaline, Bishop of Winchester,
Turstin, Superior of Glastonbury, and other ecclesiastics, by the king presenting to the abbot an ivory
knife, on the handle of which were these words :—
" Ego Willielmus Rex dedi Deo et Sanctæ Mariæ de
Tavistoc terram Wlerintune."

From Dugdale we likewise learn that Robert Old-
bridge gave to the Abbey the lands of Wynemerston,
on a stipulation that the lord abbot should pay to him
ten marks in silver, with liberty for him to take up his
abode within the walls whenever he might wish to
retire from the world ; and, in the interval, that every
day he should visit or continue in Tavistock he might
claim the allowance given to one monk, if he chose
to ask for it.

Robert Fitz Baldwin restored the lands of Passe-
ford. King Henry I. ordered Rinberg and Eudelipe,
which had been taken from the monks, to be restored.
He granted to them likewise all the churches in the
Isles of Scilly, confirmed to them by his son Reginald,
Earl of Cornwall, the tithes of which were granted to
the Abbey by the Bishop of Exeter at that period.
King Edward took the church of the island of En-
mour, in Scilly, under his protection, ordering the
constable of the castle there to guard the same from
all insults and injuries.

By deed of Odo Le Arcedeckne, knight, bearing
date the day of St. Mark the Evangelist, the seven-
teenth of Edward I., he resigns to the monks for the
health of his own soul, and the souls of all his family,
the lands of Westlydeton ; and the said monks for

the good of their own souls, in the year 1291 appropriated all the revenues of these lands to the purchase of clothes and shoes for the poor in Christ, to be yearly distributed among them on the feast of All Souls.

By an agreement between the Abbot of Tavistock and the Prior of Plympton, the latter obliged himself and his successors to do certain acts of suit and service to the former; namely, to attend the abbot, at his own charges, whenever he made his visitation within the diocese of Exeter; to provide him with sundry loaves of white bread, two flagons of wine, and five wax tapers, whenever he visited his manor of Plymstock; to present every new abbot with a palfrey and a groom during his perambulation; to confirm his rights, until the day of his instalment; and on the feast of St. Michael, to provide him with a chaplain, who was a good clerk, for the church of Plymstock.

Bronscombe, the celebrated Bishop of Exeter,[4] appropriated to our Abbey the churches of Tavistock, Lamerton, Middleton, Abbotsham, North Petherwyn, Hatherleigh, and Brent Tor. The bull of Pope Celestin, dated 1193, confirmed all donations made to this house, and all privileges whatsoever. In the year 1280, Reginald Ferrars, the Lord of Beer, and Isota of Ferrars, of Nyweton Ferrars, gave to the monks of the Abbey of Tavistock all their lands in Cornwood, on their performing the customary homage for the same.

In the second of Richard II., William Edgcumbe,

[4] His tomb, in Exeter Cathedral, still exists, and for the pure style and beauty of its execution ranks amongst the finest in Europe. The attitude in which the figure reposes, the head, limbs, and draperies remind one, in their grandeur and simplicity, of the works of Raphael.

of Cothele, resigned to the Abbey all claim on the park of Innersleigh, in the manor of Middleton, and John D'Abernon, of Bradeford, gave to the same house all his manor of Wyke, near Brent Tor, and his lands and tenements at Holywell. Many other were the benefactors to this costly foundation ; but I have here mentioned the principal.

Over this monastery presided thirty-six abbots, from its institution to the time of its dissolution. Two of these, Livingus and Aldred, were made bishops ; the latter is said to have placed the crown on the head of William the Conqueror. John Dynington, who was the superior in 1450, was charged by one of the Bishops of Exeter with too much attention to the adornment of his person, and possibly with some truth ; as he was the man who stirred the question with King Henry VI., that the abbots of Tavistock should be allowed to enjoy the privilege of wearing the pontificalia—the licence for which I shall presently copy from my brother's notices. Its particularity forms a very good illustration of the ecclesiastical vestments of the time. If, however, John Dynington had a too curious taste in his attire, it should seem he did not confine his attention to outward things of that description ; and that he was not less attentive to the edifices of his community. My brother says of him : " Dynington probably made large repairs and additions to the buildings of the Abbey, as most of the remains of these now extant are characterized by the deep label moulding, and obtusely pointed arch, which became the prevailing characteristics of Gothic architecture towards the close of the fifteenth century. The great gate of the Abbey is decorated with two minarets of this period,

and the parapet of its pointed roof is crenellated
and embattled ; certainly a misapplication of the
crenellated form, and a specimen of perverted taste."

Whilst the abbot and his monks were, as above
stated, grown rich, and had all things subservient to
their desires and their luxuries, the poor parish priest
was labouring with indigence and want. Some few
years since, among the papers in the parish chest,
was found a petition from the officiating priest to
the parishioners assembled in the vestry, absolutely
begging for a pair of shoes ! The document, which
was found and read by my husband's father, is no
longer in existence, (at least we find no traces of it)
or I should here insert it. From this petition we may
gather that the worthy monks who took such care
of their own souls, as to give away the revenues of
Westlydeton in apparel and shoes to the 'poor in
Christ,' did not consider their poor brother of the
secular clergy to be of that number, and so they let
him go barefoot. This is a trifling circumstance,
but in such trifles as these we may trace the spirit of
jealousy between the monks and the parish priests,
that commenced in the time of Dunstan, and was
never after wholly set at rest. Truly the officiating
minister was not overwhelmed with this world's
goods, and with him they seem little to have regarded the text, that those who preach the gospel
should live by the gospel ; for whilst the Abbot of
Tavistock was, in the reign of Henry VIII., honoured
with a mitre, and made a peer of the realm, by the
title of Baron of Hurdwick, (which is now one of the
titles of the Duke of Bedford, to whose ancestors the
lands of the Abbey were granted at the dissolution)
and enjoyed revenues of nearly one thousand a year,

in those days an enormous income, the poor priest
of Tavistock Church was only entitled to ten pounds
per annum.

John Banham, the abbot who received the mitre,
and was called to Parliament by Henry VIII. the
same year, maintained a long contest with Hugh
Oldham, Bishop of Exeter, about the liberties of his
church, and was so far successful that he gained the
sanction of the Pope for what he did, who excommu-
nicated the luckless Bishop but a short time before
his death; so that his body could not be buried till
this fearful sentence was removed by an application
to Rome.

I have a few observations to add concerning the
Order of monks here established during so long a
period, and then, for the present, I must say adieu.

In the Anglo-Saxon monasteries, where there was
much of true holiness, as well as of superstition, the
utmost simplicity prevailed in regard to dress, especially after the Benedictine rule had, in the ninth century, usurped that of all others in England. Here,
then, may we fancy that we see the good Livingus in
his Benedictine attire—a tunic and cowl, black in
colour, and in his day formed of the coarsest woollen
stuff; a broad belt girds his garments about the
middle, from which depends his *almonier*, or little
pouch; he carries about him a knife, a steel pen, and
a table-book to note down his thoughts; a rosary is
by his side; a cross suspended on his breast; his black
mantle is large and full, and as an abbot he has a right
to wear it without as well as within the church.

The brothers of his Order wear a black scapular as
their ordinary or working dress; they also have a
cowl, but their long woollen mantle is worn only in the

church. In addition to the knife, each monk is supplied
with a needle, and those who are most holy with a rod,
to inflict on themselves in the most literal manner

"Much castigation, exercise devout."

Hair shirts were likewise often worn; they were indeed of very ancient date, and had no doubt their
origin in the East; for St. Chrysostom mentions the
hair shirt as forming part of the dress of the Oriental
monks. I am inclined to think that such hair shirt
was not one of torture, and that Chrysostom referred
to the material of which Eastern clothing was then
generally made—the camel's and the goat's hair. In
other countries a less delicate material might have
been adopted, and become an irritating and troublesome dress when worn next the skin. But as we
know that to this day the camel's-hair shawls of India
are the softest in the world, how can we believe that
the early Eastern clothing formed of it could have
been anything like a garb of torture?

The monks in the times of the Anglo-Saxons were
bare-legged, and their 'shoon' resembled the classical
sandal. Fosbrooke in his very learned work on monachism, mentions that visiters were received among
them, the holy men "giving them water to cleanse
their hands, washing their feet, wiping them with a
towel, and inviting them to dine at nine o'clock in the
morning." And the rule of Pachomius orders "that
the feet of visiters be washed, even if clerks or holy
monks." The Benedictines were celebrated for charity
and hospitality to strangers; a noble hall is generally
found in the edifices of their Order. There was one
at Tavistock; but all account of what still remains of
the Abbey I must defer till my next letter.

LETTER XXV.

TO ROBERT SOUTHEY, ESQ.

Vicarage, Tavistock, August 29th, 1832.

THE next event which I have to communicate respecting our Abbey is its dissolution ; an occurrence
not only in this instance, but in all others throughout
the kingdom, sincerely to be regretted, for surely
the monasteries, as well as the Church, might have
been reformed without being entirely overthrown.
Old buildings, like old customs and laws, are not the

growth of a day; years of labour and generations of wisdom have been as the parents of both, and pity is it that a few months or days of innovation, and a few thoughtless or violent men, should make such destruction, and render all the toils of the past as nothing.

The benefits of the Reformation are well understood, the sins of it have been less noticed, and that good came out of so much evil was more the result of divine than human causes. God, in the wisdom of his inscrutable counsels, works by means that on a first view sometimes appear contradictory. Bad men are frequently but as his instruments, while they seem to follow the career of their own selfish or stormy passions; for in the end we generally find he but employs them, as he does the lightning and the winds, to clear away what is noxious, to purify or to renovate; when the beautiful and the serene in the moral world follow after; even as the bow of promise, a bright sun, and a refreshed earth succeed the disturbance and turmoil of the elements in that physical world which lies before our view.

That Henry VIII., when he threw off the yoke of Rome, when he repudiated a blameless wife, and overthrew monasteries and abbeys, was really a reformer for the sake of the Reformed faith, no one, I believe, of any party, for a moment even fancies. His Six Articles are sufficient proof that it was the restraining power, and not the doctrine of the Church of Rome, that he was anxious to destroy; and the cupidity, the pride, the extravagant living of his hungry dependents and courtiers, caught eagerly at the lure that such rich prizes as desecrated Church lands held out, and "Down with the monasteries for their abuses " was then the plea ; when the cry of the daughter of the horse-leech, ' Give, give,' would better have expressed the motive.

That the sixteenth century was one of great corruption, of great immorality, of much false religion, and of many enormities in its professors, cannot be denied. The time was ripe for chastisement, and God sent the storm, and idolatry and falsehood in this country fell before it. But the *immediate* effects were perhaps intended, as they were found to be, an evil. For, saving a few such men as Latimer and Cranmer, how long was it before the Reformed clergy, who succeeded the overthrow of the Popish priests, were truly worthy their high calling as guides and leaders of the flock of Christ !

Poor livings found but poor scholars and needy men to fill their place. The clergy were degraded into an impoverished and dependent body in the eyes of the people ; contempt with the vulgar was the certain consequence of such misfortunes, since base men ever look on poverty as a crime ; and though the populace were no longer allowed to feed their imagination with the splendid shows, or the candles, and the flowers, and the images of the Church of Rome, their reason was not much more enlightened than whilst it had been held in its former state of darkness. Can we then wonder that to rifle abbeys, to violate the sanctuary, to tear down the noblest monuments of piety and of art (which our forefathers in singleness of heart had offered as a habitation fit for the worship of their God) ; to commit sacrilege, deface the effigies of the great, the noble, and the good, to disturb from their place of repose the mouldering ashes of the dead, to seize the

very plate from the altar, and, like the impious king
of old, to make it subservient to the purposes of
luxury and indulgence, were things that the bold,
the avaricious, and the heartless, did without remorse;
whilst the fearful looked on and trembled. These
were the sins of the Reformation. As the poor lost
the charity of those ancient houses whose doors had
been ever open to relieve them, the old and the
pious (for there were many) who had retired from a
world of which they were grown weary, were once
more cast upon its stormy waters when they were
but themselves a wreck, and could no longer stem
the torrent, or with a safe conscience sail down the
current of the times. But these moral evils had
their date; and though days of misery, of persecution, and of sorrows 'even unto death,' intervened,
the sun of the Reformation at length came forth
from the cloud, and the harvest and the joy spread
beneath its beams.

The guardian king, who watched its progress with
so much zeal and love, was too soon snatched from
this world to one where his pure spirit was destined
to find its early and rich reward. Happy for himself,
but grievous for England, Edward died before even
his days of such glorious promise had ripened into
manhood. He lived not to bless this country with
an age 'full of years and full of honours;' but to
him may truly be applied what a French writer said
of a Dauphin of France, who also died in his youth:
"That heaven, counting his virtues, esteemed him
old, and took him to his rest."

The day of the fiery trial was next reserved for
the Reformation. The holy martyrs stood in prayer
and agony, burning at the stake, glorifying God in

the face of all the world. The Church stood the
trial and approved itself worthy, and God removed
the flaming sword from the tree of life, and gave the
olive-branch in its stead.

From that time, down to the days of Charles I.,
great and shining lights arose in succession; and not
since the days of the fathers who came after the
apostles, have, perhaps, so many truly great divines
been found in any church as in that of the Reformed
and Established Church of England. In proof of
this, who that feels a pride in the virtue, the genius,
the piety of his native land, can do other than honour
the names of Hooker, the author of the *Ecclesiastical
Polity ;*—of Fuller, whose sermons, though, like those
of the admirable Latimer, somewhat quaint, are only
less valued than his *Church History* because they are
less known ;—of Hall, venerable alike in his writings
and his life ;—of the pious and single-hearted Bishop
Andrews ;—of the apostolic Jeremy Taylor ;—the
admirable Allestree and Donne ;—of Raleigh, (the
nephew of the great Sir Walter Raleigh) who was
basely murdered in his prison, where he had been
consigned for adhering to the cause of his unfortunate
master, Charles I. ? Of this divine, Chillingworth
said " he was the most powerful reasoner he had ever
encountered ;" and Raleigh's sermon on one of the
most difficult points of doctrine—that of election
consistent with freewill—is argued with such clearness
and strength, that there needs no other proof how
well merited was the eulogium of his friend. But
what praise shall speak the excellencies of Farrindon?
of Farrindon, now slumbering in neglect, whose power
to touch the heart, though it were hard as a rock,
and make it yield a spring of living waters, has never

yet been exceeded by any writer of any age;—
of Beveridge, whose sermon on the text 'I am that
I am,' Steele (to whom many of the obsolete divines
were unknown) considered the finest in our language.
Barrow is known to every student; but not so Harris,
who preached in London during the plague, with the
fearlessness, the devotion, and the power of a true
servant of God, sent at such a moment to call all
men to repentance.

To return, however, from this digression to our
Abbey. In the notices before quoted, and written by
my brother, I find he thus speaks of the circumstances
attending its dissolution :—" John Pyryn succeeded
Banham, and, with the monks assembled in chapter,
surrendered the Abbey to the King's Commissioners
on the 20th March, 1538. Of the twenty-two signa-
tures which appear on the margin of the deed of
surrender, the following may be noted. The abbot
and the prior sign first—'Per me Joh'em Abbate,'
'per me Robertu Walsh, priore'—then indiscrimi-
nately are found—'Joh'es Harriss, sub-prior, Ryc
(Ricardus) custos,' &c. The abbot retired on a pen-
sion of one hundred pounds per annum, at that
period a very large one; the prior had a stipend of
ten pounds per annum; the sub-prior one of eight
pounds; the monks from six pounds to five pounds
six shillings and eightpence each; and two novices
were allowed two pounds per annum. The abbot
continued to reside at Tavistock,[1] in the enjoyment of
the comfortable provision which had been assigned
him : at which place in the year 1549 he made his
will, which being proved in April, 1550, we may
conclude that he died about that time.

[1] The old house in which he lived has lately been taken down.

"The dissolved Abbey of Tavistock and its dependencies were, by the King's letters patent, dated the fourth of July, in the thirty-first year of his reign, granted to John Lord Russell, Ann his wife, and their lawful heirs male, at a certain reserved rent.[2]   Lord Russell had been received into the favour of Henry VII., knighted by his successor, and created a baron of the realm; nominated Lord Warden of the Stannaries in Devon and Cornwall, Lord Privy Seal, and one of the councillors of Edward VI. during his minority.   He was constituted Lord High Steward at the coronation of that youthful monarch, and on the insurrection which broke out at Sampford Courtenay, in Devon, and which was followed by the siege of the capital of the West, Exeter, Lord Russell marched against the rebels, totally routed and dispersed them.   For these services he was shortly after created Earl of Bedford.   It is not the object of these notes to enter at length into the history of this ancient and noble house; suffice it to say, that William, the fifth descendant from the Earl, was, in the reign of William and Mary, created Marquis of Tavistock and Duke of Bedford, and his present worthy descendant, John Duke of Bedford, is in possession of the lands and ecclesiastical impropriations of the dissolved Abbey."

Having thus come to the dissolution of our Monastery, something must here be said concerning the portions of the ancient buildings that still exist, notwithstanding the havoc so largely and so repeatedly made amongst them.   For this purpose I have been looking over Mr. Bray's MS. notes, written several years since, respecting the remains of Tavistock

[2] See Farm Roll, Augmentation Office.

Abbey. These observations may not have so much interest as he could wish ; but as some of the vestiges he mentions are now no longer in existence, the notes of what he saw and described in his youth ought to be preserved. I have gleaned from a mass of papers that which follows.

" The site of the Abbey extends from east to west along the north bank of the river Tavy. The principal entrance was at the north, close to the eastern boundary. This gateway is in high preservation, with its gate at least as perfect as that at Temple Bar; to which it bears some resemblance, by having on one side a postern, or foot passage.[3] There are two other gateways to the south and west, the former of which leads to the banks of the river, where, till Guile or Abbey Bridge was erected, there was a ford ; and the latter to the abbot's gardens and stew-ponds, which still exist.[4]

" About one hundred years ago, a considerable portion of these venerable edifices was taken down, to erect on the spot the large but inconvenient building commonly called the Abbey House. This havoc was committed by a Mr. Saunders, who, not for these barbarities, however, but for building so large a house on another man's property, was and in a manner still is ridiculed, by the name of Folly Orchard being given to some grounds which he occupied with it. I

[3] Mr. Bray tells me that ever since his remembrance, till very lately, this gateway was used by a fellmonger for drying wool. Under the flight of steps leading to it was the clink; but it is now destroyed, and he believes it was of no very ancient date. The place where prisoners are now confined is situated very near, though it does not communicate with the gateway, but with the ancient guildhall.

[4] This is no longer the case; recent alterations have destroyed all but one of the stew-ponds.

never understood, as some assert, that he was the Duke of Bedford's steward; at any rate he certainly was not a *wise* one. A very old and intelligent lady of this place, Miss Adams, who remembers Saunders's wife, informs me that *part* of the building which he tore down was a school-house. Some have supposed that it was the Saxon school and Chapter-house, which Prince (who wrote not very long before Saunders committed these spoliations) thus describes: 'There is still standing the refectory, or common hall; a very spacious room, of great length, breadth, and height, lately converted into a Nonconformist meeting-house; and the Saxon school and Chapter-house, a pile of great beauty, built so round as can possibly be marked with a compass; yet withal of large dimensions, there being on the inside thereof six-and-thirty seats wrought out in the walls, all arched overhead with curious hewn and carved stone.'[5]

---

[5] Prince also says: "The abbot's palace was a glorious building, now wholly demolished; of very late years was the kitchen standing, now razed to the foundation, being a large square room, open to the roof, which was of timber so geometrically done, that even architects themselves did admire the curiosity thereof."

Recent discoveries have proved that it was the Chapter-house which Saunders, of barbarous memory, thus destroyed. In the year 1830, on making some additions to the Bedford Office, which stands close to the Abbey House (now an hotel), part of the beautiful pavement of the Chapter-house, consisting of tiles, bearing the figures of lions and fishes, was discovered. Mr Kempe says of this—"that the lion passant, or rampant, has been borne in the armorial coat of the Earls of Cornwall ever since the time of Reginald (base son of Henry I., a benefactor to our Abbey), and that by the fishes some allusion to the possessions in the Scilly Isles may be intended." I observed amongst the rubbish dug up on the spot where the tiles were found, part of a Gothic niche, beautifully carved, and still retaining its red and other colours, for it had been painted. The sight of this fragment made me but the more regret the miserable destruction which such a man as Saunders had been allowed to effect.

"The gateway S.W." continues Mr. Bray, "communicated with the gardens and pleasure-ground of the Abbey: it consists of a vaulted passage about nine paces in length and eight feet in height, between two towers that present to the front the three apparent sides of an octagon. The southern tower, called

BETSEY GRIMBAL'S TOWER.

Betsey Grimbal's, is so denominated from a tradition that a woman thus named was there murdered by a soldier. Within my own recollection there were many who pretended to show where the wall was stained with her blood; and when a child I was so little of a sceptic as firmly to believe that it was haunted, and never ventured to visit it alone. But, setting aside the want of verisimilitude in this vulgar fabrication, which from the locality of the situation should rather have suggested the story of some fair nun murdered, not by the hands of a soldier, but by some jealous monk or enamoured abbot, (as a tale I have to relate may lead one to suspect) the stains in the wall or rather in the plaster which still adheres to it in some places, are solely the effects of damp.   Probably some ironstone, of which there is a great quantity in the neighbourhood, corroded by the wet, tinged the drops of a ferruginous or red colour that percolated through the cracks.   However, allowing much for fabrication, we may fairly conclude that the story had its origin from some circumstance in which a female was concerned, and that some act of violence was committed on this spot.

"At the back of the Abbey House (now the Bed-ford Hotel) stands a porch, crowned with four lofty pinnacles, partially covered with the most luxuriant ivy.   The ceiling of the vaulted entrance is of elegantly carved stone-work.

"The upper room is also vaulted with pendent wood work.   In it is a chimney.   As there was no communication to it, the doorway in a different direction being blocked up, a passage was broken through the wall a few years since, near one of the corners, where was a hollow buttress or turret.   Here some infant bones were found ; parts of the skull, some of the vertebræ and a thigh bone, which are still in my possession.[6]   The porch here described leads to what was supposed to be the Abbot's Hall.[7]

[6] The bones above alluded to by Mr. Bray are those of a *very* young child, most probably a new-born infant.   He keeps them in a carved horn box that belonged to the famous Sir Francis Drake.   There is a passage in Fox's *Book of Martyrs*, which I well remember, though I have mislaid the note I made of it, wherein it was stated that at the dissolution of monasteries in this kingdom, the bones of infants were sometimes found in places where no such discoveries seemed likely to be suspected.

[7] Whilst copying the above from Mr. Bray's old papers, he tells me that in Lysons' *Devon*, vol. ii. p. 474, he is referred to as supposing

"In making the foundation for the Abbey House
the workmen dug up, according to tradition, a stone
coffin, or sarcophagus, containing the bones now
deposited in the church, and called the *giant's bones.*
The sarcophagus is still in existence, and in my
possession. It is very thick, but no more than four
and a half feet long in the interior, and eighteen and
a quarter inches in depth. It is not much unlike the
shape of a coffin, being larger in the middle than at
either end. The bones are of an extraordinary size,
both human thigh bones. One measures twenty-one
inches long by five inches and a half in circumference. The other is nineteen inches and a half
long, by four inches and a half in circumference. On
the authority of Mr. James Cole, the sexton, who
shows them with the church, they are said to be the
bones of Ordulph and his wife.[8] And though I
presume not to assert that Ordulph, being himself a
giant, would be content with less than a giantess for
his partner, yet it seems not improbable that the

that the apartment till within the last three years used as a ball-room,
and now taken down to give place to the new one, was the Refectory.
This supposition, which Mr. Bray mentioned to Mr. Lysons, arose from
his father having told him that it was so called in the Duke of Bedford's
rentals ; and that what Browne Willis calls the *Refectory* was the
Abbot's Hall. But he now rather doubts his father's correctness in
this particular, especially as, for the same reason, the late Mr. Bray
considered the Saxon school was under the ball-room, which does not
correspond with the description given by Prince or Willis. He is the
more disposed to think the latter antiquary right in regard to the
Refectory (still used as a Unitarian meeting-house) as the Rev. Dr. Jago,
of Milton Abbot, an aged gentleman, tells him that he recollects a
stone pulpit that was affixed to the side of the wall in this apartment.
It is well known that sermons or homilies were read to the monks
whilst at dinner ; and the custom is still observed in some religious
houses on the Continent.

. [8] William of Malmesbury expressly declares that Ordulph was of
gigantic stature.

smaller bone might have been that of his father,
Orgar, Earl of Devon.

"From the size of the sarcophagus, if we suppose
a giant was there deposited, he must have been tied
neck and heels together. It is possible indeed that
the bones might have been collected long after death,
and there placed as relics. And I am the more inclined to this opinion, as we know in what veneration
the relics of the founder of an abbey were always
held ; and that father and son, who were the co-
founders of our Monastery, were both buried in it.
There is every reason to believe [9] that the tomb of
Orgar was not only repaired, but absolutely rebuilt,
in the reign of Henry III. At that period, therefore,
the bones of himself and of his son might have been
collected and placed together. Or it is not impossible
that the pious monks, on rebuilding the tomb of their
founders, after the Abbey and its church had been
burnt and ravaged by the Danes, might even then
have exhumed and deposited their bones in one common sarcophagus, which had remained undiscovered
till the work of destruction was again commenced
within these hallowed enclosures by the barbarians
of modern times, who dug them up in forming the
foundations for the Abbey House so often named,
when that of the ancient Chapter-house was torn
down to make room for it.

"There are some interesting and picturesque remains, crowned with their lofty pinnacles, of the
buildings belonging to the Abbey, yet standing in good
preservation near the principal entrance at the north.
Amongst them may be observed a tower, remarkable
for the beauty of its masonry. The adjoining apart-

[9] See Letter xxii.

ments, in the occupation of a miller, overlook the
river Tavy; and seen from the opposite bank, present
altogether an admirable subject for the pencil of an
artist like Prout.[1]

" I have omitted to mention that the old ball-room,
erroneously called the Refectory, stood nearly north
by south : it is on the first floor ; and I have reason
to think communicated with what was considered the
Abbot's Hall, (and which Browne Willis, I doubt
not correctly, declared to have been the Refectory)
by means of a gallery. The old ball-room had also
a passage of communication with the Abbey House.
Whilst my father lived there, several years since, I
restored some of the windows, which had been plas-
tered over when the mullions of the others were
destroyed for the purpose of introducing modern
sash windows; the taste, I conclude, of Mr. Saunders,
who seems to have spared neither labour nor expense
to do all the mischief he could possibly effect. The
windows thus restored had a beautiful appearance.
The ceiling was modern, being somewhat vaulted,
but broken in the curve by a moulding, and then
becoming flat. As it was much decayed it was
taken down, when the original roof became visible,
but so little of it remained that I dared not recommend the restoration, but contented myself with
giving it an uninterrupted curve. The wood-work,
as well as I recollect, was of a trefoil form, elegantly
but not very richly carved."[2]

[1] Since this was written these ancient buildings have been appropriated to the Public Library.

[2] "It is of some importance, in investigating the ruins of abbeys, to
know where to look for the sites of particular offices. Whitaker's
account is factitious. Our authors (*History of Shrewsbury*) place them
as follows :

The following account of the parish church I copy from Mr. Bray's MS. notes, and from my brother's historical notices of Tavistock Abbey in the *Gentleman's Magazine*.

"The parish church," says the latter, "is dedicated to St. Eustace, and was erected within the cemetery of the Abbey Church. Leland thought it had not been built long before the dissolution, and that the parishioners had previously a place of worship within the Abbey Church; this indeed was not unlikely, as other examples might readily be adduced to show. The parish church of Tavistock was, however, certainly in existence in the reign of Richard II., and how much earlier I have not discovered: it appears to have been under repair in 1386. The exterior view exhibits a dark, lofty tower, under which is an archway forming a passage from the Abbey precinct into the town; four distinct roofs, extending from the tower at the west to the termination of the building, indicate a spacious interior. Among the documents to which I had access in 1827, I found and deciphered the following very early churchwarden account of the ninth year of Richard II. I shall give an extract from it on account of the curious items it contains : among these will be found a charge for collecting rushes for strewing the church against the feast of John the Baptist, and the anniversary of the dedication; for the expenses of a man and horse sent to buy wax at Plymouth for lights

"*Dormitory.*—Mostly, but not always, on the west side of the cloister.

"*Refectory.*—Generally on the side of the cloister opposite to the church, and parallel with it.

"*Chapter-house.*—Always on the eastern side of the cloister.

"*Abbot's Lodging.*—South-east of the church, though not invariably so."—*Gentleman's Magazine*, November, 1826.

in the church ; charges for materials for repairing windows, &c.; for making three painted figures in the window of the vestry; for fuel; for shutters to the great east window; for the bringing a mason to repair the said window; for drinkings to the workmen employed on the above; rents from the park of Trewelake for maintaining lights at the altars of St. Nicholas, St. Stephen, St. John the Baptist, St. Katharine; payments made to the sacrist of the parish church for offerings to the respective altars therein; to the notary, for drawing the account, &c.

"'Tavystoke. S. Compu's custod'. hujus eccli'e beati Eustachii Tavistock a festo Invenc'o'is s'c'e crucis sub anno d'ni millo ccc^{mo.} octogesimo usq' ad id'm tu'c p'x'mè sequ' ann' d'm' millo ccc^{mo} lxxxvi^{to.}

"'Empcio ceræ. Idem comput. in cxl. lib. ceræ emptis hoc anno lvi*s.* x^{d.} custos et Repa'cio Ecclie. Idem computat' in cirpis colligend' con'. festum s'c'i Johis' baptistæ iv^{d} In die dedica-c'ois eccl'ie—In bokeram emptis in repac'o'e vestementor'—In conduco'e unius viri ceram emere apud Plymouth et unius equi expens suis ibidem viii^{d.} In quar'tio calcis (lime) empt xv^{d.}—In carriag. d'ce v^{d.}—Carreragio lapid iv^{d.} (carriage of stones)—In vet. vit. (old glass) empt. iii*s.* v^{d.}—In repac'oe unius fenestræ vitre. in fine ecc'lie ii*s* iiii^{d.}—In vi. pedibus novi vitri empt. vii*s*—In focalibus (fuel) empt. ii^{d.}—In lviij. lib. plumbi empt. iv*s.* x. ob.—In vii. lib. stanni empt. xviii^{d.}—In conduco'e unius machi-onis (mason) ad d'c'am fenestram reparand—In factura trium ymaginum in fenesti in vestiario xii^{d.}—I' repa'coe trium claterium (shutters) ad magnam fenestram in fine eccl'ie vi^{d.}—In cibo et potu vi^{d.}—In libera ad opus fenest' iii^{d.} ad campanas xii^{d.} (for bell-ringing)—In rasina (resin) empt. in fatura ii (torches)—In i parva corda pro velo—In v. verg (yards) panni linei ad unum rochetum—In factura ejusd. rocheti vi^{d.}—In factura unius cartæ vi^{d.}—In libitina (a bier) empt. viii—In repa'coe vestimentorum p. a'. vi^{d.}—In vestimentis lavandis p. a' vi^{d.} Item. ad cap. red-ditis parci de trewelake xvi^{d.} Et diversis altaribus eccl'ie p'd'ce de redds. p'ci. pd'ci. viz. ad lumen sci nichi iii^{d.} ad lumen sc'i Ste'phi iii^{d.} ad lumen sci Joh. baptiste iii^{d.} ad lumen sce Katerine

iii$^{d.}$—In clerico scribent. compot. xii$^{d.}$—In emendacoe fenest
ii$^{d.}$—In pergamino (parchment) empto ii$^{d.}$ '

"The sum total of these expenses, of which I have
only given extracts, is 3*l.* 7*s.* 3*d.*; then follows:

"' Liberacio denar'—Idem computat' in liba'colo sacristæ mon-
asterii de Tavystocke pro oblacione perveniente ad altaria
ecclesie parochialis predictæ iii*s* iv$^{d.}$ per ann—Pro altari sce
Marie apud la south dor vi*s.* viij$^{d.}$ a festo invencionis sce crucis
usque ad idem festum tunc proxime sequent'. Pro altari Sci
Eustace xii$^{d.}$ per a. pro altari scæ Katerinæ xii$^{d.}$ pro altari sci
blasii iv$^{d.}$ p' altari sci Johis Baptist vi$^{d.}$ pro altari sce Trinitatis
vi$^{d.}$ d. altari sci Georgii iv$^{d.}$ pro altari sci Salvatoris in capella
Joh. dabernoun iv$^{d.}$ '

"The account is subscribed 'per me cleric' by the
notary, who, I suspect, was a wag, as, instead of his
signature, he affixes his notarial mark; a head with
an extraordinary long nose (perhaps this was intended
for his own portrait), having a quill stuck on the forehead by way of plume. Subjoined to the account is
this postscript.

"' Sepum (tallow) pro mortario (a light burning at the shrines or
tombs of the dead)—de xxxiv. lib. sepi de empeione hoc ann.
Thesaurus ecc'lie. Idem R. de cupa cum cuverculo (cup and
cover) argento et duobus angelis de auratis tenent. vit. clan.
corpus. d' m'cum (two gilt angels holding the body of our Lord
enclosed in glass); et de iv. calices cum patenis argent. Et
duobus cruetis (silver cruets) et de i pixi de argenteo pro corpore
x*s.* summa pat. Et reman i cupa cum cuverculo iv. calices cum
patenis 2 cruet' cum pixi de argenteo.'

"The paintings which formed the subject of the
engraving that appeared in the *Gentleman's Magazine*
(February, 1830) were the next relics in point of
antiquity appertaining to the church of St. Eustace.
The panels are two feet eleven inches in height, the
longer piece four feet in length, the shorter about two

feet; the figures are canopied by the most tasteful
and elegantly carved Gothic foliage; the mouldings
which divided them no longer remain, but their situation is readily observed by the vacant spaces between
the figures, and those who have a knowledge of the
Gothic style of architecture and ornament will easily
supply them. The first figure to the left hand is the
martyred Stephen, his hands uplifted, and his head
surrounded by a nimbus of glory, the distinguishing
emblem of saints; the next figure is St. Lawrence
holding the instrument of his martyrdom, the gridiron.
These are all that remain of a series of saints which
were probably at least nine in number, to correspond
with the nine grades of the angelic hierarchy, which
are distinguished with wings; of the latter remain the
personifications of the Archangeli, Cherubim, Potes-
tates, and a fourth with the crown and sceptre, the
inscription of which was probably Principatus.[3] The
style of the armour worn by one of the figures fixes
the age of the painting at about the time of Henry VI.
I believe that the whole of these figures must have
adorned compartments of the rood-loft in the parish
church, which was doubtless erected over the opening
from the church into the chancel, supporting the figure

---

[3] The five other grades were—Throni, Angeli, Seraphim, Domina-
tus, and Virtutes. All nine are represented in a window in St. Neot's
Church, Cornwall (see Hedgeland's prints), and doubtless it was these
nine orders which were painted on the Romsey altar-piece. To this
order of marshalling the heavenly host, derived by early Christian
writers from the Bible and the traditions of the Jews, Milton has frequently alluded. He makes both the Saviour of mankind and Satan
address them in the fifth book of *Paradise Lost*—

"Thrones, Dominations, Princedoms, Virtues, Powers."

And in the tenth is the following passage :

"Him Thrones and Powers,
Princedoms and Dominations ministrant,
Accompanied to Heaven gate."

of our blessed Saviour on the cross, and of his mother and John, the disciple whom he loved, standing by.

"The mysterious meaning of this arrangement was as follows: The body of the church typified the church militant on earth, the chancel the church triumphant in heaven; and all who would attain to a place in the latter must pass under the *rood;* that is, take up the cross, and then follow their great Captain through trials and afflictions. A veil or curtain was drawn over the rood and the figures attached to it, when the services of the church in which they were exhibited were completed. This explains the charge in the preceding account, of 'a little cord for the veil.'[4]

"The next parochial document appertaining to the church of St. Eustace, which I shall here notice, is headed as follows: 'The account of Thomas Holes and John Collyn, wardens of the churche of Tavistock ffrom the thirde of Maye in the yere of our Lorde Godd one thousande ffyve hundred ffower schore and eight, until the third day of Maye in the yere of our Lorde Godd one thousande ffyve hundred ffower score and nyne, that is to weete for one whole yere——.' From this I extract the following items:

" ' Receipts for the buryalle and belle.[5]

" ' Imprimis, the same accomptants doe charge themselves with the receipt of iv$^{d.}$ ffor the greate bell, upon the deathe of Margarett the daughter of Roger Dollyn.

" ' Item—Receaved upon the deathe of Agnes Drake, for all the bells and her grave, vii$s.$ iv$^{d.}$

[4] Sold a rod of iron which the curtain run upon before the rood A D. 1549—3 Edward VI. See Fuller's *History of Waltham Abbey.*

[5] This shows that the expressions used by Shakspere in his *Hamlet,* 'the bringing home of *bell and burial,*' were in the current form of his day.—*Vide Hamlet,* Act v. Scene I.

" ' Receaved of the p'shers [parishioners] of Tavystock towardes a rate made for the setting fforth of souldyers for the guardynge of the Queen's ma'tie's p'son, and towardes the mayntenaunce of the churche this yere, as appeareth by a book of p'ticulars thereof, xxx*li.* x*s.* iv^{d.} '

"A large portion of this charge was doubtless for the musters of 1588, the year of the Armada.

" ' Item.   Gave Mr. Bickell, Mr. Battishill, Mr. Knightes, and other preachers who preached at s'vall times in this p'ishe churche this yere [1588] iv*s.* viii^{d.}—Item, paide for wyne and bread this yere for the comunyon table, lix*s.* iii^{d.}

" ' Item, paide John Drake the schole master, for teachinge in the gramer schole this yere, xii*li.*—Item, paide to Nicholas Watts for wages for teachinge of the little children this yere, iiij*li.*

" ' Item, paide at the muster in August last past, xl*s.*—Item, paide by Mr Ffytz his comaundement the xvi. of June, 1588, unto a collector having the Queene's greate seale to collect with, vi^{d.}—Item, paide for a rope for one of the bells, xviij^{d.}

" ' Item, paide in August for the expenses of the soldiers at Plympton, vii*s.*—Item, paid to John Burges, for his paynes in going with the *Thrum* (the town drum) vi^{d.}—Item, paid the 6th of August and the 8th of August last past, to Mr Ffytz of the moneyes collected at the last rate xvii*li.*—Item, paide the 18 August last, to Richard Drake, towardes the charge of the tynners, vi*li.*—Item, paide James the cutler for makynge cleane strappyne and other trymmynge for the corselett and other armour of the parishe, and for a new dagger, vi*s.*—Item, paide for a new girdell, xvi^{d.}

" ' Item, paide for a book of articles at the firste visitac'on and for ffees then xxii^{d.}—Item, for writing the presentments[6] at the visitac'on and lyninge in thereof xii^{d.}—Item, paide for the expenses of the wardens, sydemen, clarkes, and others of the p'ishe at dynner that day, vi*s.* vi^{d.}—Item, paide Thomas Watts for amendinge of the Bible and the Book of Co'mon Prayer, beinge tornen in dyvers places, ii*s.* ii^{d.}

" ' Item, paide for the expenses of the constable, Mr Mohan, and of John Collyn, one of the wardens, and of Stephen

---

[6] Of Recusants refusing to attend the Common Prayer.

Hamblyn and of the Constable's man at Plympton, beinge then at the assessinge of the subsidis, the xth of Septr 1588, iii$s.$ i$^d.$

" ' Item, paide to one that collected with the broade seale, the 20th October last vi$^d.$—Item, paide to three Iryshemen, which hadd a lycence from the Earell [Earl] of Bath, vi$^d.$—To a poore man that collected for the hospital of Saynt Leonard's, vi$^d.$

" ' Paide the paver for amendinge the pavement by the conduytts and the street by the higher Churche bowe xxvii$^d.$

" ' William Gaye for killing of eight ffoxes this yere viii$s.$[7]

" ' Item, paide for a chayne and settinge in thereof, for the fastenynge of the dictionarrie in the Schole howse ix$^{d.}$[8]

" ' Item, paide Walter Burges for one planke and nayles, amendinge of the Widdow Nicholls and Walter Poynter's wyfe's seate and other seates vii$^{.l.}$ Item, paide him for coveringe of six graves in the churche this yere xviii$^d.$ Item, paide him for washinge of the churche clothes, viii$^d.$

" ' Item, for wrytinge this accompt and the accompt of the Alms-house landes, vi$s.$ viii$^d.$

" ' Bestowed on Mr. Moore the preacher for his expense, xxii^d ' "

"From a churchwarden's book, beginning 1661, I extract the following curious entries:

" ' Briefs in our parish as follow'—

"29th April, 1660. 'Collected for a company going to New England, taken by the Ostenders, 6$s.$ 6$^{d.}$'

"September 16th, 1666. 'Collected towardes the reliefe of the present poore distressed people of the towne and University of Cambridge.'

[7] The reward for the destruction of a fox was increased about a century after this time, more than threefold, as appears from the following entry: "May 18th, 1673. This day it was agreed by the masters and inhabitants of the towne and parish of Tavystoke, that whosoever shall kill any ffox within the said parish, shall receive for his or their paynes in so doing, the sum of three shillings and four pence."—*Churchwardens' Book*, 1660 to 1740.

[8] This is an amusing charge, and shows the scarcity of lexicographic tomes in that day. The reader will remember to have seen, in many parish churches, the black letter Acts and Monuments of the Martyrs, similarly attached, *pro bono publico*, 'to a chayne.' Erasmus's *Paraphrase on the Gospels* remains at the present time thus secured in Tavistock Church, the original cost of which, according to an item in another account, was fifteen shillings.

" October 11th, 1666. 'Collected towardes the reliefe of the poore inhabitants of London, who have lately suffered by the lamentable fire 11l. 5s. 9½$^{d.}$'

" ' Feb$^{ry.}$ 21st, 1668. Collected the day above written of the towne and parishe of Tavystocke towardes the reliefe and redemption of severall persons now slaves to the Turkes in Algiers and Sallay and other places 1l. 2s. 1½$^{d.}$'

" 1670, 21st, 22d, 23d, 24th November. 'Collected towardes the redemption of the present captives in Turkey, in the towne and parishe of Tavystoke.'

" The list consists of upwards of seven hundred contributors. Amount of contribution 16l. 0s. 9½$^{d.}$ [9]

" 12th July, 1674. 'Collected then the summe of 1l. 3s. 4¼^{d} fcr the fire of St. Martins in the fields, in the County of Middlesex.'

" 9th May, 1675. 'Collected then for John Forslett of Thilbroke, in the County of Cornwall, a poor captive in Ffez under the Turkes, 1l. 10s. 1½$^{d.}$'

" 24th April, 1675. 'For the fire at Redburne, in the County of Hereford, 6s. 6$^{d.}$'

" March 19th, 1675. 'To a petition for John Lawes, a captive in Tituan, 9s. 3$^{d.}$'

" 13th September, 1677. 'For the fire at St. Saviours and St. Thomas, in the County of Surrey, 27s. 9$^{d.}$'

" 27th October. 'For James Cole of Totness, a captive in Argier, 17s. 7½$^{d.}$'

" 1680, August. Another general collection for redemption of the present captives in Turkey, amounting to 6l. 18s. 5$^{d.}$

" 1681, November. Another, 'towardes the present subsistence and reliefe of the distressed Protestants of Ffrance, 6l 12s. 3¼$^{d.}$'

" ' 27th September, 1683. Paide and layd out to one M^s. Mary Danevaux fowre shillings for her charges in going to her friendes having a greate losse among nine fammilyes in the towne of Mumby, in the County of Lincoln, having seen her petition under the hands and seales of the Justices of Peace of

---

[9] At the head of this list is the Honourable Lady Marie Howard, ten shillings. She was the Lady Howard to this day so much the theme of tradition, and of whom so many wild stories are told. Some notice of her life will hereafter be given in these letters. George Howard, Esq., gave six shillings, and eight servants, nine shillings.

that County, Somerset, and Devon, to testifie it. The summe is 1400*l.*, she loste by a breache of the tyde-storme that violently destroyed heare howeses and goodes, and her husbande was lost in savinge those goodes.'

"The 'Captives in Turkey,' who appear to have been very numerous, were prisoners to the rovers of Barbary, whose piratical depredations on the seas, in the reign of Charles II., were repressed with considerable difficulty by the outfit of several naval armaments against them.

"The register of marriages, births, baptisms, and deaths is not extant at Tavistock earlier than the year 1614; but the Rev. Mr. Carpenter, of South Sydenham Damerell, in that neighbourhood, showed me the register of his church, beginning in 1539. I apprehend this is as early a register as any extant; for in the year 1538, says Stowe, 'in the moneth of September, Thomas Cromwell, Lord Privy Seale, Vicegerent to the King's Highness, sent forth intimations to all bishops and curates through the realme, charging them to see that in everie Parish Churche, the Bible of the largest volume printed in English were placed for all men to reade on,' (secured, no doubt, like the dictionary of the Grammar School at Tavistock, and the *Martyrology* in many churches, by 'a chayne,') 'and that a book of *Register* were also provided and kept in every Parish Church, wherein shall be written every wedding, christning, and burying within the same Parish for ever.' The various heads of the Sydenham Register are preceded by certain texts of Scripture, as the baptismal entries by 'whosoever was not found written in the book of life, was cast into the lake of fire,' &c. &c."

Having given the above very copious extracts from

my brother's notices of our church, and the curious churchwarden accounts (which he took the pains most minutely to examine), I shall subjoin a few observations from Mr. Bray's MS. notes in continuation; and then conclude this letter, which may be considered as one addressed to you more in your character of an antiquary than a poet; but the subjects, however recondite, belong so much to the history of this place, they ought not to be omitted.

Of the church itself, Mr. Bray says, "it consists of a nave with an aisle on each side, and a shorter one, probably additional, to the south, extending only to the chancel. This latter aisle, it has been supposed, was not carried on to the end of the chancel on account of Judge Glanville's monument, which is on that side of it. But by the carved wood-work of the ceiling, it appears to be of a more ancient date than the rest of the church. The pillars, also, have capitals enriched with leaves, whilst the others are plain. But the tracery of the windows is less ornamented than those to the north. However the windows in their general form are the same; consisting of pointed but depressed arches. The tower, which is at the west end, (though, strictly speaking, the whole of the building varies considerably from the cardinal points) is supported on four arches. Through two of these was the passage from the Abbey precincts into the town, at a spot still called Church Bow, though the arch that gave name to it has recently been taken down.

"By removing a row of old houses a few years since, the north side of the church has been opened to the street, and adds not a little to its embellishment.

"In the tower of the Church, which is plain and simple but lofty, are eight bells. They were given by the Duke of Bedford, who left it to the inhabitants of the place whether they would have an organ or bells, and they chose the latter. Formerly there were only five, which seems to have been the general number in country towns. When the poor were buried, no bell was tolled, even in an age when the tolling of a bell was thought to assist the departure of the soul to heaven, till some good old lady, whose name has unfortunately perished, gave one for the express purpose; and it was ever after called the poor-bell. Since they have been increased to eight, that among the rest was removed and probably melted; but the third bell still retains the name, and is applied to the same purpose.

"The singular custom existed here, till lately, of the sexton's carrying his spade, not shouldered, but, to use the military phrase, reversed, before the clergyman at every funeral. But this ceremony of the Church militant here on earth is now dispensed with.

"About forty years ago, a melancholy instance of the effects of superstitious credulity happened here. Two brothers of the name of Luggar sat up one Midsummer-eve in the church porch, from an idea (founded on ancient custom) that if at twelve o'clock at night they looked through the keyhole of the door, they would see all those who were to die that year walk into the church from the opposite doorway. Their imagination was so worked up that they fancied they saw *themselves* in this funeral procession. Certain it is that they both died within a very short space of time afterwards; were both buried in the same grave; and the inhabitants, by having the bells muffled at their funeral, téstified a more than ordinary commiseration of their awful fate. [1]

"In the chancel is a monument to the memory of one of the Fitz family; which, according to Prince, 'is known by tradition more than inscription, no epitaph being found thereon.' But though there is no inscription on the monument itself, on a flat stone in the pavement beneath may be distinguished the following words among others that are obliterated: 'Here lyeth John Fytz of Fytz-ford, Esquier,' with the date of 1539, or 1559: the third figure of the date being much worn, it cannot clearly be distinguished.

"Prince describes the arms of Fitz as 'argent a cross gules gutte de sang.' The arms on the canopy of the present monument do not exactly answer this description; but they have so near a resemblance that it is probable Prince may have been mistaken. They are a cross *engrailed* with five gouttes de sang on each quarter. These are on the right of the canopy; on the left are three rams; and, in front, the above coats of arms are quartered with others: the crest is a centaur. Beneath the canopy, which is supported by four columns, lies the figure of a knight in armour, with a lady by his side; the former resting his feet on a lion, the latter hers on a lamb. At the back of the monument, against the wall, a youth, probably their son, is represented kneeling, with a book before him on a desk. Some have supposed this youthful figure to be the effigy of Sir John Fitz, of whom so remarkable a story is told by Prince, and who fell on his own sword. [2] It may be such, though

---

[1] This melancholy circumstance of the death of the Luggars suggested the ballad of 'Midsummer Eve,' written by Mr. Bray, and inserted in the tale of *Fitz of Fitzford*.

[2] The story, as related by Prince, will be given in a future letter.

we have no authority, either written or traditional, to warrant the assertion.

"On the opposite side of the chancel is the monument of Judge Glanville. Prince tells us it is 'a very fair monument, so lively representing his person, in his scarlet robes, that some, at their first entrance into one of the doors there (against which it stands) have been surprised at the sight, supposing it had been living.' It is certainly very characteristic; and I have no doubt, from its resemblance to a picture of the Judge, once in my father's possession, was a striking likeness. Altogether it is one of the finest monuments I have ever seen of the Elizabethan age. His lady, Alicia, is kneeling before him, surrounded by their seven children, all of the same diminutive size, as if they were brought forth at a birth.

"Near it (of which, though now effaced, I once when some whitewash peeled off saw some vestiges) was painted against the wall, as an honorary monument, Queen Elizabeth, lying under a canopy, with the following inscription, which is preserved by Prince—

"'If ever royal vertues crown'd a crown,
    If ever mildness shined in majesty,
  If ever honour honoured renown,
    If ever courage dwelt with courtesy,
  If ever princess put all princes down
    For temperance, prowess, prudence, equity,
This! this was she, that in despight of death
Lives still ador'd, admired Elizabeth:
Spain's rod, Rome's ruin, Netherland's relief,
Heaven's gem, earth's joy, world's wonder, nature's chief.'

"In the chancel also is a slab on the pavement, dated 1740, to the memory of one of the Manatons, who, subsequently to the Glanvilles, were the possessors of Kilworthy.

"In the north aisle are the arms of an ancient family, with the following inscription—

> "'Gladius Spiritus est verus clypeus.
> Sub hoc lateat omnis tuta domus.'

"Near it is a monument of one of the Fortescues, of Buckland Filleigh, which is principally curious from the blunders of the sculptor, who seems to have corrected the text by turning one letter into another and filling up the superfluous parts by a kind of composition which is now falling off, and renders some of the words difficult to be deciphered. On the same side is the upper part of an arched tomb, too mutilated to require further notice. In other parts of the church are two or three modern tablets, and a monument lately erected by the late Mr. Carpenter, of Mount Tavy, to the memory of his father, and others of his family.[3]

"The font, of an octagonal form, each side bearing a shield, is supported on a low pillar, with a base. The upper part is enclosed with a kind of wooden pyramid, surmounted by a pelican, bearing the date 1660. Around it is 'God save King Charles II.!' with the names of Alexander Gove and John Noseworthy, churchwardens.

"On either side of the commandments, at the altar, is a border in the form of a pilaster, containing fruit and flowers beautifully carved. The figures of Moses and Aaron, as large as life, are painted in the compartments beyond, within the railing; they were

[3] Another monument to the late Mrs. Carpenter has likewise been erected by her eldest son, John Carpenter, Esq., of Mount Tavy.

executed about the time of George I., by a native of
this place named Beaumont, and considering the state
of the arts at that period, and that the artist was un-
educated as a painter, they are a very respectable
performance.[4] The altar table is of oak, richly and
beautifully carved in the Gothic style. The pulpit is
of much later date, but handsome in its decoration.
In the church is seen an iron-bound oak chest, most
probably as old as the building itself; in this were
found the ancient parish documents before noticed,
which are so numerous and so curious, that I question
if any parish in the kingdom can produce a more
interesting collection of the like nature."

Having here given you Mr. Bray's account of the
church, I shall conclude this letter with my brother's
notice of

THE SAXON SCHOOL.[5]

"No mention of such an establishment is to be
found among the muniments of the Abbey; but
Archbishop Parker refers to the existence of a Saxon
school at Tavistock, and at many other monasteries
within the realm, as a matter in the memory of persons
of his time. He says that many of the charters and
muniments of the early times being written in the
Saxon tongue, these foundations were provided in
order to communicate the knowledge of it from age
to age, lest it should at length become totally obsolete.
It is probable that the Saxon school shared the fate
of its fostering parent, the Monastery, at the time of
the Reformation, or that it merged in the grammar

---

[4] These paintings were removed at the repair of the church some
years since.

[5] *Notices of Tavistock and its Abbey.—Gentleman's Magazine*, 1830.

school still existing at Tavistock, to which no date of foundation can be assigned. Indeed it is not likely that so eminent a Monastery as Tavistock had neglected to establish a school for the instruction of the children of the poor in Latin and church music ; the mode in that day of providing that there should always be a number of persons qualified for the priesthood.

THE PRINTING PRESS.

"The noble art of printing," continues my brother, "was communicated to our land about the year 1471 ; and being first practised in Westminster Abbey, the example was soon followed by St. Augustine's, Canterbury, St. Alban's, and 'other monasteries of England,' says Stow. Among which number was the Abbey of Tavistock. Certain it is, that a translation of *Boëtius de Consolatione Philosophiæ*, undertaken at the instance of one Elizabeth Berkeley, and completed by John Walton, Canon of Osney, in 1410, was printed at Tavistock, in 1524,[6] under the editorship of Dan Thomas Rychard, one of the monks, who, by his prefix of *Dan* or Dominus to his name, was perhaps a graduate of the university, or a scholar of some note. It might, however, be a distinction added on account of the office which he bore in the monastery ; for I take him to be the same person who signs his name to the surrender, 'Rycardus custos.' The conclusion of this book (so rare that Hearne had only seen two imperfect copies of it) has the following note :

"'Here endeth the boke of comfort called in Latyn

[6] The charter of the Tinners of Devon, small quarto, was also printed at Tavistock Abbey, 1534 ; and the *Long Grammar*, containing only sixteen pages, edited by Richards.

Made in the USA
Middletown, DE
24 October 2023

41339991R00265